MCSE: Windows Server 2003 Network Infrastructure Desig

Exam 70-297

OBJECTIVE	CHAPTER
CREATING THE CONCEPTUAL DESIGN BY GATHERING AND ANALYZING BUSINESS AND TECHNICAL REQUIREMENTS	
Analyze the impact of Active Directory on the existing technical environment.	1, 2, 4
Analyze hardware and software requirements; Analyze interoperability requirements; Analyze current level of service within an existing technical environment; Analyze current network administration model; Analyze network requirements	1, 2, 4
Analyze DNS for Active Directory directory service implementation.	10
Analyze the current DNS infrastructure; Analyze the current namespace.	10
Analyze existing network operating system implementation.	2, 4
Identify the existing domain model; Identify the number and location of domain controllers on the network; Identify the configuration details of all servers on the network. Server types might include primary domain controllers, backup domain controllers, file servers, print servers, and Web servers	2, 4
Analyze security requirements for the Active Directory directory service.	3, 4
Analyze current security policies, standards, and procedures; Identify the impact of Active Directory on the current security infrastructure; Identify the existing trust relationships	3, 4
Design the Active Directory infrastructure to meet business and technical requirements.	1, 3, 4, 5
Design the envisioned administration model; Create the conceptual design of the Active Directory forest structure; Create the conceptual design of the Active Directory domain structure; Design the Active Directory replication strategy; Create the conceptual design of the organizational unit (OU) structure.	1, 3, 4, 5
Design the network services infrastructure to meet business and technical requirements.	9, 10
Create the conceptual design of the DNS infrastructure; Create the conceptual design of the WINS infrastructure; Create the conceptual design of the DHCP infrastructure; Create the conceptual design of the remote access infrastructure	9, 10

SYBEX

Exam objectives are subject to change at any time without prior notice and at Microsoft's sole discretion. Please visit Microsoft's web site (www.microsoft.com/learning) for the most current listing of exam objectives.

SYBEX

CREATING THE LOGICAL DESIGN FOR A NETWORK SERVICES INFRASTRUCTURE

CREATING THE PHYSICAL DESIGN FOR AN ACTIVE DIRECTORY AND NETWORK INFRASTRUCTURE

SYBEX

NOTE   Exam objectives are subject to change at any time without prior notice and at Microsoft's sole discretion. Please visit Microsoft's web site (www.microsoft.com/learning) for the most current listing of exam objectives.

SYBEX

MCSE:
Windows Server 2003 Active Directory and Network Infrastructure Design
Study Guide

MCSE:
Windows® Server 2003 Active Directory and Network Infrastructure Design
Study Guide

Brad Price

San Francisco • London

Associate Publisher: Neil Edde
Acquisitions Editor: Maureen Adams
Developmental Editor: Jeff Kellum
Production Editor: Elizabeth Campbell
Technical Editors: Larry Passo, James Kelly
Copyeditor: Rebecca Rider
Compositor and Graphic Illustrator: Happenstance Type-O-Rama
CD Coordinator: Dan Mummert
CD Technician: Kevin Ly
Proofreaders: Laurie O'Connell, Nancy Riddiough
Indexer: Nancy Guenther
Book Designers: Bill Gibson and Judy Fung
Cover Designer: Archer Design
Cover Photographer: Photodisc and Victor Arre

Library of Congress Card Number: 2003115678

ISBN: 0-7821-4321-0

Screen reproductions produced with FullShot 99. FullShot 99 © 1991-1999 Inbit Incorporated. All rights reserved.

FullShot is a trademark of Inbit Incorporated.

The CD interface was created using Macromedia Director, COPYRIGHT 1994, 1997-1999 Macromedia Inc. For more information on Macromedia and Macromedia Director, visit http://www.macromedia.com.

Microsoft ® Internet Explorer © 1996 Microsoft Corporation. All rights reserved. Microsoft, the Microsoft Internet Explorer logo, Windows, Windows NT, and the Windows logo are either registered trademarks or trademarks of Microsoft Corporation in the United States and/or other countries.

SYBEX is an independent entity from Microsoft Corporation, and not affiliated with Microsoft Corporation in any manner. This publication may be used in assisting students to prepare for a Microsoft Certified Professional Exam. Neither Microsoft Corporation, its designated review company, nor SYBEX warrants that use of this publication will ensure passing the relevant exam. Microsoft is either a registered trademark or trademark of Microsoft Corporation in the United States and/or other countries.

TRADEMARKS: SYBEX has attempted throughout this book to distinguish proprietary trademarks from descriptive terms by following the capitalization style used by the manufacturer.

The author and publisher have made their best efforts to prepare this book, and the content is based upon final release software whenever possible. Portions of the manuscript may be based upon pre-release versions supplied by software manufacturer(s). The author and the publisher make no representation or warranties of any kind with regard to the completeness or accuracy of the contents herein and accept no liability of any kind including but not limited to performance, merchantability, fitness for any particular purpose, or any losses or damages of any kind caused or alleged to be caused directly or indirectly from this book.

Manufactured in the United States of America

10 9 8 7 6 5 4 3 2 1

SYBEX®

To Our Valued Readers:

Thank you for looking to Sybex for your Microsoft Windows 2003 certification exam prep needs. We at Sybex are proud of the reputation we've established for providing certification candidates with the practical knowledge and skills needed to succeed in the highly competitive IT marketplace. Sybex is proud to have helped thousands of Microsoft certification candidates prepare for their exams over the years, and we are excited about the opportunity to continue to provide computer and networking professionals with the skills they'll need to succeed in the highly competitive IT industry.

With its release of Windows Server 2003, and the revised MCSA and MCSE tracks, Microsoft has raised the bar for IT certifications yet again. The new programs better reflect the skill set demanded of IT administrators in today's marketplace and offers candidates a clearer structure for acquiring the skills necessary to advance their careers.

The authors and editors have worked hard to ensure that the Study Guide you hold in your hand is comprehensive, in-depth, and pedagogically sound. We're confident that this book will exceed the demanding standards of the certification marketplace and help you, the Microsoft certification candidate, succeed in your endeavors.

As always, your feedback is important to us. Please send comments, questions, or suggestions to support@sybex.com. At Sybex we're continually striving to meet the needs of individuals preparing for IT certification exams.

Good luck in pursuit of your Microsoft certification!

Neil Edde
Associate Publisher—Certification
Sybex, Inc.

Software License Agreement: Terms and Conditions

To my loving wife, DeAnn, and daughters, Jami and Becca, whom I adore.

Acknowledgments

I would like to thank my family and friends for putting up with my constant excuses as to why I could not spend more time with them—although, I am sure some of you are glad that I was not around to bug you! I have to start by giving all of my heart and thanks to my wife, DeAnn, and to my two daughters, Jami and Becca. DeAnn, you have been amazing as you have held everything together and taken on the role of a single parent while I have been gone so much. As soon as these projects are finished, I plan on making it up to you. Jami and Becca, you two never cease to amaze me. Your accomplishments make mine pale in comparison. I wish I could have spent more time attending your games and functions, but through it all, you never let me down and you kept your compassion and faith.

To Mom and Dad, thank you for giving me the confidence to realize I could do anything I put my mind to and the work ethic with which to finish what I started. To the rest of my family, thanks for looking past my eccentricities and accepting me with open arms. A special thanks has to go to my brother, John. You are not only someone I can count on as a collaborator and someone I can bounce ideas off of, but a great friend.

To everyone at Sybex, thanks for your patience and understanding as I missed a few of those deadlines. Maureen, Jeff, and Elizabeth, you were great to work with and I hope we can do it all over again (just not too soon!). Thanks to the technical editors, Larry and Jim, for catching the errors and omissions caused by trying to finish chapters at three o'clock in the morning, and to the copyeditor, Rebecca, for transforming my words into things that shine. And to all of the staff that work behind the scenes to make sure the book and CD work, thanks for all of your hard work. Without you, the book would not look as impressive as it does.

Contents at a Glance

Contents

Chapter 8   Designing the Site Topology   265

Table of Design Scenarios

Introduction

Microsoft's Microsoft Certified Systems Administrator (MCSA) and Microsoft Certified Systems Engineer (MCSE) tracks for Windows Server 2003 are the premier certifications for computer industry professionals. Covering the core technologies around which Microsoft's future will be built, these programs provide powerful credentials for career advancement.

This book has been developed to give you the critical skills and knowledge you need to prepare for one of the design requirements of the MCSE certification in the new Windows Server 2003 track: Designing a Microsoft Windows Server 2003 Active Directory and Network Infrastructure (Exam 70-297).

The Microsoft Certified Professional Program

Since the inception of its certification program, Microsoft has certified almost 1.5 million people. As the computer network industry increases in both size and complexity, this number is sure to grow—and the need for proven ability will also increase. Companies rely on certifications to verify the skills of prospective employees and contractors.

Microsoft has developed its Microsoft Certified Professional (MCP) program to give you credentials that verify your ability to work with Microsoft products effectively and professionally. Obtaining your MCP certification requires that you pass any one Microsoft certification exam. Several levels of certification are available based on specific suites of exams. Depending on your areas of interest or experience, you can obtain any of the following MCP credentials:

Microsoft Certified Desktop Support Technician (MCDST)   This is the most recent offering from Microsoft. The program targets individuals who have very little computer experience. The only prerequisite Microsoft recommends is that you have experience using applications that are included with Windows XP, including Microsoft Internet Explorer and Outlook Express. You must pass a total of two exams to obtain your MCDST.

Microsoft Certified Systems Administrator (MCSA) on Windows Server 2003   The MCSA certification is the newest administrator certification track from Microsoft. This certification targets system and network administrators with roughly 6 to 12 months of desktop and network administration experience. The MCSA can be considered the entry-level networking certification. You must take and pass a total of four exams to obtain your MCSA. Or, if you are an MCSA on Windows 2000, you can take one Upgrade exam to obtain your MCSA on Windows Server 2003.

In addition, Microsoft just recently announced two additional specializations:

MCSA: Security on Windows Server 2003   You must take a total of six exams to get this certification. In addition to the core client and network operating system requirements, candidates must take two additional security specialization core exams, one of which can be CompTIA's Security+ exam. If you have your MCSA, you can take the Upgrade exam instead of the three core exams. However, you still need to take the two security-focused exams.

MCSA: Messaging on Windows Server 2003 You must take a total of five exams to get this certification. In addition to the core client and network operating system requirements, candidates must take one additional messaging specialization core exam. If you have your MCSA, you can take the Upgrade exam instead of the three core exams. However, you still need to take the messaging-focused exams.

Microsoft Certified Systems Engineer (MCSE) on Windows Server 2003 This certification track is designed for network and system administrators, network and system analysts, and technical consultants who work with Microsoft Windows XP and Server 2003 software. You must take and pass seven exams to obtain your MCSE. Or, if you are an MCSE on Windows 2000, you can take two Upgrade exams to obtain your MCSE on Windows Server 2003.

In addition, Microsoft just recently announced two additional specializations:

MCSE: Security on Windows Server 2003 You must take a total of eight exams to get this certification. In addition to the one core desktop networking exam and the four networking operation system exams, candidates may take three additional security-focused exams, including one security specialization design exam. If you have your MCSE, you can take both Upgrade exams (70-292 and 70-296) to satisfy the four networking operating system exams.

MCSE: Messaging on Windows Server 2003 You must take a total of eight exams to get this certification. In addition to the one core desktop networking exam, four networking operation system exams, and the one design exam, candidates may take two messaging-focused exams, both of which deal with using Microsoft Exchange Server 2003. If you have your MCSE, you can take both Upgrade exams (70-292 and 70-296) to satisfy the four networking operating system exams.

Microsoft Certified Application Developer (MCAD) This track is designed for application developers and technical consultants who primarily use Microsoft development tools. Currently, you can take exams on Visual Basic .NET or Visual C# .NET. You must take and pass three exams to obtain your MCSD.

MCSE versus MCSA

In an effort to provide those just starting off in the IT world a chance to prove their skills, Microsoft introduced its Microsoft Certified Systems Administrator (MCSA) program.

Targeted at those with less than a year's experience, the MCSA program focuses primarily on the administration portion of an IT professional's duties. Therefore, certain Windows exams satisfy both MCSA and MCSE requirements, namely exams 70-270, 70-290, and 70-291.

Of course, it should be any MCSA's goal to eventually obtain his or her MCSE. However, don't assume that, because the MCSA has to take three exams that also satisfy an MCSE requirement, the two programs are similar. An MCSE must also know how to design a network. Beyond these three exams, the remaining MCSE required exams demand that the candidate have much more hands-on experience.

Microsoft Certified Solution Developer (MCSD)   This track is designed for software engineers and developers and technical consultants who primarily use Microsoft development tools. As of this printing, you can get your MCSD in either Visual Studio 6 or Visual Studio .NET. In Visual Studio 6, you need to take and pass three exams. In Visual Studio .NET, you need to take and pass five exams to obtain your MCSD.

Microsoft Certified Database Administrator (MCDBA)   This track is designed for database administrators, developers, and analysts who work with Microsoft SQL Server. As of this printing, you can take exams on either SQL Server 7 or SQL Server 2000. You must take and pass four exams to achieve MCDBA status.

Microsoft Certified Trainer (MCT)   The MCT track is designed for any IT professional who develops and teaches Microsoft-approved courses. To become an MCT, you must first obtain your MCSE, MCSD, or MCDBA, then you must take a class at one of the Certified Technical Training Centers. You will also be required to prove your instructional ability. You can do this in various ways: by taking a skills-building or train-the-trainer class, by achieving certification as a trainer from any of several vendors, or by becoming a Certified Technical Trainer through CompTIA. Last of all, you will need to complete an MCT application.

For more information on each of these certifications, visit Microsoft's website at www.microsoft.com/learning.

How Do You Become Certified on Windows Server 2003?

Attaining an MCSA or MCSE certification has always been a challenge. In the past, students have been able to acquire detailed exam information—even most of the exam questions—from online "brain dumps" and third-party "cram" books or software products. For the new exams, this is simply not the case.

Microsoft has taken strong steps to protect the security and integrity of its certification tracks. Now prospective candidates must complete a course of study that develops detailed knowledge about a wide range of topics. It supplies them with the true skills needed, derived from working with Windows XP, Server 2003, and related software products.

The Windows Server 2003 certification programs are heavily weighted toward hands-on skills and experience. Microsoft has stated that "nearly half of the core required exams' content demands that the candidate have troubleshooting skills acquired through hands-on experience and working knowledge."

Fortunately, if you are willing to dedicate the time and effort to learn Windows XP and Server 2003, you can prepare yourself well for the exams by using the proper tools. By working through this book, you can successfully meet the exam requirements to pass the Designing a Microsoft Windows Server 2003 Active Directory and Network Infrastructure exam.

This book is part of a complete series of MCSA and MCSE Study Guides, published by Sybex Inc., that together cover the core MCSA and MCSE operating system requirements, as well as the Design requirements needed to complete your MCSE track. Please visit the Sybex website at www.sybex.com for complete program and product details.

MCSE Exam Requirements

Candidates for MCSE certification on Windows Server 2003 must pass seven exams, including one client operating system exam, four networking operating system exams, one design exam, and an elective.

You must take one of the following client operating system exams:

- Installing, Configuring, and Administering Microsoft Windows 2000 Professional (70-210)
- Installing, Configuring, and Administering Microsoft Windows XP Professional (70-270)

plus the following networking operating system exams:

- Managing and Maintaining a Microsoft Windows Server 2003 Environment (70-290)
- Implementing, Managing, and Maintaining a Microsoft Windows Server 2003 Network Infrastructure (70-291)
- Planning and Maintaining a Microsoft Windows Server 2003 Network Infrastructure (70-293)
- Planning, Implementing, and Maintaining a Microsoft Windows Server 2003 Active Directory Infrastructure (70-294)

plus one of the following Design exams:

- Designing a Microsoft Windows Server 2003 Active Directory and Network Infrastructure (70-297)
- Designing Security for a Microsoft Windows Server 2003 Network 2000 Server Technologies (70-298)

plus one of a number of electives, including these:

- Implementing and Supporting Microsoft Systems Management Server 2.0 (70-086)
- Installing, Configuring, and Administering Microsoft Internet Security and Acceleration (ISA) Server 2000, Enterprise Edition (70-227)
- Installing, Configuring, and Administering Microsoft SQL Server 2000 Enterprise Edition (70-228)
- Designing and Implementing Databases with Microsoft SQL Server 2000 Enterprise Edition (70-229)
- Implementing and Managing Microsoft Exchange Server 2003 (70-284)
- Implementing and Administering Security in a Microsoft Windows Server 2003 Network (70-299)
- The Design exam not taken as a requirement

Also, if you are an MCSE on Windows 2000, you can take two Upgrade exams:

- Managing and Maintaining a Microsoft Windows Server 2003 Environment for an MCSA Certified on Windows 2000 (70-297)
- Planning, Implementing, and Maintaining a Microsoft Windows Server 2003 Environment for an MCSE Certified on Windows 2000 (70-298)

In addition, if you are an MCSE in Windows NT, you do not have to take the client requirement, but you do have to take the networking operating system, design, and an elective exam.

Windows 2000 and Windows 2003 Certification

Microsoft recently announced that it will distinguish between Windows 2000 and Windows Server 2003 certifications. Those who have their MCSA or MCSE certification in Windows 2000 will be referred to as "certified on Windows 2000." Those who obtained their MCSA or MCSE in the Windows Server 2003 will be referred to as "certified on Windows Server 2003."

If you are certified in Windows 2000, you can take either one Upgrade exam (for MCSA) or two Upgrade exams (for MCSE) to obtain your certification on Windows 2003.

Microsoft also introduced a more clear distinction between the MCSA and MCSE certifications by more sharply focusing each certification. In the new Windows 2003 track, the objectives covered by the MCSA exams relate primarily to administrative tasks. The exams that relate specifically to the MCSE, however, deal mostly with design-level concepts. So, MCSA job tasks are considered to be more hands-on, while the MCSE job tasks involve more strategic concerns of design and planning.

The Designing a Microsoft Windows Server 2003 Active Directory and Network Infrastructure Exam

The Designing a Microsoft Windows Server 2003 Active Directory and Network Infrastructure exam covers concepts and skills related to Windows Server 2003 Active Directory infrastructure deployment and support. It emphasizes the following elements:

- Creating the conceptual design by gathering and analyzing business and technical requirements
- Creating the logical design for an Active Directory infrastructure
- Creating the logical design for a network services infrastructure
- Creating the physical design for an Active Directory and network infrastructure

This exam is quite specific regarding Windows Server 2003 Active Directory requirements and network services required to support Active Directory. It can be particular about how the network infrastructure is implemented to support Active Directory so you should be very familiar with the options available. Careful study of this book, along with hands-on experience, will help you prepare for this exam.

Microsoft provides exam objectives to give you a general overview of possible areas of coverage on the Microsoft exams. Keep in mind, however, that exam objectives are subject to change at any time without prior notice and at Microsoft's sole discretion. Please visit Microsoft's Training and Certification website (www.microsoft.com/learning) for the most current listing of exam objectives.

Types of Exam Questions

In an effort to both refine the testing process and protect the quality of its certifications, Microsoft has focused its Windows XP and Server 2003 exams on real experience and hands-on proficiency. There is a greater emphasis on your past working environments and responsibilities and less emphasis on how well you can memorize. In fact, Microsoft says a certification candidate should have at least six months of hands-on experience.

Microsoft will regularly add and remove questions from the exams. This is called *item seeding*. It is part of the effort to make it more difficult for individuals to merely memorize exam questions that were passed along by previous test-takers.

 Microsoft will accomplish its goal of protecting the exams' integrity by regularly adding and removing exam questions, limiting the number of questions that any individual sees in a beta exam, and adding new exam elements.

Exam questions may be in a variety of formats: Depending on which exam you take, you'll see multiple-choice questions as well as select-and-place and prioritize-a-list questions. Simulations and Case Study–based formats are included as well. Let's take a look at the types of exam questions and examine the adaptive testing technique so you'll be prepared for all of the possibilities.

 For more information on the various exam question types, go to www.microsoft.com/traincert/mcpexams/policies/innovations.asp.

Case Study–Based Questions

Case Study–based questions first appeared in the MCSD program and are prominent in the design-focused exams, including the Designing a Microsoft Windows Server 2003 Active Directory and Network Infrastructure exam. These questions present a scenario with a range of requirements. Based on the information provided, you answer a series of multiple-choice and select-and-place questions. The interface for Case Study–based questions has a number of buttons, each of which contain information about the scenario.

Multiple-Choice Questions

Multiple-choice questions come in two main forms. One is a straightforward question followed by several possible answers, of which one or more is correct. The other type of multiple-choice question is more complex and based on a specific scenario. The scenario may focus on several areas or objectives.

Select-and-Place Questions

Select-and-place exam questions involve graphical elements that you must manipulate to successfully answer the question. For example, you might see a diagram of a computer network, as shown in the following graphic taken from the select-and-place demo downloaded from Microsoft's website.

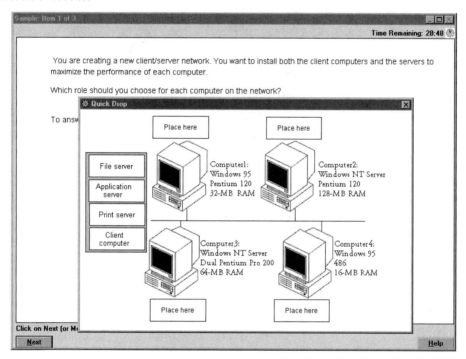

A typical diagram will show computers and other components next to boxes that contain the text "Place here." The labels for the boxes represent various computer roles on a network, such as a print server and a file server. Based on information given for each computer, you are asked to select each label and place it in the correct box. You need to place *all* of the labels correctly. No credit is given for the question if you correctly label only some of the boxes.

In another select-and-place problem you might be asked to put a series of steps in order by dragging items from boxes on the left to boxes on the right. One other type requires you to drag an item from the left and place it under an item in a column on the right.

Simulations

Simulations are the kinds of questions that most closely represent actual situations and test the skills you use while working with Microsoft software interfaces. These exam questions include a mock interface on which you are asked to perform certain actions according to a given scenario.

The simulated interfaces look nearly identical to what you see in the actual product, as shown in this example.

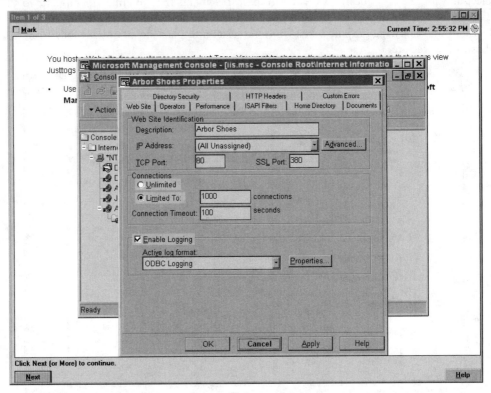

Because of the number of possible errors that can be made on simulations, be sure to consider the following recommendations from Microsoft:

- Do not change any simulation settings that don't pertain to the solution directly.

- When related information has not been provided, assume that the default settings are used.

- Make sure that your entries are spelled correctly.

- Close all the simulation application windows after completing the set of tasks in the simulation.

The best way to prepare for simulation questions is to spend time working with the graphical interface of the product on which you will be tested.

Tips For Taking the Designing a Microsoft Windows Server 2003 Active Directory and Network Infrastructure Exam

Here are some general tips for achieving success on your certification exam:

- Arrive early at the exam center so that you can relax and review your study materials. During this final review, you can look over tables and lists of exam-related information.

Exam Question Development

Microsoft follows an exam-development process consisting of eight mandatory phases. The process takes an average of seven months and involves more than 150 specific steps. The MCP exam development consists of the following phases:

Phase 1: Job Analysis   Phase 1 is an analysis of all the tasks that make up a specific job function, based on tasks performed by people who are currently performing that job function. This phase also identifies the knowledge, skills, and abilities that relate specifically to the performance area being certified.

Phase 2: Objective Domain Definition   The results of the job analysis phase provide the framework used to develop objectives. Development of objectives involves translating the job-function tasks into a comprehensive package of specific and measurable knowledge, skills, and abilities. The resulting list of objectives—the *objective domain*—is the basis for the development of both the certification exams and the training materials.

Phase 3: Blueprint Survey   The final objective domain is transformed into a blueprint survey in which contributors are asked to rate each objective. These contributors may be MCP candidates, appropriately skilled exam-development volunteers, or Microsoft employees. Based on the contributors' input, the objectives are prioritized and weighted. The actual exam items are written according to the prioritized objectives. Contributors are queried about how they spend their time on the job. If a contributor doesn't spend an adequate amount of time actually performing the specified job function, his or her data is eliminated from the analysis. The blueprint survey phase helps determine which objectives to measure, as well as the appropriate number and types of items to include on the exam.

Phase 4: Item Development   A pool of items is developed to measure the blueprinted objective domain. The number and types of items to be written are based on the results of the blueprint survey.

Phase 5: Alpha Review and Item Revision   During this phase, a panel of technical and job-function experts reviews each item for technical accuracy. The panel then answers each item and reaches a consensus on all technical issues. Once the items have been verified as being technically accurate, they are edited to ensure that they are expressed in the clearest language possible.

Phase 6: Beta Exam   The reviewed and edited items are collected into beta exams. Based on the responses of all beta participants, Microsoft performs a statistical analysis to verify the validity of the exam items and to determine which items will be used in the certification exam. Once the analysis has been completed, the items are distributed into multiple parallel forms, or *versions,* of the final certification exam.

Phase 7: Item Selection and Cut-Score Setting The results of the beta exams are analyzed to determine which items will be included in the certification exam. This determination is based on many factors, including item difficulty and relevance. During this phase, a panel of job-function experts determines the *cut score* (minimum passing score) for the exams. The cut score differs from exam to exam because it is based on an item-by-item determination of the percentage of candidates who answered the item correctly and who would be expected to answer the item correctly.

Phase 8: Live Exam In the final phase, the exams are given to candidates. MCP exams are administered by Prometric and Virtual University Enterprises (VUE).

- You will be presented with several case studies during the design exams. Each Case Study is actually a testlet. Make sure you answer all of the questions for the Case Study you are currently working on. If you move on to the next Case Study, you will no longer be able to return to the previous Case Study or any of the questions you had not answered.

- Read the questions carefully. Don't be tempted to jump to an early conclusion. Make sure you know *exactly* what the question is asking.

- For questions you're not sure about, use a process of elimination to get rid of the obviously incorrect answers first. This improves your odds of selecting the correct answer when you need to make an educated guess.

Exam Registration

You may take the Microsoft exams at any of more than 1,000 Authorized Prometric Testing Centers (APTCs) and VUE Testing Centers around the world. For the location of a testing center near you, call Prometric at 800-755-EXAM (755-3926), or call VUE at 888-837-8616. Outside the United States and Canada, contact your local Prometric or VUE registration center.

Find out the number of the exam you want to take, and then register with the Prometric or VUE registration center nearest to you. At this point, you will be asked for advance payment for the exam. The exams are $125 each and you must take them within one year of payment. You can schedule exams up to six weeks in advance or as late as one working day prior to the date of the exam. You can cancel or reschedule your exam if you contact the center at least two working days prior to the exam. Same-day registration is available in some locations, subject to space availability. Where same-day registration is available, you must register a minimum of two hours before test time.

You may also register for your exams online at www.prometric.com or www.vue.com.

When you schedule the exam, you will be provided with instructions regarding appointment and cancellation procedures, ID requirements, and information about the testing center location. In addition, you will receive a registration and payment confirmation letter from Prometric or VUE.

Microsoft requires certification candidates to accept the terms of a Non-Disclosure Agreement before taking certification exams.

Is This Book for You?

If you want to acquire a solid foundation in designing a Windows Server 2003 Active Directory and network infrastructure and your goal is to prepare for the exam by learning how to design a functional Active Directory and network infrastructure, this book is for you. You'll find clear explanations of the fundamental concepts you need to grasp and plenty of help to achieve the high level of professional competency you need to succeed in your chosen field.

If you want to become certified as an MCSE, this book is definitely for you. However, if you just want to attempt to pass the exam without really understanding how to design a Windows Server 2003 Active Directory and network infrastructure, this Study Guide is *not* for you. It is written for people who want to acquire hands-on skills and in-depth knowledge of Windows Server 2003.

What's in the Book?

What makes a Sybex Study Guide the book of choice for over 100,000 MCPs? We took into account not only what you need to know to pass the exam, but what you need to know to take what you've learned and apply it in the real world. Each book contains the following:

Objective-by-objective coverage of the topics you need to know   Each chapter lists the objectives covered in that chapter.

The topics covered in this Study Guide map directly to Microsoft's official exam objectives. Each exam objective is covered completely.

Assessment Test   Directly following this introduction is an Assessment Test that you should take. It is designed to help you determine how much you already know about designing a Windows Server 2003 Active Directory and network infrastructure. Each question is tied to a topic discussed in the book. Using the results of the Assessment Test, you can figure out the areas where you need to focus your study. Of course, we do recommend you read the entire book.

Exam Essentials   To highlight what you learn, you'll find a list of Exam Essentials toward the end of each chapter. The Exam Essentials section briefly highlights the topics that need your particular attention as you prepare for the exam.

Key Terms and Glossary   Throughout each chapter, you will be introduced to important terms and concepts that you will need to know for the exam. These terms appear in italic within the chapters, and a list of the Key Terms appears just after the Exam Essentials. At the end of the book, a detailed Glossary gives definitions for these terms, as well as other general terms you should know.

Review Questions, complete with detailed explanations   Each chapter is followed by a set of Review Questions that test what you learned in the chapter. The questions are written with the exam in mind, which means that they will cover the important topics with regard to the exam.

Case Study questions, complete with detailed explanations   Each chapter also includes a Case Study that is similar in look and feel to the types of questions you will encounter on the exam. The Case Study in each chapter is designed to test your knowledge of the topics covered in the chapter. Question types are the same as question types in the exam, including multiple choice, exhibits, and select-and-place.

Design Scenarios   Throughout the chapter you will find scenario-based exercises which present a Case Study and a few questions that help you think about how you will use the information in the chapter in designing a solution with the Microsoft products.

Real World Scenarios   Because reading a book isn't enough for you to learn how to apply these topics in your everyday duties, we have provided Real World Scenarios in special sidebars. These explain when and why a particular solution would make sense, in a working environment you'd actually encounter.

Interactive CD   Every Sybex Study Guide comes with a CD complete with additional questions, flashcards for use with an interactive device, and the book in electronic format. Details are in the following section.

What's on the CD?

With this new member of our best-selling MCSE Study Guide series, we are including quite an array of training resources. The CD offers eight Bonus Case Studies and flashcards to help you study for the exam. We have also included the complete contents of the Study Guide in electronic form. The CD's resources are described here:

The Sybex E-book for Designing a Microsoft Windows Server 2003 Active Directory and Network Infrastructure   Many people like the convenience of being able to carry their whole Study Guide on a CD. They also like being able to search the text via computer to find specific information quickly and easily. For these reasons, the entire contents of this Study Guide are supplied on the CD, in PDF format. We've also included Adobe Acrobat Reader, which provides the interface for the PDF contents as well as the search capabilities.

The Sybex Test Engine   This is a collection of questions that will help you prepare for your exam. The test engine features:

- Eight Bonus Case Studies designed to simulate the live exam. Each Case Study contains a scenario with 10 questions.
- All the Review and Case Study questions from the Study Guide.
- The Assessment Test.

Here are two sample screens from the Sybex Test Engine:

Chapter Test: Chapter 2

Mark	Time Left: 1 hr 19 min(s)	Question: 5 of 10

You are reviewing the current infrastructure and notice that all of the clients are Windows NT 4. There are five systems that use a VPN connection to gain access to the network. The VPN protocol was not documented. Which of the following protocols are probably being used? (Choose all that apply.)

☐ A. L2TP

☐ B. PPTP

☐ C. PPP

☐ D. IPX/SPX

Your Answer:

< > (Show Answer)   (Finish) 🏠 (?)

Chapter 5 Case Study

Mark		Question: 3 of 6

Back to Question

Interviews

Your company has been hired to design an Active Directory infrastructure and the network infrastructure to support it. During the interview process with some of the key stakeholders, you gathered the following information:

CEO

Currently we have a single location with all of our processes local. As we grow, we would like to keep all of the administration here in Chicago. Because the new branches are primarily retail and support offices, we will not need to have a large staff in those locations.

CIO

Most of the infrastructure that we support is located here at the corporate office. We do support some key servers at the manufacturing location. We support these servers from our main office. Because the servers are nearby, if there is a problem, we can usually be onsite within half an hour.

The new branches are going to be another issue altogether. We would like to retain the same level of administrative control over the servers in the new locations that we employ currently. Due to the geographic limitations, we may need to have some support staff at those locations. Currently, the plan is to hire staff at those locations who can provide the support for the customers, but also have an understanding of the business systems we need to put into place.

Manager of Information Technology

We have grown very quickly over the past three years and our current technologies have kept up with that growth. However, we don't think the current infrastructure is ready for the amount of growth that we are expecting within the following year. We are not afraid of moving to the latest

Background

Existing Environment

Interviews

Current Network Design

>

< > (Show Answer)   (Finish) 🏠 (?)

On the actual Microsoft exam, you will likely be presented with a total of four Case Studies, each with a varying number of questions that correspond to that Case Study. Your grade will be cumulative of all four Case Studies.

Sybex MCSE Flashcards for PCs and Handheld Devices The "flashcard" style of question offers an effective way to quickly and efficiently test your understanding of the fundamental concepts covered in the exam. The Sybex Flashcards set consists of more than 100 questions presented in a special engine developed specifically for this Study Guide series. Here's what the Sybex Flashcards interface looks like:

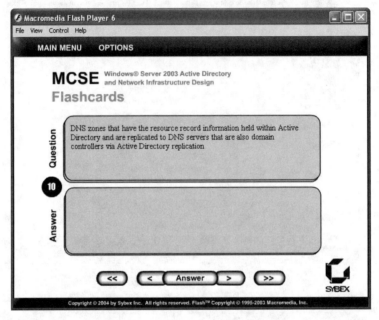

Because of the high demand for a product that will run on handheld devices, we have also developed a version of the flashcard questions that you can take with you on your Palm OS PDA (including the PalmPilot and Handspring's Visor).

How Do You Use This Book?

This book provides a solid foundation for the serious effort of preparing for the exam. To best benefit from this book, you may wish to use the following study method:

1. Take the Assessment Test to identify your weak areas.

2. Study each chapter carefully. Do your best to fully understand the information.

3. Read through all the Design Scenarios in the chapter, referring back to the text as necessary so that you understand each each fully.

4. Read over the Real World Scenarios to improve your understanding of how to use what you learn in the book.

5. Study the Exam Essentials and Key Terms to make sure you are familiar with the areas you need to focus on.

6. Answer the Review and Case Study questions at the end of each chapter. If you prefer to answer the questions in a timed and graded format, install the Sybex Test Engine from the book's CD and answer the questions there instead of in the book.

7. Take note of the questions you did not understand, and study the corresponding sections of the book again.

8. Go back over the Exam Essentials and Key Terms.

9. Go through the Study Guide's other training resources, which are included on the book's CD. These include flashcards, the electronic version of the chapter Review and Case Study questions, and the eight Bonus Case Studies.

To learn all the material covered in this book, you will need to study regularly and with discipline. Try to set aside the same time every day to study, and select a comfortable and quiet place in which to do it. If you work hard, you will be surprised at how quickly you learn this material. Good luck!

Hardware and Software Requirements

You should verify that your computer meets the minimum requirements for installing Windows Server 2003. We suggest that your computer meets or exceeds the recommended requirements for a more enjoyable experience.

The Design Scenarios in this book do not require that you have a computer to work on. These Design Scenarios are written to reinforce the topics that are presented within the chapter and allow you to make design decisions based on typical organizational needs. Pen and paper will probably be more useful for the Design Scenarios than a computer system.

Contacts and Resources

To find out more about Microsoft Education and Certification materials and programs, to register with Prometric or VUE, or to obtain other useful certification information and additional study resources, check the following resources:

Microsoft Training and Certification Home Page

www.microsoft.com/traincert

This website provides information about the MCP program and exams. You can also order the latest Microsoft Roadmap to Education and Certification.

Microsoft TechNet Technical Information Network

www.microsoft.com/technet

800-344-2121

Use this website or phone number to contact support professionals and system administrators. Outside the United States and Canada, contact your local Microsoft subsidiary for information.

Prometric

www.prometric.com

800-755-3936

Contact Prometric to register to take an MCP exam at any of more than 800 Prometric Testing Centers around the world.

Virtual University Enterprises (VUE)

www.vue.com

888-837-8616

Contact the VUE registration center to register to take an MCP exam at one of the VUE Testing Centers.

MCP Magazine Online

www.mcpmag.com

Microsoft Certified Professional Magazine is a well-respected publication that focuses on Windows certification. This site hosts chats and discussion forums and tracks news related to the MCSE program. Some of the services cost a fee, but they are well worth it.

Windows & .NET Magazine

www.windows2000mag.com

You can subscribe to this magazine or read free articles at the website. The study resource provides general information on Windows Server 2003, Windows XP, Windows 2000 Server.

Cramsession on Brainbuzz.com

cramsession.brainbuzz.com

Cramsession is an online community focusing on all IT certification programs. In addition to discussion boards and job locators, you can download one of several free cram sessions, which are nice supplements to any study approach you take.

Assessment Test

1. When a group of admins has control over resources that are all located at one location, what type of administrative model is this?

   A. Centralized/centralized

   B. Centralized/decentralized

   C. Decentralized

   D. Hybrid

   E. Outsourced

2. What type of administrative model is in place when the administrators are located close to the resources for which they are responsible, and those resources are spread out at each of the company's locations?

   A. Centralized/centralized

   B. Centralized/decentralized

   C. Decentralized

   D. Hybrid

   E. Outsourced

3. Terry is developing an Active Directory design and is in the process of interviewing some of the upper-level management from the company. The manager of information technology (IT) has told Terry that the organization is divided into teams, with each team responsible for a specific task. His IT department has several individuals who are all working on different tasks, each one responsible for supporting the IT needs of the task. What type of business model is in use?

   A. Departmental

   B. Cost center

   C. Product-based

   D. Project/service-based

4. Which of the following tools will allow you to analyze the resource usage on your servers and save the collected data within a SQL Server 7 database? (Choose all that apply.)

   A. Performance Monitor

   B. Performance Logs And Alerts

   C. System Monitor

   D. Network Monitor

5. Given the following statement, what priorities are identified? (Choose all that apply.)

    "We need to make sure that the new system still allows us to follow the federal laws put into place to govern financial institutions. Of course, we also need to continue supporting a set of software packages that have been approved for use within the Savings and Loan associations."

    A. Legal regulations

    B. Autonomy of administration

    C. Security policies

    D. Software requirements

6. When designing an Active Directory forest structure, which of the following structures is usually created if all of the company's resources are controlled by a central administrative group even though the administration may be decentralized?

    A. Organizational forest

    B. Resource forest

    C. Restricted-access forest

    D. Regional forest

7. Administrators who are identified as responsible for maintaining Active Directory are know as which of the following?

    A. Data administrators

    B. Domain administrators

    C. Forest administrators

    D. Service administrators

8. Due to their level of administrative control, service admins also have what level of authority?

    A. Data administrators

    B. Domain administrators

    C. Forest administrators

    D. Schema administrators

9. Users are required to use 8 characters for their password. Research and Development requires that 10 characters be used and that the passwords meet complexity requirements. How will you implement this?

    A. Add the Research and Development users to their own forest and set their passwords accordingly.

    B. Add the Research and Development users to their own domain and set their passwords accordingly.

    C. Add the Research and Development users to their own OU and set their passwords accordingly.

    D. Add the Research and Development users to their own group and set their passwords accordingly.

10. When interoperating with a UNIX network, which of the trust relationships can be created between UNIX and Active Directory?

    A. Forest trust

    B. Shortcut trust

    C. Realm trust

    D. External trust

11. Prior to bringing the first Windows 2003 Server domain controller online within a Windows 2000 Active Directory Domain, which utilities should be run? (Choose all that apply.)

    A. Run `ADPrep /forestprep`

    B. Run `ADPrep /prepDNS`

    C. Run `DomainPrep /prepDNS`

    D. Run `ADPrep /domainprep`

12. What are the three primary reasons for creating an OU?

    A. Control administration

    B. Assignment of group policies

    C. Object visibility

    D. Password restrictions

13. What is the definition of an OU owner?

    A. The administrative group that has the ability to control resource objects within an OU

    B. The administrative group that has been granted full control over an OU

    C. The administrative group that has the ability to control the user objects within an OU

    D. The administrative group that has the ability to create user, group, and computer accounts within an OU

14. If an OU is created for the express purpose of administrative control over printer objects, what type of an OU is this considered to be?

    A. Account OU

    B. Resource OU

    C. Security principle OU

    D. Task OU

15. When identifying an organization's objectives for using Group Policies, where should the password policy setting be applied?

    A. Default Domain Policy

    B. Default Domain Controller Policy

    C. At the site where the users are located

    D. The site where the computers are located

16. Which of the following suggestions should be followed when designing the Group Policy structure? (Choose two.)

    A. Create a GPO for each unique setting and name it for the setting used.

    B. Create a GPO for like settings and name it based on its function.

    C. Create an OU structure based primarily on the administrative needs of the company.

    D. Create an OU structure based primarily on the Group Policy needs of the company.

17. Once identified, where should the GPOs that contain the setting for corporate standards be applied?

    A. Linked to the top level OUs

    B. Linked at each of the child OUs where user and computer accounts are located

    C. At each forest within Active Directory

    D. At each domain within Active Directory

18. What condition must be met in order to nest a Global security group into another Global security group?

    A. The domain or forest must be at a minimum of Windows 2000 mixed mode, with no Windows NT 4.0 domain controllers on the network.

    B. The domain or forest must be at a minimum of Windows 2000 mixed mode with at least one Windows 2003 domain controller present.

    C. The domain or forest must be at a minimum of Windows 2000 native mode or Windows 2003 native mode.

    D. The domain must be at Windows 2003 native mode and the forest must be at a Windows 2003 forest functional level.

19. Which of the following is not an account type that can be created in Active Directory?

    A. Contact

    B. InetOrgPerson

    C. Resource

    D. Group

20. Which of the following security group would be valid when a domain is in the Windows 2000 mixed mode functional level?

    A. L-Chi-HRFiles

    B. DL-Chi-RDPrint

    C. G-Miami-MedRecords

    D. U-Acct

21. You want to control when replication occurs between domain controllers that are located on each side of a WAN link. What do you need to create in order to control the replication? (Choose all that apply.)

   A. Site

   B. Subnet

   C. Site link

   D. Subnet connector

22. Which of the following server specifications will support a domain controller that needs to support 1800 users?

   A. Single 800MHz processor, 1GB RAM

   B. Single 800MHz processor, 2GB RAM

   C. Dual 1000MHz processor, 1GB RAM

   D. Quad 1000MHz processor, 2GB RAM

23. In which of the following situations should you locate a Global Catalog server within a network location? (Choose all that apply.)

   A. You have more than 100 users authenticating.

   B. You have an application that queries a Global Catalog server.

   C. The WAN link is not reliable.

   D. You have many roaming users.

24. When choosing IP allocations options, how would you configure a DNS server within a perimeter network?

   A. With a static IP address

   B. Using an automatic private IP address (APIPA)

   C. Using dynamic host control protocol (DHCP)

   D. Using dynamic host control protocol (DHCP) with an alternate address

25. Your organization will only open IP addresses and ports for trusted systems on the Internet. You have clients who need to connect through a VPN connection to your RAS server, but you cannot guarantee the IP addresses they use when they connect. Where should you place your VPN server to support your users?

   A. In front of the firewall

   B. Behind a bastion host

   C. In the perimeter network of a three-homed firewall

   D. In the perimeter network of a back-to-back firewall

26. You have several workstations and intranet web servers within your network. You would like to configure them so that IP addressing is streamlined, yet you want to make sure they can communicate on the network if the DHCP server is unavailable. Which address allocation method should you use?

   A. Static addressing

   B. Automatic private IP addressing

   C. Dynamic host configuration Protocol (DHCP)

   D. Dynamic host configuration protocol (DHCP) with alternate IP addressing

27. Which of the following WINS replication topologies is the most efficient?

   A. Cross-server

   B. Hub-and-spoke

   C. Linear

   D. Push-allocated

28. When an attacker is attempting to determine the servers and addresses of those servers within the internal network in order to perform other attacks on the network infrastructure, what type of attack is this known as?

   A. Data modification

   B. Denial-of-service

   C. Footprinting

   D. Redirection

29. In order for DNS servers within the perimeter network to communicate with DNS servers on the internal network, you usually have to open port 53 on the firewall. Which of the following methods will allow you to keep port 53 closed and encrypt the data from an attacker trying to capture packets?

   A. Allow the DNS server to perform WINS resolution with a WINS server on the internal network instead of using hostname resolution.

   B. Configure the DNS server to use a VPN technology through the firewall.

   C. Change the port that DNS uses and open that port on the firewall instead.

   D. Only specify DNS servers that the DNS server will send zone transfers to by IP address.

Answers to Assessment Test

1. A. When administrators are located with the resources that they are administering, and no resources are located at other offices, the centralized administrative with centralized resources administrative model is used. For more information, see Chapter 1.

2. C. When the resources are decentralized and the administrators that are responsible for those resources are located local to the resources, the decentralized administrative model is used. For more information, see Chapter 1.

3. D. Most companies that are employing the project/service-based model will have employees from different business units, such as accounting and manufacturing, all working on a project so that the resources are available to efficiently complete the project. For more information, see Chapter 1.

4. A, B. Windows NT 4 has the Performance Monitor utility that will allow an administrator to log the resource usage to a database so that the information can be parsed later to determine the resource usage pattern. Windows 2000 Server provides this functionality with Performance Logs And Alerts. See Chapter 2 for more information.

5. A, D. Due to the laws that govern the Savings and Loan associations, specific needs will have to be addressed. Part of this is the certification of the software that is used within the associations as well as the legal regulations that they have to follow to insure that they are operating within the legal statutes put in place by the federal government. See Chapter 2 for more information.

6. A. Organizational forests are used when all of the resources from the company are centrally controlled. If the administrative staff is decentralized, domains can be created within the forest to allow for autonomy, or OUs can be built to organize the resources and ease administrative overhead. See Chapter 3 for more information.

7. D. Service administrators are responsible for Active Directory and making sure that it is available and configured correctly so that users can gain access to the services it provides. See Chapter 3 for more information.

8. A. Service administrators have all of the required permissions to also perform the duties of a data administrator. Although these duties are usually separated so that administration of the service and data can be divided and made more efficient, small organizations will take advantage of having the same group of administrators performing both tasks. See Chapter 3 for more information.

9. B. Account restrictions are controlled at the domain level. Although a new forest would allow the Research and Development users to have their own password policies, it is a rather drastic step to take. Creating their own domain will suffice. See Chapter 4 for more information.

10. C. Active Directory can utilize realm trusts to interoperate with a UNIX Kerberos realm. See Chapter 4 for more information.

11. A, D. `ADPrep /forestprep` adds the additional schema and object changes to the Schema Master. `ADPrep /domainprep` adds the additional changes required for Active Directory to the domain controllers within the domain where it is run. See Chapter 4 for more information.

12. A, B, C.   Password restrictions are controlled at the domain level. OUs are created to control the administrative needs of users within the domain, assign group policies to like objects, or control visibility of objects so that they are seen only by the appropriate users. See Chapter 5 for more information.

13. B.   The OU owners have the ability to control every aspect of the OU including creating, deleting, and maintaining user, group, and computer accounts as well as OUs within the OU. Once the domain owner delegates full control over the OU to a group, any member of that group will become an OU owner. See Chapter 5 for more information.

14. B.   A resource OU is created so that permissions can be delegated to administrators that need to control computer objects or shared folders or printers that have been published within the OU. See Chapter 5 for more information.

15. A.   Password policies are applied with the Default Domain Policy and cannot be overridden by any other policy within the forest. See Chapter 6 for more information.

16. B, C.   The OU structure of the company should be based on the administrative needs of the organization first and then enhanced for Group Policy use. Then by condensing the GPO settings into as few GPOs as possible, the application of GPOs will be streamlined. See Chapter 6 for more information.

17. D.   The corporate standards should be set high in the hierarchy. If set at the domain level, the settings will apply to all users within the domain. If set at the OU level, too many links may need to be applied. See Chapter 6 for more information.

18. C.   In order for Global security groups to be nested inside of other Global security groups, your domain or forest must be at a minimum of Windows 2000 native mode or Windows 2003 native mode. See Chapter 7 for more information.

19. C.   Active Directory can contain any of the following account types: User, InetOrgPerson, Contact, Computer, and Group. See Chapter 7 for more information.

20. A, B, C.   Because the domain is at the Windows 2000 native mode functional level, Universal security groups are not available for use. See Chapter 7 for more information.

21. A, C.   A site will allow all domain controllers within the site to communicate with one another as soon as an object is changed and will not compress the replicated information. A site link will allow replication to pass from one site to another and will compress the data so that the WAN link is not burdened. See Chapter 8 for more information.

22. D.   For 1500 or more users, 2GB RAM will be necessary for efficient authentication request processing. It is also recommended by Microsoft that, at a minimum, a Quad 899MHz processor system be used. See Chapter 8 for more information.

23. A, B, C, D.   All of these options are good reasons to locate a Global Catalog server in a site. See Chapter 8 for more information.

24. A.   With a DNS server, you only have the option of configuring a static address, you cannot use any of the dynamic address allocation methods. See Chapter 9 for more details.

25. A. Because the network engineers will not allow you to have the rules configured on the firewall that would allow users to connect from all addresses, you will have to place the VPN server in front of the firewall. Although this is not the most secure solution for the RAS server, the network policies will not be jeopardized. See Chapter 9 for more information.

26. D. If you configure your systems to use DHCP, then any changes to your infrastructure can be configured within the appropriate scopes in the DHCP server. If you apply alternate addressing at the client, the client can use the alternate address if the DHCP server is unavailable and the client's lease expires. See Chapter 9 for more information.

27. B. The hub-and-spoke replication topology allows WINS servers to pass replication data through a central server in order to deliver it to the other WINS servers and reduce the convergence time. See Chapter 10 for more information.

28. C. When an attacker is footprinting your network, they are attempting to determine what systems are used within your network by capturing name resolution data that specifies system names and IP addresses. See Chapter 10 for more information.

29. B. If you want to secure the DNS traffic that is sent through a firewall by DNS servers, you should configure the DNS server to use a VPN solution. Doing so will encrypt the DNS packets to keep them from prying eyes and allow you to close port 53 on the firewall. See Chapter 10 for more information.

Chapter 1

Analyzing the Administrative Structure

MICROSOFT EXAM OBJECTIVES:

✓ **Analyze the impact of Active Directory on the existing technical environment.**

  ▪ Analyze current network administration model.

✓ **Design the Active Directory infrastructure to meet business and technical requirements.**

  ▪ Design the envisioned administration model.

Configuring network protocols, building servers, and troubleshooting issues that keep the network from working as planned are all part of the daily routine. Most of us are comfortable working in that environment. But when it comes to working out issues pertaining to the administrative structure of our companies, the techno-geek in most of us is not as comfortable. Whereas the TCP/IP "map" can be held in our craniums for instant access, the administrative "map" is a bit more nebulous. The chain-of-command, the business model, the management philosophy—all are foreign concepts to most of us.

When it comes to designing an effective network infrastructure for Active Directory, we soon come to find that it becomes imperative to understand the administrative structure of the business. If you do not have a good understanding of how the business functions, Active Directory will not be rolled out effectively, and you will soon discover that a complete redesign of the directory is probably necessary. Not a fun prospect to say the least.

The administrative structure of a business falls into two categories: business models and administration models. Most business models fall into one of four categories: *departmental model*, *project-based model*, *product/service-based model* or the *cost center model*. Over the course of the next few pages, we will discuss each model and how it could impact your Active Directory design. Then we will discuss the four types of administrative structures: *centralized*, *decentralized*, *hybrid*, and *outsourced*. During these discussions, we will also look at how to identify the different models, how the models affect Active Directory design, and how to design the administrative structure.

Understanding the Administrative Structure: Business Models

Within the administrative structure, the business model is in charge of how the business is designed to function. Business models can be thought of as the DNA of a company. By identifying the business model, designers can understand how the company works, and how work is accomplished within the organization. The methodologies that Microsoft has identified follow the most common structures found in businesses today. Because Microsoft has been involved in many of the Active Directory implementations during the past four years, they have seen first hand how businesses—small, medium, and large—build their administrative structures.

The four different models that you will need to become familiar with are:

- Departmental model
- Project-based model

- Product/service-based model
- Cost center model

Each of these models will have an impact on the decision making process as the design is being reviewed.

Identifying the Departmental Model

For decades, the departmental model has been the most popular business model for companies. Based on the structure of the business units, this model reflects the internal organization of the company and the clearly delineated lines between job responsibilities. The organizational chart for this type of company will define the departments that are static and have a sole purpose within the organization. Figure 1.1 shows an example of an organization chart that you might find for the departmental model. You will more than likely find departments along the classic lines of:

Accounting   This may be broken into subdivisions such as Accounts Payable and Accounts Receivable. Accounting is responsible for handling the finances of the company.

Human Resources   The Human Resources department is usually responsible for finding and retaining employees. Responsibilities include working with the employees' insurance and retirement plans, recruiting new employees, working out differences between management and the employees, and many other personnel related issues.

Information Technology (IT)   You may find the IT department broken into different subdivisions based on the type of work that they are performing or the systems that they are responsible for, such as database management, messaging, help desk, and user account control, but you will probably find that they all fall under the same umbrella.

Marketing   Members of the Marketing department try to make the company's products appear to be the best ever. This department is sometimes also part of the Sales department.

Sales   Most companies employing the departmental model will have a product they are trying to market, whether it is a product that is being sold to an end user (consumer), or an intermediary product that is used by another firm within their manufacturing process. These individuals are responsible for finding and maintaining the customers and keeping the product "on the market."

Production   Probably the easiest way to describe the Production department is that it is the portion of the company that actually produces the product. This department is usually found in manufacturing firms, whether they build the final product or the components that go into the final product.

You will probably find other departments within a company, depending upon what type of organization it is. For instance, a hospital may have a Laboratory department and a Surgical department, whereas a manufacturing facility may have a Shipping and Receiving department and a Research and Development department. Because the departmental divisions are well defined in this business model, it is usually a simple matter of perusing the organization's organization chart to discover the departments that make up the company.

FIGURE 1.1   A departmental model organization chart

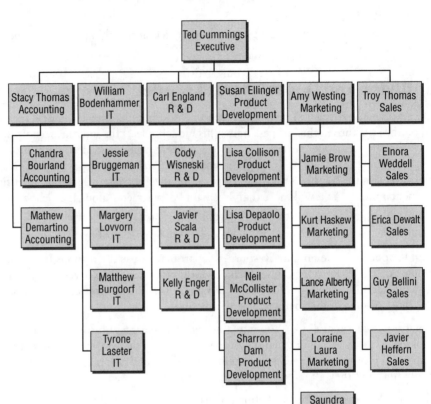

Even though the departmental model may appear to be the most straightforward of the models to design for, you will find that every company implements their administration differently. Rule number one: never use the organization chart as the basis for the Active Directory design. Although it may seem like a good idea to use the already-created structure, you will find it very difficult to build an effective administrative design or group policy deployment based on the company's organization chart. As you will find out in Chapter 4, "Designing an Organizational Unit Structure for Administrative Purposes," and Chapter 5, "Designing a Group Policy Infrastructure," an efficient Active Directory design is based on the logical and efficient organization of resources within the directory based on who is responsible for administering each resource.

Identifying a Project-Based Model

The project-based model dissolves the business units that we have been so comfortable with, and pulls job responsibilities together based upon the needs of a project. The clearly delineated lines found in the departmental model disappear when this model is employed. You will probably find accountants, electrical engineers, IT administrators, and many others working on a single project. With this model, as seen in Figure 1.2, the project is the main unit of organization. Employees are assigned to the project and work as a cohesive unit.

Depending on your viewpoint, the product-based model may not seem very efficient. Many companies have avoided organizing resources using this model because they feel that their human resources—that is, their employees—are not being utilized effectively. Having multiple individuals performing the same function on myriad projects seems redundant to many managers who would prefer to have a centralized group performing the function as seen in the departmental model. However, the project-based model allows for streamlined and efficient project management. For instance, you can have dedicated individuals working on the project instead of sharing a resource, such as an engineer from the Research and Development department, which streamlines the project; you no longer have to wait for the resource to be freed up to work on your project.

FIGURE 1.2   The project-based model

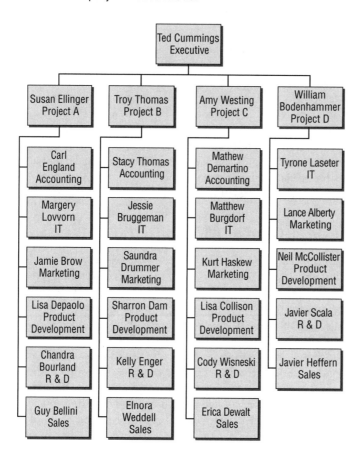

This becomes a very dynamic environment where the project teams are in a state of flux. As one project ends and another begins, the teams form, dissolve, and reform, most times with new members based on the needs of the project. If a company wants to implement a solution quickly or has specific needs on a project, this could be the best type of business model to implement.

For the network architect who is trying to develop an Active Directory and Network Infrastructure design, this is a very problematic business model to design for. Because the resources are in a state of flux, resource access and administrative control can be difficult to nail down. Your final design will have to take into account the possibility of changing resource requirements and how the administrative staff will have to approach the resource control.

Identifying the Product/Service-Based Model

The product/service-based model is basically a hybrid of the project-based and departmental models. It is prevalent in large corporations that have multiple products or services that they are bringing to market, or companies that have merged and are now supporting several products, each as its own business unit. The resources within this model do not morph as quickly as in the project-based model, but you will find that they have redundancy within the "vertical" lines of business as seen in Figure 1.3.

If you examine a large corporation that follows this model, you will probably find separate business units, each responsible for its own product or service. You may find a company that has a soft drink division, a restaurant division, and a junk food division. Each has its own marketing, research and development, and sales group, which specializes in its individual product. All the while, each division reports to the parent company, which has the final say in any decisions that impact the company.

When designing the Active Directory and network infrastructure for this type of business model, you may not have to design for the constantly changing environment as you did for the project-based model, but you will probably need to maintain specific lines of administrative control. Security will also be required, because the individual lines of the business need to be autonomous.

Identifying the Cost Center Model

The cost center model can be used with any of the aforementioned business models, but instead of the divisions working together, they "charge" each of the divisions for their services. You will usually find this in a company that uses the product/service-based model, because the hybrid nature of the business allows for more than one division to use the services of other divisions. This model appears to take on the same design as the departmental model; if you look at the organization chart, they look nearly identical. The primary difference is the interrelation between the divisions. Each division needs to be an autonomous unit with a clearly delineated set of resources. In the standard departmental model, a centralized group of administrators could potentially control all of the resources for the entire organization. With the cost center model, control of the resources has to be handled by the department or division administrators.

The most common of the chargeable departments is the Information Technology department, which charges each of the divisions for the service that it is providing for them. This charge is often called "funny money" because the money that is charged moves from one department's budget to the other division. Each department needs to make sure it has allocated enough money within its budget for the services it will take advantage of over the course of the budget's life.

When determining how to design Active Directory and network infrastructure for a company that employs the cost center model, you need to consider not only the resource requirements, but also the security requirements. Each of the cost centers needs to access only its own resources and should not be able to take advantage of other resources. At the same time, the departments need to trust the Information Services department, which will be responsible for all of the resources that reside on the systems. The other divisions will have to allow control of those resources to be administered by the Information Services staff. Designing with security in mind could make the Active Directory design a little more extensive.

FIGURE 1.3   The product/service-based model

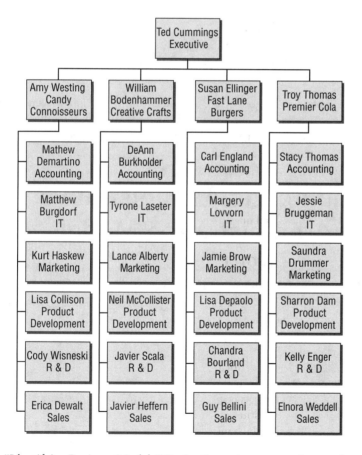

In the "Identifying Business Models" Design Scenario we are going to take a look at a company and determine which of the business models are used.

Design Scenario

Identifying Business Models

MetalFab Manufacturing has built prefabricated buildings for nearly 75 years. Their metal building designs have been widely accepted as the best manufactured in the industry. After an extremely large contract with the government to build aircraft hangars in the 1960s, they expanded their operations to include 30 manufacturing plants across the United States. Originally, all of their information processing was performed on mainframe computers. The company wished to confirm that every department was using the mainframe systems, so they started tracking usage by department and charging the departments for the total amount of processing time used. Since that time, the company has switched to personal computers at the users' desktops with servers hosting the services and data controlled by a central IT staff. To justify its existence, the IT department still charges the other departments for the use of the server systems. All access is monitored and tracked so that the usage can be calculated and reported.

1. **Question:** Which of the business models was originally used by MetalFab? **Answer:** Because each of the divisions was being charged to use the resources from the IT department, the cost center model was used.

2. **Question:** Which of the business models is MetalFab currently using? **Answer:** MetalFab has not changed the way it handles the resource requirements from the other divisions when they access the IT resources, so a cost center model is still being used.

Understanding the Administrative Structure: Administration Models

Whereas the business models define how a business is organized to perform tasks, the administration models define how the resources are organized, controlled, secured, and accessed. The four administration models are

- Centralized administration model
- Decentralized administration model
- Hybrid administration model
- Outsourced administration model

Each is supported by Active Directory, with its own advantages and disadvantages.

Identifying the Centralized Administration Model

The centralized administration model is the administrative model that most companies strive to achieve. With the centralized administration model, a core administrative group controls all of the IT assets at one central location.

Although this is the model that many companies wish they could implement, many find that they cannot for several reasons. Whether it is due to business, legal, or cultural reasons, some companies have found that this model will not fit within their organization. For example, some companies provide services or products to military divisions of our government. When these defense contracts are given out, the company that receives the contract must abide by national security regulations. Some of these regulations require that the division to whom the contract was awarded be completely isolated from the rest of the company. This keeps the information safeguarded from those individuals who do not need access to the information. This also means that the administrators of this information will probably need to be isolated from the rest of the company.

Two different structural models exist on which centralized administration is built: centralized administration with centralized resources, and centralized administration with decentralized resources. Both of these pose their own challenges and have definite advantages and disadvantages.

The Centralized/Centralized Approach

The inherent nature of the centralized administration with centralized resources model does not allow for very much flexibility. If a company has a single location with all of the employees accessing the resource from a central location, this is not a problem. As companies grow, merge with, and acquire other companies, the ability to keep all of their assets centralized becomes a challenge. Most companies find that, to reduce costs and ease administrative problems, they have to move to one of the other models discussed later. Figure 1.4 shows a simple version of this approach with all of the resources located at the Chicago office.

FIGURE 1.4   Centralized administration with centralized resources

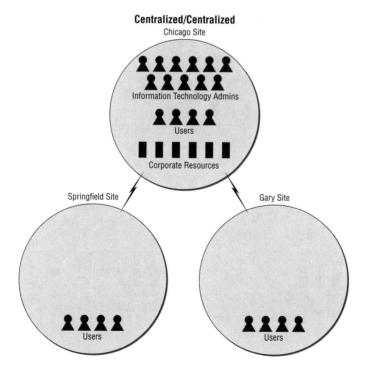

One big advantage of the centralized resources approach is that it is easy to administer. With all of the assets based at one location, administrators have all of the systems at their fingertips. Whenever a security update or a system patch needs to be applied, the systems are close by. Because all of the systems are geographically close to one another, communication problems are usually not an issue. In a local area network, the systems should have plenty of available bandwidth in which to communicate and share data.

The Active Directory design for the centralized/centralized approach is usually an easy one to decide upon. Because the resources are centralized and the administrative staff is usually grouped together, a simple, single forest design usually containing a single domain will suffice. Of course, other design criteria will come into play and may change the forest and domain structure, but it is best to start simple and add complexity as necessary.

The Centralized/Decentralized Approach

When companies discover that centralizing their resources is not efficient, they may want to decentralize their resources, yet maintain a centralized administration group. Whereas this option may not have seemed feasible as few as 10 years ago, advances in remote control administration and system automation have made this administrative model very intriguing. Figure 1.5 shows an example of an organization using this approach.

FIGURE 1.5   The centralized administration/decentralized resources approach

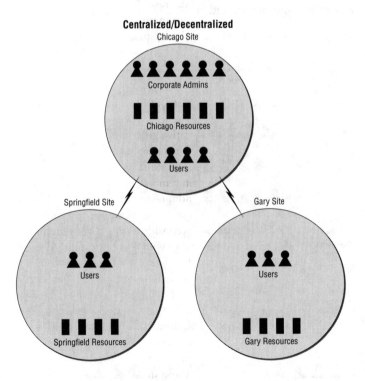

Let's face it, an administrator no longer has to be sitting in front of the system to work with it. Tools as simple as the *snap-ins* for the *Microsoft Management Console (MMC)* have made it possible for us to control systems that are located in different cities, states, or countries. Where some of the snap-ins have limitations, other administrative utilities come into play allowing us to remotely administer a system. Microsoft's *Terminal Services* is a shining example of a remote administration tool. Once the Terminal Services client is started and connects to the remote server, the administrator can perform nearly every task they could perform from a local machine. The only exception is when the administrator needs to physically replace a device or switch out removable media. And now that terminal services allows the client to connect to the console session, a remote administrator can view what is happening on the server and view any messages that may appear within the console session.

Automation tools also make an administrator's job easier and facilitate controlling remote systems from a central location. From backing up servers at predetermined times, to automating the installation of software, these automation tools end up paying for themselves. Administrators no longer have to travel to the physical location of the system in order to perform most tasks. A good example of this is utilizing Group Policy objects (GPOs) to automate software installation on a client computer or to set security requirements on a server.

The main drawback to the centralized/decentralized method stems from the fact that the administrative staff is geographically distant from the resources. If something happens to a server, the staff has to travel to the location where the resource is located in order to work on it. This means the staff will encounter times when the resource could be offline for an extended amount of time. Due to this reason in particular, companies will not adopt the centralized/decentralized model and will instead opt to use a different approach to administration. In the next section, you will find the administration theory that is the polar opposite to the centralized administration model.

Identifying the Decentralized Administration Model

Whereas the centralized model uses a core administrative group that resides in one location, the decentralized administration model spreads the administrators out around the organization to take advantage of controlling the resources at their source. An example of the decentralized model is seen in Figure 1.6. Instead of having to rely extensively on remote control or automation software, the administrators have local access to the systems they administer. Although this allows a company to have administrators located close to the systems where they can respond to problems immediately, it adds to the cost of administration. Another thing to consider is that if your organization is spread across multiple time zones, you may need to decentralize your administration. Although some companies run their data centers 24 hours a day, those that do not will need to identify whether or not they want to place administrators in those locations where the resource resides.

Employees are an expensive resource. However, some companies need to have their data available at all times, and having an administrative staff available to take care of any problem that may arise might be a small price to pay. Decentralized administration can prove a little more difficult when designing your Active Directory and network infrastructure. The delegation of administrative control takes more planning than having a centralized group that is responsible for administration. Replication of Active Directory information among the systems takes a toll on the network bandwidth, especially when wide-area connections are concerned.

FIGURE 1.6   The decentralized administration model

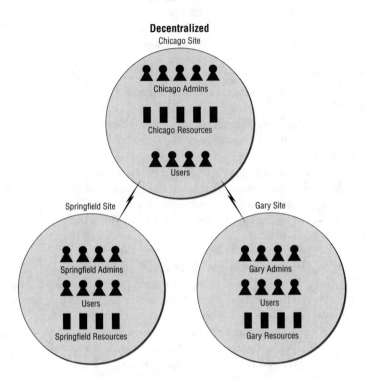

Identifying the Hybrid Administration Model

As most large companies have found, neither of the previous administrative models fits within their organization. The centralized model is far too restrictive, and response time for problems may take too long. The decentralized model allows too many administrators to have too much control across the board. The hybrid model alleviates some of these issues.

Two different methods may be employed to take advantage of the hybrid model. The first, seen in Figure 1.7, keeps most of the administrative staff centralized where they control the majority of resources, while taking advantage of a technical support staff that has the authority to work with the remote systems. These remote administrators do not have control over system policies or corporate resources. This approach allows the central staff to control all of the systems where required and a remote staff to maintain systems, perform backups, and troubleshoot issues that arise.

The second hybrid administrative method has a decentralized staff that is responsible for completely administering the systems at their locations. They have control over the users, client systems, servers, printers, and all other resources, but they will not have control over the corporate standards. Control over the standards is centralized at the corporate IT headquarters, as seen in Figure 1.8. All of the remote administrative staff will have to follow the standards as they are enforced using tools such as Group Policy.

FIGURE 1.7   Hybrid administration model for delegation of remote resources

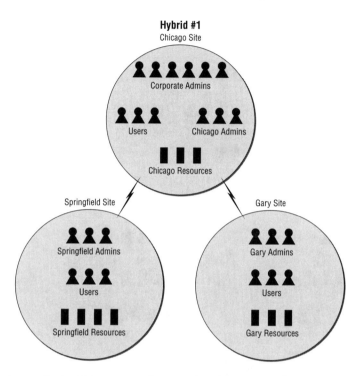

Designing an Active Directory and network infrastructure for a hybrid administrative group can be tough, yet rewarding. You need to make sure that the correct administrators have the required level of permissions for the resources they need to administer, and the correct rights to perform the tasks for which they are responsible. All the while, they should not have the right to make changes to the system policies that control and maintain the Active Directory requirements. At the same time, the central administrative group needs to have the rights to maintain the system policies that govern resource access and control.

Identifying the Outsourced Administration Model

In many companies, outsourcing the administrative staff is not an option. These companies want to have complete control over their administrative staff. They do not want to entrust their systems to employees from an outside organization, even though the outside organization may have employees who have up-to-date skill sets. For some companies, the security risks are not worth the trade-off.

For other companies, the ability to bring in employees who have a skill set that they need becomes a positive thing. The company does not have to incur the immediate expense of trying to train the employees, and the outsourced administrator can bring a skill set in that may train the current employees on a new technology.

FIGURE 1.8   Hybrid administration model for control of corporate standards

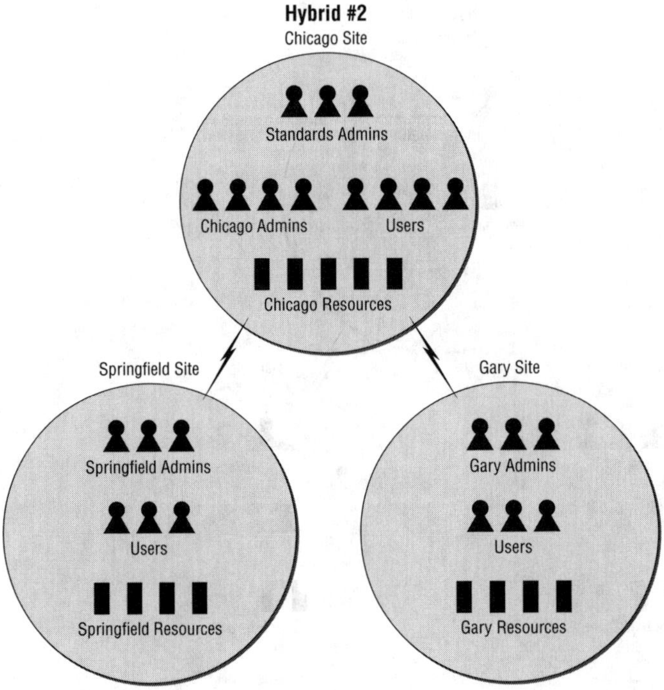

Other companies will utilize an outsourced staff so that they can reduce costs. Paying an outside firm to provide administrative resources allows a company to use the skill sets of individuals who have been trained, but also keep their own employee costs at a minimum. Figure 1.9 shows an example of using outsourced staff to provide administrative control. Human resources are expensive, not only because of the salary they draw, but because benefits they receive can cost the company quite a bit of money.

The outsourced administration model has some drawbacks. Depending on the contract that is drawn up, the outsourced employee may not be dedicated to your company. They may have other companies that they are working with, and the time that is allocated to your company may be limited. Even if the outsourced employee is dedicated to your company, they may have specific tasks and functions that they are allowed to do and not do.

When you are designing Active Directory and the network infrastructure to take advantage of the outsourced model, remember that security is an utmost priority. The process of delegating the responsibilities the administrators need while securing those resources that they should not have access to needs to be addressed. A good Active Directory design allows you to segregate the resources so that access to them is restricted. However, be aware that if you are using this model, one of the main reasons for using it is to take advantage of expertise that you may not have had in your own organization. Make sure you trust the company that is providing the outsourcing.

FIGURE 1.9   Outsourced administration model

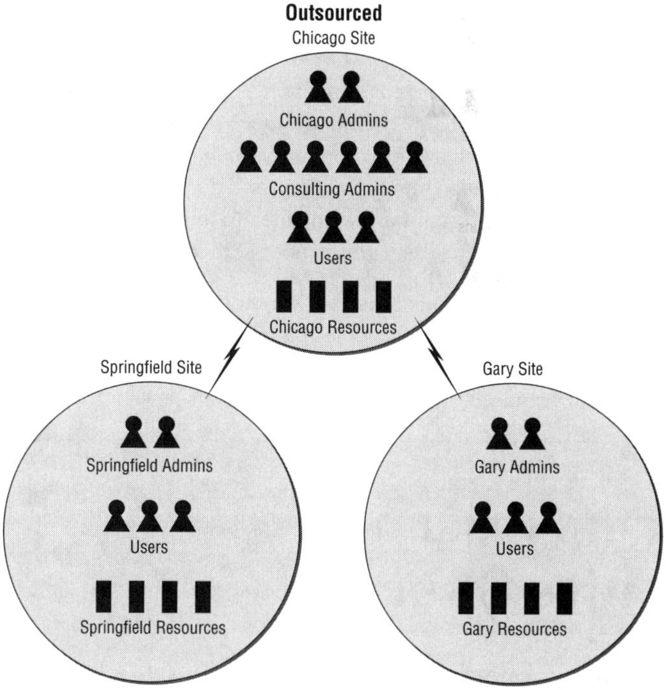

Outsourced
Chicago Site

Chicago Admins

Consulting Admins

Users

Chicago Resources

Springfield Site

Springfield Admins

Users

Springfield Resources

Gary Site

Gary Admins

Users

Gary Resources

In the "Identifying the Administrative Model" Design Scenario we are going to take a look at an organization and determine which of the administrative models are in use.

Design Scenario

Identifying the Administrative Model

Eclectic Importers' headquarters is located in San Francisco, California. They have 22 regional offices throughout the United States and 5 foreign offices. Each of the offices has its own staff that is responsible for the systems at their location. None of the offices has any control over the other offices' resources. The corporate headquarters does have ultimate control over all of the resources at all of the locations worldwide.

1.   **Question:** Which administrative model is in use at Eclectic Importers? **Answer:** Having an administrative staff at each location that is responsible for the resources located at that location falls under the decentralized administrative model. However, because the corporate administrative staff has full control over all of the resources from the headquarters, this model falls under the hybrid administrative model.

Real World Scenario

Thin Client Outsourcing

Franklin County Memorial Hospital (FCMH) decided to cut costs associated with the IT department. One method of achieving this goal involved implementing Citrix MetaFrame XP. This option allowed them to centralize their applications on several servers located in the data center and then utilize thin client workstations. They identified nurses' stations and doctors' terminals at this point, which reduced the number of backup workstations they needed to implement. The only problem came at system rollout, when they found that they were under-staffed.

Because the current staff was already overburdened with the normal day-to-day activities, FCMH decided to outsource the design, planning, and implementation of the new system. Once the system was put into place, the hospital kept these administrators on to keep the system working efficiently until the staff could be trained to take over their tasks.

Analyzing the Existing Administrative Structure

When approaching the discovery phase of the Active Directory and network infrastructure design, you need to determine what type of administrative structure the company is using. Looking back at the previous sections of this chapter, you have seen the different types of administration and business models. Each of them dictates how your design will be formulated. You can ask several questions of the organization to determine how the company is administered:

Resource Location   Where are the resources located? Why are the resources located in these areas? Are there security considerations involved in why they are located here? Are there communication issues, Wide Area Network (WAN) links, unreliable connections?

Administrative Staff   Where is the administrative staff located? Who is responsible for what resources? What level of administrative control does each administrator have? Should those administrators continue to administer the resources?

Growth Considerations   Does the existing structure allow for growth within the company? Does the existing structure allow for easy and efficient acquisitions and mergers?

The results of these questions will reinforce the administration model that is being implemented. Often you will find that the administration model that the company thought they were working with is not truly what they have currently implemented. As companies go through their lifecycle, they tend to take on an administrative model that fits the needs of the company, even though that may not be the administrative structure that was initially put into place. This is most typically seen in centralized companies.

⊕ Real World Scenario

The Morphing Administrative Model

Kinnet Company is a small company that prints custom maps for townships and villages. For years the company had all of its resources, servers, printers, and workstations in an office in one of Chicago's western suburbs. In the early 1990s, the company decided that they would open a location outside of Reno, Nevada. This remote site could better serve West Coast customers.

Most of the administration was performed from the home office. The administrators could perform most of their administrative tasks using MMC snap-ins. But for those tasks that could not be performed using the MMC, Terminal Services was used to connect to the servers and remotely administer them.

Nearly six months after the office was opened, the company decided that having one administrator on site at the Reno office was justified. This administrator would be responsible for system backups and any troubleshooting that could not be performed from the home office. The administrator in the Reno office was not given as many rights as the administrators at the home office, but could perform the functions that the other administrators deemed necessary.

When the design team started documenting the network for a Windows Server 2003 migration, they talked with the administrators, and were told that they had a centralized administration model with decentralized resources. After the design team documented the resources and the resource administration, they returned to the administrative staff and informed them that they were using a decentralized administrative model, due to the fact that the administrator in Reno had specific functions and was responsible for the systems at the remote site.

Make sure the questions you ask are open ended enough so that you can analyze them and possibly discover discrepancies with what the company thinks they are doing.

Sometimes the need for restructuring will become evident once the review of the existing structure is questioned. An outdated design could be as inefficient as a poor design. Trying to change an existing organization could be difficult, because many people are opposed to change. Reassigning job responsibilities may not go over well. Make sure you have the backing from key personnel, or know the "power" hierarchy within the company so that you can get the approval you need. Just remember, when you are aligning your allies, make sure you determine who the enemies are. You will always encounter those within an organization who are reluctant to change. Make sure you know who would like to see the project fail.

Interviewing key *stakeholders* within the organization will also yield valuable insight as to how the administration of the resources needs to be addressed. A stakeholder is anyone who is responsible for, or needs access to, a resource. Because they need to have the resource available to perform the duties for which they are responsible, you need to find out all you can about the resource. You will often find out more about the way a resource is used from those individuals who access it during their normal daily routines, but you should also talk with the administrators of the resource. Document your findings, but make sure that the information you are disseminating does not consume too much of your time. Especially in large organizations, you may need to determine who has high-level control of the resources and then break down the delegation of control when you plan the rollout of the design.

When reviewing the existing administrative infrastructure, you may want to put together a matrix containing the resources and the administrative staff that is responsible for those resources, as well as the users who need to access the resource and the level of access they need. Again, as with determining the administrative access, you may not be able to completely document every item within the organization, especially large organizations, but make sure that you know who the main groups are that need access.

 A sample matrix can be found later in this chapter under the section "Designing the Administrative Structure."

Later, in Chapter 3, "Designing the Active Directory Forest Structure" and Chapter 4, "Designing the Active Directory Domain Structure," as well as Chapter 5, "Designing an Organizational Unit Structure for Administrative Purposes," and Chapter 6, "Designing a Group Policy Infrastructure," we will look at the forest, domain, organizational unit, and site design. Within these chapters we will look at creating the documentation that specifies the administrative control and access requirements of the resource. These documents will assist you when you are designing these structures. Having the simplest design will allow us to efficiently administer the resources.

Understanding the Effect of Active Directory on the Administrative Design

Active Directory is a very flexible technology. With the initial rollout of Active Directory in Windows 2000 Server, many designers and implementers were pleasantly surprised to find that Active Directory allowed them to address nearly any administrative structure. The same flexibility that was presented within Windows 2000 Server has been brought forth in Windows Server 2003, with additional functionality.

Several technologies come into play when you look at Active Directory from an administrative standpoint. Active Directory lends itself well to a centralized administration model by allowing administrators to control all of the Active Directory resources from one central location. Active Directory presents the resources to the administrative staff in a logical view. Because all of the objects within the forest or domain can be accessed from the administrator's workstation using the Active Directory snap-in tools, it does not matter where the resources are located. Administration of these resources is efficiently controlled from any location.

Decentralized administration can be performed effectively using Active Directory. An organization can "break" their system into separate forests, domains, and organizational units (OUs) to control the administrative access to resources. The simplest decentralized model takes advantage of using a single forest with a single domain, broken into levels or OUs for administrative purposes. With this scheme, the administrators for the domain have access to all resources and are able to delegate administrative responsibilities to other personnel.

If completely separate administrative responsibilities are required, but all of the objects within the Active Directory infrastructure should be available to members of the organization, a single forest with multiple domains may be utilized. Once multiple domains are created, as seen in Figure 1.10, the administrators have rights and permissions to their own objects in their own domains, but do not automatically have access to resources in other domains. Of course access to other domains can be granted if necessary, but by default it is not.

FIGURE 1.10   Multiple domains for separation of administrative control

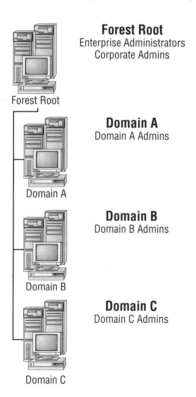

Forest Root
Enterprise Administrators
Corporate Admins

Forest Root

Domain A
Domain A Admins

Domain A

Domain B
Domain B Admins

Domain B

Domain C
Domain C Admins

Domain C

Within a multiple domain environment, issues still arise having to do with complete ownership of all of the resources within the forest. The *Enterprise Admins* group has the ability to gain access to resources anywhere within the forest. This group is a built-in group within Active Directory that resides within the forest root domain. It is "all powerful" within the forest. This is one group you should monitor very closely to make sure that only those users who are forest owners are members of the group. Once added as a member of this group, a user has the ability to modify any object within the Active Directory forest.

You may find that the political environment of the organization does not look favorably upon an all-powerful group such as the Enterprise Admins group. As we look at the risk assessment of an Active Directory design in Chapter 3, you will see that sometimes the risk of having a powerful group such as this is outweighed by the advantages of having a single schema and fewer trust relationships between multiple forests.

> Chapters 3 and 4 cover designing the Active Directory forest and domain structures. They also introduce the group interactions within these structures and specify the rights of the built-in groups.

However, if you cannot avoid the political posturing, and the company has a valid reason for not wanting to implement a single forest design (and sometimes the valid reason is that they don't trust the other administrative group!), you can create multiple forests to completely separate the administrative control over resources. Figure 1.11 shows a sample of the multiple forest structure. Sometimes a company has no choice but to implement multiple forests. Mergers and acquisitions with companies that already have an Active Directory infrastructure in place usually force the two entities to live with the multiple forest design until they can incorporate the objects from one company into the other. Legal directives also force the creation of multiple forests. Companies with military defense contracts or financial institutions that are controlled by governmental regulations find themselves building a separate forest to keep the information isolated. Several issues arise once you create a multiple forest design, and these are covered in Chapter 3, as well as in *MCSE: Windows Server 2003 Active Directory Planning, Implementation, and Maintenance Study Guide*, by Anil Desai with James Chellis (Sybex, 2003). This does become the ultimate in decentralized administration.

One note of interest: many companies have either a centralized or decentralized administrative model, yet they have implemented a multiple forest scenario. Microsoft even recommends that this practice be followed by all. A test domain should be created so that new software, patches, updates, and service packs can be tested prior to introducing them into your production environment. When taking advantage of this multiple forest scenario, the schema for the production environment will not be affected by those applications that make changes to schema attributes, and all changes to the programs that are affected by testing will not affect the systems that run the company.

Designing the Administrative Structure

After you interview the stakeholders and identify the administrative responsibilities, it is time to design the high-level overview of the administrative structure. When documenting the administrative structure, you should describe the administrative functions performed by each of the administrative groups. The documentation should also contain a breakdown of the resources and who is responsible for them. List the resource permissions at a high level. This will not be a resource-by-resource security list. For example, the administrators who are responsible for file servers at a location will be identified, but the individual shares and files will not be listed.

Real World Scenario

Research and Development

A popular home appliance manufacturer was moving from a Microsoft Windows NT 4.0 network infrastructure to Active Directory. When designing the Active Directory and network infrastructure, it was noted that the Research and Development (R&D) department was a completely autonomous business unit. For years the data that they had collected, the communication systems they used, and all of the users were kept completely separate from the corporate network. Their physical location was even separate from the corporate offices.

When the initial design phase was started, the corporate offices were included in the design, but the R&D group was not. They remained on NT 4.0 and functioned as they had done for years. When the corporate policies dictated that all of the system had to be upgraded from NT 4.0 to either Windows 2000, Windows XP, or Windows Server 2003, the initial reaction from the Active Directory team was to create a new domain for the R&D division. After all of their years of autonomy, political battles ensued. The corporate team wanted to retain a single schema for the entire enterprise, whereas the R&D team did not want to have anyone to have access to their resources.

Although access to the resources within the proposed R&D domain could be restricted to administrative staff from the R&D division, the whole idea of an all-powerful group such as Enterprise Admins scared the R&D administrators. They argued that there was no need for any of their data to be on the corporate network. For years they had maintained their own directory service with NT 4.0, and they knew how to work with Active Directory. They wanted to maintain their autonomy and have their own forest.

The battle waged on until the powers-that-be, upper management, decided that the R&D division should retain its autonomy. They had proven that they knew how to secure their resources, and those resources were not required on the corporate network. By creating the new forest, the R&D administrators had their own control over their schema and all of the administrative groups. This decentralized model is the most extreme case of a single organization having multiple forests, but the political nature of most companies can force an issue such as this.

As seen in Table 1.1, one method of documenting the administrative control is to create a resource administration matrix. The data for this matrix can be entered into a database or spreadsheet and reports can be printed out to detail the resource listing and the associated administrators or sorted so that the administrators are listed with the resources for which they are responsible.

TABLE 1.1   The Administration Matrix

Domain	Resource	Administrative Group	Permissions
Domain A		Enterprise Administrators	Full Control
		Domain A Administrators	Full Control

TABLE 1.1   The Administration Matrix *(continued)*

Domain	Resource	Administrative Group	Permissions
Domain B		Domain B Administrators	Full Control
	Exchange Server	Domain B Administrators	Full Control
		Messaging Administrators	Messaging Administration
		Messaging Techs	Server Administration
	DHCP Server	Domain B Administrators	Full Control
		Network Techs	Server Administration
	WINS Server	Domain B Administrators	Full Control
		Network Techs	Server Administration

FIGURE 1.11   Multiple forest structure

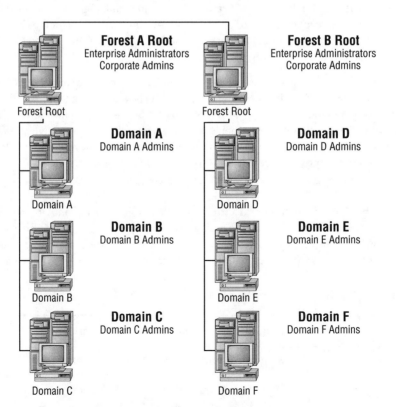

Once this information is collected and documented, you can use it when you're designing other aspects of the Active Directory and network infrastructure. Active Directory resources can be identified and grouped within OUs for easy delegation of control. This includes servers, workstations, user accounts, shared folders, printers, and other OUs. The forest and domain ownership can also be identified, aiding in the logical Active Directory design.

Figure 1.12 shows an OU design based on administrative responsibility.

Chapter 5 goes into greater detail concerning creating an efficient OU administrative design.

FIGURE 1.12   OUs designed for administrative control

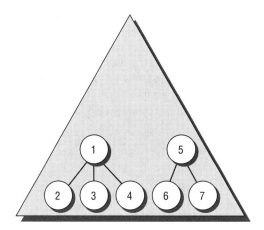

Organization Unit:	Administrator
1. Chicago	Chicago ITAdmins
2. Accounting	Chicago ITAdmins/AcctAdmins
3. Manufacturing	Chicago ITAdmins/ManAdmins
4. Information Technology	Chicago ITAdmins
5. San Diego	San Diego ITAdmins
6. Human Resources	San Diego ITAdmins/HRAdmins
7. Manufacturing	San Diego ITAdmins/ManAdmins

Summary

In this chapter, we looked at the administrative structure of a company. The administrative structure can be divided into two categories: the business model and the administration model. The business model will fall into one of four categories:

🌐 Real World Scenario

Central State Regional Board of Education

For many years the school systems that composed the Central State Regional Board of Education district were autonomous units that were able to purchase and implement any network infrastructure that they deemed necessary for their individual school system. As long as they were able to work within their budget, the RBE did not interfere. However, over the past three years support costs have been increasing due to the age of the systems and the diverse operating systems that exist throughout the district.

The decision had been made to consolidate the services under one operating system, Windows Server 2003, and a specific group of applications. Each of the schools was presented with this list. The school systems would still retain their own administrative staff and would be autonomous from the rest of the RBE school systems. After the initial political fights dissipated, the design of the new Active Directory and network infrastructure started. Because all of the schools would retain their own administrative staff but the RBE would have control over the Active Directory forest, it was decided that a hybrid model would be employed. Due to the fact that there were no special requirements for any of the school systems that would require a domain for that school, an OU structure was designed to allow the schools to have control over their resources delegated to them.

- Departmental
- Project-based
- Product/service-based
- Cost center

The administrative model will fall within the four categories:

- Centralized
- Decentralized
- Hybrid
- Outsourced

Developing an efficient Active Directory and network infrastructure design is dependent upon identifying the resources that need to be administered and the groups responsible for administering them. Once this information has been identified, the Active Directory and network infrastructure design will be mainly based upon the administrative requirements. Because Active Directory is a flexible tool, centralized or decentralized control can be easily built into its design.

Within the pages of the next chapter we will discuss the business requirements and how they affect the design. Although some of the information will carry over from this chapter to the next, this is all vital information that will help determine an efficient design for Active Directory.

Exam Essentials

Know the four business models.   The business models as identified by Microsoft are departmental, project-based, product/service-based, and cost center.

Know the four administrative models.   The four administrative models are centralized, decentralized, hybrid, and outsourced.

Know the difference between centralized administration and decentralized administration. With centralized administration, the administrative staff work as a team from one central location, even if the resources are not centrally located. Decentralized administration takes advantage of having the administrative staff distributed to where the resources are located to take advantage of efficient troubleshooting and administration.

Understand how the hybrid administration model functions.   The hybrid model has a core-centralized staff that controls all of the resources, whereas a technical support staff is decentralized to deal with issues that arise.

Know how the existing environment can affect the Active Directory design.   The current administrative model will probably be the basis for the new implementation, however, changes may occur to the administrative models due to the ease of administration when Active Directory in introduced.

Understand how Active Directory affects the administration models.   Active Directory is very flexible and can be designed to work with any of the administrative models.

Key Terms

Before you take the exam, be certain you are familiar with the following terms:

automation tools	Microsoft Management Console
centralized	outsourced
cost center model	product/service-based model
decentralized	project-based model
departmental model	snap-ins
Enterprise Admins group	stakeholders
hybrid	Terminal Services

Review Questions

1. Company A is divided into business units that make up the traditional lines of business. Some of the business units are Accounts Payable, Accounts Receivable, Human Resources, and Information Technology. What type of business model is this?

    A. Departmental

    B. Cost center

    C. Product-based

    D. Project/service-based

2. While interviewing the CIO of the company, you have noticed that he describes teams made up of employees from different divisions working together on assignments. Which of the following models is in use at this company?

    A. Departmental

    B. Cost center

    C. Product-based

    D. Project/service-based

3. Tom is working in the accounting department. Whenever he makes a request to have a report generated by the IT department, he has to determine how much the request costs and whether it fits within the monthly budget. What type of business model is this?

    A. Departmental

    B. Cost center

    C. Product-based

    D. Project/service-based

4. Mary works in the Accounting department for the Pharmaceutical division of a large corporation. Recently, she transferred from the Accounting department of the Photography division to her current position. What type of business model is employed at this corporation?

    A. Departmental

    B. Cost Center

    C. Product-based

    D. Project/service-based

5. Michelle is responsible for creating the group policies for Towneline Condominiums, Inc. She is the liaison between the Standards and Practices (S&P) group and the Information Technology (IT) staff. Her position allows her to create policies based on the standards set forth by the S&P group, but she is not allowed to assign the group policies to any of the Active Directory objects within the organization. Other administrators are allowed to assign the group policies that she creates to the OUs for which they are responsible. Which of the administrative models is employed at this organization?

   A. Centralized/centralized

   B. Centralized/decentralized

   C. Decentralized

   D. Hybrid

   E. Outsourced

6. Ted is the manager over the Information Technology group. Currently, he has twelve administrators under his control. Six of those administrators work at the corporate office and manage the servers located there. There are six branch offices, each with an administrator responsible for the servers and infrastructure at those locations. Which of the administrative models is in place here?

   A. Centralized/centralized

   B. Centralized/decentralized

   C. Decentralized

   D. Hybrid

   E. Outsourced

7. Carrie is a member of the Information Systems group at Splendiferous Foods. She is responsible for the servers at the corporate office and the two main branch offices. She works with a team of eight other administrators to support the servers at all of the locations. Because she is the "rookie" administrator, whenever there is a problem with a device at the remote locations, it is her responsibility to travel to those locations and fix the problem. What administrative model is represented?

   A. Centralized/centralized

   B. Centralized/decentralized

   C. Decentralized

   D. Hybrid

   E. Outsourced

8. Terry has been working for Driveshaft Manufacturers for several years. Until recently, he was solely responsible for the Information Technology department and all of the servers and workstations at the company. The company has recently acquired a rival and now Terry has become the manager over the Information Technology group. It has been decided that Terry will have full control over all of the resources within the company. The administrators from the company that was acquired will continue to support their systems. These systems will remain located at the new location and the administrative staff will remain there also. Terry has been given an account within their environment that will allow him to control the resources if necessary. What type of administrative model is being used?

    A. Centralized/centralized

    B. Centralized/decentralized

    C. Decentralized

    D. Hybrid

    E. Outsourced

9. Caspian's Creations employs 5,000 employees nationwide. They have locations in 37 cities. At each location, they provide servers for access to the applications required to perform the functions required by the users. Information Technology administrators are onsite at each of the locations and are given autonomy over their resources. Which of the administrative models is in place at Caspian's Creations?

    A. Centralized/centralized

    B. Centralized/decentralized

    C. Decentralized

    D. Hybrid

    E. Outsourced

10. St. Mary's Hospital Systems has hired a consulting firm to provide administrative staff to support their current infrastructure. What type of administrative model is used?

    A. Centralized/centralized

    B. Centralized/decentralized

    C. Decentralized

    D. Hybrid

    E. Outsourced

Answers to Review Questions

1. A. Any time a company has divided the business units among the traditional function format, the company is using the departmental model.

2. D. Most companies that are employing the project/service-based model will have employees from different business units, such as accounting and manufacturing, all working on a project so that the resources are available to efficiently complete the project.

3. B. In a company that employs the cost center model, each department must allocate a budget amount that will be used when using the resources of other departments.

4. C. Whenever a company has divided its businesses into distinct product lines, each with its own resources, you will probably be looking at a product-based business model.

5. D. If a company has divided the responsibilities of the administrators so that they have different levels of control to the same resources, whether those resources are centralized or decentralized, the administrative model is hybrid.

6. C. The decentralized model has the administrative staff spread out in the location where the resources are so that they can control those resources locally and efficiently.

7. B. This scenario represents the centralized/decentralized model because the administrative staff is located at one office and they are responsible for the resources at all of the locations.

8. D. Because the administrative staff is divided between the company headquarters and the acquired location and the resources are decentralized, this may seem like the decentralized model, but Terry has full administrative control over all of the resources, making this the hybrid administrative model.

9. C. Decentralized administration allows the administrators from each of the locations autonomy over their own resources. The administrators reside at the same location as the resources and do not have access to resources at other locations.

10. E. Whenever the administrative staff is brought in from another firm or the administration is provided by another firm's staff even though they may be onsite, the administrative model in place is the outsourced model.

Case Study

You should give yourself 20 minutes to review this testlet, review the diagram, and complete the questions.

Background

Insane Systems builds custom computers for their customers. They specialize in building cases that are unique and support the latest in hardware technology. They started off as a small company that provided this service to gamers who would take their cases to LAN parties to show off. Due to the fact that their systems were considered some of the most stable gaming platforms and because they provided an impressive design that gamers could show off, they started to become popular. Insane Systems started mass manufacturing some of their more popular designs and began selling stand-alone cases along with their fully configured systems. As space at the company became a premium, the office was moved from the manufacturing facility. This allowed the company to add to the amount of space that was used for the mass production line.

Existing Environment

Over the past few months, Insane Systems has been developing plans to expand their company. They have identified San Jose, California, Atlanta, Georgia, and New York City as the locations with their highest customer base. The current Chicago location will remain the corporate headquarters, but they are opening branches in New York City and San Jose. They are also in the process of acquiring a competitor's business in Atlanta. These locations will provide retail outlets as well as support. Customers will have the option of sending their systems back to the corporate office for any needed upgrades or repairs, or delivering them to one of the branch locations.

Because the company is planning on expanding, they want to make sure that the network infrastructure is in place to support their larger, distributed company. They are also concerned with the support lifetime of their current Windows NT 4.0 infrastructure. They realize they have the option of moving to a Windows 2000 Server or Windows Server 2003 infrastructure and are considering moving to Windows Server 2003 and Active Directory for two reasons: the expected support lifetime is greater than Windows 2000, and they are a technology firm that is not afraid of staying ahead of the technology curve.

Interviews

Your company has been hired to design an Active Directory infrastructure and the network infrastructure to support it. During the interview process with some of the key stakeholders you gathered the following information:

CEO Currently we have a single location with all of our processes local. As we grow, we would like to keep all of the administration here in Chicago. Because the new branches are primarily retail and support offices, we will not need to have a large staff in those locations.

CIO   Most of the infrastructure that we support is located here at the corporate office. We do support some key servers at the manufacturing location. We support these servers from our main office. Because the servers are nearby, if there is a problem, we can usually be on site within half an hour.

The new branches are going to be another issue altogether. We would like to retain the same level of administrative control over the servers in the new locations that we employ currently. Due to the geographic limitations, we may need to have some support staff at those locations. Currently, the plan is to hire staff at those locations that can provide the support for the customers, but also have an understanding of the business systems we need to put into place.

Manager of Information Technology   We have grown very quickly over the past three years and our current technologies have kept up with that growth. However, we don't think the current infrastructure is ready for the amount of growth that we are expecting within the following year. We are not afraid of moving to the latest technology, but we want to make sure that the design is stable and makes sense for us, especially if we will continue growing in the upcoming months.

Most of our processes are located here at this office, and we would like to keep it that way. We know that there will be servers that will need to be located at the remote offices, but we would like to be able to provide most of the support from this location. Remote administration tools will need to be included within the design so that we can keep our administrative costs at a minimum.

Currently we have most of our servers located at the main office, and all are located on their own high-speed backbone. We do have a server at the manufacturing site that allows the staff there to have e-mail as well as plans and orders in case we lose connectivity between the offices. This server is running Microsoft Exchange Server. Several times during the day, we replicate the public folder information to this system so that they are always up to date and do not have to dial up to the main office.

The systems at the main office are all supported by our staff of four administrators. All of the administrators are cross-trained on Windows NT 4, Exchange Server, SQL Server, our accounting software, and each of our file and print servers. We currently have five Windows NT 4 servers in place, one Exchange server at both locations, one SQL server at the main office, one server running our accounting package that interfaces with the SQL server, and one file and print server that is used by both locations. The Exchange server at the manufacturing location doubles as a print server also.

Because all of the client machines are running Windows NT 4 Workstation, we do not have to worry about supporting different operating systems. We would like to maintain that same easy administration with the upcoming system. We would like to provide the same types of services at the remote locations that we provide at the home office, although accounting will remain at the home office and will not be spread out to all of the locations.

CASE STUDY

Table

Use the following table as a resource to answer the questions.

Resources	Administrative Groups
Exchange Server—Home Office	Headquarters Administrators
Exchange Server—Manufacturing Office	San Jose Support Staff
Exchange Server—San Jose Office	New York Support Staff
Exchange Server—Atlanta Office	Atlanta Support Staff
Exchange Server—New York Office	
SQL Server—Home Office	
SQL Server—Manufacturing Office	
SQL Server—San Jose Office	
SQL Server—Atlanta Office	
SQL Server—New York Office	
Accounting Server—Home Office	
Accounting Server—Manufacturing Office	
Accounting Server—San Jose Office	
Accounting Server—Atlanta Office	
Accounting Server—New York Office	
File and Print Server—Home Office	
File and Print Server—Manufacturing Office	
File and Print Server—San Jose Office	
File and Print Server—Atlanta Office	
File and Print Server—New York Office	

Case Study Questions

1. What is the current administrative model in use?
   - **A.** Centralized
   - **B.** Decentralized
   - **C.** Hybrid
   - **D.** Outsourced

2. What type of administrative model is desired by the company for the new design?
   - **A.** Centralized
   - **B.** Decentralized
   - **C.** Hybrid
   - **D.** Outsourced

3. What type of administrative model should be suggested for the proposed corporate design?
   - **A.** Centralized
   - **B.** Decentralized
   - **C.** Hybrid
   - **D.** Outsourced

4. Using the information provided in the case study, select the resources within the existing design and write them in the right-hand column.

Resources	Resources
Exchange Server—Home Office	
Exchange Server—Manufacturing Office	
Exchange Server—San Jose Office	
Exchange Server—Atlanta Office	
Exchange Server—New York Office	
SQL Server—Home Office	
SQL Server—Manufacturing Office	
SQL Server—San Jose Office	
SQL Server—Atlanta Office	

SQL Server—New York Office	
Accounting Server—Home Office	
Accounting Server—Manufacturing Office	
Accounting Server—San Jose Office	
Accounting Server—Atlanta Office	
Accounting Server—New York Office	
File and Print Server—Home Office	
File and Print Server—Manufacturing Office	
File and Print Server—San Jose Office	
File and Print Server—Atlanta Office	
File and Print Server—New York Office	

5. Using the information provided in the case study, select the administrative staff within the existing design and write them in the right-hand column.

Administrative Groups	Administrative Groups
Headquarters Administrators	
San Jose Support Staff	
New York Support Staff	
Atlanta Support Staff	

6. Using the information provided in the case study, match the resources with the appropriate administrators for the existing design.

Resources	Administrative Groups
Exchange Server—Home Office	Headquarters Administrators
Exchange Server—Manufacturing Office	San Jose Support Staff
Exchange Server—San Jose Office	New York Support Staff
Exchange Server—Atlanta Office	Atlanta Support Staff

Exchange Server—New York Office	
SQL Server—Home Office	
SQL Server—Manufacturing Office	
SQL Server—San Jose Office	
SQL Server—Atlanta Office	
SQL Server—New York Office	
Accounting Server—Home Office	
Accounting Server—Manufacturing Office	
Accounting Server—San Jose Office	
Accounting Server—Atlanta Office	
Accounting Server—New York Office	
File and Print Server—Home Office	
File and Print Server—Manufacturing Office	
File and Print Server—San Jose Office	
File and Print Server—Atlanta Office	
File and Print Server—New York Office	

7. Using the information provided in the case study, select the resources as envisioned within the proposed design and write them in the right-hand column.

Resources	Resources
Exchange Server—Home Office	
Exchange Server—Manufacturing Office	
Exchange Server—San Jose Office	
Exchange Server—Atlanta Office	
Exchange Server—New York Office	
SQL Server—Home Office	

CASE STUDY

SQL Server—Manufacturing Office	
SQL Server—San Jose Office	
SQL Server—Atlanta Office	
SQL Server—New York Office	
Accounting Server—Home Office	
Accounting Server—Manufacturing Office	
Accounting Server—San Jose Office	
Accounting Server—Atlanta Office	
Accounting Server—New York Office	
File and Print Server—Home Office	
File and Print Server—Manufacturing Office	
File and Print Server—San Jose Office	
File and Print Server—Atlanta Office	
File and Print Server—New York Office	

8. Using the information provided in the case study, select the administrative staff as envisioned within the proposed design and move them to the right-hand column.

Administrative Groups	Administrative Groups
Headquarters Administrators	
San Jose Support Staff	
New York Support Staff	
Atlanta Support Staff	

9. Using the following table, match the resources with the appropriate administrators for the envisioned design.

Resources	Administrative Groups
Exchange Server—Home Office	Headquarters Administrators
Exchange Server—Manufacturing Office	San Jose Support Staff
Exchange Server—San Jose Office	New York Support Staff
Exchange Server—Atlanta Office	Atlanta Support Staff
Exchange Server—New York Office	
SQL Server—Home Office	
SQL Server—Manufacturing Office	
SQL Server—San Jose Office	
SQL Server—Atlanta Office	
SQL Server—New York Office	
Accounting Server—Home Office	
Accounting Server—Manufacturing Office	
Accounting Server—San Jose Office	
Accounting Server—Atlanta Office	
Accounting Server—New York Office	
File and Print Server—Home Office	
File and Print Server—Manufacturing Office	
File and Print Server—San Jose Office	
File and Print Server—Atlanta Office	
File and Print Server—New York Office	

Answers to Case Study Questions

1. A. Even though the company's resources are not centralized, the administrative staff is centralized. This falls under the centralized administrative/decentralized resources administrative model, which is still considered a centralized model.

2. A. The powers-that-be would like to keep the same administrative structure that they have become accustomed to, but that may not work out.

3. C. Using the hybrid administrative model, the current administrative staff can still control the servers and perform most of their administrative responsibilities by using tools that can perform remote administration. Support staff at the remote locations can have some administrative responsibilities and be available on site to perform functions that the central admin staff cannot because they are not on site.

4.

Resources
Exchange Server—Home Office
Exchange Server—Manufacturing Office
SQL Server—Home Office
Accounting Server—Home Office
File and Print Server—Home Office

When reviewing the case study, the only resources that were mentioned at this point included the Exchange 5.5 servers at the home office and the manufacturing site, the SQL 7.0 server, the accounting server, and the file and print server.

5.

Administrative Groups
Headquarters Administrators

Currently, the administration model is centralized/centralized and the only administrative staff in place are the headquarters administrators.

6.

Administrative Groups
Headquarters Administrators
Exchange Server—Home Office
Exchange Server—Manufacturing Office
SQL Server—Home Office
Accounting Server—Home Office
File and Print Server—Home Office

Due to the fact that the current administration model is centralized/centralized, you can easily match up the resources with the single administrative group.

7.

Resources
Exchange Server—Home Office
Exchange Server—Manufacturing Office
SQL Server—Home Office
Accounting Server—Home Office
File and Print Server—Home Office
Exchange Server—San Jose Office
Exchange Server—Atlanta Office
Exchange Server—New York Office
File and Print Server—San Jose Office
File and Print Server—Atlanta Office
File and Print Server—New York Office

In the company's expansion efforts, they have identified the resources that will be put into place at each of the locations. New resources include Exchange servers and file and print servers at each of the sites.

8.

Administrative Groups
Headquarters Administrators
Atlanta Support Staff
New York Support Staff
San Jose Support Staff

New administrative staff will be identified at each of the new locations. Although these administrators will not have as much control over resources as the corporate administrators, they will still need rights to perform tasks on the systems located at their site.

9.

Exchange Server—Home Office
Headquarters Administrators
Exchange Server Manufacturing Office
Headquarters Administrators
SQL Server—Home Office
Headquarters Administrators
Accounting Server—Home Office
Headquarters Administrators
File and Print Server—Home Office
Headquarters Administrators
Exchange Server—San Jose Office
Headquarters Administrators
San Jose Support Staff
Exchange Server—Atlanta Office
Headquarters Administrators
Atlanta Support Staff
Exchange Server—New York Office
Headquarters Administrators
New York Support Staff
File and Print Server—San Jose Office
Headquarters Administrators
San Jose Support Staff
File and Print Server—Atlanta Office
Headquarters Administrators
Atlanta Support Staff
File and Print Server New York Office
Headquarters Administrators
New York Support Staff

Once the resources have been identified, the new administrative control matrix can be prepared. All of the resources will still be administered by the headquarters administrators, and each of the site's admins will also have administrative access to the servers in their location.

Chapter 2

Determining Business and Technical Requirements

MICROSOFT EXAM OBJECTIVES COVERED IN THIS CHAPTER

✓ **Analyze the impact of Active Directory on the existing technical environment.**

- Analyze hardware and software requirements.
- Analyze current level of service within an existing technical environment.
- Analyze current network administration model.
- Analyze network requirements.

✓ **Analyze existing network operating system implementation.**

- Identify the existing domain model.
- Identify the number and location of domain controllers on the network.
- Identify the configuration details of all servers on the network. Server types might include primary domain controllers, backup domain controllers, file servers, print servers, and Web servers.

✓ **Analyze security requirements for the Active Directory directory service.**

- Analyze current security policies, standards, and procedures.

✓ **Design the Active Directory infrastructure to meet business and technical requirements.**

- Design the envisioned administration model.

✓ **Identify network topology and performance levels.**

   ▪ Identify constraints in the current network infrastructure.

   ▪ Interpret current baseline performance requirements for each major subsystem.

✓ **Analyze the impact of the infrastructure design on the existing technical environment.**

   ▪ Analyze hardware and software requirements.

   ▪ Analyze current level of service within the existing technical environment.

   ▪ Analyze network requirements.

In the previous chapter, we introduced and discussed different administrative models. As we move on through the book, these models will be referenced and noted as to how they affect, or are affected by, the design elements.

The material within this chapter is essentially the building blocks for the remainder of the book. If you do not understand how the business currently runs, what services and systems are currently in place, or the future requirements, you will not have a foundation on which to design a functional Active Directory or network infrastructure.

When put into a position where you are responsible for designing the next incarnation of your directory service and network infrastructure, you soon discover that you need to become an expert on everything related to your network. Most network administrators have a good grasp of the business practices and day-to-day activities within their organization. However, they may not have such a good grasp of the current technologies required as part of the new proposed infrastructure. That is where outside consultants can be of great benefit. Whereas some companies take on the task of designing their own infrastructure, many more decide that the current staff should continue the work they are doing, and they bring in another company that specializes in designing, planning, and implementing.

Stepping into any organization and reviewing their current network infrastructure and administrative design can be a daunting challenge. Not only are you in a position where you need to have a firm understanding of the technologies you are planning to implement, you are responsible for learning the intricacies of the current business. No two companies are created the same. Due to business practices, administrative decisions, and budget constraints, two companies that provide the same service will implement their business practices in completely different manners. This is where the knowledge of the system's administrators becomes a great benefit to the consultant.

It is critical that the entire current infrastructure is documented. Without a comprehensive outline of what is currently in place, the new design will be flawed and the implementation will most likely need to be reworked. Any redesign work that needs to take place will end up costing the company more, either in man-hours, overextended budgets, or both.

When you are determining the requirements for the organization, you need to consider several areas that make up the organizational infrastructure. Starting with the current system implementation, you need to identify what is already in place. This includes the current directory services, resources, and the administrative control over those resources. Secondly, you need to assess the *software requirements*. Finally, you need to assess the *hardware requirements* based on the currently installed systems and software. Once all of this is determined, you have the information required to start documenting the current infrastructure and making design decisions for an Active Directory and network infrastructure that is viable for the company.

Identifying the Current System Implementation

Most organizations will already have some type of network and administrative infrastructure in place. This could range from a simple peer-to-peer network where the users control their own resources, to a large multinational corporation that uses several different directory services. If you understand the current design, you will have an easier time making design decisions for the new Active Directory model.

You should also note any other projects that are currently in progress. It is rare that an organization can put everything on hold while a single project is put into place. Although it would be nice to have everything halted until Active Directory is in place and the network infrastructure is optimized, in reality we know that is not going to be the case. Make sure you investigate the changes that every project will bring and document the additional resources that will be required.

Determining Organizational Requirements

Businesses make decisions to implement a directory service and network infrastructure for many reasons. Those reasons could be as simple as a software requirement, or as complex as a need to restructure their organization's resources into one simple functional design. No matter the reason, a solid, stable infrastructure depends on a well thought out and documented design.

Several operating system and directory service vendors are on the market. Existing systems are usually put into place due to an organization's needs. Depending on the available software and hardware at the time of the installation, a company could have several vendors' products in place. If you are lucky enough to be assessing an organization that designed their infrastructure from the ground up and used a systematic approach when they integrated any new technologies, your job will be much easier than if a hodge-podge approach was taken. More often than not, however, the hodge-podge approach is what you will find. Administrators are often under the gun to implement a process that allows the users to perform their jobs. At the same time, they are responsible for the usual day-to-day activities. Quick tests of the new applications needed for the process may be run, sometimes not, and then the new system is let loose. The users begin running the applications, and when problems occur, the troubleshooting process begins. This cycle continues until the process works within the environment.

When reviewing the case studies that are presented during your exam, you will not find many questions, if any at all, that ask what type of administrative models are being used within the organization. The same is true with determining the current organizational requirements; few, if any, questions will be presented on the exam. However, you must be able to interpret the information that is presented so that you can make the correct design decisions.

Determining the Reason

The reasons for moving to, or implementing Active Directory, are varied. Some companies simply buy into the Microsoft hype and have decided that they need to join the crowd. Others need to implement Active Directory due to software requirements, such as Exchange Server 2003. Still others have decided that their current implementation of a directory service will no longer meet the needs of the organization and are adopting a single directory service design or restructuring their current implementation. You need to determine the most important reason.

Although there may be multiple reasons, the design needs to take into account the highest priority and build around it. When decisions need to be made, they should be based on the highest priority if there are any tradeoffs. The decision criteria will include domain restructuring, application support, planned obsolescence, and total cost of ownership.

Domain Restructuring

Domain restructuring is becoming a very common reason for developing a design. Numerous companies have Windows NT 4 in their organizations. Due to limitations within the Windows NT 4 domain capabilities, these companies have several domains built with trust relationships interconnecting them. Because Active Directory has the ability to support millions of objects and has more efficient administrative capabilities, the domain structure can be collapsed to allow objects from quite a few NT 4 domains to reside within a single Active Directory domain.

Application Support

Active Directory is an *extendable database*. An extendable database allows you to add objects and attributes to the default schema so that you can have a central repository for application support. Windows 2000 introduced this to the Microsoft networking environment, and software vendors started supporting this ability. Exchange Server 2003 is an application that takes advantage of the extensible nature of Active Directory. Thousands of additional *attributes*, which are the objects that define a class, and hundreds of classes are added to, or modified within, Active Directory to support Exchange Server 2003. Exchange then takes advantage of Active Directory as the directory service for which it uses to replicate information between Exchange servers and look up recipient and distribution list information.

If an organization is building its directory service infrastructure around the need to implement an application, the ramifications of "throwing" a design together may not be readily apparent. You will need to stress the importance of a careful design. The Domain Name System (DNS), Active Directory, and Organization names are extremely important and can cause problems in the future if they are not chosen correctly. For instance, if you have not registered your domain name with Internet Corporation for Assigned Names and Numbers (ICANN), and you want to use this name as your Internet presence, you will not be able to if someone has already laid claim to it. As the directory service expert, it will be your responsibility to educate the powers that be.

Planned Obsolescence

Many companies are faced with the inevitable loss of support for the legacy operating systems. As these older operating systems, such as NT 4, reach the end of their lifecycle, companies have to spend more money to keep support contracts on them. Microsoft does not release very many hotfixes or service packs for these older operating systems, which makes them subject to attacks that newer operating systems are protected from. As companies start to fear that they will no longer have support for their operating system, they are looking to upgrade to another operating system that will be supported for several more years.

Total Cost of Ownership

Total cost of ownership (TCO) is a marketing point that Microsoft likes to push, and rightfully so. TCO is based upon not only the tangible costs associated with purchasing the hardware and software, but also the intangible costs of supporting the hardware and software, such as the portion of the administrator's salary that is associated with controlling, troubleshooting, and supporting a system. If designed correctly, and administered efficiently, Active Directory can save a company's budget when it comes to efficient management and support. One example is its ability to collapse a multiple domain design into a single domain design that takes advantage of organizational units (OUs) to delegate administrative responsibilities. The administrators responsible for domains under the original domain structure can still have administrative control over the same resources as they did in the past; however, the entire structure is organized for more efficient control of the entire set of resources.

Another advantage is that Group Policies can be put into place that will control a user's environment. Standard *line-of-business applications*, which are applications used to support the business's day-to-day operations, can be rolled out to the users who need them when Group Policies are used to automatically distribute software. When an upgrade or patch becomes available, it can be rolled out in an automated fashion using group policies instead of visiting the client workstation to perform a manual install.

When designing for total cost of ownership, you need to consider where the organization wishes to concentrate their TCO efforts. Some organizations simply want to design a more efficient administrative structure. Others want to optimize their application rollout and support. Still others want to take advantage of both options.

> Chapter 5, "Designing An Organizational Unit Structure For Administrative Purposes," and Chapter 6, "Designing a Group Policy Infrastructure," are dedicated to the advantages and disadvantages of designing OUs for administrative purposes and Group Policy efficiency.

You will need to consider trade-offs during the design process, because the optimum levels of administrative delegation and efficient Group Policy application do not usually work out to be the same design.

Special Requirements

Special cases need to be considered when you are documenting the current organizational requirements, especially when a domain restructuring is in the works. Some cases involve domains that cannot be collapsed. For instance, several corporations may start their existence providing one type of service, and later expand to provide other services as well. For example, many insurance companies have started banking divisions. Due to government regulations, the two divisions of the organization have to remain separate.

These special requirements will already have an impact on the current infrastructure and will continue to affect the future implementation. Administrative, political, and geographic restrictions, legal regulations, and plans for growth are the primary implications when determining the special requirements.

Restrictions and Regulations

You may encounter administrative restrictions as you investigate the requirements. Some of the resources located in domains may reside there because of administrative restrictions. The organization may have segregated these resources so that they can only be administered by certain members of the administrative staff. However, make sure that the reason for the separation of administrative control truly justifies the need for an additional domain. Make note of the reasons for the multiple domains in your documentation. You may also want to check the regulations to make sure they have not changed since the original model was put in place. From an administrative viewpoint, it is easier to build a single domain model and use OUs to delegate administrative control.

 Design Scenario

Analyzing Organizational Requirements

RoboSystems designs and builds robotic arms that are used in manufacturing plants throughout the world. Recognized as one of the leaders in robotics, they have continued to grow during the past 10 years. Management is contemplating the acquisition of another company that has been a competitor for several years. This acquisition will allow RoboSystems to add some new products to their line and diversify their offerings. Talks between the two companies are still in the discovery stages, but the company wants to make sure that the new directory service will allow for growth of the company if the acquisition does take place.

Four administrators report to the manager of information technology and are responsible for all of RoboSystems' current system implementations. Three of the administrators are located at the company headquarters, and one is located at the manufacturing facility. The administrators at the headquarters are responsible for maintaining all of the systems within the organization, and the remote administrator at the manufacturing facility is responsible for maintaining the systems that are located at his facility.

During the interview process, you discovered the following information from key stakeholders:

CEO   We are currently in a growth mode and I am concerned about our ability to grow technologically. If our plans to acquire another company come to fruition, I want to be assured that we can support all of the processes and systems that would be needed for both entities to compete in the marketplace.
I am also expecting our company to become more competitive and am looking to lower our operating expenses. With the additional systems that we will need to support after the acquisition, we will need to support more while maintaining the same level of staffing.

Manager of Information Technology Our current network infrastructure is built on a combination of Windows NT 4 and Novell NetWare 4.11. Although we are pleased with Novell's NDS, we are looking to take advantage of applications that are only supported on a Windows-based server. Exchange Server 2003 is one of those applications. Due to Exchange's server requirements, we are looking to move to Active Directory and use Windows Server 2003 as our primary network operating system. Doing so will simplify our account management as well as allow us to concentrate on one operating system. This should reduce our administrative overhead and allow us to work more efficiently.

1. **Question:** What reasons do RoboSystems have for designing a new Active Directory and network infrastructure? **Answer:** Reduce the Total Cost of Ownership (TCO) and application support.

2. **Question:** What is the primary reason for the new design? **Answer:** Looking at the interview information from the CEO and the manager of information technology, we can determine some of the reasons for the new design. The CEO mentioned that the new system's administrative requirements should be less than the existing environment. This bit of information alone should tell you that they are looking to reduce the TCO. Of course, what CEO doesn't want to reduce the TCO of the company? The manager of IT also hints at reducing the TCO but also mentions that they want to consolidate their current systems into one directory service. Keep this in mind when reviewing the information later on, because reducing the TCO appears to be the highest priority at this point.

You will also encounter barriers that control organizations, mainly political and geographic. The political reasons affect multinational organizations more than they do domestic organizations. Although the domestic laws place some restrictions on the current designs, when *political boundaries* are crossed, specific laws cannot be broken. One in particular is the United States' *cryptographic export laws*. These laws dictate how strong the cryptographic keys can be when used outside of the United States. For the most part, these laws have been rescinded and most countries are allowed to have access to the strong keys. However, there are still some countries that are not allowed to have access to these strong cryptographic keys. Although these laws affect applications and system connectivity more than anything else, there could be legal reasons why the company has created a division between business units and created extra domains to enforce those restrictions.

 For more information about which countries are restricted due to cryptographic export laws, see the information at http://www.rsasecurity.com/rsalabs/faq/6-5-1.html.

Privacy laws are starting to become prevalent in our society as people become increasingly concerned about their privacy and identity safekeeping. Directory services, by their nature, hold information about the users in the organization. This information can be accessed by administrators and, depending on the permissions that have been assigned, users. There may be reasons to completely separate the administrative control for privacy reasons. Whereas the United States is just now starting to identify privacy concerns, other nations have already adopted privacy rules. Most European countries have specific rules pertaining to the information that can be exported. You will find that the rules that govern the data that can be sent to Europe from the United States are much more lax than the rules for exporting data from Europe to the United States.

Plans for Growth

The goal for most organizations is to make a profit and grow. Most companies do not put "reduction of size" in their mission statement. Their projections usually state that they are trying to obtain a certain amount of growth; a 10-percent increase in revenue over the same quarter from last year, a 15-percent increase in profits though the end of the year, and so on. Most corporate entities measure their viability in how much the company has grown financially. The stockholders for the company require that the company is viable and growing.

Some of the more aggressive companies attempt to acquire other businesses or merge with other entities. If plans are in the works for an acquisition or merger, the design will need to take this expansion into consideration. All of the entities concerned need to be investigated so that you will know how the units will tie together and so you can plan for the combined infrastructure.

Administrative Control

One of the most important considerations when identifying the requirements of any organization is the administrative responsibilities. More than anything else, you need to know who is responsible for the resources within the organization. Without this information, you will not know why the current domain structure is built, nor will you have a basis for restructuring the resources into an efficient directory service infrastructure.

Resources will include users, computers, shared folders, printers, domain controllers, sites, OUs, and any other physical or logical object that resides within Active Directory. You need to document what objects exist and who is responsible for each of them. In Chapter 5, we will present effective designs for administrative control. The more thorough you are at discovering and documenting information at this level, the more effective your final design will be.

One tool many administrators use when mapping the resource/administrative control is a table that outlines the resources, who is responsible for those resources, and the level of control they have over the resources. As seen in Table 2.1, when the table is created, you can easily view who is responsible for each resource. This table, usually created with a spreadsheet, will also come in handy later as you start the design of the new directory service. The information you gathered will become your documentation for designing domains and OUs.

In Chapter 1, "Analyzing The Administrative Structure," we discussed the different types of administrative control: centralized, decentralized, and hybrid. Depending on the resources the administrative staff is responsible for and the level of control they have over those resources, you can decide what type of control the company uses. If administrators need complete autonomy over their own resources, chances are the organization employs a decentralized approach. If the administration is shared over all of the resources, a centralized model is probably being employed. However, if the company does have a hierarchy of administrative responsibilities where more than one group of administrators manage the resources, each with their own level of control, the company probably uses a hybrid approach. If you review the administrative requirements carefully, you should fully understand which model is being used.

TABLE 2.1   A Sample Administrative Control Table

Server	Service/Application	Administrator (DetroitAdmins have control over all servers)
LANBDC	Backup Domain Controller	No Local Administration
NetServices	DHCP/DNS/WINS	No Local Administration
LANFNP	File and Print Server	LansingAdmins
LANINTRAWEB	Intranet Web Server	LansingAdmins

Geographic Design

If an organization only has one location, the design should be simple, with no *wide area network (WAN)* links or a need for multiple sites or site links. More often than not, the company will have multiple locations with WAN links connecting them. You may even run into large multinational corporations that not only have multiple locations and several different types of communication links connecting them, but will also have time zone differences and geo-political boundaries.

Creating a map of the corporate anatomy will assist you when you are trying to visualize how the locations communicate. Make sure you include all of the different types of communication equipment as well as the speed of the links, their reliability, and the amount of traffic currently saturating the link. Using a program such as Visio, you can create network diagrams to include within your documentation. With these documents, you will then have information that details the current network topology. Figure 2.1 is an example of a Visio diagram that shows the connections among three offices.

 Design Scenario

Determining Administrative Needs

Looking at the administrative makeup of RoboSystems that was described in the "Analyzing Organizational Requirements" sidebar earlier in this chapter, we find that there are four administrators, one of whom is located at the manufacturing facility to support the remote systems. The other three administrators have control over the remote resources also. All three of the corporate administrators are members of a group named CorpAdmins, and the administrator from the manufacturing facility is a member of the group ManAdmins. After inventorying the systems in use, the following systems were identified:

- Corporate Office resources:

  - ACCTFP = File/Print Server

  - CorpDNS = DNS Server

- CorpWINS = WINS Server

- CorpEX = Exchange 5.5

- CorpDC = NT 4 PDC

- CorpDC2 = NT 4 BDC

- CorpSQL = SQL 7 Server

- Manufacturing Plant resources:

  - ManDC = NT 4 BDC

  - ManNRS = DNS/WINS Server

  - ManEX = Exchange 5.5

  - ManFP = File/Print Server

1. **Question:** From the information gathered about the administrative structure, determine what type of administrative model is in place. **Answer:** From what you have already read about the administrative models, you can determine that the current administrative model is a hybrid model.

2. **Question:** Build an administrative control table based on the information that was gathered. **Answer:** After reviewing the systems in place within RoboSystems, you have determined the following:

Server	Service/Application	Administrator
ACCTFP	File/Print Server	CorpAdmins
CorpDNS	DNS Server	CorpAdmins
CorpWINS	WINS Server	CorpAdmins
CorpEX	Exchange 5.5	CorpAdmins
CorpDC	NT 4 PDC	CorpAdmins
CorpDC2	NT 4 BDC	CorpAdmins
CorpSQL	SQL 7 Server	CorpAdmins
ManDC	NT 4 BDC	CorpAdmins/ManAdmins
ManNRS	DNS/WINS Server	CorpAdmins/ManAdmins
ManEX	Exchange 5.5	CorpAdmins/ManAdmins
ManFP	File/Print Server	CorpAdmins/ManAdmins

FIGURE 2.1 A sample network diagram using Visio

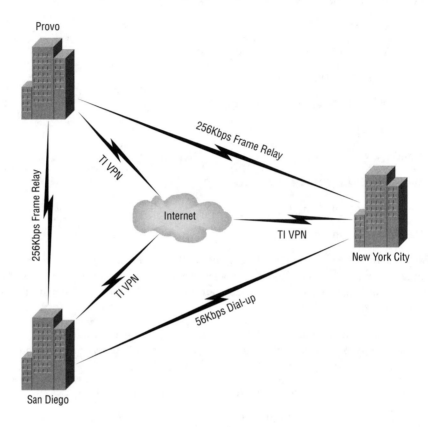

Later in this chapter, we discuss the network requirements and connection types that are used. Based on the geographic design of the network, you may end up having to use connection types that are less than optimal, but that is a trade-off that may be necessary to allow the administrative control of the resources within your organization.

Identifying the Current Software Requirements

By taking an inventory of the current software the company uses you will be able to determine what types of hardware, network, and name-resolution requirements the organization needs. You can use several methods to obtain this information, some of which are easier than others. Microsoft and other third-party companies have tools that allow you to determine what software is installed on computers within the organization. Microsoft's System's Management Server (SMS) has the ability to inventory the software installed on a client's workstation as well as the applications running on servers. Once the software is inventoried, reports can be prepared to detail the software in use. Novell has a product called ZENworks that can provide this same functionality. Other third-party companies—such as Tivoli—can also provide this for you.

One drawback of these products is that they must already exist on the network. Since many companies have not implemented one of these technologies, you will have to add it. It is rare that you will find a company that will allow you to introduce one of these products into their production environment. It is even rarer that you will be granted the budget to implement a technology that might not be used in the final rollout of the design.

Something that we will come back to time and again when we are explaining how to identify requirements is the interview process. Although prone to errors, mainly of omission, the interview process is your best tool to use when you are trying to determine what software is in place within the organization. If you are a member of the organization, you may be aware of the line of business applications that make up the business processes. However, if you are someone who is called in to assess the organization, you may not have this luxury. Sitting down with the stakeholders allows you to determine what software is in use. Even if you do have a list of the line of business applications, you should still perform interviews. You never know when you will come across a division that has implemented an application to assist them with a function, even though it was not implemented through the proper channels.

Software requirements will be based on the software issues that have dictated how the company has implemented the current design. Some software comes prepackaged, whereas other software is written in-house. You may also encounter protocol issues that may need to be addressed.

Software Issues

Software comes in two flavors: packaged and home-grown applications. Most companies will have a little of both. If a company is lucky, packaged applications that they purchase from a retail outlet will fulfill their requirements and they will not have to develop applications that are specific to their environment. Application suites, such as Microsoft Office, will play a prominent part in many organizations due to the fact that the service they provide is required by most organizations. They contain so many features that the company usually does not need any additional functionality. Other client applications used to access the server applications may only have a single function. Still other applications, such as Internet Explorer, may have a specific function they provide, such as gaining access to web pages, but they may also be used to access server-based applications that can generate and manipulate data on those servers.

Although most companies will be able to use packaged applications to some extent, some organizations will have specific requirements that packaged applications do not cover. These specialized applications are either written by in-house development staff, or contracted out for another company to develop. These applications will range from data analysis add-in macros for a spreadsheet to customer relations software. Each of the applications will have requirements for them to run.

These requirements will need to be documented along with the applications being used. These requirements will aid you when you are determining the hardware, network, and name resolution requirements. Certain applications will not need any special requirements for the network, whereas others will have specific needs. Some applications will require that a NetBIOS name resolution method be available, where others will rely on hostname resolution. Keep track of the application requirements because you will use them later when you are determining the services required and the hardware placement to make these applications work efficiently.

Protocol Requirements

If there are any software protocol requirements, make sure to note them. Most applications that have been developed for a Microsoft environment recently will take advantage of TCP/IP. Because TCP/IP has become the de-facto standard within most infrastructures, you should be familiar with the network services that need to be in place to support TCP/IP name resolution: Domain Name Service (DNS) and Windows Internet Name Service (WINS).

NWLink, Microsoft's implementation of Novell's IPX/SPX protocol, may be in place where a legacy Novell network is used. Some applications were written to take advantage of NWLink instead of TCP/IP. You may also run into applications that were written to run exclusively on a NetWare server. If this is the case, you will need to document your findings because this will pose an interesting problem for those companies that want to move to a single operating system on their network. Although Windows Server 2003 will support NWLink, you will need to determine if the application will run on a Microsoft operating system such as Windows Server 2003. You may also want to investigate the possibility of the vendor supporting a version of the application that will run on Windows Server 2003. Of course, if this is the case, the application may be very different from the NetWare version, and may require additional training, and thus more cost. If the application is not supported on a Windows Server 2003 system, you may be forced to maintain the other operating system within your design.

 Although Microsoft does not support NetBEUI on Windows Server 2003, you are able to add the NetBEUI protocol. Using a Windows XP installation, you can install NetBEUI from the Valueadd\MSFT\NET\NETBEUI folder. This solution is not supported by Microsoft, and the exam assumes that the NetBEUI protocol is not available for Windows Server 2003 systems.

Another protocol that may be in use on a legacy network is NetBEUI. This protocol is no longer supported by Windows Server 2003. Applications that require this protocol, of which there are very few, should be rewritten, or you should check for a newer version of the application that no longer uses NetBEUI. Again, if the application cannot be rewritten, a newer version cannot be found, and the business requires it, you will have to support another operating system within your design.

Do note that supporting multiple protocols can place additional overhead on your network. Although many companies have been maintaining multiple protocols for many years, it is more efficient to use a single protocol. And of course, the more efficient your network is, the more throughput you will be able to achieve.

Identifying the Current Hardware Requirements

Now that the logical requirements for the current network have been documented, you need to document the hardware requirements for the existing network. This will not simply be a document that details the hardware that is in place on the network and its capabilities; instead it will be an examination of the requirements that are necessary based on the software and the network requirements. Then, after you have documented the current hardware requirements, you will have a good idea of how much of an additional load the current infrastructure can take on. This will also be a vital resource to have when you are trying to convince the powers-that-be that you need additional resources to support the upcoming design.

When identifying the current hardware requirements, you will need to inventory the current hardware. This will include the server systems that are in place to support the organization as well as the network devices that are used to support the network infrastructure.

Identifying Hardware

Starting off, you will need to identify what hardware is in place and the capabilities of the hardware. Server, workstations, routers, switches, hubs, network throughput capabilities, WAN connectivity devices, and WAN throughput capabilities all need to be identified and documented. Again, you can use Visio to diagram what is being used within the organization.

After the hardware has been documented, you need to start testing the current load on the hardware. You can use several tools to see how many resources are being consumed on each of the devices. Within a Microsoft-based network, you can take advantage of several built-in tools to monitor your servers, workstations, and network capacity. You can use Performance Monitor in Windows NT, or Performance Logs and Alerts for Window 2000 and Windows Server 2003 to create log files that contain data about the current usage levels on your Windows-based systems. Other operating systems have utilities that you can use when you are trying to determine current usage levels. Novell NetWare has Monitor and some web-based monitoring tools that will help you document. Third-party companies also provide monitoring software that you can purchase and use to *baseline* the entire network. A baseline is the criteria for which future performance and troubleshooting is compared against. When the system is running optimally, use one of the monitoring tools to gather the current resource usage levels. These levels are then compared to performance levels when problems occur so that you can determine which of the resources may be causing the problem.

If the network is heterogeneous, you may want to purchase a third-party solution that can gather the data and store it in one central database. However, these programs are expensive. Your current budget may not have money allocated for this type of purchase. If you are lucky, however, using one of these tools will save time when you are trying to collect data from several different sources. If the current infrastructure is based on one operating system, take advantage of the built-in tools because you won't have to take a hit on your budget.

No matter what tool you decide to use, make sure the data collection is valid. Running the monitoring tool on the same system that you are monitoring skews the results because the monitoring software consumes resources. The rule of thumb is to run the monitoring software on a monitoring system. This could be a workstation that creates the logs or sends the collected data to a database. This method allows the monitored system to still function close to normal, and the monitoring system can be dedicated to collecting data. Only the network counters would be adversely affected by the additional traffic flow of data collection.

Once you have collected it, you can review the performance data from these servers and create graphs. What you are looking for are the peak usage times. This indicates how much the server is being used and how much capacity remains. Later this information will come in handy when you are deciding which servers can handle service consolidation and which may need to be replaced because they are reaching capacity for the service they provide.

As with other sections in this chapter, we are going to recommend that the information you collect here be presented in a simple format. The servers that you baseline can be entered into a table that shows the maximum resource load that occurs. You can include the graphs that you generated from the performance baseline with this documentation to substantiate the data in the table.

At this point, you should also determine the capabilities of the hardware devices that make up the network infrastructure. Router, firewall, hub, switch, and any other network device capacities need to be determined. By reviewing the manufacturer's documentation you can determine what each device is capable of. You should also run tests against these devices if you have equipment that allows you to monitor their performance. Include your findings within the documentation.

Network Requirements

Just as with the hardware requirements for the existing system, you need to collect data about the existing network infrastructure. This information allows you to detect what is currently in use on the network and have a basis to judge whether or not future growth will be allowed without compromising the efficiency of the network.

The process of collecting the network requirements will require that you monitor what traffic is currently traversing the network. Understanding the current addressing requirements so that you understand how the systems are configured and which connection types are in use will aid in the future design and plan.

Network Monitoring

Tools available from several companies will allow you to capture data as it traverses the network. These tools allow you to "see" what type of data is being sent on the network and how much of the total capacity of the network the data is consuming. Microsoft bundles a version of their network monitoring tool, Network Monitor, with Windows Server 2003, but it does not capture all of the packets on the network. It is limited to only capturing packets that originate from or are received by the system that is running Network Monitor. The fully functioning version ships with Microsoft SMS. Using this tool, packets that are traversing the network can be captured for analysis.

When capturing packets, make sure you get a good representation of the work that is being performed. Collecting a sample of network traffic between the hours of 10 A.M. and 11 A.M. and expecting that to be completely representative of the workload for the entire organization is not a valid test. For several days, sample data at different times of the day. If there are multiple locations within the organization, sample data from all of the locations, on all of their network segments to get a true reading as to how the network is being used.

When you are collecting network data be sure to collect enough data to make an informed decision during the design process, but do not collect so much that you have too much data to parse through. While collecting everything that passes on the network might seem like the ideal, you could find yourself drowning in information. Determine what traffic you want to collect, identify the systems you want to monitor, and then capture the packets.

System Addressing

Each device on the network will need a unique network address. The assignment of these addresses can either be performed manually or via Dynamic Host Configuration Protocol (DHCP). If manual addressing is employed so that the systems have static addresses, make sure to note the address ranges used within each of the network segments. You will use this information later when you are optimizing the address assignment for the new design.

Most companies take advantage of the automatic assignment nature of DHCP. Like the UNIX bootstrap protocol (BOOTP), DHCP assigns addresses to the client systems, along with any configuration options. Using DHCP dramatically eases the administrative overhead involved with configuring the addressing for a computer system. DHCP client systems send a request for address assignment across the network and the DHCP server responds with configuration information. Once the DHCP client is configured, the DHCP server keeps track of the address assignment and makes sure that no other system receives an address from its database that is already leased to another system.

You need to document where the DHCP client systems are obtaining their IP addressing configuration from. Doing so allows you to determine how DHCP is administered and controlled. It also allows you to verify the amount of data that is being transmitted across the network on behalf of DHCP. Most companies have a decentralized DHCP environment. This method allows the DHCP servers to reside close to the clients that need the address assignment. Backup DHCP servers can reside across the WAN links in case of a failure of the local DHCP server. Document the location of each of the DHCP servers and the network segments for which they are responsible, along with the current address ranges within the scope and the configuration options that are handed out with the client lease.

NetWare may introduce additional addressing concerns if the IPX/SPX protocol is used instead of TCP/IP. Until NetWare 5 was introduced, IPX/SPX was the default protocol within a NetWare environment. Many network administrators kept this protocol in place due to its installation and the efficient manner in which it ran. Some administrators would use IPX/SPX on their internal network as a security barrier. By having the internal network run a protocol different than TCP/IP, which was used within the perimeter network, they gained another layer of security. Moving these servers to a TCP/IP environment may take additional planning and time.

Connection Types

Several different options are available that allow companies to connect their offices together. Depending on how much a company is willing to pay, they can use high-speed connections between the sites. Table 2.2 lists some of the popular *connection types*.

TABLE 2.2   Connection Type Table

Connection Type	Speed of Link
Modem	Up to 56Kbps
Integrated Services Digital Network (ISDN)	64Kbps–2048Mbps
Digital Subscriber Line (DSL)—ISDN-based Digital Subscriber Line (IDSL), Asymmetric Digital Subscriber Line (ADSL), Symmetric Digital Subscriber Line(SDSL)	144Kbps–1.544Mbps
T-Carrier—Fractional	Available in 64Kbps increments
T-Carrier—T1	1.544Mbps
T-Carrier—T2	6.312Mbps
T-Carrier—T3	44.736Mbps
T-Carrier—T4	274.176Mbps
E-Carrier—E1	2.048Mbps

TABLE 2.2   Connection Type Table *(continued)*

Connection Type	Speed of Link
E-Carrier—E2	8.448Mbps
E-Carrier—E3	34.368Mbps
E-Carrier—E4	139.264Mbps
X.25	9600bps–2Mbps
Frame Relay	56Kbps–1.544Mbps
Asynchronous Transfer Mode (ATM)	25Mbps–622Mbps

You will notice that some nondomestic connection types are listed in the table. Whenever you are working on an international level, you will have to make decisions about what type of connections you will use. Although there are high-speed connections throughout the world, many locations do not support them. Thus, you may be restricted to using a modem to connect systems.

 Within Chapter 9 "Designing the Network Infrastructure," we look at the types of links that we can use for primary and backup connections when the connections are not reliable.

Virtual Private Network

One of the more popular methods of connecting clients to the internal network or connecting sites is to use a *Virtual Private Network (VPN)*. A VPN is a method of encrypting the packets sent across a nonsecure network so that the two systems can have a secure method of communication. Because it is so easy to gain access to the Internet, the Internet is being used as an extension of an organization's network. The problem with using the Internet in this manner is its inherent lack of security. VPNs are used to authenticate and encrypt the traffic between the two sites. Two main VPN types are available within Microsoft networks: *Point-To-Point Tunneling Protocol (PPTP)* and *Layer Two Tunneling Protocol (L2TP)*. PPTP can be used with nearly all Microsoft operating systems, whereas L2TP is available for Windows 2000 and later operating systems. Windows NT 4 supports L2TP with the addition of the Windows NT L2TP/IPec software available for download from Microsoft's website.

Documenting Your Findings

The data that you gather needs to be documented so that you can read through it and disseminate the valid information. These documents can take on many styles depending on the company that is performing the initial investigation of the network. Some companies simply jot the information that they find onto a piece of paper and then review the notes later when they are compiling the data. Other companies take a methodical approach and have forms for every part of the investigative process. One such form is the Connection Type form. Figure 2.2 shows an example of what this form may look like.

FIGURE 2.2   A sample Connection Type form

Connection Type Form

Organization	Date	
Prepared By	Page	of

Connection Type	Bandwidth	Connection Locations

Another form that can be used is the Subnet Allocation form. This form allows you to detail the addressing requirements for the subnets and specify how the addressing is applied—manually or through DHCP. Look at Figure 2.3 to see the data that is collected on this form.

FIGURE 2.3   A sample Subnet Allocation form

Subnet Allocation Form

Organization		Date	
Prepared By		Page	of
Location	Address Range		Allocation Type

As mentioned earlier, a map of the network layout is imperative. This map should include all of the sites within the organization, the subnets within those sites, the network devices, and enough information about the subnet so that you can cross-reference the addressing to the Subnet Allocation form. Using Visio, you can effortlessly create a network map. Look back at Figure 2.1 to review what this document may look like.

Examining the Current Infrastructure

At this point, we have been going on and on about the theory of what is necessary to document and discover about the current network. Before we end the chapter, we will run through a quick summary of the data you should be collecting. We will concentrate on two main scenarios: Windows NT 4 infrastructure and Windows 2000 Active Directory infrastructure.

Current Directory Service

Depending on the directory service that is in place, you will have to document certain information. Active Directory has the potential to hold detailed information about the resources within the network environment, whereas NT 4 does not have that ability from the native utilities. Make sure you are as detailed as possible when gathering and documenting the following information.

Windows NT 4

The Windows NT 4 directory service was very limited in the amount of information it provided. However, if Exchange 5.5 exists within the network, additional information is available. The Exchange 5.5 directory service is actually the precursor to Active Directory. It is an X.500, Lightweight Directory Access Protocol (LDAP)–compliant directory that can hold additional information about accounts that could not be held in the default NT 4 database.

Starting at the highest level, the first thing to document is the layout of the domain structure. If you are working with a simple single domain design, this will not entail very much documentation. Do take note of the domain name, because this will more than likely remain the NetBIOS domain name within Active Directory. If there are several domains within the existing structure, document all of the domains and the domain names for each. Along with this information, you should also note the reason for the domain's existence. Many organizations use domains as a method of organizing resources. Account domains hold user and group accounts and the computer accounts for the domain, usually just the domain controllers. Resource domains house the resources that the user and groups need access to. This usually encompasses the member servers that are responsible for making printers, shared folders, applications, and other resources available.

Trust relationships should also be documented at this level so that the relationship between the domains is understood. Windows NT 4 trusts are one-way nontransitive. This means that a trust only defines which domain is trusted so that users can access resources. The trust relationship will not allow users to access resources within a domain where an explicit trust is not created.

In Figure 2.4, the trust relationship between Domain A and Domain B will not allow users from Domain C to access resources in Domain A, even though a trust relationship exists between Domain B and Domain C. In order for this information to be shared, a trust would have to be configured between Domain A and Domain C.

FIGURE 2.4 Nontransitive trust relationships

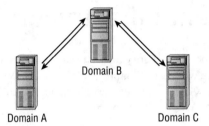

Domain B

Domain A   Domain C

For each of the domain controllers, the type of domain controller—Primary Domain Controller (PDC) or Backup Domain Controller (BDC)—should be recognized. Because the PDC is the only domain controller that can have changes made to its directory service, it will usually be located close to where the administrative staff is located. The BDCs will be located close to the client population to allow efficient authentication for the accounts. As changes are made to accounts within the domain, the PDC will replicate changes to the BDCs. Investigate the replication topology to determine when replication is allowed to the BDCs.

Figure 2.5 shows a diagram of the domain structure for a Windows NT 4 directory service and the information that you need when you are designing the upgrade of the directory service to Active Directory.

FIGURE 2.5 Windows NT 4 domain structure

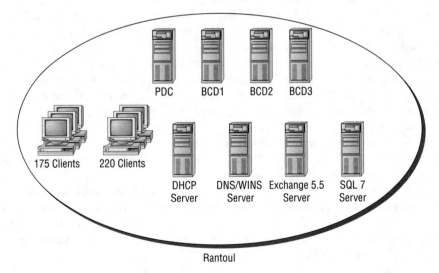

PDC   BCD1   BCD2   BCD3

175 Clients   220 Clients   DHCP   DNS/WINS   Exchange 5.5   SQL 7
                              Server   Server   Server   Server

Rantoul

Windows NT 4 Domain

Next, you need to document the administrative control over the resources on the network. This includes the domains themselves. Later you will want to review this information to determine if the current administrators still need to have control of those domains and resources. You will also be able to determine who needs to have administrative control over organizational units if the domain structure is collapsed. An example of the resource administrative design is shown in Figure 2.6.

FIGURE 2.6   Administrative delegation

Windows NT 4 Administration

Organization		Date	
Prepared By		Page	of

Domain	Administrative Group	Rights/Permissions

Windows 2000 Active Directory

The reason most organizations move from a Windows 2000–based Active Directory design to Windows Server 2003 Active Directory is to take advantage of the new and updated tools and utilities. Usually, the domain structure remains the same when moving to Windows 2003, but you are still able to rework it if you want. In fact, Windows Server 2003 has additional features that allow better integration between forests and tools that allow you to rename domains and domain controllers.

Just as in the Windows NT 4 environment, you want to document the domain structure and inter-relationships. This includes the administrative control for all of the domains and any trusts that have been created between forests, as well as shortcut trusts between domains. If any Windows NT 4 domains are still within the infrastructure, make sure to note them along with the trust path.

When documenting the administrative control that has been delegated, you not only want to identify the domain administration, but also any OUs and the delegation of authority that has been provided to other users or groups. Although this may seem like more information to document than was necessary under the NT 4 model, you will note that although there are more OUs, there are usually fewer domains, and the OUs have a better, more logical administrative design. Figure 2.7 shows an example listing of the domain and OU administrative design mapped out.

Along with the administrative layout, network services should be identified and documented. These services include domain controllers, DNS and WINS servers, file and print servers, application servers, replication bridgehead servers, and others that may be within your environment. The documentation should include a listing of the sites within the organization and the resources within those sites.

For those sites where WAN links exist, you should document the current capacity of those links along with the current amount of data throughput. Without this information, you will not be able to identify the WAN links that need to be upgraded or where additional links should be added to augment the capacity. Active Directory replication needs to travel across these links. By determining how the links are currently used, you will understand the traffic patterns and have a basis for planning the replication timing for the new design.

Using a tool such as Performance Logs And Alerts, you can monitor the traffic to identify the current traffic patterns. This aids in determining when the links are used and the peak usage times. With Network Monitor, you can capture network traffic to determine what type of traffic is traveling on the WAN and then use that information to optimize the traffic.

Software Requirements

It does not matter what operating system the software runs on, at this point, you need only identify what software is in place. Create a list of the servers and the applications and services running on those servers. A simple table should be sufficient to document this information. Table 2.3 shows an example that lists the servers, applications and services running on those servers, and the reason the application is in place. You could also add additional information to this table, such as showing who is responsible for the application or service. The reason the administrative responsibilities have not been entered into this table is that it may be considered redundant information. You should gather and document as much as you deem necessary. The more comprehensive you are, the more information you will have when making decisions.

FIGURE 2.7   Windows 2000 Active Directory administration document

Windows 2000 AD Administration

Organization	Zygort		Date	11/18/02
Prepared By	Bill Burkhardt		Page	of 1

Domain	Administrative Group	Rights/Permissions
Corp.com	Corp Admins	Full Control
Provo OU	Provo Admins	Full Control
Provo/Users OU	Provo Admins (inh)	Full Control
	Help Desk	Change Password/Reset Account Lockout
	Account Operators	User Management
Provo/Computers OU	Provo Admins (inh)	Full Control
	Tech Support	Computer Management

TABLE 2.3   Server/Software Table

Server Name	Service/Application	Reason for Implementation
FLEX1	Exchange Server 2000	Primary e-mail support for Toledo office
	Internet Information Server (IIS) 5	Required for Exchange Server 2000
	Simple Mail Transfer Protocol (SMTP) service	Required for Exchange Server 2000
	Post Office Protocol 3 (POP3) service	Required for Exchange Server 2000
	Internet Message Access Protocol, version 4 (IMAP4) service	Required for Exchange Server 2000
	Network News Transfer Protocol (NNTP) service	Required for Exchange Server 2000
	Key Management Server	Required for Exchange Server 2000
FLNRSRV	Domain Name Service (DNS)	Needed for name resolution for Toledo clients, required for Active Directory (AD)
	Windows Internet Name Service (WINS)	Toledo client name resolution for NT 4 workstations
	Dynamic Host Configuration Protocol (DHCP)	IP addressing for Toledo clients
FLDC1	AD Domain Controller	Toledo Domain Controller (DC) and GC
FLPROJ	Project 2002 Server	Toledo management Project repository

Network Requirements

The one thing to remember when documenting the network requirements for the existing system is that the documentation is for the *existing* system. Do not jump the gun and start thinking about what may need to be put into place; you are gathering this information so that you have enough data to understand how the current network performs. You will use this data so that you can determine where improvements need to be made, or where consolidation can occur.

Keeping that in mind, make sure you baseline the current servers to determine their current usage and capacity. Remember to study these servers at different times of the day so that you have a representation of how they are utilized. You can create logs to view, or you can store the data within a database so that each server and service can be disseminated with ease. Again, the more thorough you are with your data collection, the better the representation of the server's performance will be.

Make a complete inventory of the network devices: hubs, switches, routers, firewall, and any other device, whether it is a dedicated hardware device or a server performing the function. Take note of the capacities of each of these devices. The current connection types should be inventoried as well so that you know what is in place for WAN connectivity.

Summary

Understanding the business requirements and the current implementation will be the foundation upon which you build the rest of the Active Directory design. Although this may not be the most exciting part of the design process, it very well could be the most important. Be prepared to document everything you find within the existing environment, for it will all come in very handy as you move on to the other phases of the design.

Interviewing the stakeholders will allow you to glean some very important information for the design. You will learn why the new design is being called for as well as where the company's priorities lie. Later, as the design process moves on, and even later, as the planning process is undertaken, if there are tradeoffs that need to be considered, you can determine what takes precedence based on the priorities of the company.

Analyze the current administrative responsibilities for every resource within the organization. You will use this information to determine who is responsible for the resource as well as a starting point from which you can decide where consolidation of administration can occur. Later, you will review this information to determine if you can consolidate the administrative control and where you need to delegate administrative control.

The following chapter concentrates on designing the Active Directory forest structure. Using some of the data that was gathered from this chapter, you will be able to make decisions concerning the forest design you want to implement. Later, in subsequent chapters, you will continue to look back at the data gathered at this step in your process so that you can build the most efficient infrastructure based on the organization's needs.

Exam Essentials

Know the reason for the new design.   Each organization has different reasons for implementing a new design. Learn the reasons through interviews and define the highest priority reason.

Understand special design requirements.   The design could be affected by the following: domain restructuring, application support, planned obsolescence, and the reduction of the total cost of ownership (TCO).

Understand why you should document the administrative control.   The current administrative control over resources flows into the new design and dictates how the Active Directory infrastructure is created.

Understand the effects geographic locations could have on the design.   Different geographic locations could affect the site design as well as the domain design due to geopolitical reasons.

Understand the software requirements.   Software may rely on special hardware, name resolution methods, or network requirements.

Understand the name resolution requirements.   If applications or operating systems require a specific name resolution method, your design has to incorporate that name resolution.

Understand hardware requirements.   Given the operating system and the applications and services running on that operating system, make sure that the current hardware can support the software.

Know what a baseline is.   A baseline documents the current resource usage on a system. This allows you to determine how much a system can support.

Understand the system addressing requirements.   Each protocol has its own addressing capabilities. You need to identify how the systems are getting their addresses so that they can communicate on the network.

Know why you should monitor the network.   Monitoring the network allows you to identify the network traffic that is currently in use on the network and what types of packets are being sent between systems. This also allows you to determine which of the network segments are over consumed.

Key Terms

Before you take the exam, be certain you are familiar with the following terms:

attributes	line-of-business applications
baseline	Point-To-Point Tunneling Protocol (PPTP)
connection types	political boundaries
cryptographic export laws	software requirements
domain restructuring	total cost of ownership (TCO)
extendable database	Virtual Private Network (VPN)
hardware requirements	wide area network (WAN)
Layer Two Tunneling Protocol (L2TP)	

Review Questions

1. When interviewing some of the stakeholders within an organization, Pat learns that the primary reason Windows Server 2003 and Active Directory was chosen was because Exchange Server 2003 would only run on that platform. Which reason type is this known as?

   A. Application support

   B. Domain restructuring

   C. Planned obsolescence

   D. Total cost of ownership

2. What type of document details the sites, devices, and subnets within an organization?

   A. Subnet Addressing form

   B. Site Addressing form

   C. Server Location list

   D. Network diagram

3. Which of the following tools can be used to collect and save resource usage limits on a server? (Choose all that apply.)

   A. Performance Monitor

   B. Performance Logs And Alerts

   C. System Monitor

   D. Network Monitor

4. Which of the following tools can be used to collect and save network usage on a server? (Choose all that apply.)

   A. Performance Monitor

   B. Performance Logs And Alerts

   C. System Monitor

   D. Network Monitor

5. You are reviewing the current infrastructure and notice that all of the clients are Windows NT 4. There are five systems that use a VPN connection to gain access to the network. The VPN protocol was not documented. Which of the following protocols are probably being used? (Choose all that apply.)

   A. L2TP

   B. PPTP

   C. PPP

   D. IPX/SPX

6. You are preparing to document the network for Company B. You know that they have a mixed environment with Windows NT 4, Windows 2000 clients and servers, and Windows XP clients. What protocol can you safely assume is used?

   A. NetBEUI

   B. TCP/IP

   C. NetBIOS

   D. NWLink

7. What tool will allow you to inventory client systems to determine the software installed on them?

   A. System Monitor

   B. System Management Server

   C. Network Monitor

   D. Performance Monitor

8. When determining the current resources on the network, which of the following items should be documented? (Choose all that apply.)

   A. Client applications

   B. Network devices

   C. Protocols

   D. Subnet address ranges

9. Which of the following options may account for a company having a multiple domain environment? (Choose all that apply.)

   A. Legal regulations

   B. Autonomy of administration

   C. Security policies

   D. Software requirements

10. What is the term that describes collecting performance data so that you understand how a system is functioning and what the typical resource usage is?

   A. Capturing

   B. Baselining

   C. Logging

   D. Optimizing

Answers to Review Questions

1. A. Several applications require Active Directory, and Exchange Server 2003 requires Windows Server 2003 as the operating system with Active Directory in place.

2. D. The network diagram can be created with a tool such as Visio so that you can detail how the network is laid out, showing the sites, subnets, subnet addresses, network devices, and network hosts.

3. A, B. On Windows NT 4 Servers and Workstations, you can run Performance Monitor and have it log the resource usage. Windows 2000 Server and Professional and Windows Server 2003 have Performance Logs And Alerts, which provides that same functionality.

4. A, B, D. System Monitor is the only one of the listed utilities that cannot save the data. Whereas Performance Monitor and Performance Logs And Alerts only record statistics about the network segments and the server's current utilization limits, Network Monitor can capture packets to be analyzed.

5. A, B. Windows NT 4 has the option of using L2TP or PPTP for VPN connections. PPP and IPX/SPX are not VPN protocols.

6. C . Although TCP/IP is probably used, it is not safe to assume that it is definitely in place. NetBIOS will be used because there are Windows NT 4 clients on the network. NetBIOS does need some type of transport protocol for it to function, but all three of the other protocols listed will transport NetBIOS.

7. B. The System Management Server (SMS) will inventory the client system and generate reports detailing the software that is currently installed.

8. A, B, C, D. You will need all of this information when determining how you are going to design the new infrastructure. Remember the rule of thumb: document everything you find!

9. A, B, C. Legal regulations could force a company to create a completely separate domain in order to keep the data segregated. If administrators need to have control over their own resources, another domain is one of the most secure ways to keep other administrators out. If a group needs to have a different set of password restrictions, lockout policies, or Kerberos settings, a separate domain will be required.

10. B. The term baselining refers to the process of collecting data on systems so that you know how they are currently functioning. This process can be performed after a system has been set up and is running optimally so that you have a basis to start from when troubleshooting, or you can perform a baseline analysis during your data collection phase of the system upgrade so that you know how the system is currently running. This will give you a basis for knowing what the system is able to support.

Case Study

You should give yourself 20 minutes to review this testlet, and complete the questions.

Background

Insane Systems builds custom computers for their customers. They specialize in building cases that are unique and support the latest in hardware technology. They started off as a small company that provided this service to gamers who would take their cases to LAN parties to show off. Because their systems were considered some of the most stable gaming platforms and they provided an impressive design that gamers could show off, they started to become popular. Insane Systems started mass manufacturing some of their more popular designs and began selling stand-alone cases along with their fully configured systems. As space at the company became a premium, the office was moved from the manufacturing facility. This allowed the company to add to the amount of space that was used for the mass production line.

Existing Environment

Over the past few months, Insane Systems has been developing plans to expand their company. They have identified San Jose, California; Atlanta, Georgia; and New York City as the locations with their highest customer base. The current Chicago location will remain the corporate headquarters, but they are opening branches in New York City and San Jose. They are also in the process of acquiring a competitor's business in Atlanta. These locations provide retail outlets as well as support. Customers will have the option of sending their systems back for any needed upgrades or repairs to the corporate office, or delivering them to one of the branch locations.

  Because the company is planning on expanding, they want to make sure that the network infrastructure is in place to support their larger, distributed company. They are also concerned with the support lifetime of their current Windows NT 4 infrastructure. They realize they have the option of moving to a Windows 2000 or Windows 2003 infrastructure and are considering moving to Windows Server 2003 and Active Directory for two reasons: the expected support lifetime is greater than Windows 2000, and they are a technology firm that is not afraid of staying ahead of the technology curve.

Interviews

Part of the expansion of the company is a complete overhaul of their current Internet presence. They are planning on bringing all of the web development and hosting in-house. Currently a web hosting service is providing their Internet presence, and Insane Systems feels as though they could provide better marketing and support information for their customers if they had control over their own website.

  Your company has been hired to design an Active Directory infrastructure and the network infrastructure to support it. During the interview process with some of the key stakeholders you gathered the following information:

CEO

Currently we have a single location with all of our processes local. As we grow, we would like to keep all of the administration here in Chicago. Because the new branches are primarily retail and support offices, we will not need to have a large staff in those locations.

CIO

Most of the infrastructure that we support is located here at the corporate office. We do support some key servers at the manufacturing location. We support these servers from our main office. Because the servers are nearby, if there is a problem, we can usually be on site within half an hour.

The new branches are going to be another issue altogether. We would like to retain the same level of administrative control over the servers in the new locations that we employ currently. Due to the geographic limitations, we may need to have some support staff at those locations. Currently, the plan is to hire staff at those locations that can provide the support for the customers, but also have an understanding of the business systems we need to put into place.

Manager of Information Technology

We have grown very quickly over the past three years and our current technologies have kept up with that growth. However, we don't think the current infrastructure is ready for the amount of growth that we are expecting within the following year. We are not afraid of moving to the latest technology, but we want to make sure that the design is stable and makes sense for us, especially if we will continue growing in the upcoming months. And because we are losing support for NT 4, we want to make sure that we have an operating system that will be supported for a few years down the road.

Most of our processes are located here at this office, and we would like to keep it that way. We know that servers will need to be located at the remote offices, but we would like to be able to provide most of the support from this location. Remote administration tools will need to be included within the design so that we can keep our administrative costs at a minimum.

Currently, we have most of our servers located at the main office, and all located on their own high-speed backbone. We do have a server at the manufacturing site that allows the staff there to have e-mail as well as plans and orders in case we lose connectivity between the offices. This server is running Exchange 5.5. Several times during the day we replicate the public folder information to this system so that they are always up-to-date and do not have to dial up to the main office using our 56Kbps modem.

The systems at the main office are all supported by our staff of four administrators. All of the administrators are cross-trained on Windows NT 4, Exchange 5.5, SQL Server 7, our accounting software, and each of our file and print servers. We currently have several Windows NT 4 servers in place, including one Exchange 5.5 server at both locations, one SQL Server 7 server at the main office, one server running our accounting package that interfaces with the SQL server, and one file and print server that is used by both locations. The Exchange server at the manufacturing location doubles as a print server also.

Because all of the client machines are running Windows NT 4 Workstation, we do not have to worry about supporting different operating systems. We would like to maintain that same easy administration with the upcoming system. We would like to provide the same types of services at the remote locations that we provide at the home office, although accounting will remain at the home office and will not be spread out to all of the locations.

Current Infrastructure

After investigating the current infrastructure, you have determined that the following servers are in place:

Home Office

Primary Domain Controller (PDC)

Backup Domain Controller (BDC)

DHCP Server

DNS/WINS Server

Exchange 5.5 Server

SQL Server 7

Systems Management Server 2.0

File Server

Print/Antivirus Server

Research and Development File Server

Manufacturing Facility

Backup Domain Controller (BDC)

DNS/WINS/DHCP Relay Agent Server

Exchange 5.5/File Server

The Corporate Office hosts nearly 250 Windows NT 4 workstations at this point. They are interconnected by several 48-port 10/100Mbps switches. A router is used to divide the network into four virtual LANs (VLANs). One of these VLANs is the 1Gbps backbone on which the servers reside. Each of the servers is connected to a 1Gbps switch port. This location takes advantage of private IP address ranges. The servers are located on the 192.168.1.0/24 subnet. The client systems are divided among network addresses 192.168.10.0/24, 192.168.11.0/24, 192.168.12.0/24, and 192.168.13.0/24.

The manufacturing facility contains 12 Windows NT 4 workstations connected to the same switch as the servers. Because Insane Systems does not want to slow down production due to a communication failure, they have taken advantage of Exchange 5.5 Server's public folder replication. Public folders are continually updated with the latest orders. The crew foreman can access the orders locally from these public folders at any time, whether the communication link between the locations is up or not. This location uses another address range—192.168.20.0/24.

Case Study Questions

1. What is the primary reason for Insane Systems' directory service upgrade?

   A. Application support

   B. Domain restructuring

   C. Planned obsolescence

   D. Reduced TCO

2. What other reason was identified for the upgrade?

   A. Application support

   B. Domain restructuring

   C. Planned obsolescence

   D. Reduced TCO

3. When baselining the current network infrastructure, which of the following tools should be used to give Insane Systems the total network usage?

   A. Performance Monitor

   B. Performance Logs And Alerts

   C. System Monitor

   D. Network Monitor

CASE STUDY

4. Using the following address ranges and allocation types, create a Subnet Allocation form that details the current address assignment.

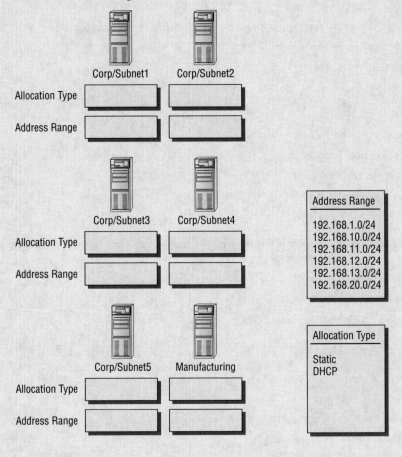

Corp/Subnet1	Corp/Subnet2
Allocation Type	
Address Range	

Corp/Subnet3	Corp/Subnet4
Allocation Type	
Address Range	

Corp/Subnet5	Manufacturing
Allocation Type	
Address Range	

Address Range

192.168.1.0/24
192.168.10.0/24
192.168.11.0/24
192.168.12.0/24
192.168.13.0/24
192.168.20.0/24

Allocation Type

Static
DHCP

5. Using the following choice, create a Connection Type form that details the current WAN connection.

```
┌─────────────────┐
│   Corporate     │
│    Office       │
└─────────────────┘


┌─────────────────┐
│  Manufacturing  │
└─────────────────┘                    **Connection types:**

                                    ┌──────────────────────────┐
┌─────────────────┐                 │   Dial-up (56Kbps)       │
│                 │                 │   T1 (128Kbps)           │
│    San Jose     │                 │ Frame Relay (1.54Mbps)   │
└─────────────────┘                 └──────────────────────────┘


┌─────────────────┐
│     Atlanta     │
└─────────────────┘


┌─────────────────┐
│    New York     │
└─────────────────┘
```

Answers to Case Study Questions

1. C. After interviewing the stakeholders, one item stands out: they fear that the operating system will no longer be supported and want to have the support that a new operating system will receive.

2. D. They wish to take advantage of a primarily centralized administrative staff so that they can keep their costs at a minimum, while having support personnel at the remote sites to take care of hands-on support needs.

3. D. While the other tools will allow the monitoring of the network to determine the current utilization patterns, Network Monitor also captures packets that are sent on the network so that the traffic patterns and the types of traffic can be documented.

4.

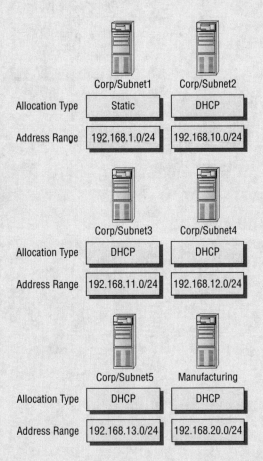

Looking at the information that was gathered from the existing network, the corporate network is comprised of 5 subnets, one for the servers, 192.168.1.0/24, and four for making up the client segments, 192.168.10.0/24, 192.168.11.0/24, 192.168.12.0/24, and 192.168.13.0/24. The manufacturing facility has a single subnet on which all of the systems reside, 192.168.20.0/24. All of the subnets use DHCP for IP configuration with the exception of the server segment where all of the systems are statically configured.

5.

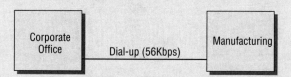

Currently, the only connection that is in place is the dial-up connection between the corporate office and the manufacturing plant. As soon as the other offices go online, they will have connections also.

Chapter
3

Designing the Active Directory Forest Structure

MICROSOFT EXAM OBJECTIVES COVERED IN THIS CHAPTER:

✓ **Analyze security requirements for the Active Directory directory service.**

 ▪ Analyze current security policies, standards, and procedures.

 ▪ Identify the impact of Active Directory on the current security infrastructure.

✓ **Design the Active Directory infrastructure to meet business and technical requirements.**

 ▪ Create the conceptual design of the Active Directory forest structure.

In the previous chapter, we took a look at the information that needs to be collected from the existing environment. Using this information, we are able to discern how the new infrastructure should be designed. Throughout the remainder of this text, we will continue referring back to the current infrastructure so that you can understand exactly what you need to have put in place as well as decide upon what is the highest priority when you are making trade-offs.

Now that we have identified the current requirements and examined the current business environment, it is time to start developing a design for the company's forest and domain structure. You have to gather and study the options you need in order to make informed decisions concerning how many forests are required for an organization and how the domain structure is created within each forest. You will encounter several design options, and you will need to investigate the options that make the design efficient and secure. This chapter starts the discussion and is based on the forest design. Chapter 4, "Designing the Active Directory Domain Structure," follows this with a discussion of the domain design.

Identifying Design Criteria

When designing the Active Directory structure, the primary design criteria is administrative control. The best Active Directory designs are based on the administrative control of the objects within Active Directory, and then the group policy structure is created. In the earliest Windows directory service structures, the domain was a security boundary as well as the unit of administrative control. That all changed once Active Directory was introduced. Although domains may still be required based on differing security needs, mechanisms are in place that allow every domain in the forest to be controlled by a central administrative group. For some companies, this makes administration easy. Other companies find that this capability causes many political battles among differing divisions. This reason alone is enough to make sure that the designer weighs all of the options available prior to making any decisions about the future Active Directory structure.

As my technical editor likes to point out, the top 4 layers of the "11 layer" OSI model are financial, political, legal, and religious!

When considering the various design options, the network architect needs to identify where control is granted within the forest. Due to the security requirements of Active Directory, identifying the users who has control over the services and objects within Active Directory becomes a priority early in the design phase. Those groups who are responsible for the resources are known as either service administrators or data administrators.

Because the service administrator has control over the entire directory service implementation for the forest, or at the very least, their own domain, they have to be an individual or group within the organization who understands Active Directory and the ramifications of making changes to the directory service. Usually senior members of the technical team are identified as the service administrators. Users who are added to the Domain Admins global group automatically have the rights and permissions to be the service administrators for the domain where the Domain Admins group resides. Users who are added to the Domain Admins global group within the forest root have the ability to add themselves to the Enterprise Admins group and become service administrators for the entire forest. Because these groups have so much power over Active Directory, make sure to monitor their membership.

Identifying Service Administrators

In an Active Directory environment, *service administrators* control the servers defined as domain controllers. Their primary responsibility is to make sure the directory service is available so that users and applications can gain access to the Active Directory. Because they are responsible for the availability of the domain controller, they have access to the configuration settings on the servers and must make sure access is not interrupted.

Service administrators must be trustworthy individuals within the organization. Because they have been granted rights that allow them to make configuration changes within the directory service, they can alter the functionality of Active Directory. Stakeholders from every domain that will be incorporated within the forest should have a voice in determining who is allowed to be a service administrator for the forest. Every domain's service administrator has control over the directory service from their own domain, but it cannot be guaranteed that administrators from other domains will not be able to gain access. If you need complete autonomy, you must consider the effects of having multiple forests. We will discuss these options in the section "Designing the Forest Structure" later in this chapter.

Due to the fact that service administrators have control over all aspects of Active Directory and can modify settings of objects, they can perform the same functions as the data administrators. In many cases, especially in smaller organizations, the service administrators and the data administrators will be the same administrators.

Identifying Data Administrators

Data administrators control the objects within Active Directory. This includes the user, computer, and group accounts, shared folder objects, printer objects, and any other objects that they have been granted authority over. Data administrators also control any of the member servers that use Active Directory. Some examples of data administrators include those users that add workstations and member servers to the domain, Exchange Server administrators, and the staff responsible for adding and modifying user accounts.

Although the service administrator has the ability to perform the same functions as the data administrator and could be the same person or group in smaller organizations, you usually find that the data administrators are individuals responsible for maintaining a specific group of objects within the Active Directory forest or domain. By delegating responsibilities to other groups within the organization, you can maximize the administrative efficiency. The service administrators can concentrate on maintaining the Active Directory structure, whereas the data administrators are only able to affect the objects for which they are responsible.

Data administrators have to trust the service administrators of the forest and domain. Active Directory does not have accounts that are solely data administrators; it is up to the service administrators to create the groups that define the data administrators. Once the rights to perform tasks are delegated to the data administrator groups, users who are added to those groups have the ability to configure the objects they are responsible for, but they do not have complete autonomy over those objects. The only way data administrators can achieve complete autonomy is to build a separate forest in which they are the service administrators as well. In the next section, we look at the different types of administration and how you can achieve data and service autonomy or isolation.

Defining Autonomy, Collaboration, and Isolation

We define a security boundary as a container that cannot be controlled by any higher-level or outside accounts. The administrators for the container do not have to worry that another account can compromise the security of the container and the objects contained within it. Because an outside account can affect the objects and configuration of a domain, the forest becomes the security boundary within the Active Directory structure. The forest root contains accounts that can affect any domain within the forest. Members of the Domain Admins group from the forest root domain have the ability to add accounts into the Enterprise Admins and Schema Admins groups, giving those accounts the ability to make changes that could affect other domains and the configuration of the entire forest.

Active Directory forests and domains are built based on the administrative needs of the organization. For some organizations, all of the resources are controlled by a central group of administrators. Some organizations have identified services and objects that need to be controlled by groups within the organization and have other groups who need rights delegated to them. Still other organizations may require complete isolation of services and resources between divisions. These administrative needs are defined as *collaborative*, *autonomous*, and *isolated* models.

Understanding Collaborative Administration

Although every administrator may not have the same level of control, as a whole, they are able to support all of the services and data for the organization. This has been identified as the collaborative model of administration. This is usually the model you find with a single domain, although you can implement a multiple domain design and allow collaborative administration to be delegated throughout.

Service and data administrators in this design share administrative responsibilities with other administrators. The domain owners have complete control over all of the services and resources within the domain. Delegation of control over the objects within the domain is granted to the data administrators, although in some cases, the service administrators are the only data administrators. Collaborative administration is found in most small companies where a single administrative group is responsible for controlling the objects within Active Directory and making sure it is available for use.

The collaborative model is not restricted to the single domain model, however. Although the single domain model is the easiest to implement collaboration, you can put the mechanisms in place to allow collaboration between domain and forests. For example, if a forest has multiple domains due to security policy requirements, the administrative staff from both domains can be added to the built-in groups that have administrative rights in the other domain. This grants the administrators from both domains the ability to control objects from either domain. Figure 3.1 shows an example of two forests with administrators from each having delegated control. You can see that the Domain Admins global group from both forests has been added to the Administrators domain local group within each domain.

FIGURE 3.1   Domain administrative collaboration

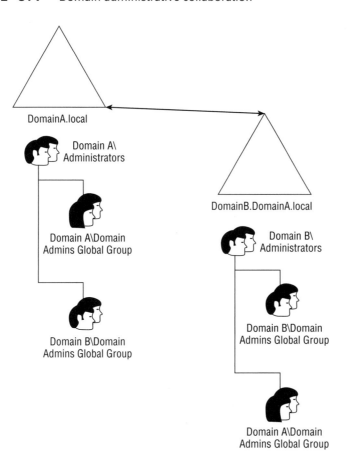

Collaboration within a multiple forest design is much more difficult, however. Because the two forests do not share the same schema and do not share information between global catalogs, assigning rights between them is difficult. Products such as Microsoft's Identity Integration Services can help tie the forests together until they can be merged. Figure 3.2 is an example of two forests tied together with a forest trust relationship. In this one-domain-per-forest example, members of the Domain Admins global group from each domain have the ability to manage objects from the other domain. If any child domains exist in either domain, you need to consider another solution.

FIGURE 3.2   Forest administrative collaboration

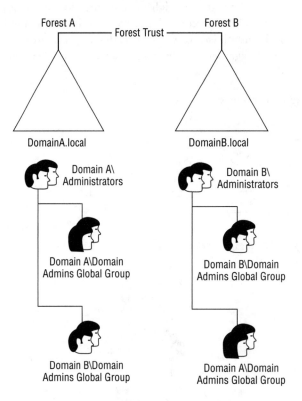

Understanding Autonomous Administration

The autonomous method of administration identifies the administrators who need to have access to the services and resources for which they are responsible but denies access to others. You usually find this type of administration when you are designing a multiple domain forest or a single domain where specific rights and permissions have been delegated to the service or data administrators at the OU level. Autonomy does not isolate the administrative staff, however. A high-level account that can take control of services or resources is always available. In a forest, that account is the Enterprise Admins group by default, although you can create and delegate control to other groups.

You can delegate service autonomy at the domain level. If you have found a reason why a portion of Active Directory needs a specific group of administrators to manage the domain controllers, you can create a domain for them. Once they have been given their own domain, the service adminis-trators can add and remove domain controllers, control the organizational unit (OU) structure, change the security policy requirements, and control how the domain is structured. The domain administrators need to accept the fact that this is not isolated control however; forest root adminis-trative group accounts will still have the power to control the domain and affect the changes they put into place.

Within a domain, the Domain Admins global group has control over all of the OUs within the domain, and other groups can be delegated control over the OUs if they need to manage them. This is known as *data autonomy*. Those administrators who need to make changes to objects within Active Directory, or work with the resources that need to utilize Active Directory, can have a domain created for them, or they can have delegated access to OUs.

Figure 3.3 shows a forest with domains that are created for data or service autonomy. You will notice that the two child domains within the forest have their own administrative groups and nei-ther of the administrative groups belong to the forest root. This safeguards the services and data within each of the domains from administrators in the other domain. If the forest root were to hold the service and data administrators for either of these divisions of the company, the service administrators from the forest root would have control over the resources of the other division. As it stands now, a separate administrative body controls the forest root and grants the divisions autonomy from each another.

FIGURE 3.3   Domains built for data or service autonomy

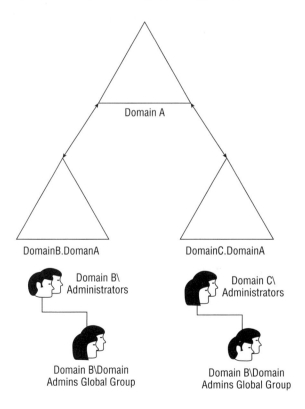

Domain A

DomainB.DomanA

Domain B\
Administrators

Domain B\Domain
Admins Global Group

DomainC.DomainA

Domain C\
Administrators

Domain B\Domain
Admins Global Group

This method of administration is usually found in the decentralized or hybrid administration models. With the decentralized model, you can create domains and delegate administrative control to those administrators who are responsible for their own partition of the directory service.

Understanding Isolated Administration

When you use the isolated administration model, you are essentially creating separate sandboxes where the administrators are selfish and won't share their toys. Although this is a harsh view of the isolated model, it accurately defines how this model functions. With this model, services and data administration needs to be performed by one administrative group and no other group should have any access whatsoever. Although this may seem like a drastic measure to take, some business practices require isolation of services and data.

If data isolation is required, the services that provide the data are also isolated. In this case, the data administrators need to take on the responsibility of the service administrator. This design may require additional staff or additional training for the administrators. Weigh the costs associated with isolation against the reasons for implementing isolation. Political reasons and posturing between departments and divisions within the organization may not be valid reasons, but legal requirements imposed by regulatory commissions are. Figure 3.4 shows an example of a forest created for service isolation.

Look back at Chapter 1, "Analyzing the Administrative Structure;" there we presented the decentralized model and discussed some of its merits and drawbacks. If you need to implement complete decentralization of resources, and those resources should not be controlled by any other administrator, you need to isolate those resources into their own forest. Again, this is a drastic measure and you should investigate other options first.

FIGURE 3.4   Forest designed for isolation

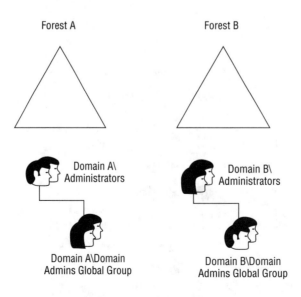

 **Design Scenario**

Identifying Owners

Cargo Container Cartage is a national delivery firm that has offices in 32 states. They have identified a need to keep each office's administration separate. However, they want to make sure that all of the offices are under the control of the national headquarters office located in St. Louis. Each of the regional offices will have an administrative staff that will be responsible for maintaining their own users and resources. All offices are interconnected via T1 connections using the national headquarters as the hub site. Currently none of the T1 links are being used at more than 30 percent capacity.

1. **Question:** Using the information provided, determine what type of administrative model is being used. **Answer:** The administrative model is a hybrid model because the administrators at the headquarters have ultimate control over the resources and the local administrative staff at the regional sites have the ability to control their own resources.

2. **Question:** Who are the forest owners? **Answer:** The administrators at the national headquarters.

3. **Question:** Who are the OU owners? **Answer:** The regional administrators.

Identifying Design Priorities

Rarely will any network architect find that every part of the Active Directory design process goes smoothly. Because the organizations are based on human wants and needs, political issues are going to arise that will cause debates over what is really required. As the designer, it is your job to separate the emotional desires from what should take priority within the design.

The interviews with key personnel should present the designer with clues as to where the organization's priorities lie. Base all of your decisions upon the priorities that you discover during these interviews. Although you may find that most of the interviews with the powers-that-be may point out that they want to keep costs at a minimum, you may find that other criteria override the "cost issue." Two other priorities, *high availability* and *reliability*, can take precedence, and you will find that they are usually mutually exclusive to the cost priority.

Because highly available solutions and reliable systems are more expensive than systems that do not provide this functionality, you need to identify where the organization stands.

Using Reliable Solutions

Reliable systems usually have mechanisms put into place for redundancy. Dual power supplies, storage partitions that take advantage of stripe sets with parity or mirroring, dual backplanes, and other technologies that provide hardware solutions to achieve fault tolerance do not come cheap. Active Directory is no exception. Because all of the domain controllers within a domain replicate the database to one another, you need multiple domain controllers. This design could dictate that multiple domain controllers are placed at high-priority sites. For additional levels of reliability, make sure you identify multiple DNS servers as well as network devices that define the physical infrastructure.

Certain domain controllers should be based on reliable systems. The *Operations Masters* are roles that only certain domain controllers can hold. The Operations Masters provide a means of controlling certain resources so that the functionality of Active Directory is not compromised. Two of these roles are only available on one domain controller within the forest:

- Schema Master
- Domain Naming Master

The other three roles are available on one domain controller in each of the domains within a forest:

- Primary Domain Controller (PDC) Emulator
- Infrastructure Master
- Relative ID (RID) Master

Because the function of each of these domain controllers is critical to Active Directory, make sure you plan to have reliable hardware for them.

> For more information on Operations Masters, check out *MCSE: Windows Server 2003 Active Directory Planning, Implementation, and Maintenance Study Guide*, by Anil Desai with James Chellis (Sybex, 2003).

Using High-Availability Solutions

Having systems that are highly available is also an expensive proposition. However, many companies that need their systems to be available at all times. Microsoft has clustering services available in the more expensive Enterprise and DataCenter Editions; you will not find clustering available in the Standard or Web editions. Also, several third-party high-availability solutions do exist, but again, they incur additional costs for the organization. If it is determined that a service must be available at all times, or a service level agreement has been put into place that guarantees availability of a service, cost is a lower priority than availability.

Whenever making trade-offs, make sure you include the stakeholders in the decision. You may come across instances when the designer should not make the trade-off; it should be left up to the stakeholders. For instance, if you are trying to determine what type of server solution you will use for your domain controllers, and you need the service to be reliable, you may end up with two solutions to choose from: the first solution is to use reliable hardware that has redundancy built in, and the second solution foregoes the highly reliable hardware for multiple servers to be used, one primary server and one backup. Both solutions may fit the organization's requirements, but the two-server solution may cost less than the redundant hardware requirements for the first option. Present the pros and cons of each of the solutions and allow the stakeholders to make the decision.

Design Scenario

Priority Identification

When interviewing management staff at Premier Pawn, a pawn shop that has ventured into the world of online sales, Tanya gathered the following information:

The Chief Executive Officer spoke of how the company had grown from a single small pawn shop in a college town to a multi-state company that became very popular due to their humorous ad placements. In the past few years, they have turned to the Internet to auction items that were in their inventory. While they are not the most recognized online auction house, the auctions have proven very popular due to the fact that the clientele trusts the Premier Pawn to deliver on the sale.

The Chief Information Officer has identified two areas that they need to improve upon with the new directory service design. Since they are moving to Exchange Server 2003 and using Internet Security and Acceleration Server, they are moving to Active Directory to support the two products. They are also taking advantage of the restructured Internet Information Server 6.0 for their web services.

The CIO also noted that since they were running auctions 24 hours a day every day of the year, they needed to make sure that the systems were functioning at all times. It is estimated that if the auctions are not accessible, the company could lose an estimated $225,000 per day in revenue. The company is willing to commit the resources to make sure that the system is always accessible to the users.

1. **Question:** What needs are identified for Premier Pawn's Windows Server 2003 Active Directory design? **Answer:** Application Support and High Availability

2. **Question:** Which of the design needs has the highest priority when choosing tradeoffs on the design? **Answer:** High Availability

Designing the Forest Structure

Before you determine the domain layout, you need to decide on the forest structure. A forest is made up of multiple domains that share the same schema, configuration container, and global catalog and are linked by two-way transitive trust relationships. Most designers try to start with a single forest design, and rightfully so. A single forest is by far the easiest structure to administer, but it allows high-level administrators to have control over all resources within the forest.

Several reasons exist for why a network architect would design a multiple forest infrastructure:

- Network administration is separated into autonomous groups that do not trust one another.
- Business units are politically separated.
- Business units must be separately maintained for legal reasons.
- You need to isolate the schema or configuration containers.

This isolation will affect Microsoft's Active Directory Application Mode (ADAM) containers also. (ADAM is also referred to as Application Data Partitions.) For more information on ADAM see the *MCSE: Windows Server 2003 Active Directory Planning, Implementation, and Maintenance Study Guide.*

- You need to limit the scope of trusts between domains.

For each of these reasons, isolation or autonomy of services or data is necessary. If data or service isolation is a requirement, you will need multiple forests. You are apt to encounter the following complications when you have a multiple forest design:

- Each forest maintains its own schema.

- Each forest maintains its own configuration container.

- Trusts and trust maintenance between domains in different forests must be manually configured.

- Replication of objects becomes manual.

Before Windows Server 2003's Active Directory came to be, having a multiple forest design was very difficult to administer if you needed forests to collaborate. Windows Server 2003's Active Directory has been beefed up with enhancements that allow you to create forest trusts, which make sharing of resources easier.

You can create forests trusts between two forests so that the resources can be accessed by accounts in the remote domain. These trust relationships can be built to control exactly where the accounts have access and which accounts can access the remote forest. New features such as partially transitive trusts and Security Identifier (SID) filtering can be used if only certain accounts need to have access.

For more information concerning SID filtering, see the white paper "Using SID Filtering to Prevent Elevation of Privilege Attacks" from the Microsoft website.

As the network architect, you need to determine if your design really needs multiple forests. Although you may find that the groups responsible for the services and data would like to have isolation, they may not really need it. Make sure everyone involved understands the costs involved in maintaining multiple directory services within the organization. Having separate service administrators for each forest incurs additional training and overlapping job responsibilities. When you create the forest design, you should take the following best practices to heart:

- When designing the forest, always start with the simplest design, the single forest.

- Determine whether the service administrators need to have service isolation or autonomy before you create additional forests.

- If collaboration is required, a single forest works the best.

- Use OUs for data autonomy instead of additional forests.
- Create a schema modification policy.

Forests can be designed based on the need to provide isolation, autonomy, or collaboration. Depending on the administrative model used, the forest takes on either an organization-based design or is built with resource separation or isolation in mind.

Implementing an Organization-Based Forest

Organization-based forests are the most common type of forest. Using this design, an organization's resources are placed within the forest and organized so that the appropriate groups have control over the resources they need. In Chapter 1, we discussed the differences among the administration models and identified some of the reasons they affect the design of Active Directory. One of the models that we discussed was the decentralized model. Although companies choose the decentralized model for several reasons, one of the primary reasons is autonomy of control. If the companies require autonomy, a department or division could have a domain created for them, or OUs could be built within a domain.

In Chapter 1, we also outlined various business models. The departmental model identifies business units that make up an organization. The product/services-based model identifies different divisions of an organization based on the products that the organization provides. Either of these two models can use the organization-based forest design.

The departmental model usually takes on a single forest design with all of the departments broken up into different domains or OUs. This allows the entire organization's resources to be administered efficiently. Using this single forest approach, all of the resources within the directory service are represented within the global catalog. No additional means of interoperating are necessary. You can achieve autonomy of control over the resources by delegating control to the owners of domains and OUs. Figure 3.5 shows an example of an organization-based forest using OUs for the business units. In this example, the manufacturing division has been given its own domain within the forest. The Model Shop and Quality Assurance departments are controlled by administrators from the Manufacturing domain, whereas the Marketing, Human Resources, and Accounting departments are controlled by administrators from the HQ domain.

The product/service-based model may take on a single forest structure with each product having its own domain. However, companies that have merged or acquired other companies may need to support multiple forests until the resources can be incorporated into a single forest design. Some organizations use a forest for each of the product lines. Creating the multiple organization forest structure allows for isolation among the product lines. Resource access can still be granted through trust relationships, but administrative control is broken apart based on the service administrators for each forest. Figure 3.6 shows an example of a company with two different business units that need to have isolation of control, yet want to allow access to resources. The forest trust is built so that the resources are available to users, but the administrative control is isolated.

FIGURE 3.5 Organization-based forest

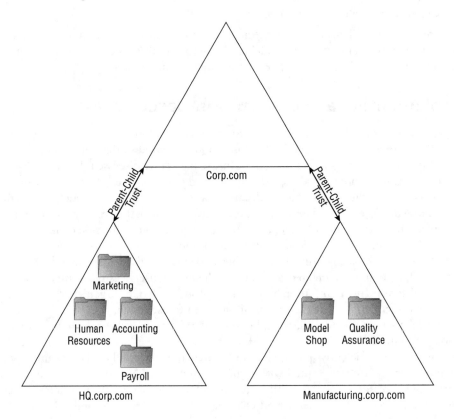

FIGURE 3.6 Isolated organization-based forest

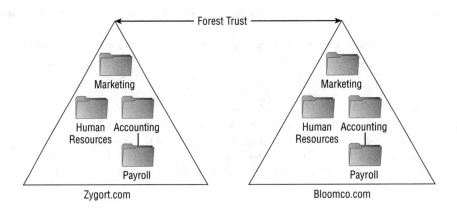

Implementing a Resource Forest

If certain resources need to be isolated from the rest of the organization, then you can create a resource forest. A *resource forest* is one in which the resources, such as shared folders, printers, member servers, and so on, are located within their own forest so that the owners of the resource can control them. Usually, the resource forest does not have any user accounts within the forest with the exception of the service administrator accounts that are required to maintain the forest.

Using this type of forest, an organization can make sure that the resources contained within the resource forest are not affected by the loss of services in any other forest. For instance, a manufacturing company that has resources in different geographical locations, especially those in different countries, may create a forest so that communication failures or a disaster at one location will not affect the resources and their reliance on the directory service. Figure 3.7 shows an example of a resource forest.

As mentioned before, having multiple forests adds to the administrative overhead. Resource forests need to have trust relationships created with the other forests. Because the directory services are isolated, the resource forest service administrators are probably different than the service administrator for other forests. Additional training and overlapping of responsibilities may occur. Decide how you will administer the additional forests prior to creating them.

Implementing a Restricted-Access Forest

A *restricted-access forest* completely separates service administrators from one another. Although you can build trust relationships to allow users to access the resources within the remote forest, the service administrators from the two forests are not allowed to administer the other forest's services. If the organization has any need for isolation of services, this is the type of forest structure that you need to build. Figure 3.8 shows an example of a restricted-access forest. Notice that no trust relationships exist among the domains that make up either forest. This not only keeps administration isolated, but access to resources is restricted to accounts within the forest only.

FIGURE 3.7   Resource forest

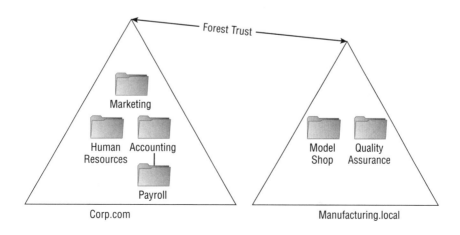

Real World Scenario

Making Use of Isolation

In order to meet the requirements of a defense contract that would bring in $28 million, Argobot had to meet the strict requirements of the contract. The primary requirement was that the specifications for the parts they would be contracted to build could only be accessed by the team that would be assigned to the project. Due to the nature of the project, the specifications dictated that the data could not be passed on the same physical network as the current business data. Complete isolation was required.

Six months earlier, Argobot had lost a contract with another firm. At that time, they had removed several pieces of machinery from an area of their building and consolidated their operations to become more efficient. The vacated area became a staging area. After discussing the network requirements for the defense contract, it was decided that the vacated area could be transformed into a separate entity within the organization. New cabling was run throughout for the new systems and all of the devices were connected to the segregated network.

Because the services and data had to be completely isolated from the rest of the organization, a new forest was decided upon. Because none of the accounts within the existing forest would have access to the new forest and a forest trust would not be built, the Defense Department isolation requirement could be met.

Windows Server 2003 was chosen as the operating system of choice, and an Active Directory forest was built for the new project. Members of the Information Technology team were chosen to be the service and data administrators for the new forest. A single domain was built and the member servers were added to support the new organization. Due to their ability to adapt quickly and meet all of the requirements of the project, Argobot won the contract.

FIGURE 3.8   Restricted-access forest

Take for example a company that has governmental defense contracts. The company may create a forest to isolate the top-secret information from the rest of the company. In this scenario, the users who need access to information from both forests may have two access terminals that they use, each terminal is a member of only one of the forests and is separated on different physical networks. Another option is to use a server-based client access tools such as Terminal Services or Citrix MetaFrame to access desktops for each of the forests. With this method, the forests would have to share parts of the same physical network, which could pose other security considerations like the ability of capturing the network packets using a network monitoring device or software.

Using the flowchart in Figure 3.9, you will be able to decide how the forest structure should be designed.

A discussion of forests cannot end without covering one of the most important parts of the forest—the schema. The schema contains the building blocks of the forest. Every domain within the forest shares the same schema so that the objects have a common set of attributes that define them. Because the schema is such an important part of Active Directory, you should not take changes to the schema lightly.

FIGURE 3.9   Flowchart to determine isolated or autonomous control

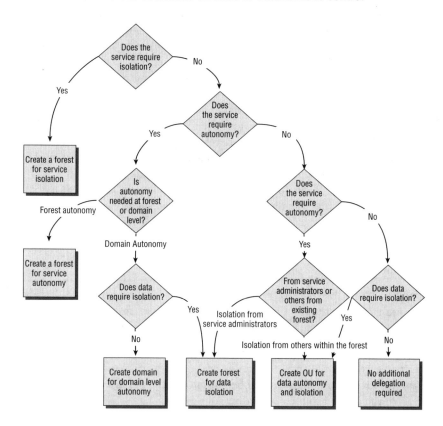

Schema Considerations

Every organization needs to create a *schema modification policy*. This policy should identify the process they need to approve schema changes, who is allowed to change the schema, and when the schema modifications should go into effect. This policy has to be followed to the letter. Because the schema holds the definitions of the attributes and objects that can be used within the forest, schema modifications can cause several problems for Active Directory as well as the network infrastructure. Something as simple as adding a single attribute to an object class can cause replication issues throughout the infrastructure.

With all of the object classes and attributes that are built into Active Directory, chances are you may never have to make any modifications to the schema, with the exception of adding Active Directory–enabled applications. Microsoft has done a very good job of identifying those objects and attributes that most companies need. Keeping this in mind, any discussion of modification should start with a thorough examination of the existing classes and objects to make sure they will not suffice.

You will encounter instances when you need to make changes. Some Active Directory–enabled applications add object classes and attributes before they will install and function. One very popular application is Exchange Server. Exchange Server 2000 and Exchange Server 2003 add several attributes and classes into Active Directory. The same holds true for ISA Server, Enterprise Edition. As more and more developers discover the benefits of storing information within Active Directory, chances are better that the schema will have to take on some updates.

The entire forest is affected by changes to the schema. Getting approval from the entire administrative staff of every domain can be difficult. You will need proof that every change is necessary. Make sure you have documented exactly what the change will provide for the company. For example, after the decision has been made to move to Exchange Server 2003, the issue becomes when, not if, the change should be made. If a developer has decided that a new attribute needs to be added to the user object class, make sure they have a valid reason for needing this attribute instead of using one of the 15 custom attributes that are available.

If changes are introduced, make sure they are made at a time when replication is allowed to propagate them efficiently and will affect the least number of services. Once a change is introduced, it will replicate to every domain controller within the forest. Potentially, propagation delays could introduce inconsistencies between sites and domain controllers. Careful planning as to when the change should be made and how replication should be enforced will minimize the issues.

In short, you should follow these rules:

- Make sure none of the existing attributes or object classes meet the needs of the organization.

- Do not grant anyone the right to make changes to the schema until they are necessary.

- Make sure to follow the guidelines of the change policy before you allow changes to the schema.

A well-defined schema modification policy reduces the problems associated with making changes. Debates will rage amongst the administrators of the domains, and the battles that need to be fought to prove the change needs to be put into place are hard enough without having to decide on all of the criteria to include within your policy.

Prior to implementing Active Directory, work into your design who will make up the schema modification approval committee. Meet with the administrators of all of the domains within the forest to gain approval of the policy. It will take buy-in from everyone who will be affected. This may not be a simple task, especially in an environment where you have service or data autonomy. Those administrators may not have a great deal of trust in other administrators. As mentioned before, make sure you have the appropriate allies so that you can get approval from the highest-level stakeholder.

Because the policy should lay out the requirements that must be met before the schema modification can occur, you should include each of the following components in the policy. Following the policy then guarantees that the modification being investigated benefits the company, and therefore it will be approved by all of the appropriate individuals.

Planning and Testing

Although planning and testing sounds like common sense, make sure you don't ignore it. A test environment is essential for a successful implementation. You can create test forests and domains that will not impact your current environment. Changes to the schema may affect applications other than the one you are making the change for. Try to account for every possibility. Within your test forest, install all of the applications used within the organization. Once the schema modification has been introduced into the test forest, thoroughly test all of the applications to determine if any problems arise.

This part of the policy should also spell out how the test forest will be built, who will be in charge, how permission to use the test forest will be granted, and what documentation will need to be completed prior to the approval of the modification. Because changes to the schema cannot be reversed easily, determining whom, when, and where changes will occur is a vital part of the Active Directory design.

Who Makes the Change?

The right to make changes to the schema is not granted to any user account. As a matter of fact, only one security principal is allowed to make changes: the Schema Admins group. Due to the sheer power this group has, it should be left without any members until absolutely necessary. Allowing an account to remain within this group would be like allowing someone to have the ability to alter your molecular DNA. The changes that could be introduced could be disastrous. Even if the user did not mean to be destructive, simple typos could introduce problems that could take months to diagnose.

The policy will specify who can control how accounts are added to the Schema Admins group. Members of the Domain Admins group in the forest root domain and the Enterprise Admins group are the only accounts who have the ability (by default) to modify the Schema Admins group membership. Therefore, the membership in these groups should be controlled and monitored. Auditing account modifications in the forest root should be enabled. This allows you to identify when a change occurred and who enacted the change.

The policy should point out who is allowed to add accounts to the Schema Admins group. Although this policy does not stop someone with the authority from implementing a change to the group, at least you have written documentation of the standards and policies that should be followed.

Plan the Roll-Out Schedule

Every network has "busy" periods when users are accessing the services and resources that reside on the network. Databases, e-mail, authentication traffic, print jobs, and many other types of data take up bandwidth on the network. Active Directory consumes bandwidth whenever replication traffic, authentication requests, or user and service queries occur. The typical daily patterns for the network traffic should be determined so that you know when the network is being used and when it is relatively silent.

For some companies, this is an easy process. They have most of their traffic occurring during the regular business hours and do not have to worry about after-hours traffic. Companies that have 24-hour cycles may not have the luxury of being able to make changes during the night because they still have a user population that needs to use the network. Large companies that span multiple time zones have even greater challenges. Changes have to be replicated to domain controllers across WAN links, through multiple sites, all at differing times.

As the person in charge of rolling out schema changes, you need to determine the best time for the roll-out. The timing of the roll-out is critical. Not only do you need to know when the change can occur due to the network bandwidth requirements mentioned above, but you need to address the propagation delay. The longer it takes for the changes to replicate, the greater the risk of having objects that are "out of sync" or built with the incorrect attributes.

Where to Make the Changes

All changes to the schema are made on the Schema Master. The Schema Master is the only domain controller that has the token that allows it to make changes to this service. You should enact any changes you need to make to the schema on this domain controller. If the change is made at another system, the change request and the authentication have to be sent to the Schema Master to take effect. Although this may not be an issue if you are adding a single attribute or object class, running the setup program for an Active Directory–integrated application such as Exchange Server 2003 sends far too much data across the network.

Summary

At this point, you should be familiar with the requirements for designing the forest structure. Starting with the service and data isolation and autonomy requirements, you can select the appropriate high-level design options. Although a lot of information is in this chapter, all of it needs to be addressed if you are going to design an efficient directory service structure. An inefficient design creates additional administrative overhead and problems when the design is implemented.

Make sure you identify who the data and service administrators are and where they need to be granted rights and permissions. Once you have determined who the administrators are and what level of control they need within the Active Directory design, determining the number of forests should be easy.

Once you have decided upon the number of forests you need to develop the root domain, domain names, and trust relationships. When developing the Active Directory infrastructure, the primary rule is to start out simple and add complexity only if it is absolutely required. The more complexity added to the design, the more administrative overhead you have when you go to implement and use the directory service.

In the next chapter, we are going to discuss the domain structure within our design. We'll compare the benefits of using a single domain to using multiple domains. Depending on the administration model you are using, you may be forced to have more than one domain. Other factors, such as the security policies, will also affect the design. But remember the forest design rules, they will show up again when designing domains.

Exam Essentials

Understand what service administrators are responsible for.   Service administrators are responsible for the configuration and maintenance of the directory service.

Understand what data administrators are responsible for.   Data administrators are responsible for maintaining the object within the directory service and the resources that need to access them.

Understand data and service collaboration.   Collaboration of data and services specifies that administrators need to share responsibilities.

Understand data and service autonomy.   Data and service autonomy specifies that the administrative staff responsible for objects and resources has control over those resources but no peer administrative account will have any level of control. Higher-level administrative accounts will still have the ability to administer the resources however.

Understand data and service isolation.   With isolation, the data or service is completely separated from any other administrative group.

Identify design priorities.   Cost will be a major factor, but do not be afraid to override the cost issue if you need reliable or highly available solutions.

Know what an organization forest is.   An organization forest is built so that the organization's structure is the basis for the forest design.

Know what a resource forest is.   A resource forest is created to isolate resources that need to have specialized administrative control or the ability to function on their own.

Know what a restricted-access forest is.   A restricted-access forest is one in which no accounts from any other forest will have access to its resources.

Understand why a schema modification policy is required.   The schema is a vitally important component of Active Directory. Special care must be taken to approve any changes that affect the schema.

Know what makes up a change policy.   The change policy states what is required for planning and testing, who will make the schema modification, when the modification can be implemented, and where is should be implemented.

Key Terms

Before you take the exam, be certain you are familiar with the following terms:

autonomous model	organization-based forest
collaborative model	reliability
data administrators	resource forest
data autonomy	restricted-access forest
high availability	schema modification policy
isolated model	service administrators
Operations Masters	

Review Questions

1. Those users who are responsible for planning, implementing, maintaining, and controlling the Active Directory forest are identified as which of the following?

   A. Data administrators

   B. Domain administrators

   C. Forest administrators

   D. Service administrators

2. Those users who are responsible for maintaining objects in Active Directory are identified as which of the following?

   A. Data administrators

   B. Domain administrators

   C. Forest administrators

   D. Service administrators

3. When creating the forest design, which of the following is the least expensive to administer?

   A. Single forest/single domain

   B. Single forest/multiple domain

   C. Two forests/single domain each

   D. Two forests/multiple domains each

4. In a single forest/single domain design, who is allowed to manipulate the Schema Admins group? (Choose all that apply)

   A. Members of the Enterprise Admins group

   B. Members of the Domain Admins group

   C. Members of the Administrators group

   D. Members of the Server Operators group

5. Josh is the manager of a new product group for Zygort Corporation. This product group is responsible for designing equipment that will be used on projects for NASA. NASA has determined that the information that must be shared with Josh's group should not be available to members of any other division within Zygort. Which of the following options best describes the design option that will be used when developing the Active Directory design for Zygort?

   A. Service isolation/new forest

   B. Data isolation/new domain

   C. Service autonomy/new domain

   D. Data autonomy/delegated OU

6. Michelle has finished the interviews she was holding with the key stakeholders from Quality Test Labs and is now building the conceptual forest design. The organization has three divisions, all autonomous from the others. Because none of the divisions interoperate, they want isolation of their resources. Each division also supports their own administrative staff. A centralized security auditing group will have access to resources in all of the domains within the organization, however. This group will reside in one Active Directory forest, but it will need to have access to resources in each forest. They will be allowed to monitor objects and resources but will not have the rights to make any modifications. Which of the forest structures is being employed?

    A. Organizational forest

    B. Resource forest

    C. Restricted-access forest

    D. Regional forest

7. Which of the following should be included in the Schema Modification Policy? (Choose all that apply.)

    A. Requirements for planning and testing changes

    B. Identifying who will be able to make the change

    C. How the roll-out schedule will be implemented

    D. Where the changes can be implemented

8. Which of the following servers would the service administrators manage?

    A. Domain Controller

    B. Exchange Server

    C. File Server

    D. SQL Server

9. Which of the following services would the data administrators manage?

    A. Domain Controller

    B. Exchange Server

    C. File Server

    D. SQL Server

10. Juan is reviewing the information he has gathered during his interview with the manager of Information Technology. He identified criteria for the upgrade to Active Directory. Exchange Server 2003 is going to be used as the primary e-mail solution. There are also requirements to keep the current administrative staff, but not add any additional staff to support the upcoming technology. The manager also mentioned the company is requiring that the directory service is available at all time. The system will be monitored and the next year's budget will be based on how they meet the requirements of an SLA. Considering this information, what will be the highest priority?

    A. Application Support

    B. High Availability

    C. Obsolescence

    D. Total Cost of Ownership

Answers to Review Questions

1. D. Service administrators are responsible for the Active Directory and making sure that it is available and configured correctly so that users can gain access to the services it provides.

2. A. Data administrators are responsible for the administration of the objects within their partition of Active Directory. They could have control over all objects within a domain, or they could be granted control at the OU level.

3. A. The single forest/single domain structure is the least costly to administer since all of the administrative functions are handled within the single structure. All of the administration models can still be supported, but you will only have to maintain one domain policy and all of the domain controller will be peers.

4. A, B, C. Because members of the domain's Administrators domain local group have the ability to change the membership of the Enterprise Admins group, and the Domain Admins group is a member of the Administrators domain local group, members from all three of these groups have the ability to control the Schema Admins group membership.

5. A. Because none of the information will be available to anyone outside of the division, and because service administrators from a forest could potentially have access to the data within an Active Directory forest, a new forest should be created to completely isolate the project data.

6. C. The restricted-access forest is built when the business units need to be isolated from one another. Trust relationships can be built so that resources from one forest are accessible by users from another, but the directory services are completely separate and administered separately.

7. A, B, C, D. All of these options should be part of the schema modification policy. If any of these components are missing, unnecessary changes could be put into place, or the network could suffer from the implementation.

8. A. Service Administrators are responsible for managing the Domain Controllers and other systems that support the directory service.

9. B, C, D. While service administrators manage the domain controllers, the data administrators will manage other servers within the organization.

10. B. While there are requirements for application support since Exchange Server 2003 will be added to the infrastructure, and reduced TCO has been identified, it appears as though the company is more interested in the availability of the directory service since they are creating an SLA for the availability of the directory service and the budget will be based on how well the requirements are met.

Case Study

You should give yourself 20 minutes to review this testlet, and complete the questions.

Background

Insane Systems build custom computers for their customers. They specialize in building cases that are unique and support the latest in hardware technology. They started off as a small company that provided this service to gamers who would take their cases to LAN parties to show off. Due to the fact that their systems were considered some of the most stable gaming platforms and because they provided an impressive design that gamers could show off, they started to become popular. Insane Systems started mass manufacturing some of their more popular designs and began selling stand-alone cases along with their fully configured systems. As space at the company became a premium, the office was moved from the manufacturing facility. This allowed the company to add to the amount of space that was used for the mass production line.

Existing Environment

Over the past few months, Insane Systems has been developing plans to expand their company. They have identified San Jose, California; Atlanta, Georgia; and New York City as the locations with their highest customer base. The current Chicago location will remain the corporate headquarters, but they are opening branches in New York City and San Jose. They are also in the process of acquiring a competitor's business in Atlanta. These locations will provide retail outlets as well as support. Customers will have the option of sending their systems back to the corporate office or delivering them to one of the branch locations.

Because the company is planning on expanding, they want to make sure that the network infrastructure is in place to support their larger, distributed company. They are also concerned with the support lifetime of their current Windows NT 4.0 infrastructure. They realize they have the option of moving to a Windows 2000 or Windows 2003 infrastructure and are considering moving to Windows Server 2003 and Active Directory for two reasons: the expected support lifetime is greater than Windows 2000, and they are a technology firm that is not afraid of staying ahead of the technology curve.

Part of the expansion of the company is a complete overhaul of their current Internet presence. They are planning on bringing all of the web development and hosting in-house. Currently a web hosting service is providing their Internet presence, and Insane Systems feels as though they could provide better marketing and support information for their customers if they had control over their own website.

Interviews

Your company has been hired to design an Active Directory infrastructure and the network infrastructure to support it. During the interview process with some of the key stakeholders, you gathered the following information:

CEO   Currently we have a single location with all of our processes local. As we grow, we would like to keep all of the administration here in Chicago. Because the new branches are primarily retail and support offices, we will not need to have a large staff in those locations.

CIO   Most of the infrastructure that we support is located here at the corporate office. We do support some key servers at the manufacturing location. We support these servers from our main office. Because the servers are nearby, if there is a problem, we can usually be on site within half an hour.

The new branches are going to be another issue altogether. We would like to retain the same level of administrative control over the servers in the new locations that we employ currently. Due to the geographic limitations, we may need to have some support staff at those locations. Currently, the plan is to hire staff at those locations who can provide the support for the customers, but also have an understanding of the business systems we need to put into place.

Manager of Information Technology   We have grown very quickly over the past three years and our current technologies have kept up with that growth. However, we don't think the current infrastructure is ready for the amount of growth that we are expecting within the following year. We are not afraid of moving to the latest technology, but we want to make sure that the design is stable and makes sense for us, especially if we will continue growing in the upcoming months. And because we are losing support for NT 4.0, we want to make sure that we have an operating system that will be supported for a few years down the road.

Most of our processes are located here at this office, and we would like to keep it that way. We know that some servers will need to be located at the remote offices, but we would like to be able to provide most of the support from this location. Remote administration tools will need to be included within the design so that we can keep our administrative costs to a minimum.

Currently, we have most of our servers located at the main office, and all are located on their own high-speed backbone. We do have a server at the manufacturing site that allows the staff there to have e-mail as well as plans and orders in case we lose connectivity between the offices. This server is running Exchange 5.5. Several times during the day we replicate the public folder information to this system so that they are always up-to-date and do not have to dial up to the main office using our 56Kbps modem.

The systems at the main office are all supported by our staff of four administrators. All of the administrators are cross-trained on Windows NT 4.0, Exchange 5.5, SQL Server 7.0, our accounting software, and each of our file and print servers. We currently have several Windows NT 4.0 servers in place, including one Exchange 5.5 server at both locations, one SQL Server 7.0 server at the main office, one server running our accounting package that interfaces with the SQL server, and one file and print server that is used by both locations. The Exchange server at the manufacturing location doubles as a print server also.

Because all of the client machines are running Windows NT 4.0 Workstation, we do not have to worry about supporting different operating systems. We would like to maintain that same easy administration with the upcoming system. We would like to provide the same types of services at the remote locations that we provide at the home office, although accounting will remain at the home office and will not be spread out to all of the locations.

Current Infrastructure

After investigating the current infrastructure, you have determined that the following servers are in place:

Home Office

Primary Domain Controller (PDC)

Backup Domain Controller (BDC)

DHCP Server

DNS/WINS Server

Exchange 5.5 Server

SQL Server 7.0

Systems Management Server 2.0

File Server

Print/Antivirus Server

Research and Development File Server

Manufacturing Facility

Backup Domain Controller (BDC)

DNS/WINS/DHCP Relay Agent Server

Exchange 5.5/File Server

The Corporate Office hosts nearly 250 Windows NT 4.0 workstations at this point. They are interconnected by several 48-port 10/100Mbps switches. A router is used to divide the network into 4 broadcast domains (i.e., VLANs). One of these broadcast domains is the 1Gbps backbone on which the servers reside. Each of the servers is connected to a 1Gbps switch port. This location takes advantage of private IP address ranges. The servers are located on the 192.168.1.0/24 subnet. The client systems are divided between network addresses 192.168.10.0/24, 192.168.11.0/24, 192.168.12.0/24, and 192.168.13.0/24.

The manufacturing facility contains 12 Windows NT 4.0 workstations connected to the same switch as the servers. Because Insane Systems does not want to slow down production due to a communication failure, they have taken advantage of Exchange 5.5's public folder replication. Public folders are continually updated with the latest orders. The crew foreman can access the orders locally from these public folders at any time, whether the communication link between the locations is up or not. This location uses another address range—192.168.20.0/24.

Case Study Questions

1. Which of the following groups will be the service administrators?
   A. HQAdmins
   B. ATStaff
   C. NYStaff
   D. SJStaff
   E. Nobody

2. Which of the following groups will be the data administrators?
   A. HQAdmins
   B. ATStaff
   C. NYStaff
   D. SJ Staff
   E. Nobody

3. How many forests will Insane Systems need for their Active Directory infrastructure?
   A. 1
   B. 2
   C. 3
   D. 4

4. Which of the following accounts should be made a member of the Schema Admins group?
   A. HQAdmins
   B. ATStaff
   C. NYStaff
   D. SJ Staff
   E. Nobody

5. Put the design criteria options that identified by the case study information in priority order.

Design Priority	Possible Options
	Application Support
	High Availability
	Obsolescence
	Total Cost of Ownership

Answers to Case Study Questions

1. A. The administrators from the headquarters located in Chicago should be service administrators because they will be responsible for Active Directory and guaranteeing its availability.

2. A. Even though the staff from the remote locations will be responsible for systems at those locations, they will not need to have Active Directory rights or permissions. If, at a later time, it is deemed necessary for the remote administrators to have rights and permissions, they can be delegated to them.

3. A. There are no requirements for isolation of services or data within the design, so Insane Systems will be well served with a single forest, which makes administration easier.

4. E. Unless a change needs to be made to the schema, this group should remain empty. Once all of the requirements of the schema change policy have been met, an account can be added to the Schema Admins group to enact the changes, but it should be removed after the change has been put into place.

5.

Design Priority
Total Cost of Ownership
Obsolescence
Application Support

Total Cost of Ownership has been identified by more than one of the administrative staff as being a priority. While the other two options, obsolescence and application support, are also a concern, the ability to reduce costs is on everyone's agenda. Since they are looking for a solution that will have support for a long period of time and they do not want to fall into the same paradox they are in with their current directory service solution, obsolescence will have a higher priority than application support since the applications they have identified could potentially run on other operating systems. The company has not identified any services which would require the additional benefits of high availability, so that option does not fall under the scope of priorities.

Chapter

4

Designing the Active Directory Domain Structure

MICROSOFT EXAM OBJECTIVES COVERED IN THIS CHAPTER:

✓ **Analyze the impact of Active Directory on the existing technical environment.**

- Analyze interoperability requirements.

✓ **Analyze existing network operating system implementation.**

- Identify the existing domain model.

✓ **Analyze security requirements for the Active Directory directory service.**

- Identify the existing trust relationships.

✓ **Design the Active Directory infrastructure to meet business and technical requirements.**

- Create the conceptual design of the Active Directory domain structure.
- Design the Active Directory replication strategy.

✓ **Analyze the impact of the infrastructure design on the existing technical environment.**

- Analyze interoperability requirements.

✓ **Design a user and computer authentication strategy.**

- Optimize authentication by using shortcut trust relationships.

✓ **Design an Active Directory naming strategy.**

- Identify Internet domain name registration requirements.
- Specify the use of hierarchical namespace within Active Directory.

✓ **Design migration paths to Active Directory.**

  ▪ Define whether the migration will include an in-place upgrade, domain restructuring, or migration to a new Active Directory environment.

After you determine what the forest structure should look like, you will need to investigate the domain structure. You will find several similarities between domains and forests when determining how many domains should be used. The primary design goal for the forest structure is administrative control. The same holds true for the domain design.

Within this chapter, we will introduce the requirements and decision criteria for domain design. We will also discuss the reasons why you would want to create multiple domains instead of using a single domain for your design.

Identifying the Domain Administrative Structure

Once your forest is designed, your domain structure can be created. The same design criteria that went into the forest design also dictates how the domains are created. For ease of administration, you should always start with the most basic design, the single domain. The need for autonomy and isolation then dictates whether you will need to create additional domains.

Domain owners have to accept the fact that they share administrative control with the forest owners. They also have to accept that some elements of administrative control are out of their control unless they are also Enterprise Admins. Certain functions such as deleting their domain or adding in an Active Directory–enabled application that modifies the schema of the forest cannot be performed by the domain owners. They have to rely on the forest owners to provide that functionality.

True isolation cannot occur unless the domain resides in its own forest and the domain administrators are also the forest administrators. Domain/forest owners need to understand that their domain/forest could become compromised by a rogue or coerced administrator. A *rogue administrator* is an individual who abuses the power that they have been granted. This abuse could be as simple as an administrator who views the information within the domain in order to glean some information about users or resources, or as devious as an administrator who intentionally damages or manipulates information. *Coerced administrators* are those who may be forced into performing a security breach within the infrastructure.

Security breaches by these rogue or coerced administrators could occur within the domain, from other domains within the forest, or from external domains via explicit trusts. Because all domains in the forest share information, a rogue or coerced administrator could modify the contents of Active Directory to allow a security breach, such as modifying the members of high-level group accounts. Domain owners should make sure that they know who the administrators are within the domain at all times. They should monitor the membership of any administrative groups. Domain owners should validate the work that the forest owners are performing and monitor the actions the forest owner performs within the domain owner's domain.

Active Directory is designed to be flexible enough that you can create a single domain to support the organization, or a multiple domain design can be utilized if necessary. In the following sections, we are going to look at the differences between the domain designs and the criteria that forces a multiple domain design instead of a single domain. We will also look at the requirements for creating multiple trees within our forest, and identify the security considerations of having a single domain compared to multiple domains, as well as the options for creating domains.

Using a Single Domain

As we have mentioned before, the simpler the design, the easier and more cost effective it is to administer and maintain the infrastructure. Domains are no exception. If the forest administrators are also the domain administrators, you may be able to implement a single domain for your organization.

If you use this approach, all of the accounts within the domain will be required to use the same account policies. Password policies, lockout restrictions, and Kerberos policies are controlled at the domain level for domain accounts and cannot be overridden at any other level within the domain. As long as this is acceptable, the single domain design will work. However, if any accounts need to have differing account policy requirements, you'll need an additional domain.

WARNING Local accounts on a member server or workstation may not have the same password and lockout restrictions that will be enforced on domain accounts. These settings can be controlled at the local security policy on the computer or at the organizational unit (OU) that contains the computer account(s). Make sure that you are periodically checking the settings at these levels to ensure that your company's standards are met.

NOTE There are programmatic methods for enforcing differing settings on specific accounts. Using Active Directory Services Interface (ADSI) scripting, you could specify that certain accounts' passwords need to be changed at a shorter interval than what the domain password policy is set for. For instance, you could enforce sensitive accounts to change their passwords at the end of a 30-day cycle while forcing other accounts into a 45-day cycle through the domain password policy.

A single domain design can accommodate any of the administrative models: centralized, decentralized, hybrid, or outsourced. In the following sections, we will look at how a single domain can support all of them.

Identifying Centralized Administration Support

As you recall from Chapter 1, "Analyzing the Administrative Structure," the centralized administrative model was divided between two different approaches: centralized administration/centralized resources and centralized administration/decentralized resources.

For the centralized administration/centralized resources model, the domain administrators will have control over all of the services and objects within the domain. The objects can be organized within OUs so that the administrative staff can apply Group Policy Objects (GPOs). This reduces the administrative load by controlling how the resource acts within the domain and how access to the resource is allowed. Centralized administration with decentralized resources works in much the same way. The resources can be grouped by location, and then subdivided based upon the GPOs that are applied to the resource.

Figure 4.1 shows an example of a single domain used for centralized administration/centralized resources, whereas Figure 4.2 shows an example of a single domain used for centralized administration/decentralized resources. The domain that is structured for centralized administration/centralized resources takes advantage of having all of the resources centrally located. In Figure 4.1, the administrative staff can have the proper permissions applied at the domain level. Whereas all of the objects within Active Directory are located within the same OU hierarchy, the permissions for the administrative staff will pass down to each object.

FIGURE 4.1   Single domain used for centralized administration/centralized resources

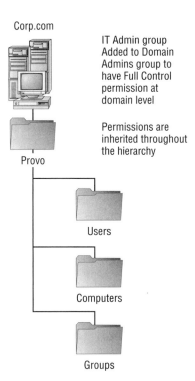

Corp.com

IT Admin group
Added to Domain
Admins group to
have Full Control
permission at
domain level

Permissions are
inherited throughout
the hierarchy

Provo

Users

Computers

Groups

For more information on using OUs for administrative control, see Chapter 5, "Designing an Organizational Unit Structure for Administrative Purposes." For more information on using OU for the application of Group Policy objects, see Chapter 6, "Designing a Group Policy Infrastructure."

In Figure 4.2, the resources are not centrally located, so the OU structure has been designed to take advantage of the location of the objects. The domain owners will have permissions assigned to them at the domain level so that they can have control over all of the objects within the domain. The administrative staff at each location can then be granted the proper permissions to manage the objects for which they are responsible. These permissions are set at the OU that represents their location.

Identifying Decentralized Administration Support

You could create additional domains to allow a separation of service or data administration. This would allow different service administrators to have control over their own domain controllers and the servers that support them. Data administrators could then have a level of autonomy over the data that they manage. Decentralized administration is also supported through OUs.

FIGURE 4.2 Single domain used for centralized administration/decentralized resources

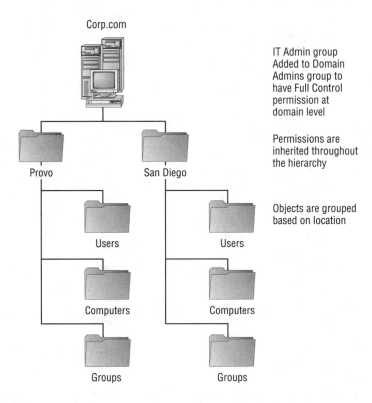

You can group resources by location and delegate the administrators of each resource administrative control. This allows access to only those administrators who need to control the resource. If Group Policy objects are to be used, the OUs can be created for administrative control and child OUs can be created to organize the objects and to assign GPOs to.

For more information on using OUs for administrative purposes, see Chapter 5.

Figure 4.3 shows a single domain design employing OUs for decentralized administration.

Identifying Hybrid Administration Support

Hybrid administration takes on the best of both the centralized and decentralized models. Objects are still organized and controlled as though they were part of the decentralized model, but those administrators who need to maintain standards and policies will have rights to the OUs within the domain.

FIGURE 4.3   Single domain using OUs for decentralized administration

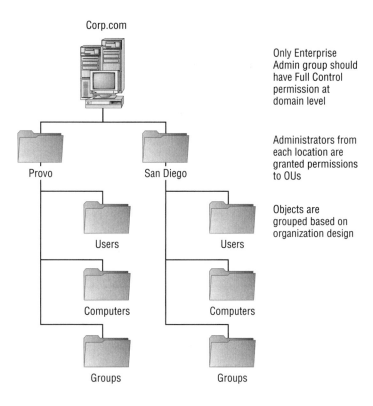

For example, if a group of administrators are responsible for creating the GPOs that will be applied to computers within the domain, they are delegated the right to create GPOs but not to assign them anywhere within the domain. This keeps them from having the power to modify the behavior of a server. The administrators responsible for the servers are then granted the right to apply GPOs to the OUs they control. They are able to read the settings on the GPO to verify that the policy is configured to work correctly but are not able to modify the policy setting. This keeps them from overriding corporate standards.

Of course there has to be a level of trust between the groups. Once applied, the GPO can still be modified, and once the policy has been created the administrator doesn't have to apply it. In a situation where policy administrators have the backing of upper management to control the resources with the policies they create, the administrators who manage the objects within Active Directory will have to abide by their rules. That does not mean that they have to blindly follow the criteria defined at the policy level. They can always question the effects of the policy if they think that the settings are incorrect.

For more information on how to control the rights users have to perform actions with or against GPOs, see Chapter 6.

Figure 4.4 shows a single domain using OUs for hybrid administration.

FIGURE 4.4   Single domain using OUs for hybrid administration

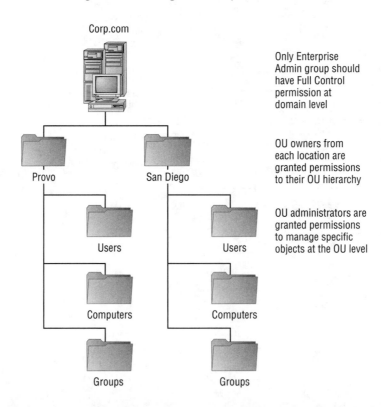

Identifying Outsourced Administration Support

Finally, the outsourced model takes on the same basic design as the decentralized model. OUs can be created to allow the outsourced administrators to have access to only those objects that they need to work with.

When making the decision to use outsourced staff, determine which of the objects they need. Separating these objects into their own OUs is a good idea because you can set permissions on the remaining OUs that will keep them out. Remember, the rule of thumb is to allow as few rights and permissions as possible. Security is of the highest concern. When you have individuals from outside companies accessing your systems, you need to make sure that they are restricted as much as possible.

Figure 4.5 shows a single domain using OUs to control outsourced administration. To control access to the resources that the outsourced administrators will manage, an additional OU has been created. The outsourced administrators can be delegated the permissions they need to perform their job functions whereas the OU owners will have permissions that are inherited from the parent OU.

FIGURE 4.5   Single domain using OUs for outsourced administration

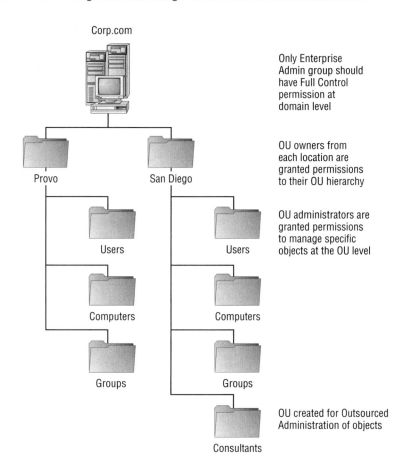

Corp.com

Only Enterprise Admin group should have Full Control permission at domain level

Provo   San Diego

OU owners from each location are granted permissions to their OU hierarchy

Users   Users

OU administrators are granted permissions to manage specific objects at the OU level

Computers   Computers

Groups   Groups

Consultants

OU created for Outsourced Administration of objects

Real World Scenario

Choosing a domain structure

Memorial Hospitals has five hospitals in two states that are supported by a single IT staff. This staff is divided into teams based upon each of the hospitals. Administrators from each team are responsible for their own hospital. The decision to move from Windows NT 4 to Windows Server 2003 was finally made and approved by the board of directors. The primary reason for the change stemmed from imminent loss of support, but the company also understood the need for lowering the total cost of ownership (TCO); moving from the Windows NT directory service to Active Directory was seen as a way of saving administrative costs. To reduce the administrative overhead, the design team decided that the existing domain structure needed to be collapsed.

Under Windows NT, the hospital had built several domains. Master user domains were created for each of the hospital units, and these were controlled by each of the administrators for the individual domains. Resources were split up into domains based on the hospital units also. The administrators administered these resources from the hospitals, but accounts had rights to perform tasks such as backing up the systems and performing routine maintenance on them.

After deciding that each of the hospitals could still control its own resources and user accounts, the board of directors dictated that a central Information Technology team would be the forest owner and would have complete service administration control. A single domain environment was envisioned with the hospital units broken into OUs—each having an administrative staff with only the appropriate rights delegated out to them.

In order to accomplish the migration, the domains were all identified and the administrative staff assigned. OUs were created based on the organizational needs, and the Windows NT domains were migrated to the new OUs. Once the administrators had rights delegated to them, they were able to perform the tasks they were responsible for just as they had when they owned their own domains. Because they were able to contain everything in a single domain forest, they were able to save administrative costs by controlling everything centrally with Active Directory.

Using Multiple Domains

You should have a compelling reason to move to a multiple domain model. Some design decisions, such as security policy requirements, force the issue. You may also need to reduce the amount of replication between office locations. Note that any time a design becomes more complex, the administrative costs increase. Although this increase is not be as drastic as maintaining multiple forests, the administrative staff needs to understand the complexities of the domain design and know how to administer the infrastructure.

Although security policy considerations force the multiple domain issue, other design criteria also dictate the move to multiple domains. If you need data or service autonomy, you can create a domain so that the domain administrators can control the data or service. When using the default administrative group memberships, administrators from other domains are not able to control resources outside of their domains.

The concept of using multiple domains for data autonomy is generally implemented to allow the organization to use decentralized administration. Because the administrators are allowed to have free run of their domains, they are able to provide all of the management of the domain and the resources within. This multiple model is often referred to as the *regional domain model* because it is most widely used in conjunction with geographically dispersed divisions of the organization. The regional domain model is more widely used when it is necessary to reduce the replication between locations than it is when the design is based on administrative needs, but both are valid concerns. Figure 4.6 shows an example of a multiple domain model that is based on regions.

You should base the upper-level domains within your design on static structures within the organization. The regional domain model works very well because the geographic locations will not change. Basing the structure on business divisions, departments, or projects may be too volatile and may cause too many changes within the infrastructure. As you bring new projects or departments online, you can merge them into the locations using OUs, or if you have an administrative or security need, you can create a child domain within the tree for the appropriate location.

FIGURE 4.6   Regional domain model

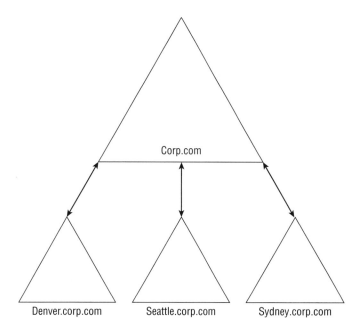

Having domains based on locations can also add additional benefits to your design. Active Directory replication is reduced between domains because the domain partition is not replicated to domain controllers outside of the domain. In a forest design where a single domain exists within the forest, every domain controller receives a copy of every object and has to replicate every change to all of the domain controllers in the domain. When multiple domains are used, by default, only the schema and configuration container are replicated to every domain controller. Although regional domains eliminate the need to replicate the domain container across wide area network (WAN) links, your design may have to account for authentication traffic across those same WAN links.

However, there are implications to the regional domain model: you probably need additional administrative staff; security principles may need to move between domains, which is not a simple task; additional GPOs need to be maintained; you need more domain controllers to support efficient authentication; and you must have more authentication paths for authentication than what you need with a single domain model. When trying to determine if this approach is the best, weigh the tradeoffs between the implications and the replication requirements to see which is more cost effective for the organization. You only create a new domain and build the trust relationship at the time the domain is put into place. Replication is an ongoing cost that will consume your network resources.

Using Multiple Trees

If an organization needs to have service autonomy and complete isolation of the directory service and data is not required, a multiple tree forest may suffice. Instead of creating a new forest to separate the divisions of a company, you can create an additional tree within the existing forest. This additional tree will have its own namespace to use, and at the same time can have its own set of service administrators who can be responsible for every domain in the tree. The administrators from the top-level domain within the tree could be added to the administrative groups in each of the lower domains to give them the ability to manage the entire tree. This will result in longer authentication paths because users need to use resources in domains from other trees. If users need to access these objects on a regular basis, you may need to create shortcut trust relationships (see the discussion on trusts later in this chapter within the "Using Trusts Between Domains" section). Figure 4.7 shows an example of a multiple tree forest.

One of the most important benefits of this design is the integrated schema. All of the trees and every domain within will share the same schema, and all of the objects will become available within the Global Catalog. Users will be able to easily search for those items they need to work with, and administrators will have control over their own resources. This model also affords administrative collaboration if necessary.

Of course, the drawback to using multiple trees within a single forest instead of using separate forests for each tree stems from the fact that complete isolation is not achieved. Administrative accounts from the root domain will be able to control resources throughout every tree within the forest because any member of the Domain Admins group from the forest root domain could add itself as a member of the Enterprise Admins group.

No matter which of the designs is chosen, you will have to address security considerations. You will be most concerned with securing the Active Directory databases and communication, but you'll also want to deal with other considerations, such as the physical security of the domain controllers and supporting hardware.

FIGURE 4.7   Using multiple trees within the forest

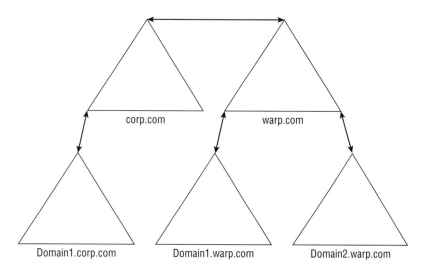

corp.com   warp.com

Domain1.corp.com   Domain1.warp.com   Domain2.warp.com

Design Scenario

Choosing a Domain Design

Jerry is trying to determine the best domain design for his company. Currently, only one business location is used within his organization. He knows that he wants Active Directory to be controlled by a single set of administrators. In addition, the Information Technology (IT) group consists of tech support staff who are responsible for maintaining Active Directory, and operations staff who are responsible for the daily backups and help desk functions.

The problem that Jerry is running into is the "group down the hall." This division works with military projects and keeps their projects to themselves. The current network infrastructure has their division completely isolated from the rest of the organization.

1. **Question:** How many domains should Jerry plan on having in his design, and why? **Answer:** Due to the isolation required for the military projects division, Jerry's company will need two domains. Each domain will reside in its own forest to maintain complete isolation.

Identifying Security Concerns

When we are discussing security, the physical access to the domain controllers is of primary concern. Anyone who has direct access to domain controller hardware could perform attacks on the devices that make up the domain controller. Something as simple as powering off the system will keep users and applications from accessing Active Directory. Service outages could cost companies downtime and lost productivity. Once the system has been powered down, an attacker could restart the system under another operating system. Once the operating system is started, the object permissions will no longer restrict access to the objects, and the attacker can gain access to information that might be deemed confidential.

If an attacker has physical access to a domain controller, she could remove the physical media on which the Active Directory database resides. Once removed from the system, the media could be introduced to another system on which attacks could be performed against the database. With the correct tools and enough time, an attacker could discover account information including the account password and properties.

Another consideration that needs to be addressed is the storage of backup media. If someone were to take the media, especially the media on which the system state had been saved, she could restore the files to another system. Once this information was restored to the new system, someone could attack the data in order to glean information about Active Directory accounts. A very talented attacker could potentially modify information within the system state for the domain controller and then use the modified information to gain access to other areas of Active Directory.

Placing the domain controllers and any other vital servers within a locked room is one of the best ways to protect the physical server. You could then grant access to the server room to administrators who need access to the servers. You could secure this room with a simple lock and key mechanism, an electronic passkey, or biometric entry devices. It is not uncommon to find hand or retina scanners controlling entry to data centers in large companies.

No matter what level of security you apply, you may still run into rogue or coerced administrators. Because the service and data administrators need to have the tools necessary for the job, your best line of defense is to hire and assign responsibilities to administrators whom you can trust. As a proactive measure, you can monitor services for abnormalities. Server monitoring programs, such as Microsoft Operations Manager or Hewlett-Packard's HP OpenView and Insight Manager, will notify administrative staff if a server is shut down, or if exceptions are noted within event logs. Auditing object access will allow you to discover if someone is accessing Active Directory objects and show what sort of access was made or attempted.

As with any monitoring, remember to be judicial. Monitoring consumes resources. The more monitoring your system performs, the more contention there will be for the resources as the services try to use them. Find an adequate trade-off level that will allow you to monitor the resources while limiting the degradation of service.

Identifying Domain Creation Considerations

At this point in your domain design, you should have the information you need to determine the number of domains your organization requires. Remember, always start with the single domain design and then create additional domains based on service and data isolation or autonomy.

Because a single domain will support all of the administration models, starting with this design will allow you to base your decisions on whether additional domains are required and why they are required.

Of course, multiple domains allow for a better security model, especially if you have service administrators who need autonomy over the resources for which they are responsible. You can then add OUs to allow data administrators to have autonomy over the resources they are managing. Before adding additional domains to the design, make sure to validate the reasons for creating them.

You should document the following information:

- Domain model
- Number of domains
- Domain functional level for each domain
- Domain used as the forest root

When deciding upon the domain functional level for each domain, you need to determine the functional level required for the domain roll-out and then a functional-level upgrade plan. Several functional levels are available, and the level that the domain can be set for will be dictated by the domain controllers within the domain.

Identifying Domain Functional Levels

Four domain functional levels can be used when configuring the domain:

Windows 2000 Mixed   A domain at this functional level supports the following: Windows NT 4 Backup Domain Controllers (BDCs), Windows 2000 domain controllers, and Windows Server 2003 domain controllers.

Windows 2000 Native Mode   A domain at this functional level supports the following: Windows 2000 domain controller and Windows Server 2003 domain controller.

Windows Server 2003 Interim   A domain at this functional level supports the following: Windows NT 4 BDC and Windows Server 2003 domain controller. Such a domain is used to facilitate upgrades from Windows NT 4 directly to Windows Server 2003.

Windows Server 2003   This functional level can only be attained when all of the domain controllers in the domain are Windows Server 2003–based.

Each domain within the forest can be set to its own functional level, regardless of the level of the other domains.

Identifying Trust Relationship Considerations

Trust relationships are used when connecting forests, domains, and remote UNIX Kerberos realms. Once trust relationships are created between structures, the accounts within those structures can be granted access to resources. You need to take some considerations into account

Documenting the Domain Design

Montgomery Printing has decided to build an Active Directory forest for their printing operations in Boston, Calgary, New Orleans, and Des Moines. Administrators from each of the operation centers are responsible for their own resources, but no administrative responsibilities are shared between operations centers. Users from each of the operations centers are allowed to access files at each of the other locations so that they do not have to duplicate work.

Each of the operations centers were originally individual companies until Montgomery Printing took them over. Even after the take-over, they retained their own staff at each location and controlled their own resources including account policies.

To retain autonomy over their own systems, a root domain was created and each operations center was made a domain beneath the root domain. Administrative staff from Montgomery Printing were identified as the Enterprise Admins group that would have the final say over how the corporate standards were enforced, and these staff could manage the forest when necessary. The four domains—one for each of the operations centers—were then managed by each of the administrative staff from the four locations.

The root domain was identified as MP.local. Each domain was then created based upon the location of the operations center: Calgary.MP.local, Boston.MP.local, NewOrleans.MP.local, and DesMoines.MP.local. Administrative staff were assigned to manage each of the domains.

Because Calgary was identified as still having Windows NT 4 BDCs that needed to be migrated, Calgary.MP.local was set to the Windows Server 2003 Interim functional level, but the other domains were set to Windows Server 2003 because all of their domain controllers were running Windows Server 2003.

when you are determining whether or not a trust should be put into place. The primary question is: Do users need to access resources within the domain/forest from the remote domain/forest? If the answer to this question is yes, you need to determine how you are going to create the trust relationship. Depending on the trust type being created, you will have options to control the level of access accounts will have within the organization.

The following sections cover the differences in the types of trust relationships that you can create within a Windows Server 2003 Active Directory environment.

Using the Forest Trust

When you are using multiple forests and your users need access to resources in remote forests, you should create a *forest trust*. A forest trust can only be created between Windows Server 2003 Active Directory forests that are running in the Windows Server 2003 functional level. By using a forest trust, you will be able to take advantage of new features available with forest and external trusts: security identifier (SID) filtering and trust authentication mechanisms (discussed later in this chapter in the sections titled "Using SID Filtering" and "Identifying Trust Authentication Allowances").

Using Trusts between Domains

When the forest is not at the Windows Server 2003 functional level, you will have to determine where you need to build trust relationships. These trust relationships are built to allow users from one domain to access resources in another domain. Three domain-based trust types exist: shortcut trusts, external trusts, and realm trusts.

Shortcut Trusts

You can create *shortcut trusts* between domains within a forest if you need to have more efficient authentication processing. Active Directory takes advantage of the shortest trust path. In Figure 4.8, users in DomainB use resources within DomainE. In this example, the shortest trust path uses DomainA, the forest root domain, and DomainD. When a user needs access to the resource within DomainE, domain controllers within each of the domains in the trust path are contacted so that the user can be granted Kerberos tickets in order to continue accessing domain controllers along the trust path, and finally, the resource.

F I G U R E   4 . 8   Trust path within a forest

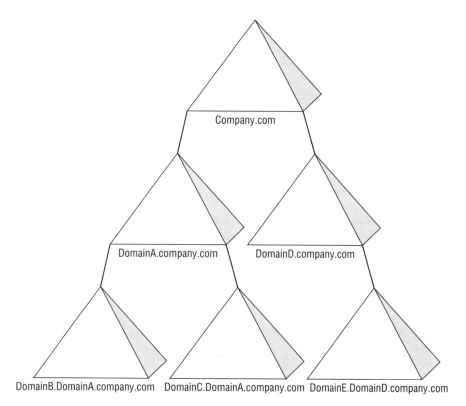

DomainB.DomainA.company.com   DomainC.DomainA.company.com   DomainE.DomainD.company.com

In Figure 4.9, a shortcut trust has been created between DomainB and DomainE. Once created, the shortcut trust is the shortest trust path to the resource. Domain controllers from DomainB and DomainE are the only ones responsible for delivering Kerberos tickets to the client, making the resource access faster and more efficient. Because these trusts are transitive, the shortest trust will be used to access the objects if the object is located within a domain that has a shorter trust path when the shortcut trust is being used instead of the parent/child trusts.

External and Realm Trusts

Two other trust types exist: *external trusts* and *realm trusts*. External trusts are used to connect two domains that reside in different forests or an Active Directory domain to a Windows NT 4 domain. A realm trust allows an Active Directory domain to have a trust relationship with a UNIX Kerberos realm.

FIGURE 4.9   Shortcut trust path

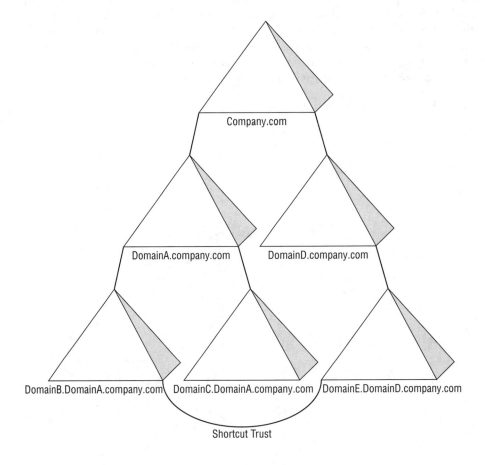

Design Scenario

Identifying Trust Relationships

Trish is responsible for maintaining two forests. Users in both forests need to access resources in each forest. Currently no trust relationships exist between the forests. Trish is reviewing the configuration of the forests and domains so that she can decide on a trust type. She wants to use the easiest method to create the trusts.

Within each forest, one domain is in the Windows 2000 Native Mode. The rest of the domains are at the Windows Server 2003 level. Users from all domains need to access resources within each forest.

1.   **Question:** What type of trust can Trish create and why? **Answer:** Trish can create an external trust. Because the forest is not at the Windows Server 2003 functional level, the forest trust cannot be used. The only other option for tying the domains together is to use an external trust between every domain. If the forest functional levels for the forests were set at the Windows Server 2003 level, a forest trust could be created that would allow access to all domains through a transitive trust.

Using these trust relationships, you can allow users from separate domains or UNIX Kerberos realms to have access to resources within your domain. The disadvantage to these trust relationships is that they are one-way non-transitive relationships. Using external trusts also allows you to take advantage of SID filtering. When planning the trust relationships you are going to use, you should understand the authentication protocols that will be used. Whenever two Windows Server 2003 domains are tied together through a trust relationship, or a UNIX realm and a Windows Server 2003 domain are tied together, the Kerberos protocol will be used to authenticate. However, any time a Windows NT 4 domain is connected through an external trust, the NT LanManager (NTLM) authentication protocol will be used.

Using SID Filtering

SID filtering is a tool that will allow you to restrict access across trust relationships. Accounts within Active Directory domains that have been put into the Windows 2000 Native Mode functional level have an attribute available known as SIDHistory. SIDHistory retains the security identifiers (SIDs) for any account that has been moved from one domain to another. Because an account obtains a new SID whenever it is moved to another domain, if SIDHistory did not keep track of the account's previous SID, the account would not be able to access the resources it had been assigned when it existed in the original domain. This could be an administrative nightmare because the administrator would have to reassign the account permissions and rights whenever a move was performed.

The SIDHistory attribute is seen as a possible security problem. A rogue administrator could modify the SIDHistory on an account to reflect another account's SID, thus gaining access to objects and resources that the rogue administrator would normally not have access to.

In order to stop this SID spoofing, SID filtering can be enabled on the trust relationship, eliminating the use of the SIDHistory attribute on objects from other domains. With SID filtering in place, the account's actual SID would be the only security descriptor that could be used across the trust relationship in the target domain.

Identifying Trust Authentication Allowances

When creating the forest trust, you will have the option of selecting whether you want forest-wide access, or if you want to specify selected accounts that will have access. If you select forest-wide authentication, as long as the user account is in the trusted forest, the account will be able to access resources within the other domain, given that the account has been granted permissions to do so. If selective authentication is chosen, the administrator will have to decide which accounts will be allowed across the trust and which resources the accounts will be allowed to access. Using selective authentication will increase the administrative overhead because the administrator will need to modify the access control every time a new user needs access to the resources.

Interoperability and Migration Strategies

As mentioned earlier, collapsing a domain structure into a single domain is a desire of many organizations when they are looking to move to Active Directory. Windows NT 4 domains are not the most efficient when it comes to organizing and supporting many users. Novell NetWare, although it is a very efficient directory service, does not have the application support that has been the key to Microsoft's growth over the past few years. Most organizations' desire to reduce their TCO has led them to make a decision of which of the directory service infrastructures they want to support.

Those that have made the decision to move to Active Directory are faced with the challenge of deciding the best course of action for migration. Many realize that challenge also entails an interoperability plan. Not everyone has the luxury of performing a single cutover migration; they need to support two directory services as a phased migration occurs. And for those who have applications they need to support that will not function on a Windows Server 2003 system, they may be faced with trying to design a long-term interoperability plan.

The following sections detail the upgrade considerations that you will need to address when you are designing the domain structure. You will need to take into account how the upgrade will be planned plus some of the concerns you will have when upgrading from Windows NT 4 or Windows 2000. Because the forest root is the most important domain within the forest—it contains the administrative accounts that control the entire forest and by default holds the Active Directory schema—you will need to make sure you have identified exactly how you want to design this domain. And every domain will need to be named appropriately. Although Windows Server 2003 allows the domain name to be changed at a later time, it is not an option you should take lightly.

Understanding Upgrade Considerations

Upgrading the current domain has some definite benefits. The accounts within the current domains will retain all of their properties when the upgrade is complete. Every account's SID will remain the same, and the group memberships will remain, as will the account properties. If the current domain design meets the requirements of the organization, an upgrade can be a relatively painless process. However, if the domain structure does not meet the design criteria, upgrading the domain may be a futile option. You may be better served to create a new domain and migrate the accounts from the existing domain to the new domain.

Understanding Restructuring Considerations

If the current domain model was put into place due to limitations of the directory service, such as those Windows NT 4 has, or the designer of the current domain structure did not implement an effective design, domain restructuring will allow you to rework the design to meet your current needs. For example, Windows NT 4 has a limit on the number of accounts that could exist within a domain and still function efficiently. Depending on the hardware that was used for the domain controllers within a Windows NT 4 domain, and taking into account replication considerations, the company may only have tens of thousands of accounts in a single domain. Due to these limitations, many administrators designed the NT 4 domain structure so that accounts and resources were divided into their own domains and trust relationships allowed users to access the resources.

Many Windows 2000 Active Directory forests were built before network architects understood many of the directory service features. In doing so, they created infrastructures that cost too much to maintain. Because Active Directory is not very forgiving, redesigning the forest was not usually an option, so the organization lived with the inefficient design. Now that Active Directory has existed for several years, network architects have gained an understanding of how it should be implemented. Creating a new directory services infrastructure and moving the accounts into it may be the best option for some organizations. You could reconfigure the forest to support the organization's needs as you move the infrastructure to Windows Server 2003's Active Directory.

Migrating the users from their existing domain to the new domain will require the use of programs, such as the Active Directory Migration Tool (ADMT), that will move all of the information correctly and allow the accounts to still have access to the resources for which they have been assigned permissions. One major complication occurs when an account is moved to another domain: when the account is created in the new domain, it is assigned a new SID. Because the resources the user had access to still identify the account's original SID as the security descriptor for permissions, the user will no longer have access to the resources. Unless you want to manually reassign permissions to all of the resources, you must make sure you follow some specific guidelines:

- The new domain must be at least at the Windows 2000 Native Mode functional level.

- The account must be migrated using the ADMT.

- You must use the ADMT that was written for use with Windows Server 2003.

Although Microsoft identifies the ADMT as the migration tool to be used, third-party utilities will provide the same functionality as the ADMT and will provide additional functionality to make the migration easier.

When using the ADMT to migrate the accounts to a Windows 2000 Native Mode functional level domain, the SIDHistory attribute for the new object will be populated with the account's original SID. The account will now have the new SID from the new domain, and the original SID from the previous domain. This allows the account to access all of the resources for which it was originally assigned and have access to new objects.

Migrating from Windows NT 4

Windows NT 4's directory service was not very efficient. The model used did not scale well for large environments, and as such, multiple domains were usually created to organize resources. *Master User Domains (MUDs)* were created to host the user accounts for the domain. MUDs were created in a Windows NT 4 environment so that the user accounts for the organization could be organized neatly. Administrators responsible for account control were made administrators of these domains so that they could modify the account requirements. In very large environments with thousands to hundreds of thousands of users, several domains would be created. Resource domains would be created to hold the resources, such as member servers. Collapsing these domains into one Active Directory domain so that the resources are arranged logically within the simplest domain model possible will help reduce the administrative overhead.

The following sections present the options available for migrating the accounts from the MUDs and resource domains into the new design.

Incorporating the Master User Domains

When updating the MUD to Active Directory, you want to retain the account SIDs. Performing an in-place upgrade of the MUDs keeps all of the properties for the accounts intact. In fact, the account is still the exact same account as it had been under Windows NT, but it has been enhanced with additional functionality due to the new features available with Active Directory.

There is a major drawback to the in-place upgrade, however. The domain structure remains the same as the NT 4 domain structure. If you had a single MUD and three resource domains, you will end up with the same domains in Active Directory. Figure 4.10 shows the original NT 4 domain structure and the Active Directory structure after the upgrade.

Upgrading a Windows NT 4 domain structure that uses multiple MUDs poses another problem. The first domain that you upgrade becomes the forest root. As the remainder of the domains are upgraded, they usually take on the role of child domains in the first tree of the forest. However, in the case of multiple MUDs, the administrators of the MUDs usually have autonomy over the accounts for which they are responsible. If one of the MUDs becomes the forest root, they will have the ability to affect the accounts from the other MUDs. Because this is usually not acceptable when you are trying to retain the same level of control, the best design option is to create an empty forest root and then upgrade the domains to be child domains within the tree.

FIGURE 4.10 Comparison of the Windows NT 4.0 domains and the upgraded Active Directory structure

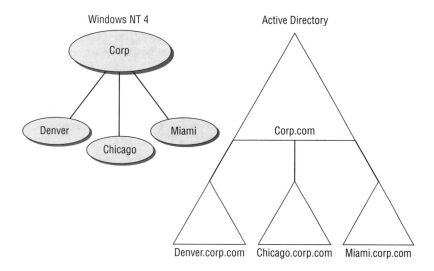

Figure 4.11 shows an example of a tree with an empty forest root and upgraded MUDs. Because the domains are controlled by different administrative groups that should not be administering objects from the other's domains, the empty forest root was created and the MUDs were upgraded as separate domains beneath the root.

FIGURE 4.11 Empty forest root and upgraded MUDs

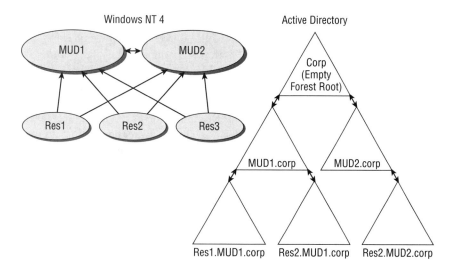

The forest root will contain the service administrator accounts for the forest, but only the forest owner will have the ability modify the membership of these accounts. The domain owners of the upgraded MUDs will still retain their autonomy over their accounts and will be able to control and maintain those accounts as they were able to under Windows NT 4.

To avoid having the same domain structure, the domains can be consolidated within a single domain structure, or a simpler multiple domain structure if necessary. Tools such as the ADMT exist to make the migration of accounts to Active Directory an easy proposition.

 For more information about these account migration tools, see the *MCSE: Windows Server 2003 Active Directory Planning, Implementation, and Maintenance Study Guide* by Anil Desai with James Chellis, (Sybex, 2003).

Because many companies were tied to the account restrictions within Windows NT 4, they had created multiple MUDs, but the same administrative staff supported all of them. Collapsing the MUDs into a single domain makes administration far easier than before and reduces administrative overhead. No longer will accounts have to be added to groups in multiple domains so that they will have the proper rights to perform their duties.

The trust relationships that are automatically created within an Active Directory forest are transitive and will allow the accounts to have access to the same resources as they had before. Due to the transitive nature of the trusts, far fewer trust relationships are required, and access to the resources is more efficient. Once the resource domains are upgraded, the users will have the same resource access as before.

Incorporating the Resource Domains

Resource domains under the Windows NT 4 model were created to delegate control to data administrators or they were required due to the account limitations of the Windows NT 4 directory service. Most organizations will want to collapse the domain structure so that the accounts and resources reside within the same domain. Unless the resources must be isolated, the domain consolidation can incorporate them into OUs that will mimic the resource domain structure. If the resources must be isolated, a resource domain can remain, giving the administrators of the resource domain autonomous control over the resource. If true isolation is required, the design requirements may dictate that a resource forest be created. For more information about resource forests, check out the section titled "Designing the Forest Structure" in Chapter 3.

Upgrading the resource domain retains the domain structure. Performing an upgrade of the domain does not allow you to restructure or collapse the domains into a smaller, more manageable design. This is the easiest of the upgrade methods, but you do not gain any administrative benefits. The domains have to be controlled separately as they were under Windows NT 4.

When looking at this migration approach, review the reasons for maintaining the same design as was previously used. One of the primary reasons for moving to Active Directory is the reduced TCO. Without reducing the administrative overhead associated with multiple domains, you will not achieve the maximum TCO savings. Figure 4.12 shows an example of a Windows NT 4 domain structure upgraded to Windows 2003 Active Directory. Note that all of the existing domains are retained within the new design. The MUD, Corp, has been upgraded to become the forest root. Each of the resource domains are upgraded as child domains so that the current administrative staff can still manage the resources. Also note that the administrative staff from Corp.com will now be able to control the objects within the resource domains.

FIGURE 4.12 Upgrading Windows NT 4 to Windows 2003 Active Directory

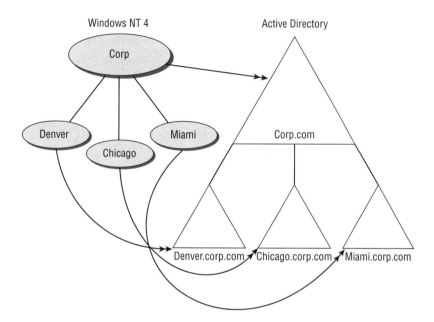

Restructuring the domains allows you to take advantage of the new features of Active Directory. If data administrators decide that they need autonomy over the resources they control, an OU can be identified in which the resources can be migrated. Delegating the appropriate rights to the OU allows the administrators to control their resources without having to worry about other administrators having rights over the resources. This does not include the service administrators, however. Remember, service administrators within the forest or domain can still access resources anywhere in the container where they have service rights. Figure 4.13 shows an example of a Windows NT 4 domain restructure under Windows Server 2003 Active Directory.

Migrating from Windows 2000

Windows 2000 Server Active Directory migration to Windows Server 2003 Active Directory can be a straightforward process. Because Windows Server 2003 Active Directory is based on the same technology as Windows 2000 Server Active Directory, the upgrade process is very straightforward. Prior to promoting a Windows Server 2003 member server to a domain controller, you need to extend the schema to support the new object classes and attributes. From the command prompt, the utility you need to run is ADPREP /forestprep, followed by ADPREP /domainprep. Once you run these and implement the new attributes and object classes, you can bring Windows Server 2003 domain controllers online and start interoperating with the domain.

FIGURE 4.13   Windows NT 4.0 restructure

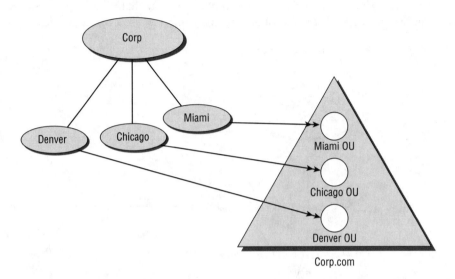

Corp.com

ADPrep is the utility that prepares the forest and all domains within the forest for the first Windows Server 2003 domain controller. If the schema for your organization has been modified, you may need to perform some additional steps. Plus, you will need to verify that the utility functioned as it should have. For more information on the steps required to prepare your domain for Windows Server 2003 Active Directory, see Microsoft Knowledgebase article 325379.

Of course, you do not have to perform an upgrade of the Windows 2000 Active Directory infrastructure. If the current design is no longer efficient enough or the design does not support the organization needs due to reorganizations, acquisitions, or mergers, you can restructure the forest to meet the needs of the organization.

Defining Domain Names

In Chapter 10, "Analyzing Name Resolution," we will discuss the name resolution requirements for the Active Directory and network infrastructure design. During this design phase, we need to identify what the domain name will be for each domain in the forest. The Active Directory namespace will follow the DNS namespace. Although Active Directory and the Windows DNS allow for the full Unicode character set, if you require interoperability with other DNS servers, you should make sure you follow the DNS naming standards, which only allow the following characters:

- A–Z
- a–z

- 0–9
- hyphen (-)

If the name that is going to be used will be used for an Internet presence, the name will have to be registered. Registering the name with a registrar, such as Network Solutions or any other registrar, guarantees that the name is reserved for the organization; no one else can use the name on the Internet. If the name is going to be a local-only name, meaning that it will be used internally within your organization and not on the Internet, then registration is not required. However, if you think you might eventually need the name for use on the Internet, register it before it is too late.

If you require an Internet presence, you need to choose how you will implement the domain names for internal and external use. Three options exist:

- A domain name that is used for internal and external resources and those resources reside in the same infrastructure

- A domain name that is used for internal resources that is the same as the external resources in different infrastructures

- A domain name that is used for internal resources that is different than the name used for external resources

Of the three, the last option is the easiest to administer. Separating the domain names from the internal and external resources allows you to have internal users accessing resources in both infrastructures without having to perform additional administration. It also allows you to protect internal resources from external users. If the first option is employed, there is a risk that the internal resources could become compromised because they are part of the same domain infrastructure as the external resources. With the second option, additional administrative overhead will occur because the replication of data between the two infrastructures will be necessary for users to access all resources.

The root domain provides the initial Active Directory domain name. This is also the root of the first tree within the forest. Most companies want this tree to define the corporate presence. All of the child domains within this tree off the root share the same namespace as the root domain. With this in mind, you will want to make sure that the name reflects the corporate image. Names should be easy for users to understand and type. Long names are not accepted very easily. Short names are easier to work with and allow you to add additional domains without making an unwieldy namespace.

Identifying the Forest Root Domain

The *forest root domain* is the most important domain within the Active Directory design. Several critical services exist within the forest root. By default, only two forest-wide single master operations exist in this domain: the Schema Master and the Domain Naming Master. Only two high-level groups reside here as well: Enterprise Admins and Schema Admins. You must carefully plan the membership of the root domain administrative accounts. Any account that becomes a member of the Domain Admins account in the forest root domain can add other accounts into the Enterprise Admins or Schema Admins groups, thereby giving them ultimate control over the forest.

🌐 Real World Scenario

Building the Domain Names

Montgomery Printing had chosen to create the domain structure based on an empty root and separate domains for each of the operations centers. To keep the Active Directory structure secure, they chose to implement a local name that would not be accessible from the Internet. Their Internet presence was registered as `montgomeryprinting.com`. The internal namespace was chosen to be mp.local to make sure that the domain name would not be too long when additional domains were added to the domain hierarchy. Each of the domains was then based upon the location of the operations center so that the users would have a simple namespace for their domain.

If a single domain is used for the design, the domain will be the forest root. All of the resources will be organized within this domain and a single domain name is all that is required. It is still imperative that the name is a meaningful name and that the domain be registered in case an Internet presence may be required using that domain name. Internal namespaces that are not seen on the Internet do not have to be registered, however, so you can create a different internal namespace to increase security. When an organization takes advantage of the single domain forest design, the forest owners are the service administrators. In this situation, monitoring of the administrative groups will be a necessity because any domain administrator can modify the membership of the forest-wide service group, Enterprise Admins.

It is possible to build a forest to allow for isolation or autonomy of services or data between organizations or divisions within an organization within the single forest design. Creating domains for each of the units of the organization allows the administrators from each business unit to control their own resources and access to those resources. The forest still needs to have a forest root, and that root contains the service accounts that have control throughout the forest. The decision then becomes, "Who has control over the forest root?" Many companies will create a "headless forest root," or a dedicated forest root that does not contain any resources or accounts for any of the business units.

This dedicated forest root domain contains only the high-level service accounts and the forest-wide master operations. Using this scenario, the Enterprise Admins and Schema Admins groups will not fall under the control of any organizational domain administrators. Of course, trusted administration staff still need to have access to the forest root, and those administrators have control over the entire forest. Carefully plan who you will allow to have control over the dedicated forest root domain.

Another benefit to this design is that by its nature, the forest will be immune to organizational changes. Acquisitions and mergers will not drastically alter the forest design. New organizational domains can be added to the forest and will not affect the existing domains. Because all of the domains can interoperate, resource access can be allowed to any account within the forest where necessary.

Summary

After deciding upon the forest design, the domain design is the next layer of Active Directory that you must define. Again, as in the forest design, the administrative responsibilities define how the domain structure is designed. Several options are available and each one needs to be judged on its ability to provide the appropriate administrative control.

Although domains can take on different designs, you also need to take into consideration the requirements for autonomy and isolation. A single domain may be the easiest to work with, but it may not provide the administrators with the kind of control over their resources that they need. Also, you will need to address issues involving migrating the existing domain, trust relationships, and security.

Windows NT 4 and Windows 2000 pose different challenges when you are upgrading or migrating Active Directory to Windows Server 2003. The domain naming structure has to be determined as well as the upgrade strategy. The first part of this strategy involves determining how the forest root domain will be created and then how the remaining domains will be integrated into the forest/domain. Once the domain design has been determined, you will need to create the trust relationships that are required to facilitate authentication to all of the domains.

Once all of domain design considerations have been worked out, the design team needs to drill down one more layer and take a look at the administrative capabilities of OUs. In the next chapter, we are going to discuss how OUs allow you to control administrative access to objects within domains, and how they are more versatile than the forest or domain structures.

Exam Essentials

Know why a single domain should be used.   This is the easiest model to administer. Because the single domain can support all of the administration models, it can be used in most cases.

Know why a multiple domain structure should be implemented.   If data or service autonomy or data isolation is required, or if specific security policy requirements exist for a division of the company, a multiple domain environment will be required.

Know the different trust types and when to use them.   Forest trusts exist between Windows 2003 functional level forests; shortcut trusts connect two domains (in the same forest) in order to shorten the authentication path; external trusts can be created in order to tie a domain in an Active Directory forest to a domain in another Active Directory forest or a Windows NT 4 domain; and realm trusts connect UNIX realms to Active Directory.

Identify the interoperability options.   Windows NT 4, Windows 2000 Server, and Windows Server 2003 can all interoperate. The functional levels of the domains and forests will be determined based on what type of domain controllers are in use.

Identify the migration strategy options.   When migrating to Active Directory, the Windows NT 4 domains and Windows 2000 Server Active Directory can be upgraded to Windows Server 2003 Active Directory to maintain the same domain and forest structure, or they can be restructured to take advantage of the new features of Active Directory.

Understand the options when creating a forest root domain.   When creating the forest root domain, the service administrators of the root domain have the ability to modify the Enterprise Admins and Schema Admins groups. To keep other administrative staff from having this level of control, the root domain can be created as a dedicated root with only a small number of administrators.

Key Terms

Before you take the exam, be certain you are familiar with the following terms:

coerced administrators	external trusts
forest root domain	forest trust
Master User Domains (MUDs)	realm trusts
regional domain model	rogue administrator
shortcut trusts	SID filtering

Review Questions

1. Which domain type boasts simple design and ease of administration?

    A. Master User Domain

    B. Single domain

    C. Forest domain

    D. Multiple domain

2. What is the name of the utility that allows you to move computer and user accounts from one domain to another?

    A. Active Directory Merge Utility

    B. Active Directory Migration Tool

    C. Active Directory Domains and Trusts

    D. Active Directory Users and Computers

3. If you require different account policies between remote offices, which of the following must you do?

    A. Use a single forest/single domain model, place the remote branch in a resource OU, and define account policies on that OU.

    B. Use a single forest/multiple domain model and define account policies on each domain.

    C. Use a single forest/multiple domain model, configure OUs in each domain, and match their names exactly. Configure account settings on the main OU and those settings will replicate to the other OU in the other domain.

    D. Use a multiple forest/multiple domain model and define account policies on each forest.

4. While migrating from an NT 4 domain to a Windows Server 2003 Active Directory domain, which type of trust will you create to start the migration?

    A. Forest trust

    B. Shortcut trust

    C. External trust

    D. Internal trust

5. You are the administrator of a large multiple domain forest. Users from one domain use printers and databases from another domain on a regular basis. The two domains reside in different trees within the forest. You need to design a more efficient authentication process than what is provided through the default trust relationships. Which of the following will allow you to do this with the least administrative effort?

    A. Move all user accounts to the root of the forest.

    B. Create matching accounts in the other domains that the user will need access to.

    C. Create two-way domain trusts between the two domains.

    D. Create a shortcut trust between the two domains.

6. What feature in Active Directory allows a user to retain the security identifier for an account that has been moved from one domain to another?

    A. SIDHistory

    B. SID filtering

    C. SID lookup

    D. SID attribute

7. Which of the following criteria must be met for SIDHistory to work after an object has been moved to another domain in the same forest? (Choose all that apply.)

    A. The domain must be in Windows 2000 Native Mode.

    B. You must use the ADMT tool or a compatible third-party application.

    C. The account must have the SIDHistory attribute enabled before the migration, which is accomplished from the ADMT tool.

    D. The ADMT utility must be the version for Windows 2003.

8. When adding a Windows 2003 domain controller to an existing Windows 2000 native mode domain, which of the following steps would you take before you bring the new Windows 2003 domain controller into the network? (Choose all that apply.)

    A. Run ADPrep /forestprep

    B. Run ADPrep /prcpDNS

    C. Run DomainPrep /prepDNS

    D. Run ADPrep /domainprep

9. Which of the following single master operations roles are, by default, located only in the forest root? (Choose all that apply.)

    A. Global Catalog

    B. Schema Master

    C. Domain Naming Master

    D. Infrastructure Master

    E. Primary Domain Controller (PDC) Emulator

10. For security reasons, you would like to disable the SID History feature. How would you do this?

    A. Disable the trust between the domains.

    B. Remove the SIDFiltering attribute from the forest root domain.

    C. Enable SIDFiltering on the trust between the domains.

    D. Configure Group Policy to disable SIDHistory and apply it to the OU where the users reside.

Answers to Review Questions

1. B. Single domains are the easiest to administer and easiest to design and configure.

2. B. The Active Directory Migration Tool copies accounts from one domain to another, whether that domain is a Windows NT 4–, Windows 2000–, or Windows 2003–based domain. If you want to populate the SIDHistory attribute when you are using this utility, the target domain has to be at least at the Windows 2000 functional level.

3. B. Each domain has a Default Domain policy that enforces the account policy restrictions. These restrictions cannot be overridden at any other level within the domain. If a group of users have password policies, account lockout restrictions, or Kerberos policy requirements that are different from the domain standard, a new domain will be required.

4. C. An external trust is a trust that is created between domains in different forests. An example would be a trust between an NT 4 domain and a Windows Server 2003 Active Directory domain.

5. D. Shortcut trusts are created between domains in a forest to provide a more efficient authentication process. Active Directory automatically measures the shortest trust path to the other domain.

6. A. SIDHistory is an attribute in a Windows 2003 domain that allows a resource to retain the security identifier from one domain after being moved to another.

7. A, B, D. SIDHistory only works if the following requirements are met: the domain must be at least Windows 2000 Native Mode; the account must be migrated with the ADMT utility; and the ADMT utility must be the version for Windows 2003.

8. A, D. Before you can bring a Windows 2003 Active Directory domain controller into an existing Windows 2000 network, you must extend the schema. This is done by running the commands ADPREP /forestprep and ADPREP /domainprep.

9. B, C. Of the five single master operations roles, the Schema Master and Domain Naming Master are forest level roles and you can only have one per forest. The other three roles—Relative Identifier (RID) Master, Infrastructure Master, and Primary Domain Controller Emulator—are limited to one per domain. In a multiple domain model, you may have more than one RID Master, Infrastructure Master, or PDC Emulator, but you will only have one Schema Master and one Domain Naming Master.

10. C. The SIDHistory attribute is seen as a possible security problem. A rogue administrator could modify the SIDHistory attribute on an account to reflect another account's SID, thus gaining access to objects and resources that they would normally not have access to. In order to stop this SID spoofing, SID filtering can be enabled on the trust relationship, eliminating the use of the SIDHistory attribute on objects from other domains. With SID filtering in place, the account's actual SID would be the only security descriptor that could be used across the trust relationship in the target domain.

Case Study

You should give yourself 20 minutes to review this testlet and complete the questions.

Background

Insane Systems builds custom computers for their customers. They specialize in building cases that are unique and support the latest in hardware technology. They started off as a small company that provided this service to gamers who would take their cases to LAN parties to show off. Because their systems were considered some of the most stable gaming platforms and they provided an impressive design that gamers could show off, they started to become popular. Insane Systems started mass manufacturing some of their more popular designs and began selling stand-alone cases along with their fully configured systems. As space at the company became a premium, the office was moved from the manufacturing facility. This allowed the company to add to the amount of space that was used for the mass production line.

Existing Environment

Over the past few months, Insane Systems has been developing plans to expand their company. They have identified San Jose, California, Atlanta, Georgia, and New York City as the locations with their highest customer base. The current Chicago location will remain the corporate headquarters, but they are opening branches in New York City and San Jose. They are also in the process of acquiring a competitor's business in Atlanta. These locations will provide retail outlets as well as support. Customers will have the option of sending their systems back to the corporate office for upgrades or repairs, or delivering them to one of the branch locations.

Because the company is planning on expanding, they want to make sure that the network infrastructure is in place to support their larger, distributed company. They are also concerned with the support lifetime of their current Windows NT 4 infrastructure. They realize they have the option of moving to a Windows 2000 Server or Windows Server 2003 infrastructure and are considering moving to Windows Server 2003 and Active Directory for two reasons: the expected support lifetime is greater than Windows 2000, and they are a technology firm that is not afraid of staying ahead of the technology curve.

Part of the expansion of the company is a complete overhaul of their current Internet presence. They are planning on bringing all of the web development and hosting in-house. Currently a web hosting service is providing their Internet presence, and Insane Systems feels as though they could provide better marketing and support information for their customers if they had control over their own website. Insane Systems would also like to change the name of their website to better represent their name in the marketplace. They own the name `insane-systems.com`.

Interviews

Your company has been hired to design an Active Directory infrastructure and the network infrastructure to support it. During the interview process with some of the key stakeholders, you gathered the following information:

CEO   Currently we have a single location with all of our processes local. As we grow, we would like to keep all of the administration here in Chicago. Because the new branches are primarily retail and support offices, we will not need to have a large staff in those locations. The Atlanta office has an existing network that we would like to merge into our network.

CIO   Most of the infrastructure that we support is located here at the corporate office. We do support some key servers at the manufacturing location. We support these servers from our main office. Because the servers are nearby, if there is a problem, we can usually be on site within half an hour.

The new branches are going to be another issue altogether. We would like to retain the same level of administrative control over the servers in the new locations that we employ currently. Due to the geographic limitations, we may need to have some support staff at those locations. Currently, the plan is to hire staff at those locations who can provide the support for the customers, but also have an understanding of the business systems we need to put into place.

Manager of Information Technology   We have grown very quickly over the past three years and our current technologies have kept up with that growth. However, we don't think the current infrastructure is ready for the amount of growth that we are expecting within the following year. We are not afraid of moving to the latest technology, but we want to make sure that the design is stable and makes sense for us, especially if we will continue growing in the upcoming months. And because we are losing support for NT 4, we want to make sure that we have an operating system that will be supported for a few years down the road.

Most of our processes are located here at this office, and we would like to keep it that way. We know that some servers will need to be located at the remote offices, but we would like to be able to provide most of the support from this location. Remote administration tools will need to be included within the design so that we can keep our administrative costs to a minimum.

Currently, we have most of our servers located at the main office, and all are located on their own high-speed backbone. We do have a server at the manufacturing site that allows the staff there to have e-mail as well as plans and orders in case we lose connectivity between the offices. This server is running Exchange 5.5. Several times during the day we replicate the public folder information to this system so that they are always up to date and do not have to dial up to the main office using our 56Kbps modem.

The systems at the main office are all supported by our staff of four administrators. All of the administrators are cross-trained on Windows NT 4, Exchange 5.5, SQL Server 7, our accounting software, and each of our file and print servers. We currently have several Windows NT 4 servers in place, including one Exchange 5.5 server at both locations, one SQL Server 7 server at the main office, one server running our accounting package that interfaces with the SQL server, and one file and print server that is used by both locations. The Exchange server at the manufacturing location doubles as a print server also.

The Atlanta office currently has a Windows NT 4 domain, and we will migrate that domain into our forest. Administration of this new forest will also be moved to our Chicago branch. We will have a very small IT staff in the Atlanta office who will need control of user and computer accounts located in that office. The users in the Atlanta office will also require different password and lockout restrictions than the other offices.

Because all of the client machines are running Windows NT 4 Workstation, we do not have to worry about supporting different operating systems. We would like to maintain that same easy administration with the upcoming system. We would like to provide the same types of services at the remote locations that we provide at the home office, although accounting will remain at the home office and will not be spread out to all of the locations.

Current Infrastructure

After investigating the current infrastructure, you have determined that the following servers are in place:

> **Home Office**
>
> Primary Domain Controller (PDC)
>
> Backup Domain Controller (BDC)
>
> DHCP /DNS/WINS server
>
> Exchange 5.5 Server
>
> SQL Server 7
>
> Systems Management Server 2
>
> File server/Print/Antivirus server
>
> Research and Development File server

The following shows the graphical representation of the Home Office's layout:

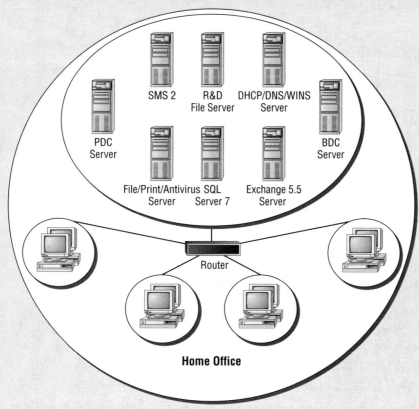

Atlanta Office

Primary Domain Controller (PDC)

Backup Domain Controller (BDC)

WINS server

File server

The following shows the graphical representation of the Atlanta office's layout:

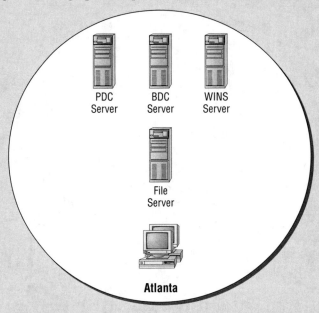

Manufacturing Facility

Backup Domain Controller (BDC)

DNS/WINS/DHCP Relay Agent server

Exchange 5.5/File server

The following shows the graphical representation of the Manufacturing facility's layout:

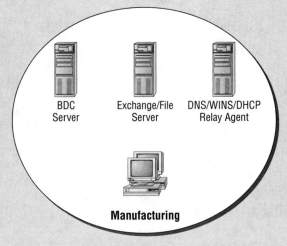

The Home Office hosts nearly 250 Windows NT 4 workstations at this point. They are interconnected by several 48-port 10/100Mbps switches. A router is used to divide the network into 4 VLANs. One VLAN is the 1Gbps backbone on which the servers reside. Each of the servers is connected to a 1Gbps switch port. This location takes advantage of private IP address ranges. The servers are located on the 192.168.1.0/24 subnet. The client systems are divided between network addresses 192.168.10.0/24, 192.168.11.0/24, 192.168.12.0/24, and 192.168.13.0/24.

The manufacturing facility contains 12 Windows NT 4 workstations connected to the same switch as the servers. Because Insane Systems does not want to slow down production due to a communication failure, they have taken advantage of Exchange 5.5's public folder replication. Public folders are continually updated with the latest orders. The crew foreman can access the orders locally from these public folders at any time, whether the communication link between the locations is up or not. This location uses another address range—192.168.20.0/24.

Case Study Questions

1. How many domains will be required to support the design?

   A. 1

   B. 2

   C. 3

   D. 4

2. What is the best option for moving the objects from the Atlanta domain into your new Active Directory forest?

   A. Create a shortcut trust between the domains and add accounts from the Atlanta domain to groups in the Insane Systems domain.

   B. Create a two-way trust between the domains and run the ADMT utility to merge the users and computers from the Atlanta domain to the Insane-Systems domain.

   C. Create a forest trust between the domains and run the ADMT utility to merge the users and computers from the Atlanta domain to the Insane-Systems domain.

   D. Do an in-place migration of the Atlanta domain and specify that it should join the existing forest (either as a child domain of the existing tree or as a new tree).

3. Prior to the migration, what kind of trust should you set up between the Atlanta office and the Chicago office if you want to allow Atlanta users to access Chicago resources?

   A. Forest trust

   B. Shortcut trust

   C. Realm trust

   D. External trust

4. Which administrative model best describes this environment?

   A. Centralized

   B. Decentralized

   C. Hybrid

   D. Outsourced

5. Prior to migrating the user accounts to the new Active Directory domain, at which functional level should the domain be set?

   A. Windows 2000 Native Mode functional level

   B. Windows 2000 Mixed Mode functional level

   C. Windows Server 2003 functional level

   D. Windows Server 2003 Interim functional level

Answers to Case Study Questions

1. B. Because all of the resources will be administered from the headquarters location in Chicago, a single forest is all that is necessary. The password and account lockout restrictions of the Atlanta office require an additional domain, as password and lockout settings are controlled at the domain level and cannot be overridden.

2. D. Because the Atlanta domain is going to be migrated to the forest, an in-place upgrade of the domain can be planned for in the design. As the upgrade is being performed, you can make it a domain within the forest.

3. D. Forest and shortcut trusts are not allowed between NT 4 and Active Directory domains. A realm trust is used with UNIX Kerberos realms. An external trust can be built to allow the accounts to have access to their original resources until they are moved.

4. B. Because there are administrative accounts within the Atlanta office control their own resources, the administrative model is decentralized.

5. A. If the user accounts will need to retain their original SIDs so that they will still maintain access to their resources from the original domain, the minimum functional level for the domain will have to be set at the Windows 2000 Native Mode functional level.

Chapter

5

Designing an Organizational Unit Structure for Administrative Purposes

MICROSOFT EXAM OBJECTIVES COVERED IN THIS CHAPTER:

✓ **Design the Active Directory infrastructure to meet business and technical requirements.**

  ▪ Create the conceptual design of the organizational unit (OU) structure.

✓ **Design an OU structure.**

  ▪ Design an OU structure for the purpose of delegating authority.

So far we have looked at the options available for creating forests and domains. Chapter 4 introduced the domain creation options. Several options are available when deciding on how to create the domain structure, foremost is the administrative needs of the organization.

Once the domain structure has been developed, the objects that represent the resources within the domain can be organized. This organization of objects can be for the ease of delegating administrative responsibilities, the efficient application of group policies, or a combination of the two. You will need to consider trade-offs when deciding how to deal with the domain organization. Within the chapter, we will discuss designing with administrative control in mind. In Chapter 6, "Designing Organizational Units for Group Policy," we will detail the options available when you are designing for efficient application of group policies.

You must understand how the organization is administered when you are determining how the organizational unit (OU) structure will be designed. If you do not understand how the organization is administered, the OU structure you create may not be as efficient as it could be, nor will it remain effective over time. An unwieldy or faulty design could create more administrative problems than it helps alleviate.

In this chapter, we are going to discuss the options that are available for creating an OU hierarchy that is manageable, efficient, and helps reduce the administrative costs associated with maintaining an organization.

The Basics of Organizational Units

Active Directory introduced one of the most useful objects into the Windows realm; the organizational unit (OU). This versatile tool allows administrators not only to organize resources within the Active Directory structure, but to delegate administrative control to users who are not members of any administrative group. When OUs are used within a domain, users can be granted control to resources that they need to manage and at the same time, gain autonomy over those resources. Users who do not have administrative control over OUs or objects within those OUs will not be able to affect resources within the OUs.

To have complete control over an OU, you must first be delegated Full Control permission. This delegation is provided by the domain owner and can be granted to users or groups. For efficiency's sake, you should create a group that will manage the OU and then delegate permissions to this group. You can then add user accounts that need to manage the objects, otherwise known as the *OU owners*, to the group with Full Control permissions.

OU owners control all aspects of the OU that they have been given authority over, as well as all of the objects that reside within the OU tree. Like the domain owner, they will not be isolated from outside influences, because the domain owner will have control if the need arises. However, this autonomy of control over the resources allows the OU owner to plan and implement the objects necessary to effectively administer their OU hierarchy. This includes delegating administrative control to those users who need to be *OU administrators*.

OU administrators are responsible for the specific objects within their OU. Usually they will not have the ability to create child OUs. Their control will more than likely be limited to working with a specific object type within the OU. For example, the OU owner could delegate the ability to work with computer accounts to the technical support staff. This would allow the technical support staff to create and delete computer objects within the OU, but they would not be able to control or modify user objects within the OU. Controlling user objects could be delegated to a Human Resources employee who is responsible for creating user objects when a person is hired, and disabling and deleting objects when a person is discharged.

In the following sections we take a look at some of the design options that are available when creating OUs. This includes the choices that should be made so that changes within the organization will not adversely affect the OU structure.

Understanding the OU Design Options

The OU design should be predicated on the administrative structure of the organization, not the departmental organization as seen on the company's organization chart. Most companies do not base the administration of resources on the organization chart. Usually, the IT department is responsible for objects within the company no matter which department is using the resource.

Although this centralized approach is the most basic method of controlling the objects within Active Directory, some organizations cannot utilize one single administrative group that has power over all of the objects. Other organizations will not have a centralized administrative team; instead they will have decentralized control over objects. In such cases, design decisions will have to be made that will dictate where the objects will reside within the OU structure. Microsoft has identified five design options when developing the OU design. These five allow the OUs to be designed by location, organization, business function, location then business function, or organization then location.

OUs Based on Location

If an organization has resources that are centralized, but the administrative staff is based at different geographic locations, the OU design should take on a location-based strategy. Using this strategy, the OU structure is very resistant to reorganizations, mergers, and acquisitions. Because all of the objects are located beneath the top-level OU, which is based on company location as seen in Figure 5.1, the lower-level OUs can be modified and the objects moved within the OUs to accommodate the changes. Consider the alternative: having domains that are used to host the objects. Moving objects between domains has many more implications because the security ID of the objects will have to change as will the domain owners.

However, some disadvantages to the location-based strategy exist. Unless the inheritance of permissions has been blocked, administrative groups that are granted authority at an upper-OU level will have the ability to affect objects in the lower-level OUs.

The location-based strategy works well within organizations that are using the departmental model but have geographically dispersed resources. In this manner, administrators located in the same site as the resources will have control over the objects that represent them in Active Directory.

FIGURE 5.1   OU structure based on Location

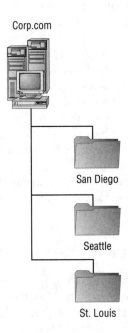

OUs Based on Organization

If the administrative structure has an administrative staff that reports to divisions and is responsible for the maintenance of the resources for that division, the OU structure can be designed so that is takes advantage of the departmental makeup of the company as seen in Figure 5.2. Using this design strategy makes the OU structure much more vulnerable to change within the organization should a reorganization occur. However, it does allow departments to maintain autonomy over the objects that they own.

This strategy is usually employed whenever the cost center, product/service-based or project-based business models are employed. This allows for the resources to be grouped so that the cost centers are separate OU structures. The product, service, or project resources can likewise be isolated within an OU tree, and those administrators who are responsible for the resources can be delegated the ability to control the objects within Active Directory.

OUs Based on Function

Smaller organizations that have an administrative staff who has specific functions they provide to the organization typically use an OU design strategy based on job functions as seen in Figure 5.3. In these smaller organizations, the administrators will have several job responsibilities. Building the OU structure based on the job responsibilities allows the controlled objects to be grouped together based on the tasks that need to be administered. This type of OU deployment is resistant to company reorganizations, but due to the way the resources are organized, replication traffic may be increased.

FIGURE 5.2   OU structure based on Organization

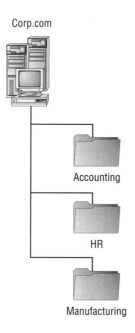

FIGURE 5.3   OU structure based on Function

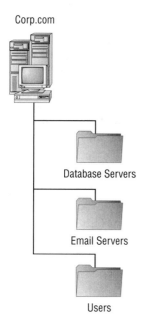

This strategy can be employed with any of the business models. Because it is usually implemented in smaller companies, a single administrative group such as Information Technology is responsible for maintaining all of the objects. The functions can be broken out based on the staff responsible for maintaining user objects, group objects, shared folders, databases, mail systems, and so on. Of course the administrative staff will have to be trusted by all divisions if this model is employed, but usually in the smaller companies, this is not as much of an issue.

OUs Based on Location and Organization

Two hybrid methods of organizing resources exist. Each one is based on a combination of the location of resources and the method the company uses to organize the objects.

OUs Based on Location, Then Organization   When you use an OU design strategy that is first based on location and then organization, the upper-level OUs are based upon the location of the objects within the directory, and the lower-level OUs are broken out by the organization's departmental structure as seen in Figure 5.4. This strategy allows the organization to grow if necessary, and has distinct boundaries so that the objects' administration is based on local autonomy. Administrative staff will need to cooperate if administrative groups are responsible for the departments within the OU structure, because if this is the case, OU owners will have control over all of the objects within the OU tree.

Large companies that employ the departmental business model may have several locations within the company that have administrative staff controlling the resources. If this is the case, the OU owner for the location can control all of the accounts that are OU administrators for the individual departments within that location. This allows the OU owner to control users within the location for which they are responsible, while still maintaining control over their location. OU administrators would only be able to affect objects within their department at that location.

OUs Based on Organization, Then Location   With an OU design strategy that is first based on organization and then location, the OU trees are based upon the organization's departmental makeup with the objects organized based on location, as seen in Figure 5.5. Using this strategy, the administrative control of objects can be delegated to administrative staff responsible for objects at each of the locations, whereas all of the resources can be owned by a department's own administrative staff. This allows for a strong level of autonomous administration and security; however, the OU structure is vulnerable to reorganization because the departmental design of the company could change.

Very large companies using the cost center–based, product/service-based, or project-based business models may create an OU tree that is based on the organizational makeup of the company and then have a decentralized administrative staff that is responsible for the resources within different geographic regions. This allows for more efficient control of the resources while still allowing the OU owners to have a level of autonomy over the objects that represent their resources within the company.

FIGURE 5.4   OU structure based on Location, then Organization

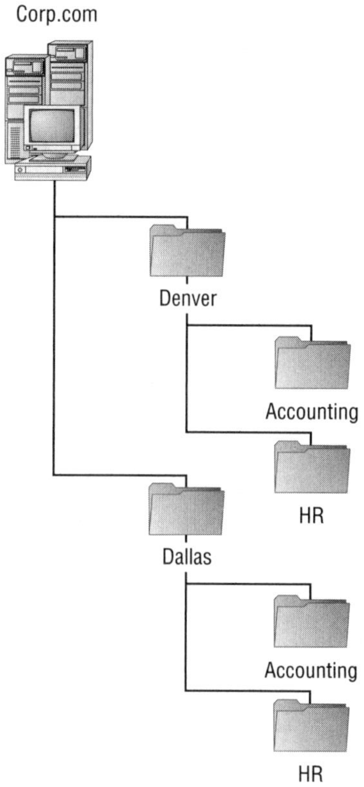

Choosing the Best OU Design Approach

You will notice that each of the design options has its own unique set of advantages and disadvantages. To choose the best design for your company, you will have to weigh the pros and cons of each strategy so that you come up with a design that is the best fit for your environment. If your company is not going to undergo many reorganizations or mergers and acquisitions, you may want to choose a design that makes the delegation of control easiest for your current administrative model. Company reorganizations could force a reevaluation of the departmental makeup within the organization, thus forcing the OU hierarchy to change. Projects that are completed or abandoned will also force the OU structure to change. You may not want to rework the OU structure every time management decides they want to try running the business in a new fashion.

You will find that the adage "The only constant is change" will probably ring true no matter what strategy you employ, so try to employ the strategy that appears to be the least likely to change but reflects the way the administration is provided.

FIGURE 5.5 OU structure based on Organization, then Location

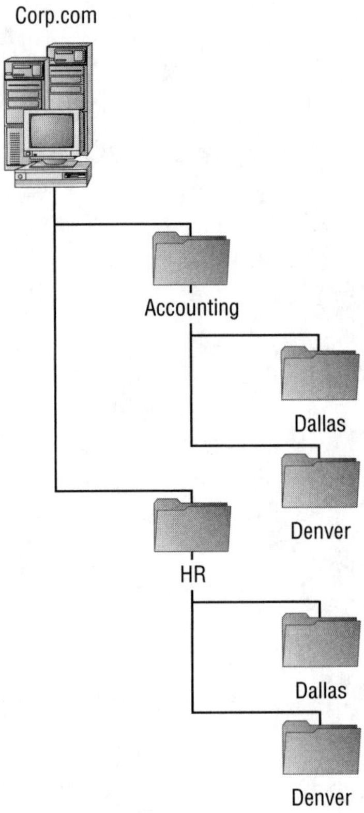

Corp.com

Accounting

Dallas

Denver

HR

Dallas

Denver

Understanding OU Design Criteria

Back in Chapter 1, "Analyzing the Administrative Structure," we discussed the interviews that should take place and the information you should collect about who is responsible for controlling resources. This is where that information will start coming in very handy. As a matter of fact, OUs are built based on three criteria:

- Autonomy over objects
- Efficient Group Policy application
- Control object visibility

Designing the OU structure to take advantage of efficient Group Policy application will be discussed in Chapter 6.

Design Scenario

Choosing the OU structure

Kentucky Clay manufactures ceramic fixtures such as sinks, bathtubs, and toilet bowls. They are in the process of migrating their Novell 3.12–based network to Windows Server 2003 Active Directory. Currently they have a large Information Technology staff located at their headquarters in Prospect, KY. The Prospect plant is the original location for the company and they manufacture toilet bowls here. Over the past few years the company has expanded its operations by building two new plants and acquiring three competitors. Each of these plants, four of which are located in other cities in Kentucky and one in Ohio, manufacture different products.

The IT staff in Prospect is responsible for all operations. Most of the systems are centrally located within the data center at the headquarters. Each of the plants hosts their own systems that allow them to run their daily operations. The daily updates are then sent to the headquarters for processing. Kentucky Clay is not convinced that the wide area network links that they are leasing from the telecommunications companies are reliable enough to support a truly centralized approach, so the systems that are critical to the functioning of the plants are located onsite. These systems support the plant functions only, since all of the administrative processing is performed at headquarters. Each remote plant has an administrative staff who is responsible for the daily maintenance of their systems.

The design team would like to maintain a single domain structure if possible. They have determined that the changes they will be making to objects within Active Directory will be minimal, thus reducing the need for extensive replication throughout the locations. They are now looking at the OU design options and are trying to determine which strategy to employ.

1. **Question:** Which of the OU design strategies would you suggest that Kentucky Clay implement? **Answer:** Location-based.

2. **Question:** When you specify your strategy of choice, what explanation would you give them for your decision? **Answer:** Since the resources are going to be located at each plant along with the administrative staff who is responsible for maintaining them, the location-based option is the most optimal. This will allow you to organize the resources located at each plant into their own OUs and delegate permissions to the groups responsible for them.

Object Autonomy

Object autonomy should be the primary criteria by which most organizations design their OUs. Giving the OU owners the ability to control the objects for which they are accountable allows them to perform their job functions. At the same time, they will feel comfortable knowing those objects are not controlled by other OU owners or administrators from outside their OU structure, with the exception of the forest's and domain's service and data administrators. Once a group is identified as the OU owner, they can control the accounts to which administrative control within the OU tree can be granted.

Real World Scenario

Delegating resonsibilities

The domain owner for domain corp.com has decided to create an OU structure for the Accounting department. Melissa is in charge of the group that is responsible for all of the servers, workstations, and resources within the Accounting department. Several people report to Melissa, all of whom are responsible for different resource types. The domain owner has decided that Melissa will become the OU owner and will be responsible for maintaining the Accounting OU structure. The domain owner creates an OU named Accounting and then delegates full control over the OU to Melissa. Melissa is now able to create additional OUs beneath her Accounting OU. She is also able to delegate control to members of her group. She will need to identify how she wants to organize the objects within the OU structure.

You will note that the top-level OU is based on the division of the organization that Melissa is responsible for. When a company is taking advantage of decentralized or hybrid administration, they can break the OU structure down into location-based or organization-based OUs, or a combination of the two, to effectively grant the administrative staff the permissions to manage their resources. Since Melissa is the owner of the OU and she has others who report to her, she can delegate permissions to those users so that they can perform their functions.

Controlling Visibility

When controlling *object visibility*, OUs can be used to hide objects from users when they are searching within Active Directory. By hiding the objects that users do not need access to, you can add a level of security to those objects. If users do not have the List Contents permission to an OU, they will not be able to view any of the objects within the OU. You can hide printers that they do not need to use and shares that should not appear in search results in this manner. You can also hide user and group objects from other administrators.

When you design the OU structure, you should always start with designing for administrative control, and then take visibility of objects into consideration. The primary goal of the OU design is to make administration of objects as efficient and easy as possible. Once you have completed the administrative design, you can address visibility requirements.

For example, take a company that has a printer that restricts users, with the exception of a few authorized individuals, from being able to print to it. This printer is used to print accounts payable and payroll checks. Only a few Accounts Payable employees are allowed to send print jobs to this printer. Also, some shares on the Accounts Payable server are exclusive for use by Accounts Payable staff. Because these resources need to be isolated from the rest of the organization, they should not show up when users from other departments perform searches within Active Directory.

The Accounts Payable department is part of the Accounting Division of the company. Because the company has all of the accounting resources located at the corporate office, the corporate Information Technology department is responsible for maintaining the objects in Active Directory. Other departments have staff located at other offices, and each of those offices has administrative staff responsible for maintaining the resources.

During the design phase, the design team decides to use the Location, Then Organization design approach. This allows them to assign control over all resources to the administrative groups that need to be owners of the OU hierarchy, and then grant other levels of control at the departmental level for those administrators that control a subset of resources. The initial design looks like Figure 5.6.

FIGURE 5.6   OU design for administrative purposes

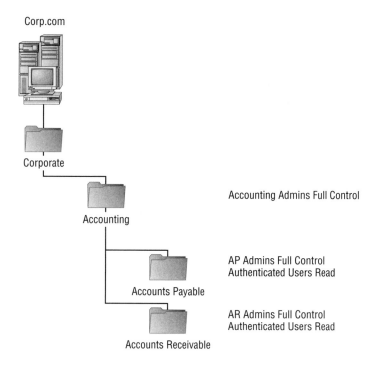

The objects that were initially identified as needing to be hidden from users need to be placed within an OU that will not allow users to view its contents. For a user to be able to "see" the objects within an OU, at the very least they will need the List Contents permission granted to them. If they do not have this permission, the objects contained within the OU will not show up in their searches. Since this permission is included in the standard Read permission, accounts with Read permission will be able to list the contents of the OU.

Because users need to view objects within the Accounts Payable OU, the permissions to that OU cannot be changed. Instead, a child OU is created to control visibility of the objects. The users within Accounts Payable department who need to work with the objects will be able to see them when they access Active Directory tools or perform searches, but no one else will. It should be noted that the AP Admins still need to be able to maintain the objects within the OU, so their permissions will either need to be re-added to the access control list, or the existing permissions will need to be copied directly to the OU with the unnecessary accounts and permissions then removed. The final OU design for Accounting will look like Figure 5.7.

FIGURE 5.7   OU design with OU created to control visibility

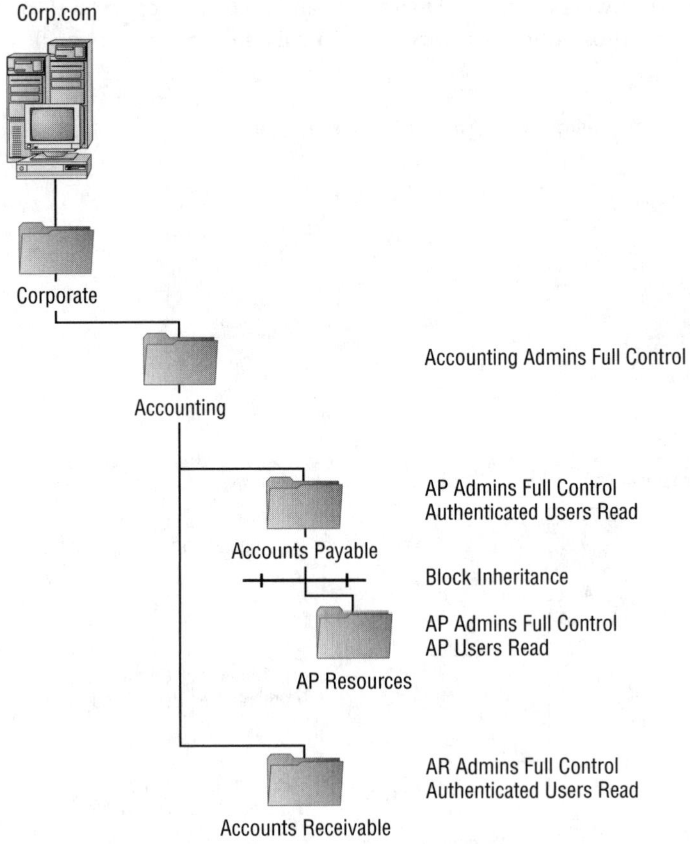

Corp.com

Corporate

Accounting — Accounting Admins Full Control

Accounts Payable — AP Admins Full Control
Authenticated Users Read

Block Inheritance

AP Resources — AP Admins Full Control
AP Users Read

Accounts Receivable — AR Admins Full Control
Authenticated Users Read

As we have mentioned, the primary reason to create an OU structure is to have the ability to control administrative abilities and make administration of resources more efficient. Because there is only one way to delegate administration of resources and there are many options to control group policies, as you will be seen in Chapter 6, the administrative design should take precedence.

Options for Delegating Control

Users do not usually have the ability to view OUs. They use the Global Catalog to find objects that give them access to the resources within the network. OUs are designed to make administration easier for the administrative staff within the company. Keep this in mind when you are creating your OU structure. Build it with administration as the top priority; you can address other issues later.

Because so much power can be wielded when a user is allowed to become an OU owner, they should be trained on the proper methods of delegation. This means that anyone who is allowed to delegate control to another user should understand the two methods of delegating permissions—object-based and task-based—as well as how inheritance affects the design. If OU owners are not properly trained on how to delegate control, the OU structure may be at a security risk with users who have too much power, or on the opposite extreme, with users who do not have the proper amount of authority to administer the objects they are supposed to control.

The OU owners are responsible for making sure that the appropriate users and groups have the ability to manage the objects they are responsible for. In the following sections, we will look at the options available to make sure those users and groups are properly configured for the access they need.

Understanding Delegation Methods

Object-based delegation grants a user control over an entire object type. Objects within Active Directory include users, groups, computers, OUs, printers, and shared folders. If a user needs to have control over computer accounts, you can use the Delegation of Control Wizard to allow Full Control permission only over computer objects within the OU. You may have another user who administers the User and Group objects within the OU. This level of control can be delegated as well.

Take, for instance, a company that has a remote office that manages its own users and resources but is controlled by the parent company. To keep the staff at the remote location from having too much control within the domain, an OU can be created to host the objects for that location. Then users from the remote office can be identified as the responsible parties and can have control over the objects delegated to them. If one user is responsible for adding new computers and maintaining systems and another is responsible for maintaining the User and Group objects, the Delegation of Control Wizard will allow you to easily set up the permissions required for them to perform their jobs. The Delegation of Control Wizard will only allow you to assign permissions, it will not allow you to revoke those permissions. If you want to revoke the permissions you will have to access the Access Control List on the OU to remove the account or change the permissions granted to the account.

 For more information on how to use the Delegation of Control Wizard within the Active Directory administration tools, see *MCSE: Windows Server 2003 Active Directory Planning, Implementation, and Maintenance Study Guide* (Sybex, 2003).

Task-based delegation grants a user the ability to perform specific functions against objects within the OU. Controlling objects at this level is more difficult to manage and maintain, but sometimes you may find it necessary. Take for instance a case where a company has a Help Desk department and one of its job duties is to reset passwords for users. However, you don't want them to modify any of the user properties. If you delegate the ability to work with user objects, the Help Desk personnel will have too much power. Instead, you can delegate the ability to reset passwords at the task level, locking them out of having the ability to affect the objects in any other way.

As mentioned earlier, however, it is much more difficult to manage the permissions granted at the task level than it is the object level. You will need to make sure that you are documenting the groups to which you are delegating permissions. Otherwise, you may find it problematic to try to track down where permissions are applied and troubleshoot access problems. As a best practice, try to design the OU structure so that you can take advantage of object-based delegation as much as possible.

Understanding Account and Resource OUs

In some Windows NT 4 directory service structures, the user accounts and resources are divided up into their own domains, based on the administrative needs of the domain owners. Because the domain is the administrative boundary within NT 4, the user account administrators have control over the account domain. Resource administrators have domains that are made up of the resources they are responsible for maintaining, usually systems that provided database, email, file, and print services, to name a few.

Depending upon the administrative needs of the organization, delegation of the sublevel OUs should follow a few rules:

The OU owner will have full control.   The OU owner will have the ability to work with any object within the OU tree for which they are the owner. Once the domain owner delegates full control to the top-level OU for the OU owner, the OU owner will be able to take ownership of any object within that OU tree.

The OU admin can only control objects for which they have been granted permissions.   The OU owner should only delegate the ability to work with the object types that the OU admin needs to modify. If the OU admin is an account admin, then only user and/or group object permissions should be granted. If the admin is a resource admin, only the appropriate object type should be delegated to them. OU admins should not have the ability to affect OUs, but only the objects within them.

Account OUs and *resource OUs* can provide the same functionality that account and resource domains provided under NT 4. Account OUs will hold the user and group accounts that are used when accessing the resources. Resource OUs will host the resources that users will need to access within the domain. These could be computer accounts, file shares, shared folders and contacts. You can build an OU structure that allows the user, group, and resource objects to be separated based on the staff that needs to have administrative control over them.

Let's look at an example of a company that has divided the OU structure based upon locations, with each location having users, and resources having local staff to support them. A domain owner creates an OU for the location Denver and delegates full control and OU ownership to Linda. Linda will be responsible for maintaining the OU hierarchy from this point on, although the domain owners will have the ability to modify and maintain the design if things go wrong. The manager of Information Technology decided that the OU owner accounts will be members of a group created within another container in the domain that the domain owners control. In this case, an OU is created within the OU named OU_Owners. Figure 5.8 shows an example of the design so far.

The Denver location does not have a large body of users and computers. After discussing the current administrative needs of the company, the forest owners decided that all of the users will reside within their own OU, groups will reside within another, and computers will have their own OU also. Appropriately, the OUs are named Users, Groups, and Computers, all located within the Denver OU.

FIGURE 5.8   The OU structure after top-level OUs have been created

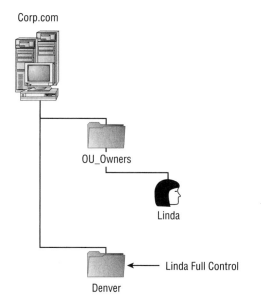

Linda identifies the OU administrators that will be responsible for maintaining the users and groups. She also identifies which users will be responsible for maintaining the systems used at the Denver location. Although all of the objects could reside within the same OUs, there could be reasons why object types should be separated. Reasons could include Group Policy application or administrative control. For this example, we will discuss the implications of administrative control.

 The application of Group Policy will be discussed in Chapter 6.

The user accounts for Denver are maintained by two Human Resources personnel and three IT staff members, all of whom are located in the Denver office. The HR personnel are responsible for creating and deleting the objects representing the accounts, whereas the IT staff members maintain the objects. The IT staff is also responsible for creating, deleting, and maintaining group accounts within the Denver location. The corporate Help Desk is responsible for resetting passwords for the users if necessary. Once the level of responsibility is identified, Linda creates two groups for maintaining user accounts. The first group she creates is the HR Account Admins group; the second is the IT Account Admins. She creates both of these groups in the Denver OU so that she can maintain them. The Corporate Help Desk group already exists within another OU that is maintained by the forest owners.

To the HR Account Admins group, she delegates the task permissions necessary to create and delete the user object type at the Users OU. She gives the IT Account Admins group the task permissions it needs to perform all actions against the user object type within the Users OU, with the exception of creating or deleting them. And finally, she grants the Corporate Help Desk group the ability to reset the passwords on the user object type.

The only group that needs delegated rights to the Groups OU is the IT Account Admins group. Because they have the ability to create, delete, and manage the groups, they are granted Full Control permissions to the group object type in the Groups OU.

Computer accounts for the Denver location are controlled by a group of four administrators. These administrators are responsible for installing and removing the systems from the network and domain, and also for every aspect of maintaining those systems. Once the administrative need is identified, a group should be created so that permissions can be granted to it. Linda creates the Systems Admin group within the Denver OU so that she can maintain the membership of the group. Then the group is delegated Full Control permissions to the computer object type within the Computers OU. After Linda performs all of these actions, the OU hierarchy looks like the representation seen in Figure 5.9.

Understanding Inheritance

Inheritance allows the permissions set at a parent level to be assigned at each child level automatically. The inheritance of object permissions from the parent object to the child object eases some of the administration headaches. Permissions set at the parent level are propagated to the child levels by default. Any object created within an OU will inherit the applicable permissions from the OU. With this being the case, whenever an account is granted permissions at the OU level, all of the child OUs and objects within those OUs inherit the settings.

FIGURE 5.9   The OU structure after permissions have been delegated

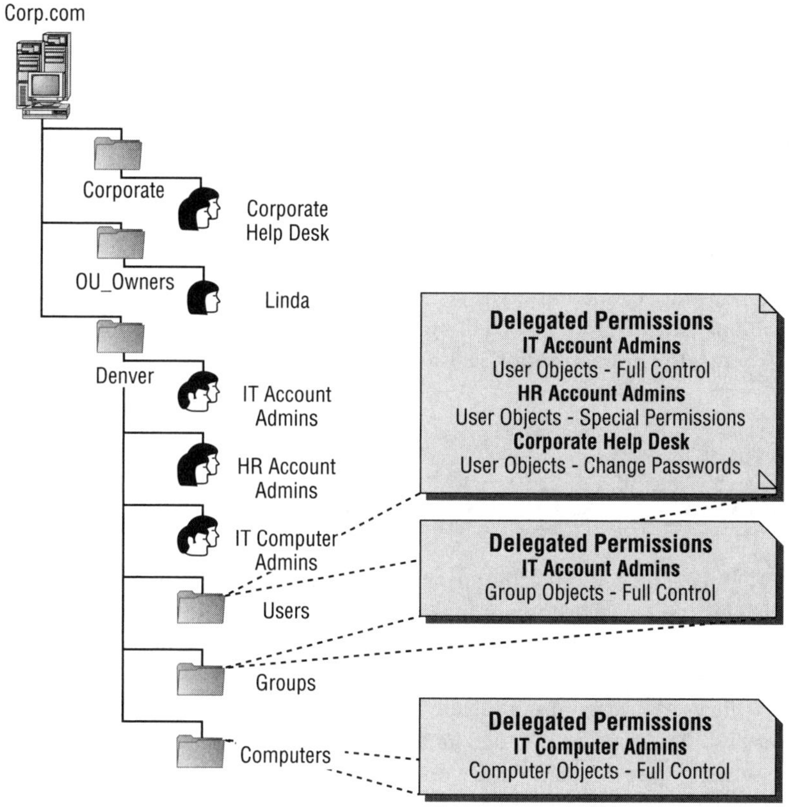

OU owners have the ability to control all of the objects within their OU tree after the domain owner delegates the appropriate permissions to the top-level OU. In the preceding Denver example, Linda is able to create the child OUs Users, Group, and Computers. After delegating the appropriate permissions to the groups that will administer the objects, she can pretty much take a hands-off approach to the administration of those objects. However, if the need arises, she can still enforce some level of control over the objects. For instance, if an OU admin makes a mistake when creating an object or modifies an object incorrectly, Linda could use her authority to troubleshoot and correct the problem.

There will be occasions when the permissions set at higher levels within Active Directory are not the proper permissions needed at a lower level. If this is the case, inheritance can be blocked, which means that permissions set at the parent level will no longer pass to the child objects. When blocking the inheritance of permissions, the administrator who is initiating the block can choose whether or not to copy the inherited permissions to the object or remove them completely. If the inherited permissions are removed from the object, only the permissions that are explicitly set at the object level will apply. This could restrict an upper-level OU owner, OU administrator, domain owner, or forest owner from being able to perform actions against the object. If this happens, the OU owner, domain owner, or forest owner has the ability to reset the inheritable permissions on the object or objects that were affected.

The blocking of inheritance could be problematic for those users or groups who do not have the power to change the inheritable permissions setting. If inheritance is blocked to objects that a groups needs to have control over, they will not be able to effectively maintain those objects. At this point, the OU owner could step in and change the inheritance on the OU or object, or change the effective permissions on the objects that the group needs to control. Trying to troubleshoot inheritance issues can be time consuming and difficult, so try to limit the amount of inheritance blocking you use within your design.

Creating an OU structure for a brand new design can be challenging. Developing a design that allows the administrative functions to be performed easily is of the utmost priority. However, very few organizations have the option of creating a brand new design. An existing infrastructure probably already exists. If the organization is using a Windows NT 4 domain environment, you need to consider several design options.

Migrating from NT 4.0

Windows NT 4 had some serious limitations when it came to administrative control. If a user needed to change user passwords or control group membership, their user account needed to be added to either the Account Operators group, or worse yet, to the Domain Admins group. The Account Operators group allowed the user to perform these two functions, but it also allowed the user to create users and groups and delete those same types of accounts. It was probably too much power in some cases. If a user account was added to the Domain Admins group, the user had far too much power throughout the domain.

With the granular level of control granted to accounts in Active Directory, you can allow a group of users to manage objects with only the level of control that they need. What this means is that you no longer have to add a user into a group that has too much power just so they can perform a single function. For many administrators that have a Windows NT 4 domain, this will probably be one of the most intriguing options available with Active Directory.

The following sections explain the options available whenever migrating Windows NT 4 account domains to Active Directory account OUs as well as migrating Windows NT 4 resource domains to Active Directory resource domains.

Migrating Account Domains

When you develop a design that includes migrating accounts from a Windows NT 4 Master User Domain (MUD), the first thing you need to decide is whether the current domain owners retain their control over the accounts. You may discover that the migration might entail defining different administrative personnel. This could be because the migration is collapsing the administrative structure, giving control over objects that define the accounts to a different group. Another reason you may need to define different personnel to manage the objects could be because NT 4 allows users to have too much control when they are added to the default groups. Review the required level of control each of the users will need and base the migration on that.

If the current domain owners will retain the same level of control in the new design, you can create an OU so that you can migrate the accounts directly into it. The new domain owner can then delegate control of the OU to the accounts that were originally the NT 4.0 domain owners, thus making them OU owners. Figure 5.10 shows a representation of this migration.

FIGURE 5.10   Migrating NT 4 MUD to OU, keeping the same administrative groups

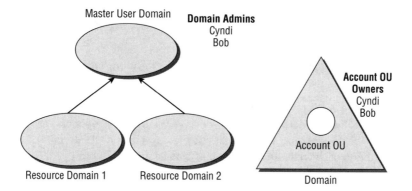

The ability to collapse the NT 4 domain structure is a benefit of Active Directory that many administrators want to take advantage of. Taking multiple MUDs and reducing them into a single domain where the accounts can be organized into OUs makes for a much simpler administrative design. Making the design as simple as possible will reduce the administrative costs, thus allowing the administrators to work with the accounts efficiently with fewer issues pertaining to setting and maintaining permissions.

In our Denver example, during the Active Directory design phase, another company is being acquired. The accounts and resources from this company will be migrated into the new Active Directory design. The designers have decided that the new accounts will fit in nicely with the current design options that they have chosen, user accounts will be migrated into the Users OU, and the groups will migrate to the Groups OU.

Migrating Resource Domains

Resource domains are the repositories for the computer accounts that hold the organization's resources. These resources include databases, e-mail, web servers, file shares, print devices, and management software, to name a few. Within the NT 4 domain structure, resource domains were usually created so the administrators who maintained the systems could control them and be isolated from the user accounts that were managed by other administrators. Other organizations that had a large number of accounts within the organization would divide the resources up into their own domains. Trust relationships would allow user accounts from MUDs the ability to access and maintain the resources.

Design Scenario

Migrating from Windows NT 4

Kryton Composites has used Windows NT 4 for several years. As the company has grown and added personnel and locations, they have had to change their initial Windows NT 4 domain structure from a single domain model to a multiple-domain model that incorporates two MUDs and four resource domains. The resource domains are based on each of the four factory locations: Tulsa, OK, which is also the corporate headquarters; South Bend, IN; Rebecca, GA; and Herrin, TN. Each of the locations has a single administrative group that is responsible for the resources at that location but does not have control over user and group accounts.

In the new design, the administrative staff from each of the locations should still have the ability to maintain the servers, workstations, shared folders, and printers, but should not have the ability to create or delete user and group objects or OUs.

The administrative staff at the corporate office will have control of all user and group objects and will be responsible for creating and maintaining the domain and OU structure. They want to make administration of the user and group objects as easy as possible.

1. **Question:** Which accounts should be identified as the OU owners? **Answer:** The administrative staff at the corporate headquarters will become the OU owners. They will be responsible for creating and maintaining the OU structure for the company.

2. **Question:** Which accounts should be identified as the OU administrators? **Answer:** Each of the administrative groups at the factory locations will be the OU administrators because they will be responsible for the objects within their OUs.

3. **Question:** When migrating the accounts from the MUDs, what type of OU structure would best fit their needs? **Answer:** Either of two options would work. First, you could create a function-based OU structure with the user and group objects from each of the locations separated into their own OU. Secondly, you could use a location-based design that would take advantage of the factory locations, each with an OU to contain the user or group objects.

4. **Question:** When you are migrating the resource objects from the resource domains, what type of OU structure would best fit their needs? **Answer:** Because each of the factory locations has its own administrative staff, the OU structure that will work best is the one that is location based. Using this structure, each of the administrative groups from each location can be delegated the level of control that they need over their own resources within their own OU structure.

5. **Question:** What OU structure would you suggest Kryton Composites use? **Answer:** The most efficient design, and the one that will not be affected greatly by any kind of reorganization, would be the location-based design. Because the account and resource OU structures can take advantage of this type of structure, you can create a single OU design that will be the same for all administrators and will not be confusing. At the same time, you can delegate the permissions at the top level of the OU hierarchy, and the inheritance will allow the administrative groups to control and maintain the objects for which they are responsible.

Usually, when a resource domain was created, an account from one of the trusted MUDs would be used to administer the resources. By adding an account to the built-in administrative groups in the resource domain, you could manage the user objects within the MUD where all of the user accounts reside and retain administrative control within the resource domain.

Some of the same options exist for migrating resource domains into resource OUs. You need to decide whether or not the resources will still be controlled by the same groups in the new design. If not, when you migrate the resources, migrate them to an OU where the new administrators have had control delegated to them. This is usually the case when you are merging with another company or your company has just acquired another. The resources from the company that you are now working with may fall under your jurisdiction, or your resources may be controlled by the other company.

If the resources are still under the control of the same administrative staff, you can migrate them to their own OUs within the appropriate OU tree. The decision about which OU tree will be used will be based on which group will be identified as the OU owner. The new OU can be created as a child OU within the OU structure based on who the OU administrators will be and whether the original NT 4 domain structure will be mimicked.

Some organizations will decide to keep the same structure so that the resources are grouped within a child OU of the account OU that has authority over the resources. The inheritance of permissions will allow an administrator at the account OU to have control over the resource OU also. Of course, the permissions inherited will only be those that are set at the parent level. If a group is granted the ability to create and delete user objects in the account OU, they will not have the ability to work with computer objects in the resource OU. If you do not want members of the group to have the ability to affect computer objects in the account OU, you will have to delegate the permission explicitly at the resource OU level.

In keeping with our Denver location scenario, the small company that the organization has recently acquired needs to have the resources moved into the Active Directory structure. Because the OU design for the account domains has been completed, the resource's migration method needs to be determined. Linda has worked with the Active Directory design staff to work out the OU requirements for her Denver OU tree. The manager of IT has decided that the resource domains will no longer fall under the same administrative staff for the original company. Some of the employees of the company that was acquired will stay on with the new company, but many decided to take positions at other companies. Because the resources will all fall under the IT Computer Admins' responsibility, the decision is made by the IT manager to migrate the resources to the Computers OU.

Summary

OU design takes administrative control into consideration before building the OU structure for Group Policy application. This allows for an organization to build an efficient administrative design, thus reducing the amount of administrative overhead that will be incurred by the organization. If properly planned out, the administrative control of the objects within Active Directory will be very straightforward and easy to maintain.

OUs will also allow you to easily upgrade or restructure Windows NT 4.0 domains into a single administrative unit. The original domain owners could become OU owners and the account and resource domains can either take on the same structure that was utilized within the NT 4 environment, or the entire structure can be redesigned and collapsed into a new administrative design.

In the next chapter, we are going to look at strategies used in designing an OU structure to allow for the efficient application of group policies. Because group policies and administrative designs do not always work out to be the same design methodology, we will also look at some of the trade-offs that you may have to make to design the best of both worlds.

Exam Essentials

Understand the OU owner role. The OU owner is a group that has been assigned the Full Control permission and is responsible for controlling and maintaining the OU tree.

Understand the OU admin role. The OU admin is the group that is responsible for a specific function within the OU, such as maintaining user or group objects.

Know what the five OU design options are. OU designs are based upon location, organization, function, or two combinations of location and organization.

Know what object autonomy is and how it is achieved. Object autonomy is granted to OU owners when they are given control over their OU tree. OU owners from other OUs will not have control over the resources that are managed by any other OU owner.

Know what object visibility is and how it is achieved. Object visibility is the ability to view objects within Active Directory, and it is controlled by giving the permission to list the contents of an OU to those users who need access to the object.

Understand object-based delegation. Object-based delegation grants a group the ability to work with all aspects of a specific object type, such as a user object or computer object.

Understand task-based administration. Task-based administration grants a group the ability to perform specific functions on an object type, such as changing the password on a user object.

Know what an account OU is. Account OUs consist of user objects and group objects.

Know what a resource OU is. Resource OUs consists of computer objects and shared folders, printers, and other resources that are published in Active Directory.

Understand how inheritance works. Inheritance allows for the permissions that are set at a parent OU to be passed down to a child OU and to all of the objects that reside within these OUs.

Know the two migration options when you are migrating Windows NT 4 domains to OUs. Windows NT 4 account and resource domains can be migrated so that they retain their original design configuration and the same groups can manage them, or they can be restructured so that the OU structure is more efficient and the groups that administer them are changed.

Key Terms

Before you take the exam, be certain you are familiar with the following terms:

account OUs

inheritance

object autonomy

object visibility

object-based delegation

OU administrators

OU owners

resource OUs

task-based delegation

Review Questions

1. When a member of the Domain Admins group grants a user Full Control permissions to an OU, what is that user considered to be?

   A. OU admin

   B. OU delegate

   C. OU controller

   D. OU owner

2. When a user is given the permission to control and maintain user objects within an OU, what role is the user considered to have?

   A. OU admin

   B. OU delegate

   C. OU controller

   D. OU owner

3. When an OU structure is created based on the geographic makeup of the company, what type of structure is this?

   A. Location-based

   B. Organization-based

   C. Function-based

   D. Location/organization-based

4. Tom is an administrator for XYZ, Inc. His job responsibilities include installing and maintaining computers at the Houston office. Within Active Directory, the top-level OUs are based on the city where the resources are located, with child OUs based on the departments at each office. What type of structure is used at XYZ?

   A. Location-based

   B. Organization-based

   C. Function-based

   D. Location/organization-based

5. Susie is the user and group administrator for 24Hr Coffee. Within Active Directory Users and Computers, she has access to the top-level OU Accounts. Within this OU she can manipulate and control the user and group objects, but within the Workstations, Servers, and Resources OUs she cannot perform any functions. What type of OU structure is being used at 24Hr Coffee?

   A. Location-based

   B. Organization-based

   C. Function-based

   D. Location/organization-based

6. Cari works for the Help Desk. When users call with password problems, she is able to reset their passwords using a custom taskpad. What kind of delegation is being used?

    A. OU-based

    B. Rights-based

    C. Object-based

    D. Task-based

7. When an OU is created for the sole purpose of hosting users or groups, what type of OU is it?

    A. Account OU

    B. Resource OU

    C. Security principle OU

    D. Task OU

8. When an OU is created for the sole purpose of hosting computers, shared folders, or printers, what type of OU is it?

    A. Account OU

    B. Resource OU

    C. Security Principle OU

    D. Task OU

9. Prestige Plastics has seven plants within the United States. Each of the plants maintains its own resources so that it can function even if it cannot reach resources at the corporate office in Jefferson City, MO. Each plant is equipped with a T1 connection to the corporate office. The administrative team in Jefferson City can control all of the resources at all of the plants, but the administrative teams at each of the plants only have control over their own resources. Based on the information given, what OU structure would you suggest?

    A. Location-based

    B. Organization-based

    C. Function-based

    D. Location/organization-based

10. Within an Active Directory structure, what is the easiest way to hide a large number of objects from users but keep administration easy for administrators?

    A. Create a separate forest for the objects and do not create a trust relationship between forests.

    B. Create a separate domain for the objects and disable the trust relationship for the domain.

    C. Create a separate OU for the objects and assign the List Contents permission for only the accounts that need access.

    D. Add the objects into the Restricted Groups container.

Answers to Review Questions

1. D. The OU owner is an account that has been granted Full Control permissions to an OU. This permission is usually assigned to a group and then the user account is added to the group.

2. A. The OU admin is an account that has been granted the ability to perform specific functions to objects within an OU. This permission is usually assigned to a group and then the user account is added to the group.

3. A. One of the most popular OU structure types, the location-based design, allows the resources to be grouped based on the geographic distribution of the organization. This type of design is resistant to reorganizations, mergers, and acquisitions.

4. D. Because the administrative functions are based on the physical location of the objects and the resources themselves are grouped based on the organization's departmental arrangement, the location/organization-based OU structure is being employed.

5. C. The administrative control that is delegated in this example is based on the administrative function for which the users or groups are responsible.

6. D. Task-based delegation assigns specific permissions that an account will be able to use on an object. Using this method, specific functions can be assigned to users so that they do not have too much power over objects. It is also more difficult to troubleshoot permission problems when task-based delegation is used.

7. A. An account OU is created so that permissions can be delegated to administrators who need to control the user or group objects and will have an OU for that purpose.

8. B. A resource OU is created so that permissions can be delegated to administrators who need to control computer objects, shared folders, or printers that have been published within the OU.

9. A. Location-based would be the most appropriate structure because the administrative structure is set up to take advantage of administrators at each location having control over their own resources.

10. C. If the objects are placed within the same forest, they will share the same Global Catalog, which will allow those users who do need to view the objects the ability to search for them. If the permissions are set on the OU so that the users who need to view them have the List Contents permission, the users will be able to search for the objects while those who have not been granted that permission will not see that they exist.

Case Study

You should give yourself 20 minutes to review this testlet and complete the questions.

Background

Insane Systems builds custom computers for their customers. They specialize in building cases that are unique and support the latest in hardware technology. They started off as a small company that provided this service to gamers who would take their cases to LAN parties to show off. Because their systems were considered some of the most stable gaming platforms and they provided an impressive design that gamers could show off, they started to become popular. Insane Systems started mass manufacturing some of their more popular designs and began selling stand-alone cases along with their fully configured systems. As space at the company became a premium, the office was moved from the manufacturing facility. This allowed the company to add to the amount of space that was used for the mass production line.

Existing Environment

Over the past few months, Insane Systems has been developing plans to expand their company. They have identified San Jose, California, Atlanta, Georgia, and New York City as the locations with their highest customer base. The current Chicago location will remain the corporate headquarters, but they are opening branches in New York City and San Jose. They are also in the process of acquiring a competitor's business in Atlanta. These locations will provide retail outlets as well as support. Customers will have the option of sending their systems back for any needed upgrades or repairs to the corporate office, or delivering them to one of the branch locations.

Because the company is planning on expanding, they want to make sure that the network infrastructure is in place to support their larger, distributed company. They are also concerned with the support lifetime of their current Windows NT 4 infrastructure. They realize they have the option of moving to a Windows 2000 or Windows 2003 infrastructure and are considering moving to Windows Server 2003 and Active Directory for two reasons: the expected support lifetime is greater than Windows 2000, and they are a technology firm that is not afraid of staying ahead of the technology curve.

Part of the expansion of the company is a complete overhaul of their current Internet presence. They are planning on bringing all of the web development and hosting in-house. Currently a web hosting service is providing their Internet presence, and Insane Systems feels as though they could provide better marketing and support information for their customers if they had control over their own website.

Interviews

Your company has been hired to design an Active Directory infrastructure and the network infrastructure to support it. During the interview process with some of the key stakeholders, you gathered the following information:

CEO   Currently we have a single location with all of our processes local. As we grow, we would like to keep all of the administration here in Chicago. Because the new branches are primarily retail and support offices, we will not need to have a large staff in those locations.

CIO   Most of the infrastructure that we support is located here at the corporate office. We do support some key servers at the manufacturing location. We support these servers from our main office. Because the servers are nearby, if there is a problem, we can usually be onsite within half an hour.

The new branches are going to be another issue altogether. We would like to retain the same level of administrative control over the servers in the new locations that we employ currently. Due to the geographic limitations, we may need to have some support staff at those locations. Currently, the plan is to hire staff at those locations who can provide the support for the customers, but also have an understanding of the business systems we need to put into place.

Manager of Information Technology   We have grown very quickly over the past three years and our current technologies have kept up with that growth. However, we don't think the current infrastructure is ready for the amount of growth that we are expecting within the following year. We are not afraid of moving to the latest technology, but we want to make sure that the design is stable and makes sense for us, especially if we will continue growing in the upcoming months. And because we are losing support for NT 4.0, we want to make sure that we have an operating system that will be supported for a few years down the road.

Most of our processes are located here at this office, and we would like to keep it that way. We know that some servers will need to be located at the remote offices, but we would like to be able to provide most of the support from this location. Remote administration tools will need to be included within the design so that we can keep our administrative costs to a minimum.

Currently, we have most of our servers located at the main office, and all are located on their own high-speed backbone. We do have a server at the manufacturing site that allows the staff there to have email as well as plans and orders in case we lose connectivity between the offices. This server is running Exchange 5.5. Several times during the day we replicate the public folder information to this system so that they are always up to date and do not have to dial up to the main office using our 56Kbps modem.

The systems at the main office are all supported by our staff of four administrators. All of the administrators are cross-trained on Windows NT 4, Exchange 5.5, SQL Server 7, our accounting software, and each of our file and print servers. We currently have several Windows NT 4 servers in place, including one Exchange 5.5 server at both locations, one SQL Server 7 server at the main office, one server running our accounting package that interfaces with SQL Server, and one file and print server that is used by both locations. The Exchange server at the manufacturing location doubles as a print server also.

CASE STUDY

Because all of the client machines are running Windows NT 4 Workstation, we do not have to worry about supporting different operating systems. We would like to maintain that same easy administration with the upcoming system. We would like to provide the same types of services at the remote locations that we provide at the home office, although accounting will remain at the home office and will not be spread out to all of the locations.

Current Network Design

After investigating the current infrastructure, you have determined that the following servers are in place:

Home Office Primary Domain Controller (PDC)

Backup Domain Controller (BDC)

DHCP server

DNS/WINS server

Exchange 5.5 Server

SQL Server 7

Systems Management Server 2

File server

Print/Antivirus server

Research and Development File server

Manufacturing Facility Backup Domain Controller (BDC)

DNS/WINS/DHCP Relay Agent server

Exchange 5.5/File server

The Corporate Office hosts nearly 250 Windows NT 4 workstations at this point. They are interconnected by several 48-port 10/100Mbps switches. A router is used to divide the network into four VLANs. One of these VLANs is the 1Gbps backbone on which the servers reside. Each of the servers is connected to a 1Gbps switch port. This location takes advantage of private IP address ranges. The servers are located on the 192.168.1.0/24 subnet. The client systems are divided between network addresses 192.168.10.0/24, 192.168.11.0/24, 192.168.12.0/24, and 192.168.13.0/24.

The manufacturing facility contains 12 Windows NT 4 workstations connected to the same switch as the servers. Because Insane Systems does not want to slow down production due to a communication failure, they have taken advantage of Exchange 5.5 Server's public folder replication. Public folders are continually updated with the latest orders. The crew foreman can access the orders locally from these public folders at any time, whether the communication link between the locations is up or not. This location uses another address range—192.168.20.0/24.

Case Study Questions

1. What type of OU structure should be used to efficiently administer the active directory objects?

   A. Location-based

   B. Organization-based

   C. Function-based

   D. Location/organization-based

2. Who should be identified as the OU owners?

   A. Corporate (Chicago) administrators

   B. New York resource administrators

   C. San Jose resource administrators

   D. Atlanta resource administrators

3. Who should be identified as the OU administrators? (Choose all that apply.)

   A. Corporate (Chicago) administrators

   B. New York resource administrators

   C. San Jose resource administrators

   D. Atlanta resource administrators

4. Insane Systems has chosen to use a single domain design. The Accounting department is only going to be located at the corporate headquarters. Some of the objects that Accounting has access to should not be seen by other users within the company. Is this single domain structure still the best design, or should another option be considered?

   A. You should still use single domain with OUs to control administration.

   B. You should use two domains, to separate the Accounting functions from the rest of the corporate resources. Use OUs within the domain holding the corporate resources.

   C. You should use four domains, one for each location to host their own objects, and use OUs to organize objects within the domain.

   D. You should use two forests so that the objects that Accounting needs to hide from other users can be completely separated from the rest of the organization's resources.

5. When designing the OU structure, you will want to create a design that will be efficient for the administrative staff. Using the following diagram, place the appropriate labels on the OUs according to the OU structure that best meets the needs of Insane Systems (there may be labels or OUs that are not required to complete this).

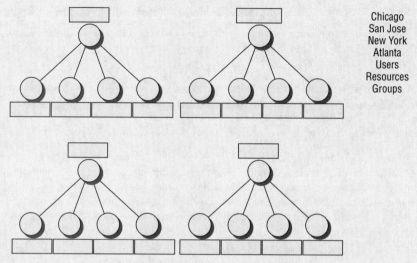

Chicago
San Jose
New York
Atlanta
Users
Resources
Groups

6. When migrating accounts from the existing Windows NT 4.0 domain, where in the hierarchy should they be migrated (there may be labels or OUs that are not required to complete this question)?

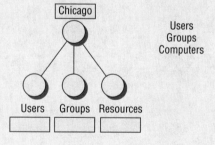

Users
Groups
Computers

Answers to Case Study Questions

1. A. Location-based will be the most appropriate structure because the administrative structure is set up to take advantage of administrators at each location having control over their own resources.

2. A. The corporate administrators will have the ability to control all of the objects within the new Active Directory design. They will be able to control the OU structure as well as have complete control over the users, groups, and resource objects.

3. A, B, C, D. Those users who have been identified as resource administrators for each location will be added to a group that has been delegated the authority to work with the resource objects. Although the corporate administrators were defined as the OU owners, OU owners have the ability to provide administrative control over the objects, which they do provide to the corporate resources.

4. A. The single domain option is still the most efficient for Insane Systems. The OUs can be used to control administrative delegation over the appropriate objects, and if the Accounting department needs to control what objects are available for users, another OU could be created with the accounting objects organized within it. The accounting users could then be granted the List Contents permission and any other appropriate permission to the objects so that they can find them within Active Directory.

5.

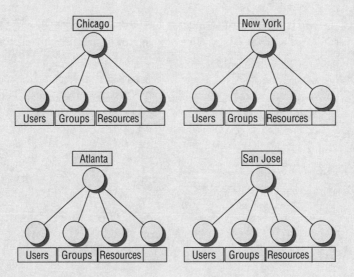

Insane Systems design should take advantage of the location-based OU structure, so the top-level OUs will be based on the locations of their branches. Beneath each of the location OUs, an OU should be created for the user and group objects and another for the objects that represent the resources at each location. This allows the user accounts to be organized based on their location; the OU owners for each location can maintain the user and group objects. The resource objects can be placed in the resource OUs where inheritance will allow the OU owners to still have control of them, but the OU administrators can be delegated the ability to maintain the resource objects if necessary.

6.

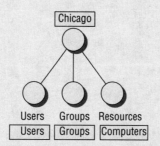

The user and group accounts within the existing domain represent the corporate accounts that are used in the Chicago location. Migrating these users and groups to the Users and Groups OU within the Chicago OU will keep them organized correctly. Moving the computer accounts to the Resources OU within the Chicago OU will allow the administrative staff to control the resources as they currently do.

Chapter 6

Designing Organizational Units for Group Policy

MICROSOFT EXAM OBJECTIVES COVERED IN THIS CHAPTER

✓ **Design an OU structure.**

- Identify the Group Policy requirements for the OU structure.

✓ **Design a strategy for Group Policy implementation.**

- Design the administration of Group Policy objects (GPOs).
- Design the deployment strategy of GPOs.
- Create a strategy for configuring the user environment with Group Policy.
- Create a strategy for configuring the computer environment with Group Policy.

Organizational unit (OU) design should always start with the administrative requirements for the organization. In Chapter 5, "Designing an Organizational Unit Structure for Administrative Purposes," we discussed how to designate who will have control of the OUs based on the requirements for maintaining the objects within Active Directory. By making administrative control the highest design priority, you make administration easier for those who need to maintain objects and reduce the cost of administrative overhead.

After the requirements for administration have been addressed, the design team will need to identify how Group Policy Objects (GPOs) will be applied within the infrastructure. Because group policies can be applied in many different ways, the administrative structure that has been decided upon should not be affected by the application of Group Policy. However, you may encounter instances when the OU design will be enhanced due to the GPOs that need to be applied.

In this chapter, we are going to concentrate on the different ways that GPOs can be applied and the design decisions that you will need to consider when you are identifying the settings and restrictions that you want to have enforced on users, groups, and computers. Because the designer has several options available when they are using GPOs, including security settings, user restrictions, and software deployment, they will have to make decisions in order to guarantee that the design is the most efficient possible.

Group Policy Overview

Group Policy has proven to be one of the most widely used Active Directory technologies, and at the same time, one of the most misunderstood and misused. Many administrators have taken advantage of GPOs in order to control the security of systems and to distribute software to users and computers but do not fully understand the options that are available when using GPOs. Understanding the settings that can control security, restrict user sessions and desktops, deploy software, and configure the application environment should be the top priority when you are using GPOs. Options that affect how the GPOs are applied need to be understood as well; some of the options we will discuss include blocking inheritance, enforcing settings, applying settings to specific users or systems, and filtering out the accounts that do not need to have settings applied to them.

To make your job much easier, Microsoft has introduced a freely downloadable utility: the *Group Policy Management Console (GPMC)*. The GPMC simplifies the task of administering the GPOs used within your organization. From one location, all of the GPOs from any domain in any forest of the organization can be controlled and maintained. You can download the utility from Microsoft's website. As you can see in Figure 6.1, once this utility is installed on a system, the Group Policy tab on the properties page of a site, domain, or OU will no longer show the GPOs linked at that object. Instead, a button to open the GPMC appears there. The GPMC is added to the Administrative Tools menu also.

FIGURE 6.1   The Group Policy tab after the Group Policy Management Console is added.

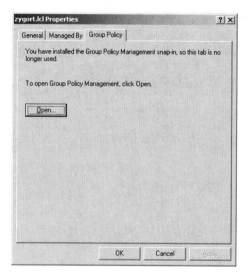

 For more information about the Group Policy Management Console and how to download your copy of this tool, go to http://www.microsoft.com/windowsserver2003/gpmc/default.mspx.

Do note that the GPMC will only function on Windows XP and Windows Server 2003 operating systems. Any administrators within the organization who need to use this utility will require a workstation running Windows XP or else they will need to work from a server where the GPMC has been added. Figure 6.2 shows the GPMC. Notice how the group policies are all organized beneath the Group Policy container. This allows you to go to the container and work with any of the GPOs that you are using in Active Directory. Also note that the domain and all of the sites and OUs are organized within the console so that you can see where of the GPOs are linked.

Of course the real power of the GPMC is the ability to run sample scenarios and to determine which GPOs are being applied to a user or computer. As you are designing the GPOs that will be used within the organization, take the time to test the effects the GPO will have on users and computers when applied in conjunction with other GPOS. Figure 6.3 shows an example of the GPMC's Group Policy Modeling section.

In the following sections we are going to take a look at what the company wants to use GPOs for. This will include the security needs, software installation options and user restrictions that will be used to control the user's environment.

FIGURE 6.2   Group Policy Objects within the GPMC

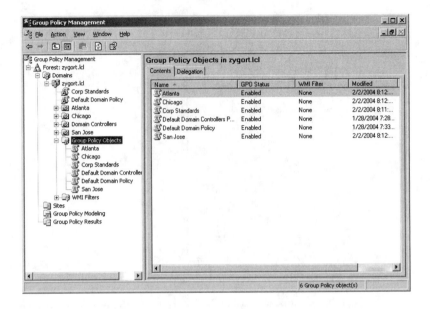

FIGURE 6.3   Group Policy Modeling

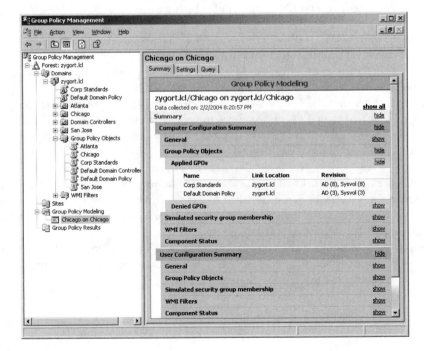

Understanding the Company's Objectives

Before sitting down and designing the OUs that you will use for implementing GPOs, you must understand the needs of the organization. Although every Active Directory rollout will have password requirements, lockout restrictions, and Kerberos policies applied, that is usually where any similarities between organizations end. The first thing you should do is document the administrative structure of the organization. The previous chapters within this book have dealt with designing and documenting the administrative responsibilities, and you should have a good idea of how the OU structure is going to look from Chapter 5.

Base your Group Policy design on this administrative design as much as possible. Most organizations find that if they create their OU structure based on the administrative functions, the Group Policy requirements follow along pretty well. Although you may still have to build OUs for special purposes, the basic design should already be put into place. The special purposes could include special software that a subset of users from a department need to use, or restrictions on the systems that temporary employees will have.

A good Group Policy design starts with defining exactly what actions GPOs will perform for your organization. Because GPOs are primarily an administrative tool, you can ease some of the administrative load from the staff and allow the system to control users' environments. Some of the areas that can be controlled are security, software installation, and user restrictions.

Identifying Security Needs

One of the first types of settings that will need to be determined are the security settings that will be enforced for users and the systems to which they connect. When Windows Server 2003 is configured as a domain controller, the security policy for the domain requires users to use *strong passwords*, which are password that do not use words that can be found in a dictionary and utilize several different types of characters. Microsoft has identified strong passwords as those that follow these guidelines:

- Are at least seven characters long

- Do not contain your username, real name, or company name.

- Do not contain a complete dictionary word.

- Are significantly different from previous passwords. Passwords that increment (*Password1, Password2, Password3* ...) are not strong.

- Contain characters from at least three of the following four groups:

    - Uppercase letters, such as A, B, and C

    - Lowercase letters, such as a, b, and c

    - Numerals, such as 0, 1, 2, and 3

    - Symbols found on the keyboard (all keyboard characters not defined as letters or numerals), including the following:` ~ ! @ # $ % ^ & * ( ) _ + - = { } | [ ] \ : " ; ' < > ? , . /

Training users on the proper methods of creating and using passwords can prove to be difficult. For instance, turning on the complexity requirements that force a user to have strong passwords usually ends up with the user writing their password down on a piece of paper or a sticky note and placing it close to their computer. You should implement corporate standards that identify how passwords should be protected and the ramifications of not following the policy. Of course, training the users and explaining the reason passwords are a vital defense mechanism can aid in the acceptance of the password policy.

Account lockout restrictions are another defense mechanism that should be used. Any time a brute-force attack is made against an account, the account lockout policy prevents the attackers from being able to make too many attempts at discovering the password. Most companies have this setting configured to allow between three and five attempts before the account is locked. Once it is locked, the attacker does not have the ability to try any additional passwords against the account for as long as the account is locked. This brings us to the second part of account lockout restrictions: you should always leave the accounts locked until an administrator unlocks them. Although this increases the administrative load to some extent, and more times than not the lockout is due to the user forgetting their password or having the Caps Lock key turned on, at least the administrator is notified of the possible attack. And just to make sure that you are not allowing an unauthorized user access to another user's account, you will need to put procedures in place that will help you identify the user who needs their account unlocked. This is especially true if they call to have their account unlocked and they mention that they cannot remember their password. Before changing the password, you will need to authenticate the identity of the user.

Aside from the account policies that can be set, other requirements also need to be identified. For instance, you may have users who need access to servers that hold confidential information. If users need to use an encrypted connection when accessing the data, you can specify the Internet protocol security (IPSec) policies that will be enforced by using GPOs. For example, if a user within the Payroll department needs to modify the salary and bonus structure for an employee, and the employee data is hosted on a server that you want to make sure is only accessed when IPSec communication is used, you can create an OU, IPSec Servers, for the payroll departments server and any other servers that require IPSec communication. You can then create a Group Policy object for the IPSec Servers OU that enforces the Secure Server IPSec policy and apply it to all servers in the IPSec Servers OU. Another OU can be created for the workstations within the Payroll department, Payroll Clients OU. The Group Policy object that is defined for the Payroll Clients OU could have the Client IPSec policy assigned to it, which would turn on IPSec communication whenever connecting to the Payroll servers, or any server that requests an IPSec channel.

 For more information on security, see Exam 70-293, *Planning and Maintaining a Microsoft Windows Server 2003 Network Infrastructure*, by Susan Sage London and James Chellis (Sybex, 2004).

Identifying Software Installation Needs

Using GPOs to roll out software can drastically reduce the administrative efforts required to install and maintain software within the organization. At the same time, it can increase the load upon the network to a point that is not acceptable. You need to determine if the benefits gained from having automated installation of software outweigh the network overhead required. Of course, no matter how much you may want to use GPOs to push software to client machines, some instances will occur when the network infrastructure will not allow it. This is especially true if you use wide area network (WAN) links between locations and the software distribution point is located on a server on the other end of the slow link.

A *Service Level Agreement (SLA)* could affect the rollout of software. SLAs are contractual obligations that dictate the amount of service availability that is required for servers or workstations. In some cases, software can take several minutes to install. If SLAs are in place and they restrict the amount of time that it takes to install an application, you may be forced to manually install the application for the user during times when they are not using the system. Another alternative is to link the GPO after hours and have the software installation assigned to the computer. Due to the fact that the software installation client-side extension is not included in the periodic refresh of GPOs, any changes that you make to the software installation options within a GPO are not processed on the client. Using remote access tools, you could then restart the user's computer, which would initiate the installation of the software.

If you determine that you are going to assign or publish applications to users or computers, you need to identify which applications are required. Most applications written by commercial software vendors within the last few years take advantage of Microsoft's IntelliMirror technology and are supported by Group Policy. Make sure the software is stamped with Microsoft's seal of approval. If Microsoft has certified the software to run on Windows Server 2003, the application will support IntelliMirror.

Work with each department within the organization to determine their software requirements. Understanding the software needs of the organization helps you identify which software packages need to be rolled out through a GPO. You may need to make some trade-offs. If every user within the organization needs to have a specific application such as antivirus software, it may be easier to create a system image that includes that operating system and the software. Using a third-party disk imaging utility, you can create a generic image of a system that includes all of the software and the appropriate system settings for the organization. Whenever the tech staff builds a new client system, the image is placed on the hard drive of the new computer, and when the computer is rebooted, it is configured with the default settings and software. This is a very quick and usually painless method of getting systems online in short order. However, you will encounter some drawbacks.

If devices on the new hardware are not supported at the time the image was originally created, the new hardware may not start up correctly and you will be left trying to install the correct drivers. As new software packages are identified as required for the organization, you may have to rebuild the image to support the software, which then brings us back to the advantages of Group Policy software deployment. Although operating systems cannot be deployed through a policy (that is a function of Remote Installation Services [RIS]), new and updated software can be. Of course Microsoft Systems Management Server (SMS) will also roll out software to client machines, and will do so with more efficient management options. One of the benefits of SMS that Group Policy has yet to implement is the ability to push the software package out at a predetermined time.

After determining which of the deployment options you are going to use, you then need to determine which software packages are going to be rolled out with Group Policy and how you are going to accomplish this.

Identifying User Restrictions

User restrictions limit what actions a user can perform on their workstation or control the applications that are allowed to run. For some companies, not many settings are required. The users have control over their workstations and the administrators may only control the account policies that are put into effect with the *Default Domain Policy*, which is where the password requirements, account lockout settings, and Kerberos policy settings are configured. Other companies take full advantage of using GPOs to restrict their users from being able to access any of the operating system configuration options. Some companies even force all of the systems to have the corporate background.

As extreme as it may sound, the fewer configuration options that a user is allowed to access, the less the user can affect, and possibly change for the worse. Desktop restrictions can remove the icons for My Computer and My Network Places, or can change what the user sees from the context menu when the right mouse button is used on these icons. The Display properties can be locked out so that the user cannot choose a monitor refresh rate or screen resolution that is not supported by the video subsystem. Start menu items can be restricted so that the user does not have the ability to open the Control Panel and modify settings within the operating system.

 For more information about Group Policy and the settings that you can use to control a user's environment, see the Group Policy section within the Windows Server 2003 Technical Reference on the Microsoft website.

You should identify which operating system configuration settings the users within the organization really need to work with, and how much power they need to wield over their workstations. Whereas it may take you a little longer to plan out the Group Policy settings that need to be applied to groups of users, the administrative headaches that these restrictions will alleviate will be worth the trouble. As you are designing the Group Policy settings that will be used to control and assist the administrative structure, remember the golden rule: keep it simple.

Creating a Simple Design

The underlying design goal, aside from supporting the organization's objectives, should be to create a Group Policy design that is as simple as possible. A simple design will allow for more efficient troubleshooting and processing of Group Policy settings. The fewer Group Policy settings that need to be applied to a computer or user, the faster the computer will start up, the quicker the users will be able to log on to their systems and, since a small GPO can be 1.5 MB in size, network traffic will also be reduced. If problems arise due to Group Policy conflicts or inappropriate settings, if the design is simple, it is easier for an administrator to troubleshoot the problem.

When determining the best and most efficient use of GPOs, you should review the requirements of the users who will be affected and then try to consolidate settings into the fewest number of GPOs possible. Then make sure you are taking advantage of the natural inheritance of Active Directory and are not using too many options that change the inheritance state.

Identifying User Requirements

Determine what you need to provide for the users and their computers. Every company's requirements will be different. Understanding how employees function on a day-to-day basis and what they need in order to perform these functions will aid you in determining the Group Policy settings you need to enforce. You will need to determine which settings need to be applied based on employees' job functions and job requirements, as well as identify the corporate standards that should be put in place.

Corporate Standards

Corporate standards are usually the easiest settings to figure out. These are the settings that should be set across the board for every employee and computer. Corporate standards are settings that you define in order to control the environment so that no employee is allowed to perform actions that are prohibited. Settings that make up these standards include the password policy, account lockout policy, software restrictions, Internet Explorer Security Zone settings, and warning messages that appear when someone attempts to log on.

Corporate standards are settings that should be applied as high in the *Group Policy hierarchy* as possible. The Group Policy hierarchy consists of the three levels at which a GPO can be linked; site, domain and organizational unit (OU). Since the GPO settings are inherited from each of these levels, by linking the GPO at the highest level within the hierarchy where it applies, you will be able to enforce the settings over a large number of objects with the fewest number of GPOs.

Most designs apply the corporate standards at the domain level so that every user logging on and every computer starting up will have the policy applied to it. To make sure that these settings are imposed upon every user and system, the Enforced setting should be enabled on the GPO that represents the corporate standards. This way, if another administrator configures a GPO with settings that conflict with the corporate standards and links the new GPO to an OU, the corporate standards will still take precedence.

Don't modify the Default Domain Policy to include the settings for the corporate standards. Although this may seem like a logical place to enforce the settings because the Default Domain Policy affects all users and computers within the domain, the new Default Group Policy Restore Command, dcgpofix.exe, will not retain the settings that have been modified since the domain was created.

 NOTE For more information about the Default Group Policy Restore Command, dcgpofix.exe utility, see the section "Options for Linking Group Policies" later in this chapter.

If multiple domains exist within the organization, chances are the corporate standards will apply to them also. The GPMC will allow you to copy a GPO from one domain to another. Using this functionality, you can create a duplicate GPO that can be linked to a domain. This will alleviate having to link a single GPO to multiple domains. Whereas this is not an issue when you have domain controllers within a site that host the GPOs, if you have to pull the GPO from across a WAN link, you could increase the user's logon time considerably.

Job Function

Employees have specific functions that they provide for the company. An employee within the Human Resources department provides different functions than a temporary employee providing data entry for the Marketing department. Identify what the employees require to perform their jobs. Document your findings, and then compare what is the same among all employees within an OU and what is different. You may be able to create a single GPO for a department that applies to all of the users and computers and then link it at the parent OU for the department. Those settings that are specific to a subset of users or computers can then be added to a GPO that is linked to the child OU where the user or computer accounts are located.

Organize all of the settings required by employees within a department and create a GPO named after the department. That GPO can then be linked to the department. Other settings that are specific to a subset of the users within that department can either be linked to the OU and configured so that only those users receive the settings, or linked to a child OU if the users and computers are distributed for administrative purposes.

Job Requirements

There may be specific job requirements that must be met by users or computers that are different even though the job functions may be very similar. Whereas all members of the Human Resources department will need to access the training materials and benefits documents so that they can assist employees when necessary, a subset of Human Resources personnel may have access to the employee database. If this database resides on a server that requires IPSec-encrypted communication, only the appropriate Human Resources personnel should fall under the control of the GPO that provides the appropriate IPSec policy settings. By linking a GPO to the server's OU that enforces the servers to require IPSec for communication and another GPO linked at the Human Resource's client OU that uses the IPSec client policy, the Human Resources personnel will communicate securely with the servers.

System requirements may be different for users depending upon their job requirements. You may have users who need to use modems to connect to remote systems. Other users may need to have access to administrative tools. Exceptions to restrictions that are applied at the domain or parent OU may need to be overridden for these users. Make sure you document the special needs of every user.

Minimizing Group Policy Objects

If you use as few GPOs as possible, you will be able to troubleshoot problems that arise much more easily than if several GPOs could affect users and computers. Policy settings that are related, such as software restrictions that affect a large group of users, should be added to the same GPO. By adding settings to a single GPO instead of using multiple GPOs to enforce the settings, you will reduce the GPO processing time.

SLAs are starting to become more widespread. As systems become more and more vital to the operation of the company, the need to have these systems online becomes mandatory. Although we think of SLAs controlling servers and server maintenance, SLAs that affect workstations are also being put into place. Some of these dictate the amount of time that a user will have to spend for applications to load and the amount of time spent waiting for logon to complete. This may sound picky to some individuals, but there are financial institutions, brokerage firms, and other organizations that require their workstations to be available at all times so that they can perform their duties.

If your organization falls under an SLA, you will need to determine how long it takes to process the GPOs you are planning. By combining settings into a single GPO, you will decrease the amount of processing time required to process the settings. If the settings are spread out among several GPOs, all of the settings for each of the policies will have to be processed.

Try to determine if you can condense the settings into a single policy, and if you cannot, try to condense to the fewest policies possible. Of course, this is a practice that you should follow whether you are working under an SLA or not. Users do not like to wait to gain access to their systems. The faster they are able to see their logon screen and then have access to their desktop, the happier they are. And the happier the users are, the better your day will be!

Another method of making your GPOs more efficient is to disable part of the GPO from processing. Each of the two sections that you can configure settings in, computer and user, can be disabled. When you do so, you are essentially telling the system to ignore any of the settings in that section. Since the client-side extensions do not have to parse through the GPO to determine what needs to be enforced or disabled, the GPO will process faster, thus reducing the time it takes for the computer to reach the logon screen or the user to log on to their system.

Consider the following scenario. Company X has identified several settings that they want to use. They create a GPO for each of the settings so that they can name the GPO based on the setting that will be used. When finished, they have 14 unique GPOs. When the employees start their computers and log on, all settings in the 14 GPOs need to be processed. Company X starts receiving calls from their users who complain that the startup and logon times are excruciatingly long. After identifying which of the settings can be condensed into individual GPOs, they end up with 3 GPOs and no further complaints from the users.

Identifying Interoperability Issues

Windows XP and Windows Server 2003 are the only operating systems that can take full advantage of the new Group Policy settings in a Windows Server 2003 Active Directory environment. Windows XP can take advantage of all of the new client specific settings whereas Windows Server 2003 can take advantage of all of the new server-based settings. For users running Windows 2000 Professional or servers running Windows 2000 Server, there will be over 200 possible settings that will not be processed on those platforms. When you are editing the settings for a GPO, make sure each of the settings specify to which operating system platform the setting will apply.

Windows Management Instrumentation (WMI) Filters provide additional functionality to a Group Policy application. By specifying operating system or system options, you can control which computers a GPO will apply. For instance, if you want to make sure that a system has enough free space on a partition or volume in order to install software, you can specify that the free space must exceed the minimum requirement for the application. Figure 6.4 is an example of a GPO that uses a WMI filter to control the installation of software to partitions or volumes with enough free space. If the requirement is not met, the application installation setting is ignored. Again, Windows XP and Windows Server 2003 can take advantage of WMI Filters but Windows 2000 cannot. If a WMI filter is in place that controls whether a GPO is applied and the computer is running Windows 2000, the WMI filter is ignored and the settings are applied.

Real World Scenario

Minimizing Logon Time

Ornament Retailers Association (ORA) is a group of retailers that sell out-of-print Christmas ornaments. ORA recently implemented Group Policy in Active Directory. They decided to utilize many features of Group Policy, including controlling security, restricting user desktops, and deploying software.

ORA decided to create five levels of user access and created a GPO for each group. They designed it so that a user would log on, and depending on what group they were a member of, they would get a custom Desktop and Start menu from the Folder Redirection portion of Group Policy. All GPOs were then linked to an OU that contained all of the company's users. After the GPO implementation, users started complaining about very slow logon times. This was unacceptable due to a SLA in place that stated that logon times would take no longer than one minute. Some logons were taking from five to seven minutes.

After further investigation, it was found that the only difference among all five of the policies was the appearance of the Desktop and Start menu. All other settings were exactly the same.

ORA decided to streamline their policies and reduce the number that they use. They found that they could reduce their policies to just one at the Users OU, as folder redirection can be defined by group.

ORA reduced their logon time greatly by streamlining their GPOs.

FIGURE 6.4 WMI filter for detecting adequate drive space

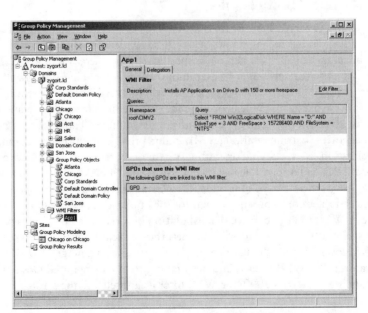

Other operating systems, such as Windows NT 4, Windows 95, and Windows 98, will not process GPOs. If you wish to control computers running these operating systems, you will have to use System Policy Editor. This means that you will have to support two different technologies when trying to set user restrictions. Another drawback comes from the fact that only a small subset of settings are supported by System Policies. In order to efficiently control the systems and users within your environment, try to determine an upgrade path for the older operating systems.

Designing for Inheritance

Just as permissions are inherited from a parent OU to the child OU, Group Policy settings will also pass down through the hierarchy. Taking advantage of *inheritance*, you will be able to create a Group Policy hierarchy that allows you to efficiently apply GPOs to your organization and make it easy for your staff to troubleshoot issues arising from GPOs. You have several options when you are using inheritance. You should implement best practices that will allow inheritance to work as it should and then only use the options that change the default behavior when necessary. The more the options for enforcing, blocking, and filtering are used, the harder it is to troubleshoot the design.

Organizing OUs

Use the OU structure that is based on the administrative requirements as much as possible. Only create additional OUs if it makes the application of Group Policy easier to maintain and troubleshoot. For instance, if you look at Figure 6.5, an OU structure has been created that allows the Engineering department administration to be broken out into two departments: Graphic Design and Model Shop. Each of the departments has a different internal administrative staff responsible for maintaining the user and computer accounts. Within the Model Shop, some employees work with the Research and Development department to build prototypes. For users to access the plans from the Research and Development (R&D) servers, which are placed in an OU that has the required IPSec policy applied, they need to use IPSec-encrypted communication. The GPO that allows the IPSec client policy is applied to the R&D Model Shop OU, where the user accounts are located, giving them the ability to access the plans from which they need to build. The rest of the Model Shop employees' accounts are placed with the Users container.

Define Corporate Standards

Once the settings for corporate standards have been identified and configured within a GPO, they should be linked high within the hierarchy, preferably at the domain level. Once linked, the Enforced option should be set so that lower-level GPOs do not override any of the standards. Figure 6.6 shows a domain with the Default Domain Policy and the Corporate Standards policy. Notice that the Corp Standards GPO has the Enforced option turned on. Figure 6.7 shows the inheritance of GPOs at the Accounting OU. Notice that the Corp Standards GPO is the GPO with the highest priority within the list due to its Enforced setting.

FIGURE 6.5 OU structure enhanced for Group Policy application

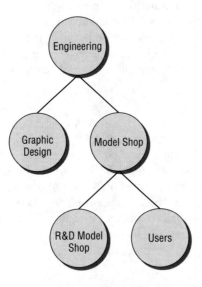

FIGURE 6.6 Corporate Standards GPO enforced at the domain level

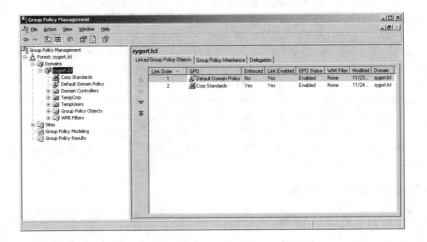

Use Blocking and Filtering Sparingly

The *Block Inheritance* option stops the natural inheritance of settings from GPOs higher in the hierarchy. When you use this option, you will block every GPO setting from any parent object with the exception of the domain account policies. Once blocked, the only way that a GPO's settings will override the Block Inheritance option is if you apply the Enforced option. The Enforced option takes precedence over any Block Inheritance option that it encounters, but it is only applied to an individual GPO. You will need to set the Enforced option for every GPO that needs to override the blockage.

FIGURE 6.7   Corporate Standards affecting the Accounting OU

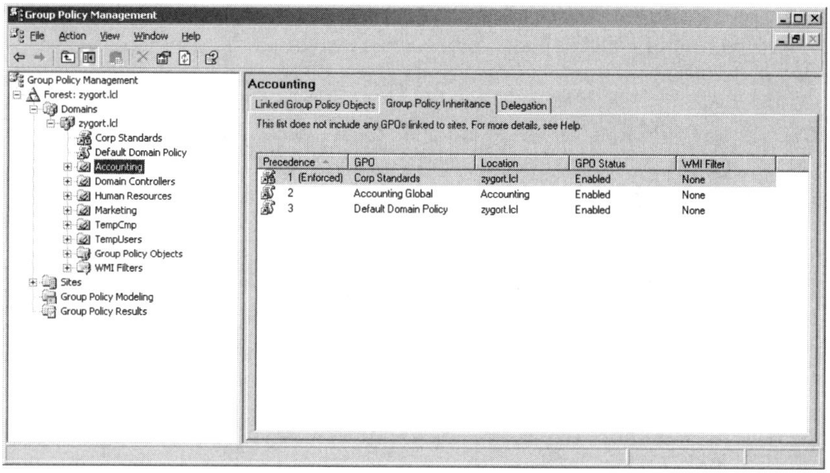

Filtering is the process of specifying to which accounts the GPOs will apply. By default, the Authenticated Users group will have the GPO applied to it at the location where the GPO is linked. This may work in some instances, but for most applications, you will not want every account within the OU to be under the GPO's control. For instance, if the user account that has administrative rights to the OU is located within the OU and the GPO restricts the use of administrative tools, the administrative user will not have access to the tools they need to perform their job. Decide upon which accounts will need to have the GPOs applied to them and create a group based on that need. Do not add the administrative users to the group for the user accounts; instead, create another group for the administrators to be members of. Configure the Security Filtering option to include the group to which the GPO will be applied.

Prioritizing

If more than one GPO is attached to a site, domain, or OU, you will need to determine the *processing priority* for each. The processing priority specifies the order to which GPOs are processed. As the GPOs are processed, the GPO with the lowest processing number, which is the highest priority, will override any of the other GPOs' settings that are linked to the same location with the exception of those GPOs that have the Enforced options enabled. Compare Figure 6.5 with Figure 6.8. In Figure 6.9, the processing priorities of the three GPOs linked at the Accounting OU are set so that the Accounting Registry & File GPO has the lowest processing priority. Yet because the Enforced option is set, you can see in Figure 6.5 that the Group Policy Inheritance tab lists it with a higher priority than the other two GPOs.

Enabling Loopback

Some computers within an organization should only be used for certain purposes. Kiosks will have access to public information, but because they are usually accessible to the general public, you may not want such computers to have the ability to access sensitive corporate information.

You may encounter other computers that need to have user settings applied to the computer no matter which user is logged on. To enforce these settings, the *loopback* feature is used. Once enabled, the settings from the User Configuration portion of the Group Policy object that is applied to the computer's OU will take precedence instead of the User Configuration settings at the user's OU.

FIGURE 6.8   Priorities for GPOs attached to the Accounting OU

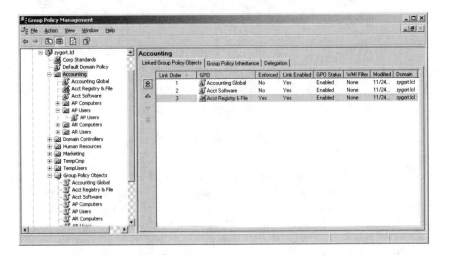

FIGURE 6.9   Processing order for GPOs at the Accounting OU

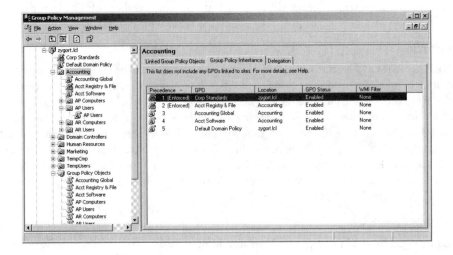

There are two methods of applying the settings once loopback processing has been enabled. The first, Merge, consolidates all of the settings from the user's and computer's GPOs, and any settings that conflict, the computer's setting will apply. The second method is Replace. When Replace is chosen, the user's settings are not processed. Instead, the computer's settings are applied, thus restricting the user account to just those settings that are allowed by the computer's GPO settings.

Options for Linking Group Policies

At this point in your MCSE studies, you should know that GPOs can be linked at the site, domain, or OU level. Although there are reasons you would want to do so, linking at the site or domain level is usually not suggested. Linking at the OU level allows you to efficiently control the GPOs and how they are applied to users and computers. Of course there are always exceptions.

The primary exception is the security settings that are applied at the domain level. You'll recall that the Default Domain Policy is where the password requirements, account lockout settings, and Kerberos policy settings are configured. These settings are then applied throughout the domain and cannot be overridden. This is the reason that a separate domain must be created if any settings within these options need to be different between user accounts.

As a general rule, you should not make changes to the Default Domain Policy with the exception of setting the account policy options settings. If any settings will define corporate standards other than the account policy settings and you want to apply them at the domain level, create a new policy for these settings. Although this goes against the recommendation that you use the fewest GPOs possible, it will allow you to have a central point to access the account policies for the domain and separate out any other policy settings that are applied. Another reason is that this gives you the ability to re-create the Default Domain Policy if it becomes damaged.

Included with Windows Server 2003 is a utility called `dcgpofix.exe`. This command line utility will re-create the Default Domain Policy and the Default Domain Controller Policy if necessary. It will not create either policy with any modified settings; it will only re-create the policy with the initial default settings that are applied when the first domain controller in the domain is brought online. Keeping this in mind, only make changes to the security settings that are applied to either of these two policies and make sure the settings are documented. After running `dcgpofix.exe`, the settings that define the corporate security standards can then be reset.

If you were to add settings to the Default Domain Policy, and then run `dcgpofix.exe`, the settings would be lost and you would have to re-create them. However, if you were to create a new Group Policy and add the settings to it instead, when the Default Domain Policy is re-created, the new Group Policy would not be affected. The same rule holds true for the Default Domain Controllers Policy. Because some settings should be applied to domain controllers to ensure their security, do not edit the settings on this Group Policy. The `dcgpofix.exe` utility can be used to regenerate this policy as well.

For more information on dcgpofix.exe and how to regenerate the Default Domain Policy and Default Domain Controllers Policy, look within the Windows Server 2003 Help files.

Design Scenario

Defining GPOs

Amber Film Distributors is planning an Active Directory infrastructure that will tie together all of their wholesale distribution warehouses. A single forest with a single domain design has been decided upon. The OU structure is based upon departments within the organization. Each department has child OUs based upon the locations where the department is located. They are in the process of deciding upon how much they are going to use GPOs to maintain their environment. Some of the settings that have been decided upon are listed here:

- Every user in the domain will need to use strong passwords and have an account lockout setting of three attempts.

- Every user must have antivirus software installed on their system.

- The Accounting computers will have an accounting software package installed.

- The Human Resources personnel can only access the Human Resources database server using IPSec encryption.

- All users will have the Control Panel option removed from their computers with the exception of technical administrators.

1. **Question:** When deciding upon the settings that will be used within the corporate standards GPO, which of the settings should be combined? **Answer:** The software installation setting on the GPO making up the corporate standards will include the antivirus software. Another GPO should be created for the removal of the Control Panel options. Password and lockout restrictions should be set within the Default Domain Policy.

2. **Question:** Where should the GPOs for corporate standards be linked? **Answer:** They should be linked at the domain level so that all users in the domain will have the policies applied to them.

3. **Question:** Which user accounts should have the policies applied to them? **Answer:** The corporate standards GPO that includes the antivirus software installation setting should be set so that authenticated users have it applied to them whereas the GPO with the Control Panel removal setting should be applied to a group that includes all users in the domain with the exception of any administrative user accounts.

4. **Question:** Are there special GPOs that should be linked to OUs? And if so, which setting should be added to GPOs linked to those OUs? **Answer:** The Accounting OU should have a GPO created that includes the software installation for the accounting software. The Human Resources OU should have two OUs, one for client workstations and one for servers. A GPO that requires IPSec communication should be linked to the servers OU and another GPO that uses the IPSec client policy should be linked to the workstation OU.

As a general rule of thumb, when planning where the policies should be linked, if the policy applies to a large number of users, link it at the parent OU. If the policy applies to a discreet subset of users, link the policy at the child OU. This should alleviate the need to have elaborate filtering and blocking schemes that will affect the natural inheritance of GPOs.

Creating the OU Structure

When creating the OU structure, you need to base it primarily on administrative needs. Although we keep hitting on that point, it cannot be stressed enough. You should build the OU structure to make the administration of the domain as easy and efficient as possible. You can create GPOs to take advantage of the administrative structure of the OUs, and you can create additional OUs if the Group Policy requirements dictate it, but do so sparingly.

Two containers exist within Active Directory: the Users container and the Computers container. If a user or computer account is created and an OU membership is not specified, then the user account is created in the Users container and the computer account are created in the Computers container. GPOs cannot be set on these containers. The only GPOs that will apply to these users are the settings applied at the site or domain level. If you are following the recommendation that GPOs be applied at the OU level as much as possible, these users and computers will not be under the jurisdiction of GPOs that would otherwise control what the accounts can do.

To avoid this scenario, Microsoft has included two utilities with Windows Server 2003: redirusr.exe and redircmp.exe. As you can probably tell from their names, these utilities redirect the accounts to OUs that you specify instead of the default containers. However, there is one caveat to using these utilities: the domain has to be at the Windows 2003 functional level. Unfortunately, not many organizations are ready to move to this functional level. Those that have had the good fortune to change their domain functional level to Window 2003 will find that they can take advantage of creating new OUs for controlling those new user and computer accounts.

For more information about the redirusr.exe and redircmp.exe commands, see TechNet article 324949, Redirecting the Users and Computers Containers in Windows Server 2003 Domains.

After redirecting new accounts to the new OUs, the rest of the OU structure needs can be identified. Most of the OU structure should already be designed because it is based on the administrative structure of the organization. In Chapter 5, we discussed creating the top-level OUs based on a static aspect of the organization. This still holds true for Group Policy design. If the top-level OUs are based on either locations or functions, the structure is resistant to change. The child OUs can then reflect the administrative requirements. This allows for the administrative staff to have efficient control of those objects they need to manage.

GPOs will use this structure, but other OUs may need to be created to further enhance the Group Policy requirements. Do be careful when you create additional OUs to implement Group Policy. The more layers in the hierarchy, the harder it is to manage the objects within. Remember, the key to the OU structure is to make administrative tasks easier. Investigate all of the possible options when you are determining how to apply GPOs.

New OUs should be added to the OU structure only if they enhance the application of GPOs and make the assignment of settings and restrictions to a group of users or computers easier than if they were linked at an existing OU. Use the Group Policy Modeling Wizard within the GPMC to determine if the application of policies is going to work as you expect it to. Experiment with the linkage of GPOs at those OUs that you already have defined. View the results and see which accounts are adversely affected before determining that an additional OU is required. You may find that filtering the GPO to a new group that you create allows you to assign settings to those users within that group while keeping the users within the OU instead of creating a new OU to host them.

Those users who need to create and link the OUs will need the appropriate rights delegated to them. You will also need to identify how you are going to maintain the GPOs and monitor how the GPOs are administered. Once the OU structure has been identified for applying Group Policy, the staff who will be responsible for the creation and maintenance of the GPOs will need rights delegated to them and training provided. If you are delegating the ability to perform specific functions to those users who are working with GPOs, you can give them the ability to create GPOs, edit GPOs, and link GPOS. One user could have the ability to perform all three functions, or you could break the functions up so that only certain users can perform an individual task. The following section will describe how you can design your GPO management for delegated administration.

Identifying Administrative Requirements

In smaller organizations, the same administrator who creates user accounts will maintain the servers and work with the GPOs. Such an administrator, sometimes known as the Jack-of-All-Trades administrator, does it all. For this type of administration, identifying who is going to perform the tasks is simple. That administrator has to make sure that they are trained to perform the tasks at hand. In larger environments, however, one administrator cannot do it all. Usually specific tasks are assigned to users, and they are responsible for their own little piece of the organization. In this case, the users who are delegated the tasks of maintaining GPOs have to be trained on the proper methods of maintaining the Group Policy infrastructure.

Training Users

Different users can be assigned to create GPOs than those who are allowed to link the GPOs. In larger organizations where specialized job functions are assigned to employees, or in organizations that use the hybrid administrative model, users who are in charge of corporate standards can be allowed to create unlinked GPOS and modify GPOs with the settings determined by the corporate administration. The domain and OU owners are then responsible for linking the appropriate GPOs to their OUs or domains.

When you delegate the permission to perform actions on GPOs to users other than administrators who already have that ability, you need to make sure that you are giving the users permission to do so only for the portion of Active Directory that they are responsible for. Within the GPMC, you can delegate the ability to link GPOs at the site, domain, or OU level. By changing permissions within the discretionary access control list for the GPO, you can control who is able to edit the GPO. By granting someone the Read and Write permissions, that user could modify settings within the GPO. Figure 6.10 shows the Delegation tab within the GPMC for an OU.

FIGURE 6.10   Delegation tab for an OU

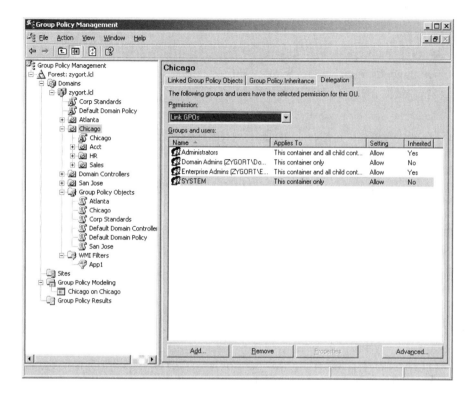

There is a special group that exists to make the task of delegating the creation of GPOs easier; the Group Policy Creator Owners group. When a user is added to this group, they will be able to modify any GPO that they create, but they will not be able to link the GPO anywhere within Active Directory unless they have been delegated the right to do so at a site, domain, or OU.

When employees are granted the ability to create, modify, and/or link GPOs, they should be trained on the proper methods of handling their responsibilities. Guidelines for the functions that can be performed should be explained to the OU owners, domain owners, and forest owners. Without a basic set of guidelines, users could inadvertently make changes or create GPOs that will not function properly within your environment. Document the guidelines that you want to use and make sure everyone involved understands them.

The Group Policy administration training methodology should include best practices for the following topics:

- Creating GPOs

- Importing settings

- Editing settings

- Linking GPOs

- Setting exceptions for inheritance

- Filtering accounts
- Using the Group Policy Modeling Wizard
- Using the Group Policy Results Wizard
- Backing up and restoring GPOs
- Learning which settings apply to specific operating systems
- Using WMI filters
- Handling security templates

If users understand how each of these work, they will have a better understanding of why GPOs should be implemented the way they are, and as a result, the troubleshooting required to determine problems should ease. The more training and understanding that goes on before the users are allowed to create and maintain GPOs, the less time will be spent troubleshooting later in the life cycle of Active Directory.

Identifying Required Permissions

For the most part, GPOs should be linked at the OU level. This allows you to use the most versatile method of controlling how the settings are applied. Sometimes you will find that the best method of applying policies is performed if the policy is linked at the site or domain level. As mentioned previously, the account policies are always set at the domain level. You may also find a reason to link them at the site level, such as when all computers at the site need to have an IPSec policy applied to them.

In order for a GPO to be linked at the site level, the administrator who is performing the linking has to have enterprise-level permissions or have the permission to link to the site delegated to them. Adding an account to the Domain Admins global group or Administrators domain local group at the root domain or Enterprise Admins universal group is not a recommended practice unless that administrative account is the forest owner.

Administrative staff responsible for linking at the domain level will need to be members of the Domain Admins global group or have the Manage Group Policy Links permission delegated to them. Members of the Domain Admins global group will also be able to use the GPMC and edit any GPOs for their domain. To have access to GPOs for any other domain, they will need permissions delegated to them for the objects within the other domains, or they will need to be members of the Enterprise Admins universal group.

Policies linked at the OU level require the administrative staff to be members of the Domain Admins global group for the domain or have the proper permissions delegated to them to work with GPOs.

Controlling Change Management

No discussion of GPOs would be complete without touching on the need to have *change management procedures* in place. Change management procedures are rules that are used to control when and where changes can be made to GPOs. GPOs assist in the administrative control over users and computers and should be treated as a critical part of your Active Directory environment.

🌐 Real World Scenario

Controlling Group Policy Application

Karlee Hospital is in the design phase of their Windows 2003 Active Directory upgrade. The forest and domain designs have already been decided upon; an empty root forest will be created to host the forest administrators only. Each of the entities that make up the organization has a subdomain structure based on the business units. The forest root domain uses the domain name `karlee.local`. The insurance division has a domain called `insurance.karlee.local` and the clinic has `clinic.karlee.local` as its domain name.

Several administrators responsible for the rollout of Active Directory have been identified as the forest owners. It has been decided by the design team that they will not have the time to oversee the Group Policy structure for all of the organizations. Domain owners will have the ability to control GPOs within their domain and have the right to delegate out the ability to create and link GPOs to administrators within the domain.

Administrators who are OU owners are allowed to create, link, and maintain GPOs. They are also allowed to run the Group Policy Modeling Wizard to determine if the GPOs will work correctly within the hospital's environment. Prior to making any changes to the GPO structure, however, they need to submit a change request to the forest owners who will in turn verify that the change is necessary.

Changing a setting within a GPO could affect the way users are allowed to work or how they are controlled within the network. Without change management procedures in place, users who control GPOs will not have the proper procedures to follow when implementing changes.

In the following sections we will discuss what goes into the change management procedures and why they are important.

Change Procedures

When setting up your change management procedures, you should create a Group Policy change approval committee. The members of this committee should understand how GPOs function and know the Group Policy requirements of the organization. Earlier in this chapter, in the section Understanding the Company's Objectives, we discussed the organization's objectives and why they need to have GPOs. This committee should follow the objectives and make sure that any changes follow the requirements of the organization.

Before creating a change request, the user who is requesting the change should identify exactly why the change should be enacted. Sometimes this change could be something as simple as a change to the menu options available on the Start menu, or as extensive as a new software rollout. Most medium and large companies create a change request form that the user has to fill out and submit.

The change request form should contain the reason for the change request and when it needs to be implemented. It should also include information that will identify the users or computers affected by the change. This information is necessary so that proper testing of the change can take place. Without proper testing, changes could affect the users or computers in unforeseen ways.

Backing Up and Restoring GPOs

While reading through this text, you may think that this section is pretty basic, but there are still things that need to be said about backing up and restoring GPOs. Any change to a GPO could have detrimental effects on the users and computers to which the policy is applied. Having a good backup of the original GPOs will allow you to replace a misconfigured or damaged policy very quickly.

A feature of the GPMC is the ability to back up and restore GPOs without having to retrieve them from a system backup. The backup function will back up both the Active Directory GPO and the Sysvol Group Policy Template. When restored, both parts of the GPO are returned to their proper locations. Part of the change procedures that are put into place should include training the technical staff who are responsible for maintaining GPOs on how to back up and restore using the GPMC.

At the same time, a procedure should be put into place that will identify how the backups will be saved. Sometimes problems with a change will not manifest themselves for days or weeks. Once a change is discovered, there should be a way to reverse it so that the original settings are available once again. Creating a backup scheme that will allow you to keep several revisions of GPOs could save you from administrative hassles and help maintain SLAs.

In the "Linking GPOs" Design Scenario, you will need to identify the requirements for the users to be able to create and link GPOs at different levels within an organization's Active Directory.

 Design Scenario

Linking GPOs

Tom is responsible for linking GPOs within Active Directory. However, he is not allowed to create the GPOs; this is the responsibility of two members of a Standards and Practices Committee— Susan and DeAnn. After DeAnn creates a GPO and Susan has thoroughly tested it using the Group Policy Modeling Wizard, they notify Tom that he needs to link it to a site within Active Directory.

1. **Question:** What level of permissions is required by Susan and DeAnn? **Answer:** They need to be members of the Group Policy Creator Owners group or be granted permission to create GPOs in a specified domain. If they have the proper permissions to do so, they will be able to work with the GPOs they create, but will not have the ability to link them.

2. **Question:** Which utilities could Susan and DeAnn use? **Answer:** They need to have the GPMC in order to run the Group Policy Modeling Wizard. DeAnn could use the Group Policy Object Editor in the MMC to create the GPO.

3. **Question:** What permissions must Tom have to link the GPO? **Answer:** Because Tom is linking the GPO to a site, he must either have Enterprise-level administrative rights or have the Manage Group Policy Links permission delegated to him for that particular site.

Summary

Although the design basis for OUs should be the administrative structure of the organization, Group Policy will also play a part in the final design. Additional OUs may need to be created so that the appropriate settings and restrictions can be enforced automatically within the Active Directory structure, while alleviating some of the administrative requirements imposed upon the staff who maintain user and computer accounts.

Understanding what settings need to be applied based on an organization's objectives is key to a well-designed OU structure for a Group Policy application. You should identify the security requirements, software installation needs, and user restrictions that are to go into effect. The design should take on the simplest approach possible. Make sure to condense settings into as few GPOs as possible while following the corporate standards and identifying the requirements of each job function and the responsibilities of those functions.

Using the natural inheritance will make the GPO structure easy to maintain. Those users who are allowed to maintain GPOs should be trained on how to effectively manage GPOs using this inheritance. They should also be trained on how the company maintains the GPOs and what is required before a change can be made to the GPO structure.

In the next chapter, we are going to delve into the naming requirements for accounts in Active Directory as well as how to control the resources to which those accounts have access. We will use the information we have learned up to this point to design an account strategy. This strategy will make sense for all who need to provide administrative control over objects within Active Directory and the network resources that the objects represent.

Exam Essentials

Understand the company's objectives. The company's objectives will be based on the requirements defined by the company. These objectives will be based on the security requirements, software installation needs, and user restrictions.

Be able to create a simple design by identifying user requirements. The design should take into account what the user requires to perform their function. The users will be limited by and controlled by the corporate standards, the employee's job functions, and the job requirements.

Be able to create a simple design by minimizing GPOs. Settings for GPOs should be condensed into as few GPOs as possible to make computer startup and user logon times acceptable.

Be able to use natural inheritance in your design. Planning for the inheritance of settings and minimizing the options that change the inheritance of settings will make troubleshooting of GPO problems easier.

Understand the linking options for Group Policy. GPOs can be linked at the site, domain, or OU level. When linked, they will follow the natural inheritance unless the options for Enforced, Block Inheritance, or Filtering are used.

Identify administrative requirements for creating the OU structure.   All users should be trained on how GPOs function and should understand the company's best practices that are used when maintaining the Group Policy structure.

Be able to create a change management procedure.   GPOs are a vital part of most company's Active Directory implementation. A change management procedure should be put into place so that the changes can be tested and approved prior to their implementation.

Key Terms

Before you take the exam, be certain you are familiar with the following terms:

account lockout restrictions	inheritance
block Inheritance	loopback
change management	processing priority
corporate standards	Service Level Agreement (SLA)
Default Domain Policy	strong passwords
filtering	user restrictions
Group Policy Management Console (GPMC)	

Review Questions

1. After assigning an application in a GPO that is linked to an organizational unit, you instruct the users to look for the application in their Start menu. They do not see the application. What do you need to do in order for the application to show up?

   A. From a command prompt, issue the command `gpedit /refreshpolicy machine_policy`

   B. Change the rights for the user in question, giving them the Apply Group Policy right.

   C. Instruct the user to reboot their computer.

   D. Instruct the user to logoff and logon again.

2. To which of the following locations can GPOs be linked? (Choose all that apply.)

   A. Sites

   B. Domains

   C. Forests

   D. OUs

3. A member of your administration team has edited the Default Domain Policy and the edit had an adverse affect. How can you restore the Default Domain Policy to its original settings?

   A. Use the `dcpgofix` utility.

   B. Restore the Default Domain Policy from the system state of the latest good backup.

   C. Restore the Default Domain Policy by using the Group Policy Management Console.

   D. Restore the Default Domain Policy by using Automated System Recovery.

4. If you want to delegate authority to link GPOs at the domain level but do not want to add the user to the Domain Admins group, which of the following permissions should you give them?

   A. Group Policy Administrator permission

   B. Group Policy Owner permission

   C. Manage Group Policy Links permission

   D. Group Policy Edit permission

5. You have edited the Default Domain Policy and decide that you should make a backup of your changes in case something happens so that you can easily restore it. Which utility should you use to back up and restore the Default Domain Policy?

   A. Automated System Recovery (ASR)

   B. `dcgpofix`

   C. Windows 2003 Backup

   D. GPMC

6. You decide to set account lockout restrictions via Group Policy. Where will you link the GPO?

   A. At the site level

   B. At the domain level

   C. At the OU level

   D. At the forest level

7. You have all of your users separated into OUs based on job function and department. You decide to create a GPO and configure it to publish an application to everyone in the Accounting group so that when they click on a file that is associated with the application, the application will automatically load onto their system. Your accounting staff has ten employees in the main office, and one each in two other branches. Both branches are connected via a fast WAN connection that is not overconsumed. The application is only 2.5 MB and you have determined that it will not adversely affect the WAN link. Where is the best place to link the GPO?

   A. Link it to the main office site at the site level, and have the other two users in accounting install the software via a network share.

   B. Link it to the Accounting OU and do nothing more.

   C. Link it to the domain and instruct the accounting users to install the software. You should tell them to let you know when it is installed so that you can remove the link from the GPO.

   D. Link it at the forest level and set security on the install directory to only allow the Accounting group.

8. You have a network that consists of ten locations. All locations have sites defined. All users are grouped into OUs by job function and department. You have three domains in your forest. Your Atlanta, Detroit, and Cleveland offices have their own domains. Each of the ten offices holds users from every department in the company. You decide to implement IPSec settings for the Atlanta office, and you create a GPO with those settings. Where can you link the GPO? (Choose all that apply.)

   A. At the site level

   B. At the OU level

   C. At the domain level

   D. At the forest level

9. Software can be installed automatically by Group Policy as long as which of the following requirements is met?

   A. The software is in a compressed format to reduce bandwidth across a WAN link.

   B. The software was written to take advantage of IntelliMirror.

   C. The forest is at Windows 2003 forest functional level.

   D. The user installing the software has the Group Policy installation right.

10. You are the administrator of a Windows Server 2003 forest that has three domains. You would like the members of the Domain Admins global group from the other domains to create GPOs for their own domains, but you would like final approval before they are implemented on the live network. The domain admins at the forest level should be the only users who have the ability to apply GPOs. What would be the best choice for this situation?

A. Remove the users in question from the Domain Admins group of their respective domains.

B. Add the Domain Admins group from the remote domain to the Forest Admins group of the forest and take away the Link Group Policy Object right.

C. Remove the Link Group Policy Object right from the users in the Domain Admins group for each child domain.

D. Create a new group called Group Policy Test. Add all Domain Admins groups from all domains to that group. Remove the Link Group Policy Object right from the group.

Answers to Review Questions

1. D. Application assignment takes effect at logon only, so the user will need to log on and log off their computer for the changes to apply.

2. A, B, D. GPOs can only be applied to sites, domains, and OUs.

3. A. The command line utility dcgpofix.exe is a new utility that is included with Windows Server 2003. It allows an administrator to restore the Default Domain Policy.

4. C. In order to link GPOs at the domain level, a user will need to be a member of the Domain Admins global group, or have the Manage Group Policy Links permission delegated to them.

5. D. The GPMC allows you the ability to back up and restore GPOs. This utility lets you back up and restore custom GPOs, as well as the built-in Default Domain Policy and Default Domain Controllers Policy. If you have modified the Default Domain Policy or the Default Domain Controllers Policy, the GPMC's backup and restore policy can recover the changed policies so that you do not lose your changes. This is a better solution than dcgpofix, because dcgpofix will only let you restore the Default Domain Policy and Default Domain Controllers Policy back to their default settings. Windows 2003 Backup will back up and restore the system state of the server, but not individual GPOs and ASR will back up and restore the operating system in case of a disaster, but just like Backup, it will not back up the individual GPOs.

6. B. Although there are guidelines when it comes to linking GPOs, there are also times when linking at certain levels is required. Some settings, such as account lockout settings, can only be set at the domain level. You will not be able to set any of the account policy, lockout policy or Kerberos policy settings anywhere but the Default Domain Policy.

7. B. Based on the criteria listed in the question, it would make the most sense to link the GPO at the Accounting OU. The majority of users are located in one office, and only two users are located at remote branches. Both of those branches have fast connections, so installation is not going to overconsume bandwidth on the WAN links.

8. A, C. Because the Atlanta office has its own domain and its own site, either of these locations would suffice.

9. B. IntelliMirror is a Microsoft technology that Group Policy takes advantage of to push out software packages. In order for Group Policy to automate application installation, the software must be written with IntelliMirror in mind.

10. C. The Domain Admins group will have rights to edit GPOs for their own domain. If you remove the Link Group Policy Object right from the users in the Domain Admins group, they will be able to edit existing GPOs and create new GPOs, but they will not be able to implement new GPOs. (However, smart administrators will be able to change their permissions back!)

Case Study

You should give yourself 20 minutes to review this testlet, and complete the questions.

Background

Insane Systems builds custom computers for their customers. They specialize in building cases that are unique and support the latest in hardware technology. They started off as a small company that provided this service to gamers who would take their cases to LAN parties to show off. Because their systems were considered some of the most stable gaming platforms and they provided an impressive design that gamers could show off, they started to become popular. Insane Systems started mass manufacturing some of their more popular designs and began selling standalone cases along with their fully configured systems. As space at the company became a premium, the office was moved from the manufacturing facility. This allowed the company to add to the amount of space that was used for the mass production line.

Over the past few months, Insane Systems has been developing plans to expand their company. They have identified San Jose, Atlanta, and New York City as the locations with their highest customer base. The current Chicago location will remain the corporate headquarters, but they are opening branches in New York City and San Jose. They are also in the process of acquiring a competitor's business in Atlanta. These locations will provide retail outlets as well as support. Customers will have the option of sending their systems back to the corporate office for upgrades or repairs, or delivering them to one of the branch locations.

Because the company is planning on expanding, they want to make sure that the network infrastructure is in place to support their larger, distributed company. They are also concerned with the support lifetime of their current Windows NT 4 infrastructure. They realize they have the option of moving to a Windows 2000 or Windows Server 2003 infrastructure and are considering moving to Windows Server 2003 and Active Directory for two reasons: the expected support lifetime is greater than Windows 2000, and they are a technology firm that is not afraid of staying ahead of the technology curve.

Part of the expansion of the company is a complete overhaul of their current Internet presence. They are planning on bringing all of the web development and hosting in-house. Currently a web hosting service is providing their Internet presence, and Insane Systems feels as though they could provide better marketing and support information for their customers if they had control over their own website. Insane Systems would also like to change the name of their website to better represent their name in the marketplace. They own the name `insane-systems.com`.

Interviews

Your company has been hired to design an Active Directory infrastructure and the network infrastructure to support it. During the interview process with some of the key stakeholders, you gathered the following information:

CEO   Currently we have a single location with all of our processes local. As we grow, we would like to keep all of the administration here in Chicago. Because the new branches are primarily retail and support offices, we will not need to have a large staff in those locations. The Atlanta office has an existing network that we would like to merge into our network. System design, research and development, and patent information come from the Atlanta office, so a secure connection from Atlanta to Chicago must be implemented.

CIO   Most of the infrastructure that we support is located here at the corporate office. We do support some key servers at the manufacturing location. We support these servers from our main office. Because the servers are nearby, if there is a problem, we can usually be onsite within half an hour.

The new branches are going to be another issue altogether. We would like to retain the same level of administrative control over the servers in the new locations that we employ currently. Due to the geographic limitations, we may need to have some support staff at those locations. Currently, the plan is to hire staff at those locations who can provide the support for the customers, but also have an understanding of the business systems we need to put into place. We would like to automate software installations to the remote offices due to the lack of IT staff.

Manager of Information Technology   We have grown very quickly over the past three years and our current technologies have kept up with that growth. However, we don't think the current infrastructure is ready for the amount of growth that we are expecting within the following year. We are not afraid of moving to the latest technology, but we want to make sure that the design is stable and makes sense for us, especially if we will continue growing in the upcoming months. And because we are losing support for NT 4, we want to make sure that we have an operating system that will be supported for a few years down the road.

Most of our processes are located here at this office, and we would like to keep it that way. We know that some servers will need to be located at the remote offices, but we would like to be able to provide most of the support from this location. Remote administration tools will need to be included within the design so that we can keep our administrative costs to a minimum.

Currently, we have most of our servers located at the main office, and all are located on their own high-speed backbone. We do have a server at the manufacturing site that allows the staff there to have e-mail as well as plans and orders in case we lose connectivity between the offices. This server is running Exchange 5.5. Several times during the day we replicate the public folder information to this system so that they are always up to date and do not have to dial up to the main office using our 56Kbps modem.

The systems at the main office are all supported by our staff of four administrators. All of the administrators are cross-trained on Windows NT 4, Exchange 5.5, SQL Server 7, our accounting software, and each of our file and print servers. We currently have several Windows NT 4 servers in place, including one Exchange 5.5 server at both locations, one SQL Server 7 server at the main office, one server running our accounting package that interfaces with the SQL Server, and one file and print server that is used by both locations. The Exchange server at the manufacturing location doubles as a print server also.

The Atlanta office currently has a Windows NT 4 domain, and we will migrate that domain into our forest. Although administration of the forest will be moved to the Chicago branch, administration of the Atlanta domain will reside in the Atlanta domain. We will have a very small IT staff in the Atlanta office who will need control all aspects of the Atlanta domain. Administrators of the Atlanta domain will have control over the Atlanta domain only and will not have administrator access to any other domain or any other part of the forest. All communication between the Atlanta office and the Chicago office will take place via an IPSec connection. The users in the Atlanta office will also require different password and lockout restrictions than the other offices.

Because all of the client machines are running Windows NT 4 Workstation, we do not have to worry about supporting different operating systems. We would like to maintain that same easy administration with the upcoming system. We would like to provide the same types of services at the remote locations that we provide at the home office, although accounting will remain at the home office and will not be spread out to all of the locations.

Existing Infrastructure

After investigating the current infrastructure, you have determined that the following servers are in place:

Home Office

Primary Domain Controller (PDC)

Backup Domain Controller (BDC)

DHCP server

DNS/WINS server

Exchange 5.5 server

SQL Server 7

Systems Management Server 2

File server

Print/Antivirus server

Research and Development File server

Atlanta Office

Primary Domain Controller (PDC)

Backup Domain Controller (BDC)

WINS server

File server

Manufacturing Facility

Backup Domain Controller (BDC)

DNS/WINS/DHCP Relay Agent server

Exchange 5.5/File server

The Corporate Office hosts nearly 250 Windows NT 4 workstations at this point. They are interconnected by several 48-port 10/100Mbps switches. A router is used to divide the network into four broadcast domains (VLANs). One of these broadcast domains is the 1Gbps backbone on which the servers reside. Each of the servers is connected to a 1Gbps switch port. This location takes advantage of private IP address ranges. The servers are located on the 192.168.1.0/24 subnet. The client systems are divided between network addresses 192.168.10.0/24, 192.168.11.0/24, 192.168.12.0/24, and 192.168.13.0/24.

The manufacturing facility contains 12 Windows NT 4 workstations connected to the same switch as the servers. Because Insane Systems does not want to slow down production due to a communication failure, they have taken advantage of Exchange 5.5's public folder replication. Public folders are continually updated with the latest orders. The crew foreman can access the orders locally from these public folders at any time, whether the communication link between the locations is up or not. This location uses another address range—192.168.20.0/24.

Case Study Questions

1. You want to install the administrative tools on the computers of all members of the IT department, in all locations. What is the best way to accomplish this task?

    A. Create a GPO to assign the `adminpak.msi` program to users. Link the GPO to the OU that holds the IT user objects.

    B. Place the `adminpak.msi` on a network share and instruct administrator users to install it from that location.

    C. Create a GPO to assign the `adminpak.msi` program to computers. Link the GPO to the OU where the IT computers reside.

    D. Create a GPO to assign the `adminpak.msi` program to computers. Link the GPO to the domain where the IT computers reside.

2. How would you ensure IPSec communication between the Atlanta and Chicago offices? (Choose all that apply.)

    A. Create a GPO with the IPSec settings and link it to the Atlanta site.

    B. Create a GPO with the IPSec settings and link it to the OU.

    C. Place all of the servers from the Atlanta office into an OU and link the GPO to that OU.

    D. Place the server providing the VPN connection to Chicago in an OU and link the GPO to that OU.

3. Once corporate standards are applied and defined in a GPO, where should that GPO be linked?

    A. At the OUs where the user accounts reside in each domain within the forest.

    B. At the domain level of the root domain of the forest.

    C. At the sites for each location.

    D. At the domain level of each domain in the forest. It should be copied and linked at each domain in the forest.

4. Assign the following group policies to the appropriate locations within Active Directory.

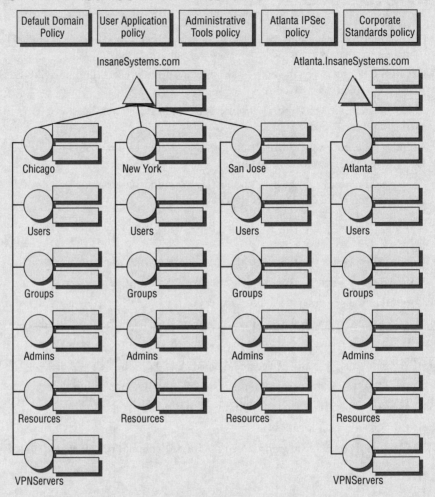

Answers to Case Study Questions

1. A. Group Policy allows you to define a GPO that contains software installation settings and to link that GPO to an OU, a site, or domain. Because you are planning on rolling out the administrative tools only to users with administrative needs, you should create a GPO that has the software installation option set for users and link it to the OU where the administrative users are located.

2. B, D. The communication between the two locations needs to be encrypted, but internal communication between clients and servers within the Atlanta office was not defined as needing encrypted communication. Therefore, a server acting as a VPN server would best fit the needs, and the IPSec GPO should be applied to it.

3. D. Corporate standards are settings that will apply to all users in the domain. When a user logs on to the domain, these settings should take effect, no matter where the user logs on. In order to accomplish this, the same settings must be in place on all domains in the forest. The GPO should be copied to all domains and linked at the root of each domain.

4.

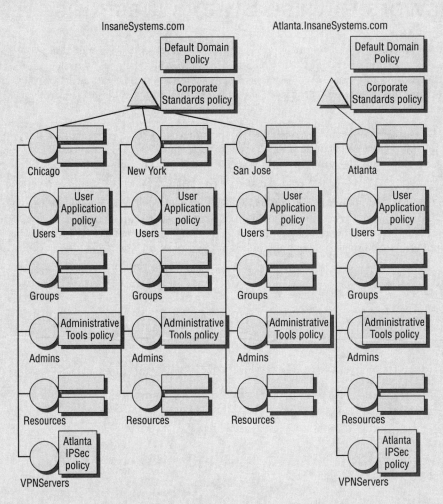

The Default Domain Policy will always be applied at the domain level. The Corporate Standards GPO should be linked at the domain level also so that all users are under the control of these settings. Because each of the locations will be using a standard set of applications, the User Application policy should be copied to each domain and linked to the Users OU. The Administrative Tools GPO should be linked at the Admins OU so that all of the administrative staff will have the administrative tools added to computers where they log on. The Atlanta IPSec policy should be copied to each domain and linked to the VPNServers OU in each domain.

Chapter

7

Designing Accounts Access and Management

MICROSOFT EXAM OBJECTIVES COVERED IN THIS CHAPTER

✓ **Design a security group strategy.**

- Define the scope of a security group to meet requirements.
- Define resource access requirements.
- Define administrative access requirements.
- Define user roles.

✓ **Design a user and computer authentication strategy.**

- Identify common authentication requirements.
- Select authentication mechanisms.

✓ **Design a user and computer account strategy.**

- Specify account policy requirements.
- Specify account requirements for users, computers, administrators, and services.

Forests, domains, and organizational units (OUs) make up the pieces of Active Directory that we have discussed up to this point. Starting at the highest level in the logical structure of our Active Directory infrastructure, we have made design decisions that have led us to a functional design that will allow us to have an efficient administrative structure. When combined with group policies, these decisions can ensure that the management of user, group, and computer accounts is just as efficient.

As we evaluated the administrative needs of an organization, we identified the resources that need to be managed and the employees who will manage the objects. Using this information, we can continue to build on our design by determining which accounts—User, Group, and Computer—need to be identified and the policies that we will use to create and manage them. This chapter introduces the options for account creation policies, group management policies, and the options for administrative control.

Planning Account Creation

As with any part of the design phase, you should determine the requirements for creating specific objects. This time, we are going to discuss the account creation options. Every organization will approach this differently; however, you should follow a few guidelines when creating User, Group, or Computer accounts.

Table 7.1 shows the five types of accounts within Active Directory.

TABLE 7.1 Accounts within Active Directory

Icon	Account Type	Description
	User	Allows a person to be authenticated by Active Directory or on a local computer and lets them access the resources.
	InetOrgPerson	Similar to the User account type, but also allows for integration with other LDAP-based directory services such as Novell's NDS or IBM's iPlanet servers.
	Contact	Represents a person who is external to the Active Directory forest While a contact cannot be granted permission to access objects, they do show up in address books and can be added to distribution lists when Exchange is implemented.

TABLE 7.1   Accounts within Active Directory *(continued)*

Icon	Account Type	Description
	Computer	Represents a physical computer that is member within the Active Directory forest.
	Group	Made up of a collection of User, Computer, or Group accounts that have the same resource access requirements.

When using Active Directory Users and Computers to create accounts, make sure that the name of the account reflects what the account represents and the type of account it is. A *naming strategy* consists of the rules that need to be followed when you are identifying an account. As you can see from the preceding descriptions, each of the account types has a unique icon that represents it within the management tools, so you will be able to tell a User account from a Computer account. Groups can pose an interesting problem, however. When we discuss group creation later in this chapter under the section "Determining Group Requirements for Resource Access," you will find that multiple group types as well as scopes can be chosen based upon the functionality they require. All groups appear within the management tools with the same icon. The naming strategy you employ needs to address this.

Another rule you should follow involves populating as much account information as possible. This includes the Description field. Many designers will not address this field within the design specifications because they think it is superfluous. Although a good naming strategy should make identifying accounts easy, you'll come across instances when accounts will have names that are very close to the same—the description could be the only way to tell them apart.

You should always start determining your account creation strategy based upon the existing account structure. This allows you to understand how the current accounts are created and what the current policies are. It will also allow you to conclude where the limitations of the strategy lie.

In the following section, we will look at how to identify the current account structure, as well as how to determine a naming strategy and an account authentication policy.

Identifying Current Account Structure

At this point within the design phase, you should have already identified the resources that exist within the organization so that you could make the proper decisions for designing the forest, domain, and OU structure. You also should have identified the administrative design as well as those employees who perform the administrative functions. If an organization is currently running another network operating system, such as NT 4, Windows 2000, Novell NetWare, or even a Windows peer-to-peer network, you may be able to transfer some of the current design to the new design.

You should study the current naming strategy for all of the account types in use. Some may not exist within the current design. For example, a peer-to-peer environment may not include Group accounts; the resources may have access granted directly to User accounts. A Windows NT 4 equivalent to the InetOrgPerson account does not exist, and is not available in a Windows 2000 Active Directory domain until the schema has been modified by running adprep to update the forest.

Where groups are concerned, make sure you document the existing group structure including nested groups if applicable. Again, what types of groups are used and how they can be used depends on the operating system. For example, a Windows peer-to-peer environment may not use groups at all, but if it does, it will not allow group nesting. All of the groups within a Windows peer-to-peer network are local to the computers where the resources are located. Windows NT allows group nesting within a domain to make resource access easier. Anyone familiar with the Windows NT AGLP principle understands that User accounts (A) are organized within Global groups (G), which are nested within Local groups (L), to which permissions (P) are granted to provide access to resources.

Document what you find within the existing environment so that you can use it later. If you have this information, you will be able to discuss the current strategies with the stakeholders and have a basis on which to build the new environment. It will also allow you to identify the deficiencies in the current design and make recommendations on ways to enhance the new design.

Identifying a Naming Strategy

All accounts need to have a unique name for which they are identified within the forest. With this in mind, you will need to identify how similar accounts will be named or how you will identify them when you are searching for them. User and InetOrgPerson accounts can be the most problematic when you are trying to determine a name, but Computer and Group accounts can prove problematic when you are trying to locate them within the directory. For these reasons, your naming policy should spell out the requirements for naming each type of account.

Naming User, Contact, and InetOrgPerson Accounts

A user's account should identify who the user is. This makes the user feel comfortable when they are logging in as well as making it easy for users to locate other user accounts. Administrative staff will need to easily identify each user, and other users will probably need to send e-mail to their fellow employees. A User account is usually identified using

- First Name, initial, or subset of first name
- First initial of last name, last name, or subset of characters from last name
- Additional characters to make account name unique

In small organizations, you may be able to use just the first name for the user. However, this solution makes the naming of user accounts for employees who have the same name difficult. If you have two users named Gina, you will need to identify how each of the names will be unique. Making one Gina and the other Gina1 will probably not make the second Gina very happy. Using a naming convention that uses the user's first name and first initial of their last name may work for some companies, but the same issues could arise. For example, Tom Smith and Tom Sanders could pose problems. And, as you might have guessed, inverting this naming convention so that the initial of the first name and the full last name is used as the account name will pose problems with users who have names such as Sandy Jones and Steve Jones.

Other options that companies employ include using the entire name of the user or adding their employee number to their account name. The first option works well until you have two John Petersons or Sue Johnsons. In this case, an incremental number at the end of the name or adding the middle initial to the name may work, but it may be confusing when you want to modify an account. The former option will guarantee that the account is unique, but it may be a little impersonal to some users. Of course, impersonal does work for some companies; the employee ID number is used as their logon ID.

No matter what option you choose, you will run into limitations. Make sure you sit down with the design team and choose a naming convention that everyone agrees upon. Once you have agreed, make sure that everyone responsible for creating accounts understands the naming convention so that all accounts will follow it.

The user accounts that will be used to allow users to have access to the network and network resources should follow a naming convention that is easy for them to accept and use. Other user accounts will exist within your environment that will be used for special purposes. Two of these special purposes are service accounts and temporary employees.

Service Accounts

A *service account* is a User account created for the sole purpose of allowing an application's background services to interact with the operating system. For many applications to function properly, the developers write a service program that runs in the background to provide needed functionality to the application. Although some of these services use the LocalService or NetworkService accounts, others require a special account to be created.

When creating service accounts, you should make sure a policy is in place that dictates how the account will be named. These names do not have to be user friendly as they do for a user account, but they should be descriptive enough to detail what the account is used for. That being said, because the service accounts are usually assigned generous permissions so that they can permit the service to access the resources, the name of this account should also be cryptic enough that someone trying to determine what the account name is will have a difficult time doing so.

Although every company will have their own ideas concerning the naming of service accounts, one option would be to prefix the service account name with SRV-. The application that requires this service could then be appended; for instance, an Exchange Server 2003 Information Store service might use the name SRV-Exch. Of course, this is not very cryptic, and a hacker could attempt to use this account to gain access to the network or attempt a denial of service attack on the service. To keep the service accounts hidden and secure, there are cases where companies have decided upon a service identity plan in order to hide the service accounts.

Using a service identity plan, the service, or the application that the service provides functionality for, is given a code name. For example, SQL Server could be assigned a code of 1S75. Combine this with the SRV- prefix, and you have a service account for SQL Server of SRV-1S75. This would allow the administrators to search for the service accounts within Active Directory by specifying SRV as the first letters of the account name, but it would keep the actual service name cryptic enough to safeguard it. Of course the disadvantage of this is trying to determine which accounts are used for which service, so the documentation for the service accounts will have to be good, or you could create an OU specifically for containing the service accounts so that you know where they are located within the directory.

Temporary Employees

Temporary employees are individuals who are hired for a short period of time. Whenever a company employs temporary employees, they experience a greater rollover in personnel. The staff members who are responsible for maintaining the accounts for temporary employees will be required to create and delete these accounts on a regular basis. Having a naming convention that identifies these employees will reduce the amount of time necessary to locate their accounts within the directory, and help prevent someone from adding their accounts into resource groups where they do not belong.

A long-standing tradition with Microsoft best practices is to name the temporary employees' User accounts starting with a prefix T_. This provides the administrative staff with an efficient method of searching for the temporary accounts when they need to add or remove them from a resource or delete them when their term has expired.

Naming Computer Accounts

Computer accounts need to be identified within Active Directory just as any other account does. Computer accounts can be added to groups or directly to an object's access control list (ACL), so that an administrator will need to search for the Computer account. As with the User account, the Computer account should be named in a manner that will make it easy to search for and identify.

In a large organization, naming Computer accounts can be difficult. Descriptive names for the computers may be hard to come up with. Servers are generally given a descriptive name, but workstations are often overlooked. In the past, it was not uncommon to see workstation names that were the result of a random generation of alphanumeric characters. Although this may not have seemed like a bad idea under Windows NT, with the tools that are available under Windows Server 2003 and Windows XP, remote desktop control utilities are becoming more widely used. The users whom are responsible for assisting users through these utilities may need to find the systems by name. Unless the naming convention is easy to understand, good documentation will need to be maintained.

Some of the more common naming options for Computer accounts involve naming them after the user who they are assigned to or the location where they are used. Servers are usually identified by the services they provide. The following are some recommendations for naming both servers and computers.

Naming Servers

Server names can identify the service they provide. In small organizations, this name will probably consist of the service and an identifier to make the name unique. For example, domain controllers could be named DC1 and DC2. Exchange servers would be named EX1 and EX2. Although this may work in a small environment, trying to use this same convention in a large organization may be difficult.

To further identify servers within a large organization, you may want to name the servers for the service they provide *and* the location of the users for whom they provide the service. If you use this method, you will be able to identify the servers for a centralized or decentralized administrative model.

For example, take a company that has centralized resources with users who are located in offices at different locations. The server names could have a prefix for the service they provide, like EX for Exchange, which is followed by a location code for the accounts that use the server, such as CHI for Chicago. In this case, the EXCHI server would be the Exchange server hosting the mailboxes for the users in the Chicago office.

A company that employs decentralized resources can also take advantage of this scenario. They will be able to identify the service the server provides and the location for which it functions. A Microsoft SQL 2000 server residing within the Fort Worth branch could be identified as SQLFW.

With either of these two options, if more than one server provides the same service in the same location, you will have to determine how you are going to uniquely identify the server. And just as with the naming of the service accounts mentioned earlier, those companies that identify their servers with an alphanumeric naming convention will need to make sure they have documentation to make it understandable. Clustered servers also provide you with a challenge because you need to determine how you will name the virtual server that the users "see," and the physical servers that provide the functionality.

Naming Workstations

Several options are available when it comes to naming workstations. Some organizations name the workstation for the user who uses it. Others name the workstation based on a location such as a phone extension the computer is next to or the cubicle number where the workstation resides. Still others use a random workstation name and keep track of the workstations in a database.

No matter what strategy you employ, you will need to keep good documentation so that the administrative staff knows which workstation they are working with in Active Directory. For those workstations that are running Windows XP Professional as their operating system, the Remote Desktop is available for administrators to work with. Any of the administrative staff who needs to manage the workstation from the Remote Desktop client will have to know the name of the workstation to which they are attaching.

Naming Group Accounts

As with the other account types, you should name groups in a manner that will allow you to identify what each is used for. The names you choose for groups should be very easy to search for and understand. Groups are used to organize accounts so that the members all have the same level of permissions for a resource. Unless the person naming the group really understands what it is used for, they might assign inappropriate permissions to a user.

Three group scopes exist within the two group types: distribution and security. Of the two group types, the security group is the most versatile. Security groups are used to provide access to resources and as distribution lists. Distribution groups are used solely by e-mail programs, such as Exchange, as distribution lists.

Most organization will organize the distribution groups within an OU that is used explicitly for maintaining distribution lists. These groups should be named based upon the need for the distribution list. When using Exchange, these groups will appear in the address lists users use when sending mail. Having a name that is descriptive as possible will make finding the group easier for the user.

Security groups are both a blessing and a curse for administrative staff. Though they can make assigning rights and permissions easier, the design and planning of these groups can be frustrating and time consuming. The primary reason for using a security group is to allow members of the group to have access to resources. When users no longer need access to a resource, their account can be removed from the group membership. When new users need access, they can be added to the group and be given all of the rights and permissions that are assigned to the group.

 Group strategies are discussed in the section "Determining Group Requirements for Resource Access" later in this chapter.

The group's name should identify the group and help differentiate it from other groups within the organization. A policy should be created that designates how group names will be generated. This policy should include the following options:

- The group's scope
- The group's purpose
- The group's owner

The naming convention for the group should use the group's scope, such as G for Global groups, DL for Domain Local groups, and U for Universal groups. The purpose could be a general identification of the group's usage such as Printer03Print. The group's owner could be the business unit it is used in or the location of the resource, such as ATLHR for the Atlanta Human Resources division.

You should make sure that the naming convention is easy to understand and perform searches on. When you go to name the resource, make sure the most general portion of the name is at the beginning of the name. The most specific portion of the name should appear at the end of the name. This will allow the groups to be listed within dialog boxes in alphabetic order, and you will be able to find them easier.

Group names and descriptions can have a maximum length of 256 characters. Although this may seem as it is very generous and you could name a group with an extremely well documented name, you should take other limitations into consideration. For instance, when viewing the group name in dialog boxes, you will only be able to see around 20 characters without having to scroll or expand the column. Also, the Properties pages will only show approximately 50 characters of the name. Anything beyond that will not show and you will not be able to scroll to see it. You should always plan to have the most descriptive part of the name fall within the first 20 characters of the name. As a general rule, the name should be short enough to make out from all of the dialog boxes, yet long enough to be descriptive.

For instance, if you have a printer named Printer03 in the Atlanta Human Resources Department, and you want to assign users the Print permission on it, you could create a Domain Local group and name it DL-ATLHR-Printer03Print. This would allow you to sort the list of groups and locate all of the Domain Local groups. Within the resulting list, you would find all of the Atlanta Human Resources groups sorted together.

Another method employed by large companies that have many geographic locations is to use the location name first and then the scope, with the purpose last. In our preceding printer example, the name would then be created as ATLHR-DL-Printer03Print.

No matter what naming convention you choose, make sure you enforce it. If any of the groups do not follow the naming convention, searches will be very difficult. Stress the importance of this to anyone who has the ability to create groups. You will find that some individuals have their own ideas of what makes for a descriptive name. If they do not follow the criteria you set forth in your policy, the policy is useless.

Real World Scenario

Naming Conventions

Randi is planning an upgrade of her current Windows NT 4 domain to a Windows Server 2003 forest. She inherited a network that has grown very fast. Her company has also bought other companies throughout this growth period and the network has grown to incorporate these new domains.

She currently has many resource domains in her NT 4 environment but would like to restructure this when she moves to the Windows Server 2003 forest. Groups in the different domains all have different naming conventions. For example, a separate domain exists for Randi's users in the Atlanta region. The sales people in the Atlanta office are in a group named Sales. Sales people in her Chicago office are in a group called SalesGroup. This has been very confusing to her and to other administrators.

When planning her authorization strategy, Randi decided to move to a more cohesive and easier-to-administer naming convention for groups. She would also like to make the design so that it is easy to incorporate new domains or forests, and the domains that reside in them. Because her new domain will be a Windows Server 2003 domain in Windows 2000 Native mode functional level, she can place users in Universal groups.

Randi plans to define the groups by group type first, then department, then location, then job responsibility, and so on. Some examples will include the following:

- G-Sales-Atlanta-Internal Sales

- G-Sales-Atlanta-Widget Sales

- G-Sales-Atlanta-Robot Sales

- G-Sales-Atlanta-Welder Sales

- G-Sales-Chicago-Press Sales

- G-Sales-Chicago-Widget Sales

Using this naming convention, Randi is able to quickly identify the group types within her directory service and determine what they are used for and where the geographic location they apply.

Identifying an Account Authentication Policy

For security purposes, you should implement *account policies* that will safeguard the user accounts and resources. An account policy controls how passwords are used and how many times the user account can unsuccessfully attempt to authenticate within the domain before it is locked out. The account policy should be strict enough that the user accounts are protected from being attacked, yet not so restrictive that the users become frustrated when they try to access the network. Two parts make up the account policy: the password policy and the account lockout policy.

In conjunction with the account policy, you will need to determine how users will authenticate to the domain. You should specify how the user logs in, whether it is with the pre–Windows 2000 username or with the User Principle Name (UPN), as well as whether another form of authentication will be used, such as a biometric device. If using a smart card, you can dictate that the user has to have the smart card to authenticate with, but it is up to you to put a standard in place that states that the users will use either a pre–Windows 2000 logon or a UPN to log on. And the training that goes on to inform them on how to use a UPN will be up to you also.

Understanding the Password Policy

A user's password is the first line of defense against unwanted access into network resources. A password policy controls how the passwords can be used within the domain. Users should be informed of the importance of using strong passwords and be told how they can protect their passwords. Strong passwords use more than the standard lowercase letters from the keyboard. A strong password will use a combination of uppercase letters, lowercase letters, numerals, and special characters. Using a combination of these characters increases the possible combinations of characters within the password and dramatically increases the amount of time it will take an attacker to discover what the password is.

WARNING   Of course, no combination of characters is going to be effective if the user leaves their password out in broad daylight. No options within the password policy will remove yellow sticky notes from the bottom of keyboards or the sides of monitors. Make sure you stress the importance of keeping a password secure and secret.

Within a domain environment, the password policy for domain accounts can only be set at the domain level. A GPO linked to a domain's root controls the policy for every account within the domain. If there are any reasons why the password policy should be different for any set of users, another domain will need to be constructed to host the new policy.

Figure 7.1 shows the password policy options within the account policy container of the Default Domain Policy.

The password policy consists of six settings (each of these settings can be used in conjunction with the others to create very strong password protection for accounts within the domain):

Enforce Password History   The *Enforce Password History* setting allows Active Directory to store the previous versions of users' passwords. When a user changes their password, the new password is compared to the previous passwords to ensure that the user is not trying to reuse an old password.

FIGURE 7.1   The Default Domain Policy password policies

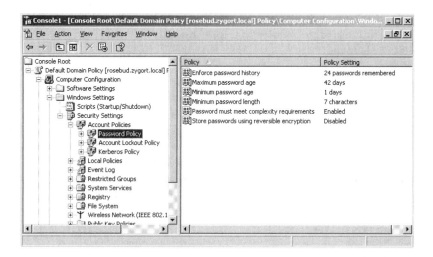

Maximum Password Age   The *Maximum Password Age* setting allows you to define exactly how long a password may be used before another password has to be defined for the user.

Minimum Password Age   The *Minimum Password Age* setting defines how long a password must be used before it can be changed.

Minimum Password Length   The *Minimum Password Length* setting defines the number of characters that must be included within a password.

Password Must Meet Complexity Requirements   The *Password Must Meet Complexity Requirements* setting enforces the use of strong passwords. When enforced, the password must include at least three of the four character types: uppercase, lowercase, numeric, and special characters.

Store Password Using Reversible Encryption   The *Store Passwords Using Reversible Encryption* setting is used in conjunction with digest authentication. If digest authentication is required for IIS, the user's password is stored in clear text within Active Directory.

Of the six settings, the first five are commonly used within an Active Directory environment. A solid password policy will use all five of these policy settings. The default settings within a Windows Server 2003 domain are shown in Figure 7.1. Notice that the setting for password history is set to 24 passwords. Users will have to use 24 different and unique passwords before they can reuse any of them. Now note that the minimum password age is set to one day. This setting keeps the user from changing the password 24 times on the day that the password was initially changed just so that they can use the same password over again.

The maximum password age should be set long enough that the users will not become upset because they have to change their passwords too often, yet short enough that attempts to break in using the password will be thwarted by the would-be intruder having a new password to work against. The 42 days set by the initial security policy should be effective enough for most companies, although you may want to relax it some depending upon user feedback. Whatever you choose for this setting, make sure you get the proper backing from upper management to keep it in place. If they understand the need for constantly changing passwords, the users will have to abide by the policy.

The password length is another setting that users will complain about. The default setting of 7 characters is not extreme. Most organizations will use from 6 to 10 characters for password lengths. The longer the password, the more combinations of characters will be required to break it.

Finally, the setting that will cause the most complaints within the user community is complexity requirements. This setting alone will stop the use of pet names, nicknames, and favorite colors for passwords. Once you implement these, users will have no choice but to come up with creative passwords based on the character requirements. The downside to this setting is that users will start writing down their passwords, which leaves a paper trail. Passwords written on a piece of paper stuck under the keyboard are just as unsafe as using a password that is weak.

Understanding the Lockout Policy

The *lockout policy* for the domain controls the number of unsuccessful attempts someone can make with a user account before the account is locked from use. This thwarts an attacker who is attempting to figure out a user's password by entering several words. Figure 7.2 shows the default settings that are applied when Active Directory is installed.

FIGURE 7.2 The Default Domain Policy lockout settings

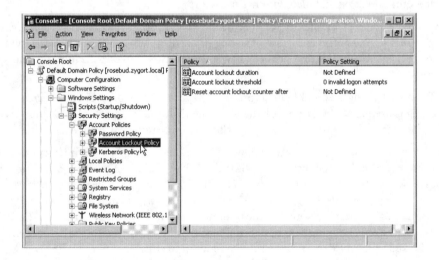

The lockout policy has three default settings (as with the password policy, each of the settings works in conjunction with one another to enforce a strong lockout policy):

Account Lockout Duration The *Account Lockout Duration* setting specifies how long an account will remain locked out before the system automatically unlocks the account. A setting of 0 will not allow the account to unlock automatically; instead, an administrator will have to manually unlock it.

Account Lockout Threshold The *Account Lockout Threshold* setting defines the number of incorrect password entries that can be made against an account before the account is locked out.

Reset Account Lockout Counter After The *Reset Account Lockout Counter After* setting defines the amount of time that the lockout counter will continue to increment incorrect logon attempts. If this setting is configured for 5 minutes, the counter will not reset the bad attempts for a 5-minute period, even if the user successfully authenticated.

You will notice that the Default Domain Policy does not have the lockout restrictions enforced. This should be one area that you specify to be enforced when you design your account policy. Without these settings, attackers will have unlimited attempts at breaking into an account. Most organizations will allow three to five attempts before locking the account. Make sure your policy is generous enough that users will not complain too loudly about it, yet strict enough to be secure.

In conjunction with the lockout threshold, you will need to specify how long the account will remain locked out. The Account Lockout Duration setting will allow the account to reset automatically if you choose a number of minutes for the account to remain locked. This saves the administrator the frustration of having to manually unlock accounts; however, allowing the account to unlock automatically does not throw up a red flag to the administrator. If an administrator is inundated with telephone calls first thing Monday morning from users yelling at him because their accounts are locked out, that may indicate that his network has been attacked. Consider setting this option to 0 if you are concerned about possible attacks.

Understanding Log-on Options

In an Active Directory environment, it does not matter whether the users log on using their UPN or pre–Windows 2000 username—the Kerberos service is responsible for authenticating their account. However, the method of authentication is different, and when you can use each type of logon will be dictated by the functional level of the domain. And then there are the alternative methods of authentication that add an additional level of security. Using devices such as smart cards and biometrics allows for multifactor authentication.

The log-in options that a user can use are:

Username/Password Using the username/password combination is the traditional method of authenticating. User accounts are given a pre–Windows 2000 username that can be used to authenticate them. The combination of username and password that is provided during logon is validated by the Kerberos service on a domain controller within the domain that is specified during logon.

User Principal Name/Password The User Principal Name/password combination allows you to authenticate to the domain just as you would with the username/password combination, but before the authentication request can be sent, a query is sent to the nearest Global Catalog server, which provides the appropriate username and domain name for the account.

Design Scenario

Determining the Authentication Requirements

Donna is designing the authentication standards for the company. So far she has identified that the internal auditors would like to have passwords that are a minimum of eight characters, that complex passwords must be used, and that users must not be able to use the same password within a two-year span of time. They have also specified that they would like to enforce lockout restrictions that would lock a user's account if the password was entered incorrectly more than five times; at this point an administrator would be required to unlock the account.

1. **Question:** Which of the default settings for the domain will need to be updated for Donna's password policy design to meet the auditor's requirements? **Answer:** Within the password policy, the only change that will be required is changing the Minimum Password Length setting to 8. All of the rest of the settings meet or exceed the auditor's requirements.

2. **Question:** Which of the default settings for the domain will need to be updated for Donna's lockout policy design to meet the auditor's requirements? **Answer:** The Account Lockout Threshold setting will need to be set at 5 and the Account Lockout Duration setting will have to be set to 0.

Multifactor Authentication   *Multifactor authentication* uses an additional layer of security when the user attempts to authenticate. A user's account is associated with a certificate that identifies the user. If a smart card is used, the user is prompted to enter a Personal Identification Number (PIN) at the Windows logon screen. If the PIN is correct, the certificates stored on the smart card are compared with the certificates within Active Directory. Devices such as SecureID will generate a key value that is used to prove the authenticity of the person.

For organizations that need a higher level of protection, multifactor authentication should provide the security that they need. Multifactor authentication can be used within domains at any functional level, as can the username/password option.

In the "Determining the Authentication Requirements" Design Scenario, you will determine the authentication requirements for a particular scenario.

Determining Group Requirements for Resource Access

There are two group types within Active Directory: security and distribution. When creating a group, you will need to determine exactly what the group will be used for. Distribution groups are used for e-mail. An e-mail program such as Microsoft Exchange Server can use distribution groups as distribution lists once they have been mail-enabled. Security groups are used to grant the members of the group access to objects and resources. You will create security groups to allow users with the same resource access needs to be grouped together.

When using groups, you cannot assign access to resources using a distribution group; only a security group has that functionality. A security group can be mail-enabled, however, so the members of a security group can have access to resources and be members of a distribution list all at the same time. So why would you want to use a distribution group? Distribution group membership is not considered when a user logs on, so it does not affect the generation of the access token for resource access. If users need to be grouped together for the sole purpose of receiving the same mail messages, create a distribution group and add the user accounts to it.

Identifying User Access and Group Strategies

Just like the forests, domains, and OUs that we have been discussing, groups can be categorized as account groups and resource groups. Account groups are used to organize user accounts that need the same level of access to resources. Resource groups are used to grant access to a resource to the members of the account groups or user accounts that are added to the membership of the resource group. You can use one of three strategies when assigning permissions to accounts, and these two types of groups are used differently with each one.

Account/Discretionary Access Control List (A/DACL)

Using the *account/discretionary access control list (A/DACL)* strategy, user accounts are added directly to the DACL of the resource. Because groups are not used, the administrator will have to add the user's account to the DACL of every resource that the user needs to work with. In large organizations with several resources, the administrator may mistakenly omit an account from a resource's DACL, thus keeping the user from working effectively. This will also generate one of those nasty phone calls that we administrators love to receive.

When adding users directly to the DACL, the administrative staff who is responsible for maintaining user access to resources will have to document the permission assignment carefully. When a user leaves the company or moves to another position where they do not need to have access to the resources they formerly had, the account will have to be removed from each DACL individually. This can be time consuming, and if any DACLs were missed, the user could have access to resources they should not have access to.

Even though we are warning you against using the A/DACL strategy, there are times when it is a viable solution. Take, for instance, the scenario where the administrator of a resource wants to allow a user to have permission to access the resource, but not to view the membership of groups. If you are unsure of whether or not there are additional members of the group that should not have access to the resource, from a security standpoint, it may be best to add the individual user account to grant permissions.

Account Group/Discretionary Access Control List (AG/DACL)

The *account group/discretionary access control list (AG/DACL)* strategy allows groups to be created that will be used to organize user accounts that have the same resource access requirements. These account groups are then assigned permissions that let them access the resources by adding the group account to the DACL of the resource and then setting the appropriate permissions.

In some cases, this strategy may work very well. If a user account needs to have access to a resource, the account can be added to the account group. If the permissions need to be revoked from a user, their account can be removed from the group, thus stripping them of their ability to access the resource. Administrators only need to document the access granted to the groups and add or remove the user accounts to the membership of the group to control the user's access.

The proper AG/DACL strategies are as follows:

Accounts—Local group—permissions (ALP)   This strategy uses Local groups to which permission are applied, and then adds the user's account to the membership of the Local group. Using this strategy, the administrator for a server could create the Local group and maintain the membership. The Local group is only on the local system, however, and is not an object within Active Directory, so the group can only be used on the server where it was created.

Accounts—Domain Local group—permissions (ADLP)   This strategy uses the Domain Local group type, which is located in Active Directory. As with the Local group, the permissions are applied to the Domain Local group and users who need to access the resource are added to the group membership. In Native mode and higher functional levels, the domain local group can be used for accessing any resource within the domain; however, if the domain is in mixed mode, you can only use Domain Local groups for resources on the domain controllers.

Account—Global group—permissions (AGP)   The Global group type is another Active Directory–based group. Permission to access resources can be granted to this group type and the users who need access to the resource are added to the group membership. The disadvantage to using this group type to assign permission to resources is that the membership can only include accounts from the domain in which the group resides. Accounts from other domains will have to be added to another group in order for it to have access.

Account Group/Resource Group (AG/RG)

Using the *Account group/Resource group* (AG/RG) strategy allows the administrative staff the most flexibility, but it is also the most time consuming, and sometimes the most confusing of the strategies. Plus, this strategy employs the most groups and may become unwieldy when you try to identify the proper groups to which you need to grant permission or add user accounts.

When you are using this strategy, the *Resource group* is added to the ACL and the proper level of permissions is applied. A Resource group is a group that you use to allow permission to objects. User accounts that need the same level of resource access are organized as members of the *Account group*. Account groups are used to organize users and other groups (in native mode and higher) that have the same resource access needs. Once the Account group is made a member of the Resource group, all of the members of the Account group are granted the proper level of access to the resource. Although this may seem like a simple concept here on paper, some mechanisms in Active Directory can cause confusion when you are designing the group strategy.

The first limitation is the functional level of the domains where the groups are needed. If a domain is not at the Windows 2000 Native mode or higher, you won't be able to use universal security groups. At first, this may not seem like such a drawback because you still have the ability to use Domain Local security and Global security groups, in a large forest. However, you will soon find that you may be performing too many group administration tasks. Universal groups can alleviate some of the group management you will have to perform.

Windows 2000 Native mode functional level or higher is also required for some of the security group nesting options. If you are not at one of these functional levels, Global security groups can only be made members of Local or Domain Local security groups. If the functional level has been raised for the domain to the Windows 2000 Native mode or Windows Server 2003 levels, then Global security groups can be made members of other Global security groups.

When using the AG/RG strategy, administrators have a choice of several nesting options. As mentioned earlier, which functional level the domain is at will dictate whether or not some of the nesting options are available. When implementing an AG/RG strategy, the groups with a scope of Global or Universal are considered account groups. Security groups with the scope of Domain Local or Local are considered Resource groups.

The AG/RG strategies are:

Accounts—Global group—Local group—permissions (AGLP) All domains, even those in the mixed mode functional level are able to use the AGLP nesting strategy. As with all of the AG/RG strategies, the accounts that need access to the resource are added to the appropriate Global security group. As shown in Figure 7.3, the Local security group is added to the DACL of the resource and the proper permissions are specified. Once the Global group is added as a member of the Local security group, the user accounts that are members of the Global security group can then access any resources for which they have granted permissions to the Local security group.

FIGURE 7.3 Example of AGLP

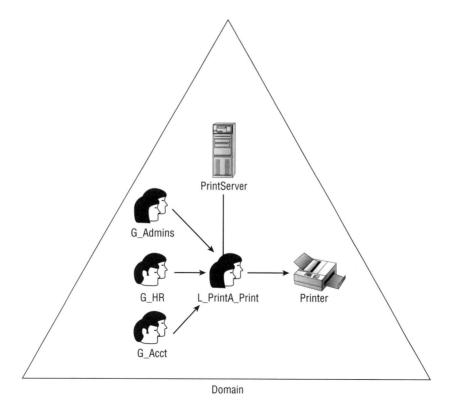

You still have the ability to use Universal Distribution groups within a Mixed mode domain. The limitation only applies to Universal security groups.

The limitation to this strategy is that the local account can only be accessed on the local machine. Local groups are not part of Active Directory and will not show up in Active Directory queries. For users to have control over Local groups, they will need to have administrative authority to the local system where the Local group resides.

Accounts—Global group—Domain Local group—permissions (AGDLP)   All domains, even those in the mixed mode functional level, are able to use the AGDLP nesting strategy. As with all of the AG/RG strategies, the accounts that need access to the resource are added to the Global security group. As shown in Figure 7.4, the Local security group is added to the ACL of the resource and the proper permissions are applied. Once the Global security group is added as a member of the Domain Local security group, the user accounts that are members of the Global security group are then given the permissions of the Local security group.

FIGURE 7.4   Example of AGDLP

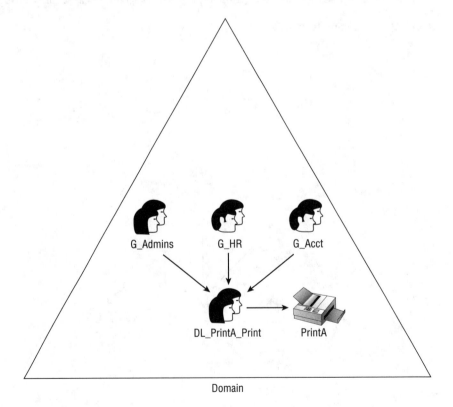

Domain Local groups are part of Active Directory and will show up in Active Directory queries. Users can be delegated control to manage group accounts within Active Directory. Because these accounts are part of Active Directory, additional groups will appear in queries making it more confusing when you are trying to locate the proper groups.

Accounts—Global group—(Global group)—Universal group—Domain Local group—permissions (AGUDLP)   Universal security groups and the ability to nest Global security groups are only available when the domain is at the Windows 2000 Native mode functional level or higher. Once the domain is at one of these functional levels, you can use the AGUDLP nesting strategy. This strategy, as seen in Figure 7.5, is usually only employed when several domains are within the forest. Using this method, users are still made members of a Global group, and the Domain Local group is added to the DACL of the resource.

The benefit of using the Universal group comes from the fact that you can add many Global groups from any domain in the forest to the Universal group, which in turn is made a member of the Domain Local group. Now if another Global group from another domain needs access to resources, you can add that Global group to the membership of the Universal group, which will give the members of the Global group the access they need to all of the resources from all of the Domain Local groups of which the Universal group is a member.

Using nesting, you could keep stacking the groups, such as AGGUDLP or AGGUDLDLP.

FIGURE 7.5   Example of AGUDLP

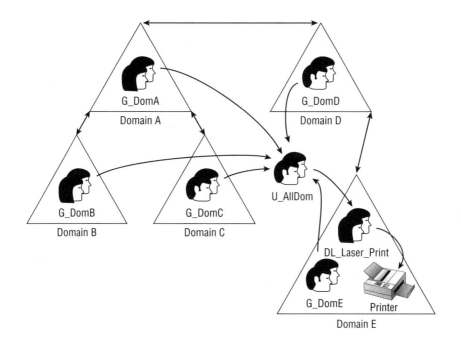

🌐 **Real World Scenario**

Laid-Back Admin

Ron is an administrator in a large enterprise network. He is one of the administrators in charge of network printers; that are available to factory users. The print server that he manages contains 50 printers. 35 of the printers are located on the shop floor. They print reports and job details for the shop foremen. All foremen should be able to print to all printers on the shop floor so that they can print reports anywhere in the factory. Ten of the printers are located in the administration area and are available to all members of the administrative groups. 5 printers are defined for management only, and all 5 should be available to all members of the management groups.

Ron implemented an AG/RG. He created three printer groups: one called DL-ShopPrinters, one called DL-AdminPrinters, and one called DL-ManagementPrinters. He then added user account groups to these printer groups to define access to the printers. The DACL on each printer only has to be edited one time.

Recently, the company decided to implement a new application that the administration staff will use to send reports out to the foremen. Ron now needs to add the 10 users from the administration staff to all 35 printers.

Because Ron implemented an AG/RG authorization method, he simply added the account group that includes the user accounts of the administration staff to the DL-ShopPrinters resource group. All users from the administration staff instantly had access to all 35 printers located in the shop.

Identifying Group Creation Options

By default, members of the Domain Admins, Enterprise Admins, and Account Operators groups have the ability to create groups. In some cases, these groups will suffice. For instance, a centralized administrative group that is responsible for all account creation, user, and group accounts could have their accounts added to the Account Operators group and have the ability to perform their job.

There are occasions when this strategy will not suffice. The Account Operators group may have too many rights associated with it for the job responsibilities of users who need to maintain groups. Account Operators also allows user accounts to be created and maintained. If maintaining user accounts is a separate job responsibility from the users who maintain group accounts, you will have to create groups based on job functions.

The preferred method of delegating the ability to maintain group accounts is to create an OU in which the group accounts will reside. Then you should create a group that will be granted the ability to maintain group accounts. This group should reside in an OU other than the OU that the users manage. That will keep them from having the ability to change the functionality of their group. Once the OU and the group exists, run the Delegation of Control Wizard to assign the proper permissions to the group.

Design Scenario

Designing Resource Access for the Forest

Carl has a large number of users who need to access a domain-based DFS root. All of the users are from throughout the two-tree, 12-domain Active Directory design he is working on. He wants to make the administration of the user access and group management as easy as possible.

1. **Question:** Which of the strategies should he employ? **Answer:** Account Group/Resource Group (AG/RG).

2. **Question:** Which of the nesting options would make administration easiest for Carl? **Answer:** Accounts—Global Group—(Global Group)—Universal Group—Domain Local Group—Permissions (AGUDLP).

3. **Question:** How is this nesting option implemented? **Answer:** Global groups from each domain are created and user accounts that have the same resource access needs are made members of the group. A Domain Local group is created. This Domain Local group is added to the ACL of the resource and the appropriate permissions are applied. A Universal group is created and added to the membership of the Domain Local group. The Global groups from all of the domains are added to the membership of the Universal group to complete the chain.

Make sure that you document your changes. There isn't a "tell me what I did wizard" or a "take it back wizard".

The OU that you create to hold groups will really only be used to hold the groups and delegate permissions to those users who need to maintain them. GPOs do not affect groups; they only affect computers and users, so this OU will be for administrative purposes only.

After you have decided who will have permission to create and maintain the groups, make sure that those users understand the policies you have set forth concerning the naming conventions for groups. Other administrators will need to find the groups when adding them to the DDACL of the resources for which they maintain access. If the naming convention is followed, maintaining access to resources should be easy to control.

In the "Designing Resource Access for the Forest" Design Scenario, you will learn how to design a resource access for a forest.

Designing a Group Creation Strategy

As you are deciding upon the policies that you will implement for naming conventions and delegation of authority, you will also need to determine the strategy you will employ for resource access. You will need to create a guideline for group membership and nesting that will meet the requirements of your organization. You will start by identifying which resources the users will need to access, the level of access they will require, and then the strategy that you will implement to allow that access.

Identifying Resource Access Needs

Resources exist for a reason. Printers, folders, files, databases, e-mail, and many other resources exist within the network, and users will need to have access to those resources in order to perform their job functions.

You will need to determine the resources that exist within the organization. Even in small organizations, this can be a time consuming task, let alone what you will run into in a large organization. This is not a task that you will be able to perform on your own. Assign other users to documenting the resources that they are responsible for and which users need to have access to them. Once you have identified all of the resources on the network, you can look at the users who need to access them.

Look for users who need the same type of access to resources. These users will become the members of a group who have the same requirements. Try to keep the number of these groups to a minimum, but make sure that you do not allow user accounts to become members of groups where they do not belong.

Think of employees that have basically the same functions, such as accounting employees. There will be files that all of the accounting employees need access to, so you can include all of them into one group. You will also have resources that only a subset of employees, such as Accounts Payable, need to access. In this case you could add only the Accounts Payable staff members to the group.

Determining the Level of Access Required

The next thing you should do is review the access requirements for users. When determining the type of access different users need to the same resource, you should keep documentation for each level of permission. Once you have determined the level of permission required for each different type of user, you can create a security group for each of the access requirements. Add those security groups to the DACL of the resource and apply the appropriate permissions.

For example, a graphics design company may have a folder called PromoArt that contains sample artwork that they present to prospective clients. Members of the sales team need to be able to show the clients the artwork. Members of the Design team need to be able to modify their own artwork, but not any of the other artists' work. The Art department managers need to be able to add and remove artwork from these folders as they determine which designs are going to be used for promotional purposes. Members of the IT department are responsible for maintaining the server that the design folder is on. They will need to have access to the directory so that they can back it up and restore it if necessary. They will also need to manage the permissions for those accounts that need to have access to the designs.

Domain Local groups could be created that allow for all of the specific permissions that the accounts will need. Because the Sales team needs Read permission, a group DL_PromoArt_Read is created. The Design team members and the Art department managers need to modify the artwork, so a Domain Local group named DL_PromoArt_Mod is created. Finally, because the IT group maintains the folder, a group named DL_PromoArt_FC is created.

Designing for Efficient Nesting

When using Windows XP Professional as the client operating system within your domain, you can allow a user to be a member of about 120 groups without having to change registry entries to allow more. However, the more groups that a user is a member of, the longer it takes for the user to log on to their system because the access token generation will take so long. Try to keep the group membership of a client to a minimum so that you will not incur long logon times.

You should try to use group nesting to your advantage. A well-thought-out design will allow you to streamline your administrative overhead. You should try to design so that you are nesting groups based on the *most-restrictive/most-inclusive strategy*. By using the most-restrictive/most-inclusive strategy, you create groups that will include the fewest number of users where you want to control the membership, and then you add that group to other groups that allow less restrictive access to other resources. Take for instance a department where the management team has access to all of the resources that the employees of the department has. You could add the management team into a Global group and then add that Global group into another Global group that contains the department's employees.

For instance, you may have an Accounting division that includes an Accounts Payable and an Accounts Receivables department. There may be resources that the entire Accounting division needs to access. You'll also have resources that only the individual departments will need access to. You can create a group for the Accounting division managers and call it G_AcctManagers. The Accounts Receivables and Accounts Payables staff could be added to the groups G_AcctRec and G_AcctPay, respectively. You could create another group that would include all of the Accounting division staff so that they could access common resources, called U_AcctAll.

If the domain is at least at the Windows 2000 Native mode functional level, you could nest the groups to make administration easy. The G_AcctPay and G_AcctRec groups could be added to the membership of U_AcctAll. Now any new member of either G_AcctPay or G_AcctRec will have access to the resources that U_AcctAll has. Then, by adding the G_AcctManagers group to the membership of G_AcctPay and G_AcctRec, the members of G_AcctManagers would have access to the resources from all three groups. Figure 7.6 shows a representation of this strategy.

If a new Accounts Receivables employee is hired, their account can be created and added to the G_AcctRec group. Once added, the new user will have access to all of the resources provided to members of the G_AcctRec group and the U_AcctAll group. If a new manager was hired for the Accounting division, the user account for the manager could be added to the G_AcctManagers group. Assuming this was the case, the new manager would have access to all of the resources from all of the following groups: G_AcctManagers, G_AcctPay, G_AcctRec, and U_AcctAll.

If you can follow this strategy for all of the groups within your organization, you should be able to add and remove most user accounts with very little trouble. You'll have to plan more as you study the combinations of groups and evaluate the best nesting procedure, but the long-term administration will be much easier.

FIGURE 7.6   Nesting groups for efficient resource access

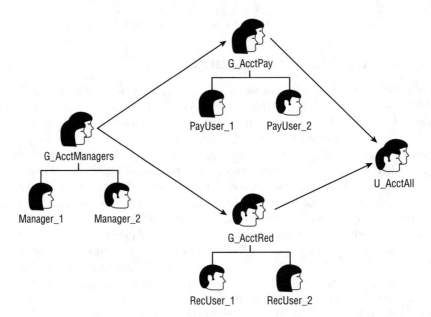

Summary

To make it easy for administrators and users to identify accounts within Active Directory, an organization should develop a naming strategy. This strategy should allow employees with the same name to be differentiated. Computer names should identify the computer and its purpose and group accounts should identify the group's scope, purpose, and owner.

The account authentication policy should identify the password and account lockout settings that will be enforced in order to keep the organization's resources secure. The method of authentication should also be determined. The typical sign-on measures, username or UPN and password, can be used in most cases, but if a more secure method of authentication is required, multifactor authentication using smart cards or biometrics may be necessary.

It can be difficult to decide upon the best method of allowing users to access resources. You should determine the resource access requirements for users and then form a group strategy. Usually, administrators find the AG/RG strategy the easiest to use, but the A/DACL or AG/DACL options are available also.

This puts an end to the Active Directory design portion of the book. Starting with the next chapter, we will be looking at the options available for the network infrastructure design that will be necessary to support the Active Directory design.

Exam Essentials

Understand what types of accounts can be created.   There are five types of accounts that can be created within Active Directory: User, InetOrgPerson, Contact, Computer, and Group.

Understand the need to uniquely identify accounts.   Account names should identify who the user or computer is to make it easier to understand which accounts are being used and managed.

Know why prefixes for service and temporary accounts are recommended.   Service and temporary accounts should be identified with a prefix so that they can be found easily within the directory.

Understand the group naming strategies.   Group names should include the scope of the group, the group's purpose, and the group's owner.

Know what makes up an account authentication policy.   An authentication policy is made up of the password and lockout policies, as well as the methods used to authenticate it.

Know the settings used within the password policy.   The settings are Enforce Password History, Maximum Password Age, Minimum Password Age, Minimum Password Length, Password Must Meet Complexity Requirements, and Store Password Using Reversible Encryption.

Know the settings used within the lockout policy.   The settings are Account Lockout Duration, Account Lockout Threshold, and Reset Account Lockout Counter After.

Know the resource access strategies that can be employed to give users access to resources.   The three resource access strategies include account/discretionary access control list (A/DACL), account group/discretionary access control list (AG/DACL), and account group/resource group (AG/RG).

Understand the group creation options.   Domain Admins, Account Operators, and Enterprise Admins all have the ability to create and manage groups. You can also delegate the permission to create and manage groups to users who you do not want to add to the membership of these groups.

Key Terms

Before you take the exam, be certain you are familiar with the following terms:

account group	Minimum Password Length
account group/discretionary access control list (AG/DACL)	most-restrictive/most-inclusive strategy
account group/resource group	multifactor authentication
Account Lockout Duration	naming strategy
Account Lockout Threshold	Password Must Meet Complexity Requirements
account policies	Reset Account Lockout Counter After
account/discretionary access control list (A/DACL)	resource group
Enforce Password History	service account
lockout policy	Store Passwords Using Reversible Encryption
Maximum Password Age	temporary employees
Minimum Password Age	

Review Questions

1. Which of the following are security groups scopes that can be used in a Windows 2003 forest? (Choose all that apply.)

   A. Local

   B. Domain Local

   C. Global

   D. Enterprise

2. Hallie would like to add a Global security group named Central Accounting to another Global security group called Central Administration. She cannot do this. What could be the reason?

   A. The domain is not operating at a minimum of Windows 2000 Mixed mode functional level.

   B. The domain is not operating at a Windows 2000 Native mode functional level.

   C. The "Group Nesting" option is not enabled in the forest.

   D. The Central Accounting group is in domain that is not operating at Windows 2003 functional level.

3. You would like to create a group in which the users and computers that need access to a resource will be made members. What type of group will you create?

   A. User list group

   B. Access control list

   C. Resource group

   D. Account group

4. What type of group would you create if you want to define access to a new print device on your network?

   A. Resource group

   B. Account croup

   C. Access control group

   D. Principal group

5. You are the network administrator of a small network that consists of about 30 users. You define access to all resources on the network by assigning permissions to the individual users who need access to each resource. What type of resource authorization method does this describe?

   A. Role-based authorization method

   B. Account group/DACL method (AG/DACL)

   C. User/DACL method

   D. Account group/Resource group method (AG/RG)

6. When designing an access control strategy for your network, you define access to printers by groups. You create a group for each printer on your network. When adding new users to your network, you add the user to the Account groups that are needed by that user, then add them to the Printer groups so that they have access to printers without changing the DACL on each individual printer. What type of resource authorization method is this an example of?

    A. Role-based authorization method

    B. Account group/DACL (AG/DACL)

    C. User/DACL method

    D. Account group/Resource group (AG/RG)

7. By default, what security groups have the ability to create security groups and delegate group object permissions? (Choose all that apply.)

    A. Domain Admins

    B. Enterprise Admins

    C. Domain Local Admins

    D. Account Operators

8. Which of the following are group types in Active Directory? (Choose all that apply.)

    A. Security

    B. Uscr

    C. Computer

    D. Distribution

9. When designing the group naming strategy, which of the following criteria should be part of the group name? (Choose all that apply.)

    A. Group purpose

    B. Group permission

    C. Group scope

    D. Group owner

10. You are naming your groups according to their scope. Which of the following security groups could be used when a domain is in the Windows Server 2003 functional level? (Choose all that apply.)

    A. L-Chi-HRFiles

    B. DL-Chi-RDPrint

    C. G-Miami-MedRecords

    D. U-Acct

Answers to Review Questions

1. A, B, C. Security groups are used to organize user accounts, computer accounts, and other types of accounts into manageable units. Security groups available in Windows 2003 include Local, Domain Local, Global, and Universal.

2. B. You can only nest Global security groups if your domain is running in a Windows 2000 Native mode or higher forest functional level.

3. D. An Account group is a security group that contains the User accounts and Computer accounts that have a common access requirement to a resource.

4. A. A Resource group is a security group that is added to the discretionary access control list for a resource.

5. C. In a small environment, the account/DACL method of resource authorization is acceptable. In this environment, you define access to a resource by adding individual user accounts to the DACL of a resource.

6. D. The AG/RG authorization method is often used in large environments to make administration easier. When defining access by Account groups and Resource groups, you can save time by defining access to resources by groups, rather than by adding individual users or groups to the DACL of the resource.

7. A, B, D. By default, the members of Domain Admins, Enterprise Admins, and Account Operators have the ability to create group objects and delegate group object permissions.

8. A, D. There are two group types within Active Directory: security and distribution. You should create groups based what the group will be used for. Distribution groups are used for e-mail. An e-mail program such as Microsoft Exchange Server can use distribution groups as distribution lists once they have been mail-enabled. Security groups are used to organize users and grant them access to objects and resources. Security groups can be mail-enabled and used for distribution purposes. You will create security groups to allow users with the same resource access needs to be grouped together.

9. A, C, D. The three criteria that make up a functional naming strategy that will allow an administrator to easily locate the group within Active Directory and understand what the group is used for are the group's scope, purpose, and owner.

10. A, B, C, D. All of the options are correct because the domain is in a Windows Server 2003 functional level. They would also be available in the Windows 2000 Native mode functional level.

Case Study

You should give yourself 20 minutes to review this testlet and complete the questions.

Background

Insane Systems builds custom computers for their customers. They specialize in building cases that are unique and support the latest in hardware technology. They started off as a small company that provided this service to gamers who would take their cases to LAN parties to show off. Because their systems were considered some of the most stable gaming platforms and they provided an impressive design that gamers could show off, they started to become popular. Insane Systems started mass manufacturing some of their more popular designs and began selling stand-alone cases along with their fully configured systems. As space at the company became a premium, the office was moved from the manufacturing facility. This allowed the company to add to the amount of space that was used for the mass production line.

Existing Environment

Over the past few months, Insane Systems has been developing plans to expand their company. They have identified San Jose, California, Atlanta, Georgia, and New York City as the locations with their highest customer base. The current Chicago location will remain the corporate headquarters, but they are opening branches in New York City and San Jose. They are also in the process of acquiring a competitor's business in Atlanta. These locations will provide retail outlets as well as support. Customers will have the option of sending their systems back to the corporate office, or delivering them to one of the branch locations for repairs and/or upgrades.

Because the company is planning on expanding, they want to make sure that the network infrastructure is in place to support their larger, distributed company. They ware also concerned with the support lifetime of their current Windows NT 4 infrastructure. They realize they have the option of moving to a Windows 2000 or Windows 2003 infrastructure and are considering moving to Windows Server 2003 and Active Directory for two reasons: the expected support lifetime is greater than Windows 2000, and they are a technology firm that is not afraid of staying ahead of the technology curve.

Part of the expansion of the company is a complete overhaul of their current Internet presence. They are planning on bringing all of the web development and hosting in-house. Currently a web hosting service is providing their Internet presence, and Insane Systems feels as though they could provide better marketing and support information for their customers if they had control over their own website. Insane Systems would also like to change the name of their website to better represent their name in the marketplace. They own the name `insane-systems.com`.

Interviews

Your company has been hired to design an Active Directory infrastructure and the network infrastructure to support it. During the interview process with some of the key stakeholders, you gathered the following information:

CEO   Currently we have a single location with all of our processes local. As we grow, we would like to keep all of the administration here in Chicago. Because the new branches are primarily retail and support offices, we will not need to have a large staff in those locations. The Atlanta office has an existing network that we would like to merge into our network. System design, research and development, and patent information come from the Atlanta office, so a secure connection from Atlanta to Chicago must be implemented.

CIO   Most of the infrastructure that we support is located here at the corporate office. We do support some key servers at the manufacturing location. We support these servers from our main office. Because the servers are nearby, if there is a problem, we can usually be on site within half an hour.

The new branches are going to be another issue altogether. We would like to retain the same level of administrative control over the servers in the new locations that we employ currently. Due to the geographic limitations, we may need to have some support staff at those locations. Currently, the plan is to hire staff at those locations who can provide the support for the customers, but also understand the business systems we need to put into place. We would like to automate software installations to the remote office due to the lack of IT staff.

Manager of Information Technology   We have grown very quickly over the past three years and our current technologies have kept up with that growth. However we don't think the current infrastructure is ready for the amount of growth that we are expecting within the following year. We are not afraid of moving to the latest technology, but we want to make sure that the design is stable and makes sense for us, especially if we will continue growing in the upcoming months. And because we are losing support for NT 4.0, we want to make sure that we have an operating system that will be supported for a few years down the road.

Most of our processes are located here at this office and we would like to keep it that way. We know that sometimes servers will need to be located at the remote offices, but we would like to be able to provide most of the support from this location. Remote administration tools will need to be included within the design so that we can keep our administrative costs to a minimum.

Currently, we have most of our servers located at the main office, and all are located on their own high-speed backbone. We do have a server at the manufacturing site that allows the staff there to have e-mail as well as plans and orders in case we lose connectivity between the offices. This server is running Exchange 5.5. Several times during the day we replicate the public folder information to this system so that the systems are always up to date and do not have to dial up to the main office using our 56Kbps modem.

The systems at the main office are all supported by our staff of four administrators. All of the administrators are cross-trained on Windows NT 4, Exchange 5.5, SQL Server 7, our accounting software, and each of our file and print servers. We currently have several Windows NT 4 servers in place, including one Exchange 5.5 server at both locations, one SQL Server 7 server at the main office, one server running our accounting package that interfaces with the SQL server, and one file and print server that is used by both locations. The Exchange server at the manufacturing location doubles as a print server also.

The Atlanta office currently has a Windows NT 4 domain, and we will migrate that domain into our forest. Although administration of the forest will be moved to the Chicago branch, administration of the Atlanta domain will reside in the Atlanta domain. We will have a very small IT staff in the Atlanta office who will need control all aspects of the Atlanta domain. Administrators of the Atlanta domain will have control over the Atlanta domain only and will not have administrator access to any other domain or any other part of the forest. All communication between the Atlanta office and the Chicago office will take place via an IPSec connection. The users in the Atlanta office will also require different password and lockout restrictions than the other offices.

Naming conventions for groups are very confusing right now, and adding the Atlanta domain only added to this confusion. Groups in the current domain are named Sales, IT, Accounting, and so on. Groups in the Atlanta domain are also named Sales, Accounting, and so on. We would like to rename groups to define the use of the group. All groups should be prefixed with the group type—Global, Domain Local, or Universal—so that it is easy to locate the group in Active Directory. Domain Local groups should be named according to the location of the resource, the resource name, and the permissions granted. Global groups should be named according to the location of the users who are members of the group. When the domain is moved to Windows Server 2003 functional level, the Universal security groups should be named for the groups that will be included as members.

LAN Administrators in the root domain of the forest are responsible for creating GPOs but do not have access to link them at any level. Domain Admins in each domain are responsible for testing and linking the GPO to their own domains only. Forest owners will also have access to link GPOs at any level of any domain in the forest.

Because all of the client machines are running Windows NT 4 Workstation, we do not have to worry about supporting different operating systems. We would like to maintain that same easy administration with the upcoming system. We would like to provide the same types of services at the remote locations that we provide at the home office, although accounting will remain at the home office and will not be spread out to all of the locations.

Current Infrastructure

After investigating the current infrastructure, you have determined that the following servers are in place:

Home Office

Primary Domain Controller (PDC)

Backup Domain Controller (BDC)

DHCP Server/DNS/WINS Server

Exchange 5.5 Server

SQL Server 7

Systems Management Server 2

File server/Print/Antivirus server

Research and Development file server

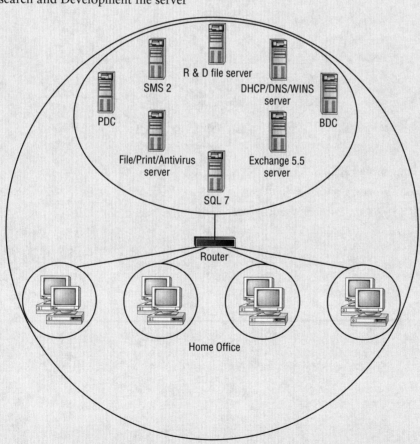

Atlanta Office

Primary Domain Controller (PDC)

Backup Domain Controller (BDC)

WINS server

File server

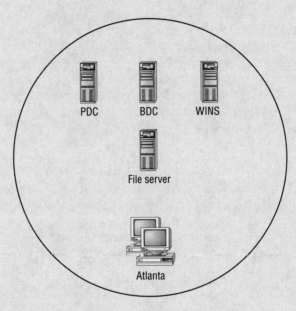

Manufacturing Facility

Backup Domain Controller (BDC)

DNS/WINS/DHCP Relay Agent server

Exchange 5.5/file server

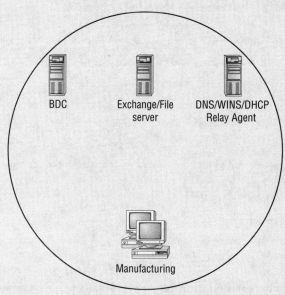

The corporate office hosts nearly 250 Windows NT 4 workstations at this point. They are interconnected by several 48-port 10/100Mbps switches. A router is used to divide the network into 4 VLANs. One of these broadcast domains is the 1Gbps backbone on which the servers reside. Each of the servers is connected to a 1Gbps switch port. This location takes advantage of private IP address ranges. The servers are located on the 192.168.1.0/24 subnet. The client systems are divided between network addresses 192.168.10.0/24, 192.168.11.0/24, 192.168.12.0/24, and 192.168.13.0/24.

The manufacturing facility contains 12 Windows NT 4 workstations connected to the same switch as the servers. Because Insane Systems does not want to slow down production due to a communication failure, they have taken advantage of Exchange 5.5's public folder replication. Public folders are continually updated with the latest orders. The crew foreman can access the orders locally from these public folders at any time, whether the communication link between the locations is up or not. This location uses another address range—192.168.20.0/24.

Case Study Questions

1. During the initial rollout of Active Directory, while Windows NT 4 backup domain controllers exist, which of the group nesting options will be available for use? (Choose all that apply.)

   A. AGLP

   B. AGDLP

   C. AGUDLP

   D. AGGUDLP

2. Which of the following group name structures would work best according to the information you have gathered?

   A. Atl-DL-SalesPrinter-Print, Atl-G-Sales

   B. DL-Atl-SalesPrinter-Print, G-Atl-Sales

   C. DL-SalesPrinter-Print-Atl, G-Sales-Atl

   D. SalesPrinter-Print-DL-Atl, Sales-G-Atl

3. Bill is trying to determine the most efficient method for adding membership to groups in order to grant access to a printer. He needs to design access while the domain is still in mixed mode. He has created the following groups. The users from the Maintenance department will need to print to the printer that is connected to their domain controller. Put the groups in order so that you have defined which accounts are added as members of the groups required to grant access. Place the group that is added to the other at the top of the list. All of the options might not be used.

Groups	Groups
	L-Print1-Print
	DL-Print1-Print
	G-Maintenance
	U-Maintenance

4. When designing resource access, you should have a plan in place for when the domain is moved into Windows Server 2003 functional level. At that point, which of the following nesting options for security groups will be available for use? (Choose all that apply.)

   A. AGLP

   B. AGDLP

   C. AGUDLP

   D. AGGUDLP

5. After a domain has been changed to the Windows Server 2003 functional level, which of the following group names could be used and would be appropriate for use by Insane Systems? (Choose all that apply.)

    A. DL-Chi-SalesPrinter-Print

    B. U-HRUsers

    C. Chi-G-TechSupport

    D. AcctPay-U

Answers to Case Study Questions

1. A, B. While Windows NT 4 backup domain controllers exist, the domain functional level will be at the Windows 2000 Mixed mode or Windows 2003 interim mode domain functional level. At those levels, nesting of Global security groups and Universal security groups is not available.

2. B. According to the interview with the Manager of Information Technology, the naming strategy they would like to employ utilizes the group type—Domain Local, Global, and so on—as the first part of the name, then the location where the group is utilized, and then the purpose of the group.

3.

Groups
G-Maintenance
DL-Print1-Print

   In mixed mode, the only nesting for security groups that is available involves making a Global security group a member of a Domain Local or Local security group. To ease administration, you would use a Domain Local group instead of a Local group because the printer is located on the domain controller.

4. A, B, C, D. Once all of the Windows NT 4 and Windows 2000 domain controllers are removed, you can place the domain in Windows Server 2003 functional level, which will allow for all of the nesting options. Global security groups can become members of other Global security groups, and Universal security groups are available.

5. A, B. Once the domain is in Windows Server 2003 functional level, the Universal security groups can be used. According to the naming convention that was specified by the Manager of Information Technology, the only two options that meet the convention are DL-Chi-SalesPrinter-Print and U-HRUsers.

Chapter

8

Designing the Site Topology

MICROSOFT EXAM OBJECTIVES COVERED IN THIS CHAPTER:

- ✓ **Design an Active Directory directory service site topology.**
    - ▪ Design sites.
    - ▪ Identify site links.
- ✓ **Design an Active Directory implementation plan.**
    - ▪ Design the placement of domain controllers and global catalog servers.
    - ▪ Plan the placement of flexible operations master roles.
    - ▪ Select the domain controller creation process.
- ✓ **Specify the server specifications to meet system requirements.**

So far, we have dealt with Active Directory and the design process involved in creating an efficient Active Directory infrastructure. Our primary focus was to ease the administrative burden. The technologies that are available for use within an Active Directory environment allow administrators to design their directory service so that they will be able to easily locate and maintain objects no matter which type of administrative model is employed. By using Group Policy objects (GPOs), they can automate some of the administrative functions so that they can use their time more productively.

Starting with this chapter, we will discuss the physical components of Active Directory and the network infrastructure. Whereas the Active Directory design is based on the administrative needs of the organization, the network infrastructure design is based upon the need to effectively support Active Directory. If the network infrastructure does not support the needs of the directory service, the system will function poorly and users will not be happy with the decision to move to Active Directory.

Site topology is the first part of the network infrastructure that we will visit. Although the objects that make up the site topology are logical objects within Active Directory, they are based on the physical subnets within the network. We will also cover how to determine where site boundaries are required and the links that define the replication topology.

Domain controller and Global Catalog placement is also an issue that needs to be addressed. Some sites will have domain controllers, whereas others will not. There will be domain controllers that hold the single master operations roles, and you will need to determine which servers will hold those roles. When deciding upon which servers will provide domain controller and Global Catalog services, you will need to take the hardware requirements to support the services into consideration.

Determining the Site Topology

Active Directory employs a multimaster replication technology that allows nearly every aspect of the directory service to be modified from any of the domain controllers within a domain. Changes that are made to one domain controller within the domain are replicated to all of the other domain controllers within the domain. This replication allows all the domain controllers to act as peers and provide the same functionality. However, this same replication can cause issues when you are trying to keep WAN traffic to a minimum.

To reduce the amount of WAN traffic generated by replication, you will need to create sites within Active Directory that define the servers that are well connected. The domain controllers that are all members of the same site will update quickly, whereas replication to domain controllers in other sites can be controlled as to when and how often the replication will occur.

Another advantage to using sites is that client traffic can be contained within the site if there are servers that provide the service that the user needs. User authentication occurs with domain controllers that are located in the same site as the computer that the user is logging onto. In addition, you can make queries to a Global Catalog server and access the Distributed File System (DFS) shares within the same site as the user's computer.

Within a site, the *Knowledge Consistency Checker (KCC)*, a background process that runs on all domain controllers, creates connection objects that represent replication paths to other domain controllers within the site. These connection objects are created in order to produce an efficient replication path to all of the domain controllers within the site. An administrator can also create connection objects manually. If a manual connection is created, the KCC will build other connections around the manual connection to allow for replication redundancy. Do note, however, if you create a connection object that does not allow for efficient replication, the KCC will not override your efforts. As domain controllers are brought online or sites are created, the KCC is responsible for creating the connection objects to allow replication to occur. If a domain controller fails, the KCC will also rebuild the connection objects to allow replication to continue.

The KCC is also responsible for generating the intersite connection objects. When a site connector is created to allow replication between two sites, one domain controller is identified as the *Intersite Topology Generator (ISTG)*. The ISTG is responsible for determining the most efficient path for replication between sites.

As you should remember from studying for previous exams, domain controllers that are placed in different sites do not automatically replicate to one another. To give them the ability to replicate objects to one another, you have to configure a site connector. Once the site connector is created, the domain controller that is defined as the bridgehead server for the site will poll the bridgehead server from the other site to determine if there is any data that needs to be replicated. Because data that is replicated between sites is compressed to conserve network bandwidth, you may want to designate a server to be the bridgehead server. Bridgehead servers should have enough available resources to perform the compression and decompression of data as well as send, receive, and redistribute the replicated objects.

Bridgehead servers are chosen according to their globally unique ID (GUID). If you do not select a domain controller to be a preferred bridgehead server, then the domain controller with the highest GUID is selected. The same holds true if you have multiple domain controllers that are configured to be preferred bridgehead servers—the one with the highest GUID is selected. The remaining domain controllers will wait until the bridgehead server goes offline, and then the ISTG will appoint one of the remaining domain controllers according to the GUID value.

Only one domain controller in each site will become the ISTG. The domain controller with the highest GUID in the site will become the ISTG for the site. It is responsible for determining the bridgehead server and maintaining the connection objects between bridgehead servers in each of the other sites.

In the following section, we are going to look at the options and strategies that you need to consider when designing the site topology to support your Active Directory design.

Understanding the Current Network Infrastructure

Very few organizations will be starting fresh with Windows Server 2003. Unless it is a brand-new business, some type of network will already be in place. In Chapter 3, "Designing the Active Directory Forest Structure," we discussed some of the information you should have gathered about the existing infrastructure. Most of the information gathered at that time dealt with the directory service aspect of the current infrastructure. To build an effective site topology for the Active Directory design, you will also need to know how the current infrastructure supports the user and computer base. Once you have identified the current network infrastructure, you can create the site and site link design.

Identifying the Current Network Infrastructure Design

Networks are made up of well-connected network segments that are connected through other less-reliable or slow links. For a domain controller to be considered well connected to another domain controller, the connection type will usually be 10Mbps, or greater. Of course that is a generalization. Some segments on your network may have 10Mbps or higher links between systems, but if the links are saturated, you may not have enough available bandwidth to support replication. The inverse is also true, you may have network connections that are less than 10Mbps that have enough available bandwidth to handle the replication and authentication traffic.

Look over the existing network and draw out a network map that defines the subnets that are well connected. Some organizations have a networking group that is responsible for the network infrastructure and a directory services group that is responsible for the Active Directory infrastructure. If this is the case, you have to make sure that the two groups work closely together. From the group that is responsible for maintaining the network infrastructure, find out the current physical topology of the network. Gather the information about the location of routers, the speed of the segments, and the IP address ranges used on each of the segments. Also note how many users are in each of the network segments and the types of WAN links that connect the locations. This information will prove useful as you design the site topology.

As an example, consider a company that has a campus in Newark with four buildings and two remote locations: Albuquerque and New Haven. All of the buildings in Newark are connected via an FDDI ring. The two remote locations are connected to Newark via T1 connections. Figure 8.1 shows the network map, which also lists the user population at each location.

For those organizations that have more than one domain, you will need to determine where the user accounts reside. A site can support users from multiple domains as long as those domains are members of the same forest. On your network map, if you have more than one domain, designate the number of users from each domain. In our previous example, if the Research and Development department has its own domain for security purposes, the network map may look like Figure 8.2.

Don't confuse the logical representation of your network with the actual physical entities. You could still have domain controllers from multiple forests within the same physical subnet, but the Active Directory objects that define them can only exist within one forest.

FIGURE 8.1   Network map

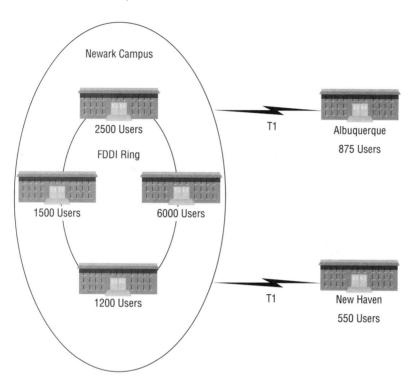

Newark Campus

2500 Users

T1

Albuquerque
875 Users

FDDI Ring

1500 Users

6000 Users

1200 Users

T1

New Haven
550 Users

Designing Sites to Support the Active Directory Design

Once you have created the network map, you can begin designing the required *sites*. Sites are collections of well-connected subnets that are used to control Active Directory replication or manage user and application access to domain controllers and Global Catalog servers. As with every other Active Directory object, you should determine a naming strategy for sites and site links. A site's name should represent the physical location that the site represents. The location could represent a geographic location for organizations that have regional offices, the buildings within an organization's campus or distinct portions of a building. Once you have defined the naming strategy, make sure all of the administrators who have the ability to create sites understand the strategy and follow it.

You need to create a document that details the sites that will be used within the design. This document should include the name of the site, the location that the site represents, the IP subnets that are members of the site, and the WAN links that connect the sites.

If you look at Figure 8.2, you can see that the information that was gathered about the current infrastructure is shown in the network map. You need to use this information to create the site design, as shown in Figure 8.3. Notice that the primary locations are identified as sites within the design. Newark, New Haven, and Albuquerque are all identified as sites. Each of the

IP subnets from the buildings at the Newark campus is shown as included within the Newark site; the IP subnets from the office in Albuquerque are included in the Albuquerque site; and the IP subnets from the office in New Haven are included in the New Haven site.

FIGURE 8.2 Multiple domain network map

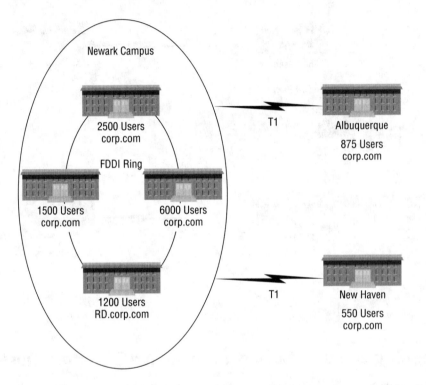

FIGURE 8.3 Site design layout

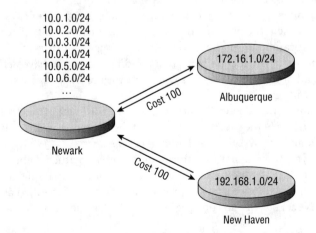

The WAN links that connect Albuquerque and New Haven to the Newark campus are shown on the site design layout. But because the Newark campus is considered a single site, the FDDI connections between the buildings are not considered WAN links at this point. Later when we address the replication needs, this may change.

You should also consider including information about the WAN links on the site layout. This information should include the locations that the WAN link connects, the speed of the link, the available bandwidth on the link during normal operation and how reliable the link is. You may also want to consider including information concerning when the link is used the most, when the off-peak hours are and whether the link is persistent or a dial-up connection. This information will help you to determine the replication schedule.

Once the initial site choices are made based upon the network requirements, you will need to determine if you should create sites to support user and application requirements. Users sitting at workstations that are Active Directory aware will authenticate to a domain controller from their domain, if there is one within their site. If their site does not have a domain controller for their domain, they will authenticate with a domain controller within another site. All domain controllers determine if any sites exist that do not contain domain controllers from their domain when they are brought online. If some sites match this criteria, the domain controller then determines if it is located within a site near the site without a domain controller. The domain controller determines this based on the cost of the site link or site link bridges that connect the two sites. If it is determined that the domain controller is close to the site, it registers a service locator (SRV) record for the site.

For more information on how to configure domain controllers to register their services to other sites, see Knowledge Base articles 200498 and 306602.

As an example, Company G has two domains: `corp.com` and `RD.corp.com`. Five sites exist within their environment: A, B, C, D, and E. Figure 8.4 shows the site layout and the site links that connect them. Within the sites, there are domain controllers for each of the domains. Note that site C does not contain a domain controller for `RD.corp.com`. In this case, as domain controllers start up, they will check the configuration of the domain to determine whether or not a site exists without a domain controller from their own domain. When domain controllers from `RD.corp.com` start up, they will recognize that site C does not have a domain controller. They will then determine whether they should register SRV records for the site based upon whether or not they are in a site that is considered to be the nearest. Since site B has the lowest cost value over the site link to site C, `RDDCB1.RD.corp.com` will register SRV records on behalf of site C. When users from the RD.corp.com domain authenticate from a computer in site C, they will authenticate with the nearest domain controller, `RDDCB1.RD.corp.com`.

Active Directory replication can consume a considerable amount of network resources within a site. Replication traffic is not compressed between domain controllers that exist within the same site. If the available network bandwidth will not support the replication traffic that you are anticipating, you may want to look into dividing up IP segments so that you can control the replication moving between the domain controllers. Once additional sites are created, site links can then be configured. Replication traffic that passes across site links is compressed to conserve bandwidth if the data exceeds 50KB.

FIGURE 8.4 Determining the nearest site

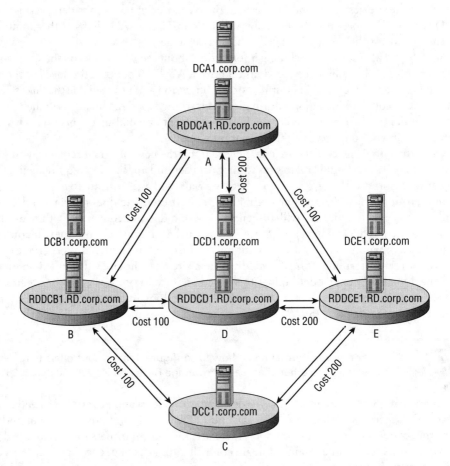

Another consideration is application support. Applications such as Exchange Server 2003 require access to a Global Catalog server. If you want to control which Global Catalog server an Exchange server will use, you could create a site and place the two servers within the site to control the traffic between them. For example, within our `corp.com` domain, we have an Exchange Server 2003 server that is located within Building 1 of the Newark campus. We have specified that a domain controller within Building 2 is to be used by the Exchange server when it sends queries to a Global Catalog server. In order to control the requests, another site is created that includes Building 1 and Building 2. Figure 8.5 represents the site design once the change has been made to support our decision.

Designing Site Links and Site Link Bridges

Because we have identified the WAN links that connect the sites within our design, we can decide easily on the *site links* that we will need to support the design at this point. Site links are objects that are created to connect sites so that replication can be controlled. You also need to address other considerations such as replication, log-on authentication control, and application support.

FIGURE 8.5   Site design to support application requirements

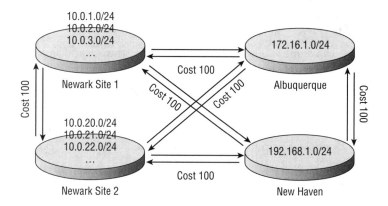

Site link bridges are collections of site links that allow replication traffic from domain controllers in one site to pass to domain controllers in another site when no explicit replication partners exist in the intermediary site that connects them.

In the following sections we are going to spend some time reviewing the options that are available for sites and site link bridges.

Site Links

By default there is one site link created when the first domain controller is installed. This site link is called DEFAULTIPSITELINK, but it can be renamed to conform to your naming strategy. This site link uses Remote Procedure Calls (RPC) for replication. You could take advantage of using this site link for all of the sites that you have within your infrastructure if they all have the same replication requirements. For example, if all of the sites are connected by WAN links that have approximately the same available bandwidth and they all use RPC for replication, then simply rename this site link to conform to your naming strategy and make sure all of the sites are included.

Another reason you may want to create additional site links is to control when the replication can occur. You may have some sites that need to have objects updated at different schedules. Using site links, you can create a replication schedule between sites. You cannot define which physical connection a site links uses in order to control the replication traffic over specific network links. For instance, if you have a T1 connection and an ISDN connection to a branch office and the ISDN connection is only used as a backup communication link if the T1 goes down, you cannot create two site links with two different costs, one for each of the communication links.

When creating the site link, you have the options of choosing the following:

Protocol used for replication   Two protocols can be used for replication of objects: IP and SMTP. When selecting IP, you are really specifying that you want to use RPCs to deliver the replicated objects. You can select SMTP if the domain controllers that you are replicating data between are not within the same domain. If the domain controllers are within the same domain, the file replication service (FRS) has to use RPCs to replicate the Sysvol data. Since FRS requires the same replication topology as the domain partition, you cannot use SMTP between the domain controllers within a domain. You can use SMTP if you want to control the replication between Global Catalog servers or domain controllers that are replicating the schema and configuration partition data between domain controllers.

Name of the site link   The name should follow your naming strategy and should define the sites that are connected using the link.

Connected sites   These are the sites that will explicitly replicate between bridgehead servers in each listed site.

Schedule   The schedule consists of the hours when replication can occur and the interval—how often you want to allow replication to occur during the hours that replication data is allowed to pass between the bridgehead servers.

Cost of the connection   A value that determines which link will be used. This cost, or priority, value is used to choose the most efficient site link. You will use the combination of site links with the lowest total cost to replicate data between any pair of sites.

Note the replication patterns when you are trying to determine the schedule. You could cause a good deal of latency to occur if the schedule is not compatible. For example, a company may have a central office that acts as the hub for the regional office. The regional offices are responsible for replication to the branch offices in their region. Figure 8.6 shows the schedule for the Atlanta central office, the Sydney and Chicago regional offices, and the Exmouth, Peoria, and Bloomington branch offices. Because all of the domestic U.S. links have approximately the same bandwidth availability, you could create a single site link that uses a 15-minute interval. You could then create a separate site link between Atlanta and Sydney that has the replication interval set for every two hours so that replication does not adversely affect the WAN links. Between the Sydney and Exmouth sites, another site link uses a 1-hour interval to control traffic. Depending on the connection objects that are created by the KCC, the total propagation delay for an update in Chicago to reach Exmouth could be three and a half hours. And that is only considering the replication interval. The schedule on the site link could be configured to allow replication traffic to flow only during the evening hours. If you have a schedule that is closed off for a portion of time, the propagation delay will increase even more. You need to make sure that this will be acceptable within your organization.

FIGURE 8.6   Replication schedules based on site links

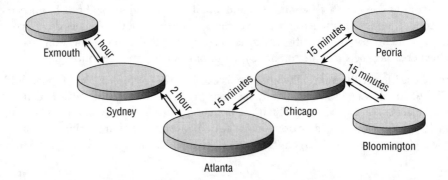

You should also plan the cost of site links carefully. The default site link cost value is 100. If all of the communication links have the same available bandwidth, you could leave the default cost on all links. However, if different bandwidth constraints occur on any of the communication links, you will need to adjust the cost values. One method of determining a valid cost for site links is to divide 1,024 by the base 10 logarithm of the available bandwidth as measured in kilobits per second (Kbps). In doing so, you will find cost values that correspond to the entries in Table 8.1.

TABLE 8.1   Example of costs for available bandwidth

Available Bandwidth in Kbps	Cost Value
4096	283
2048	309
1024	340
512	378
256	425
128	486
64	567
56	586
38.4	644
19.2	798
9.6	1042

Site Link Bridges

In Windows Server 2003 Active Directory, site link bridging is enabled for all site links by default, making replication transitive throughout sites. In Figure 8.7, note that there are domain controllers in all three sites from `corp.com`. Site B is the only site that does not have a domain controller from `RD.corp.com`. With site link bridging enabled, replication from domain controllers for `RD.corp.com` in site A will pass to `RD.corp.com` domain controllers in site C.

FIGURE 8.7   Site Link Bridge

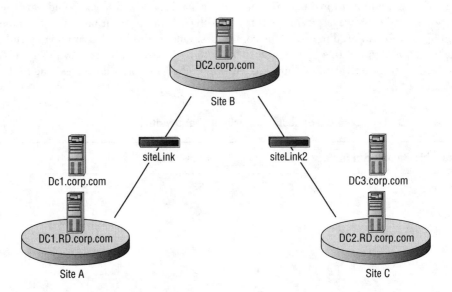

If you have a network infrastructure that is fully routed and all of the locations can communicate directly with one another, then you can leave this default setting turned on. However, if you have locations where not all of the domain controllers are able to communicate directly to one another—for instance, if they are separated by firewalls—you may want to turn off the site link bridging. You may also want to turn it off if you want to manually control where it is allowed. If you have a large, complex network, you could turn off the bridging and create your own site link bridges by defining which site links will be included in a bridge.

Firewalls that exist within your organization's network infrastructure could also pose challenges. There may be rules in place that will only allow specific servers to communicate with internal resources. If you do have a firewall in place you may need to turn off site link bridging so that you can control the site links that will pass replication traffic from site to site.

Remember that the site link does not define any physical network links. The physical connections are determined by how the domain controllers are connected to one another. A site link cannot detect if a physical link is down and thus will not reroute the traffic immediately. Determine your site link's costs based upon the paths on which you would like replication to occur when using bridging.

For more information on creating site links and controlling site link bridging, see the *MCSE: Windows Server 2003 Active Directory Planning, Implementation and Maintenance Study Guide,* by Anil Desai with James Chellis (Sybex, 2003).

In the "Determining Site Topology" Design Scenario, you will determine a site topology for a specific scenario.

In the next section, we start discussing domain controllers, what server specifications are recommended, and where they should be located. This includes servers that will be domain controllers for the domain and those that will also be Global Catalog servers.

Determining Domain Controller Specifications and Placement

Domain controllers are probably the single most important server type within your organization. Without them, you would not have a nice unified database that holds the objects used for authentication, stores application information, and provides centralized security control.

To have this functionality available to users, you need to determine where you will place domain controllers within your environment. This includes the domain controllers you will use primarily for authentication purposes, those designated as Global Catalog servers, and those that hold the master operations roles. You can start choosing the hardware you will use for a domain controller and then base the number of domain controllers required for each site on the hardware, or you can determine how many domain controllers and Global Catalog servers you would like to locate at each site and determine the hardware you will need to support the design. Finally, you will need to determine how the domain controllers will be created, because you may have domain controllers that will be installed in remote locations. You may not want to have the initial replication occur across a WAN link.

Determining Domain Controller Specifications

Although it is best to test the hardware you would like to use as domain controllers to determine how they perform when they are supporting users, some general guidelines, shown in Table 8.2, can give you an idea of how many domain controllers you will need to support your infrastructure. The values you find on the following pages are according to Microsoft's calculations. We decided to include them for a reference since there are many companies that are continuing to use their existing hardware instead of purchasing new systems. As a rule of thumb, always test your hardware before implementing the system. Newer processors, bus speeds, memory speeds and drive subsystems work more efficiently than the older technologies. As with anything, your mileage may vary.

TABLE 8.2   Processor and Memory Specifications for Domain Controllers

Number of Users	Processor(s)	Memory
1–499	Single 866Mhz or faster	512MB
500–1499	Dual 899Mhz or faster	1GB
1500+	Quad 899Mhz or faster	2 GB

If you use Table 8.2 to determine how many domain controllers are required to support the Newark campus in our example from earlier in the chapter, you will remember that there were 11,200 users within the Newark site. If you assumed that the hardware the company wants to purchase for domain controllers has dual 2000Mhz processors with 1GB of RAM each, then you would need to have at least 8 domain controllers. With the faster processors that you have included within the system, you will probably be able to exceed the recommendations in Table 8.2, but the memory or network subsystems may cause a bottleneck. Again, your best bet is to test the hardware that you plan on using to see what type of performance you can get out of it.

As far as the amount of drive space you will need to support your domain controller goes, there are also guidelines you can follow. For every 1000 users, you will need 0.4GB of disk space. For the 12,625 users of `corp.com`, you will need approximately 5.05GB of disk space.

As a rule of thumb, if the domain controller is also used as a Global Catalog server, you will need to have enough drive space to support half of the drive space requirements from each of the other domains. In a scenario where a company may have three domains—DomainA with 10,000 users, DomainB with 18,000 users, and DomainC with 4,000 users—the space requirements for each of the domains would work out as shown in Table 8.3.

TABLE 8.3 Global Catalog Drive Space Requirements

Domain	Domain Requirements (# Users/1000 * .4)	Total Space Required (Domain + (Total of Other Domains /2))
DomainA	4GB	8.4GB
DomainB	7.2GB	10GB
DomainC	1.6GB	7.2GB

You will need additional drive space for the transaction logs that are generated as the domain controller performs its functions. All transactions that occur on the domain controller are performed in memory. These transactions are written sequentially to the transaction logs so that the data is safeguarded in case the domain controller fails before the transaction is committed to the database.

Once you have determined what the server specifications for your domain controllers should be, you need to determine where they will be located. In the following section you will find the reasons for locating domain controllers in sites and what happens when a domain controller is not located in a user's site.

In the "Calculating the Database Size" Design Scenario, we are going to estimate the drive space requirements based upon the objects that will make up the Active Directory database.

 Design Scenario

Calculating the Database Size

Argobot Mechanations is preparing to expand operations. They are in the process of upgrading their network infrastructure, which will implement Windows Server 2003 Active Directory as their directory service. Currently they have three divisions within their organization. The main division is their robotics line, which employs 4,500 people. The second division is the Research and Development department (R&D), which will become its own domain. R&D employs 500 users. Robotic Techs is the third division, and it operates as a subsidiary to Argobot Mechanations. This division employs 6,000 users and will also be a separate domain.

1. **Question:** When you are planning the drive space requirements for the domain controller, how much drive space will be consumed? **Answer:** Argobot Mechanations should have 1.8GB, R&D should have .2GB, and Robotic Techs should have 2.4GB.

2. **Question:** When planning the drive space requirements for the Global Catalog, how much drive space will be consumed? **Answer:** Argobot Mechanations should have 3.1GB, R&D should have 2.3GB, and Robotic Techs should have 3.4GB.

Choosing Domain Controller Placement

Choosing where domain controllers will be placed can be difficult. You should take several things into consideration before deciding to place a domain controller at a location. Security, replication traffic, and user authentication should all be taken into account. When determining the placement at the design phase, some questions will help you determine which site the domain controller should be placed in:

Will the domain controller by physically secure at the location?   If the domain controller will not be locked away, the computer could be physically attacked and the drives containing the database could be compromised. In some small organizations, this may not be as important a consideration as in large companies, but it should be considered nonetheless.

Can the domain controller be administered by local staff?   If the staff members from the location do not have the ability to manage the domain controller, will you be able to provide remote access capabilities to the domain controller? Built-in tools allow an administrator to manage the domain controller remotely, and you need to determine if having those tools loaded is worth the trade-off of having the domain controller located at another location where it can be managed by local administrators. Make sure that your network infrastructure will allow you to connect to the remote servers because firewalls and connectivity issues could limit your access to the domain controllers.

Is the WAN link reliable?   If the link is not reliable enough, you need to determine if you can get by without a domain controller for the site. We recommend that you do not allow for a site to be left without a domain controller if the WAN link is unreliable. However, if security concerns are greater than the users' ability to authenticate for a short period of time, or the user base is small enough that you cannot justify the cost of a domain controller, you may choose to have them authenticate to a domain controller in another site away from the users.

If you are allowing authentication across the WAN link, is the logon performance acceptable?   If it is, you should be able to host a site without a dedicated domain controller. However, if users are complaining about logon times, consider moving the domain controller to their site so that they can authenticate more efficiently. You may have to consider a trade-off between local authentication and replication traffic. Replication traffic in large domains or domains that have many Active Directory updates could consume too much of the available bandwidth. If the logon traffic is less than the replication traffic, it may make more sense to not locate the domain controller within the site.

You may encounter cases when domain controllers from the forest root will be placed within a site even though users from the forest root will not be authenticating within that site. If resources are located in another domain, having a domain controller from the forest root in the same site as the users will alleviate some of the WAN traffic caused by the Kerberos ticket passing that is going on. Of course, creating a shortcut trust between the domains that are affected may be a more efficient solution in a small environment, but locating a forest root domain controller within the site will alleviate traffic and the need for multiple shortcut trusts if there are several domains that the users are accessing.

After determining where the domain controllers should be placed, you should determine where Global Catalog servers are needed. The following section details the reasons for having a Global Catalog in a site.

Choosing Global Catalog Placement

Global Catalog servers provide functionality to users as well as applications within the domain. Global Catalog servers are responsible for collecting information about the objects that exist in the domain partition of other domains in the forest. Although this is just a subset of the attributes for the objects, this could still be a considerable amount of information. Once a domain controller is specified as a Global Catalog server, additional replication will occur so that information from the other domains will populate the database. You need to determine if this additional replication is going to affect the performance of the network links.

When determining if you should have a Global Catalog server placed within a site, you should consider how much the Global Catalog server will be used and whether applications within the site need to use a Global Catalog server. The following questions should be asked to determine whether or not a Global Catalog should be placed within a site:

Are there any applications, such as Exchange 2000 Server or Exchange Server 2003, located within the site?   If this is the case, you will want to locate a Global Catalog server within the same site as the application since the LDAP queries being posted to the Global Catalog server will probably consume more bandwidth than replication. Test the network requirements to determine which will consume more bandwidth. If the WAN link is not 100 percent reliable, you should always have the Global Catalog server local, otherwise the application will not function properly when the link goes down.

Do you have more than 100 users located within the site?   If you have more than 100 users within a site, you will need to determine if stranding them without having the ability to access a Global Catalog server if the WAN link goes down is an acceptable option. You will also need to determine if the query latency is worth the cost savings of keeping the Global Catalog server at another location and not dedicating hardware for the site in question.

Is the WAN link 100 percent available?   If you do need application support and the user base is less than 100 users, you could have those users access a Global Catalog server in the remote site if the WAN link is reliable. Although no WAN link will ever be 100 percent available, the higher the reliability of the link, the better your chances of being able to support the user base from a remote site. If the WAN link is not always available and there are not any applications that rely on the Global Catalog server, you could implement universal group membership cacheing to alleviate some of the problems associated with user authentication.

Are there many roaming users who will be visiting the site?   If many roaming users will be logging on at the site, you will want to locate a Global Catalog server within the site. Whenever a user logs on, the user's universal group membership is retrieved from the Global Catalog server. However, if the user population at the site is relatively static, you may be able to implement universal group membership cacheing on a domain controller.

One of the new features of Windows Server 2003 is *universal group membership caching*. This feature is only available when the domain is in the Windows 2000 Native mode or a higher functional level, and only Windows Server 2003 domain controllers provide this functionality. The benefit of using universal group membership cacheing is that a domain controller does not have to be made a Global Catalog server in order to provide the user with their universal group membership, which is required to log on. As users authenticate, the domain controller contacts a Global Catalog server from another site to retrieve the required information. The group membership is then cached on the domain controller ready to be used the next time the user logs on. Because the domain controller does not have to provide Global Catalog services, replication across the WAN link is reduced.

Universal group membership cacheing is not meant for sites with large user populations, nor is it meant to be used where applications need to access a Global Catalog server. A maximum of 500 users is supported using this cacheing method. Also, the cached data is only updated every 8 hours. If you are planning on performing group membership changes on a regular basis, your users may not receive those changes in a timely manner. You can reduce the timeframe for updating the cache, but in doing so you will be creating more replication traffic on your WAN link. Make sure you weigh the trade-offs before you decide where you will place a Global Catalog server.

Another Active Directory technology whose location needs to be determined is the master operations roles. Because only specific servers support the master operations functions, you should know the criteria for their placement.

Choosing Master Operations Placement

Back in Chapter 4, "Designing the Active Directory Domain Structure," we discussed the master operations roles and their functions within the forest. Due to the importance of the master operations, you should carefully choose where the domain controllers holding each of these roles are placed. The following sections discuss what guidelines you should take into consideration.

Operations Masters in a Single Domain Forest

Within a single domain forest, the infrastructure master does not play a very important role. As a matter of fact, its services are not used at all. Because you will not have any remote domains for the infrastructure master to compare domain information to, it will not matter if the domain controller is a Global Catalog server or not. In fact, in a single domain environment, all domain controllers could be enabled as Global Catalog servers because there will not be any additional replication costs.

By default, the first domain controller within the domain will hold all of the master operations roles and will also be a Global Catalog server. You should also designate another domain controller as a standby server. You do not have to configure anything special on this domain controller. Just make sure that all administrative personnel are aware of your preference to use a specific server as the standby in case the first fails. Then, if a failure of the first server does occur, you can quickly seize the master operations on the second server. Make sure that the two systems are located close to one another and connected via a high-speed connection. You could even create connection objects between the two systems so that they replicate directly to one another, ensuring that their directories are as identical as possible.

Operations Masters Site Placement in a Multiple Domain Forest

The five master operations roles will have to be placed on domain controllers where they will be the most effective. You should take certain criteria into consideration when you are deciding on which site these domain controllers will be placed.

Schema Master

The schema master role is not one that is used very often. Typically, the only time the schema master needs to be online after the initial installation of Active Directory is when you are making changes to the schema. When you are planning the placement of the schema master, place it in a site where the schema administrators have easy access to it. Also take into consideration the replication that will be incurred when a change is made. For this reason alone you may want to place the schema master within a site that has the most domain controllers within the forest.

Domain Naming Master

As with the schema master, the domain naming master is not used very often. Its role is to guarantee the uniqueness of domain names within the forest. It is also used when removing domains from the forest. For the domain naming master to perform its function, you should locate it on a global catalog server, although with Windows Server 2003 this is not a requirement as it was in Windows 2000.

The domain naming master and the schema master can be located on the same domain controller since neither of the roles will impact the way the domain controllers function. And as with the schema master, it should be located close to where the administrative staff can access.

Relative Identifier (RID) Master

The RID master is responsible for generating and maintaining the RIDs used by the security principles within the domain. Each domain controller will contact the RID master to obtain a group of RIDs to be used as the accounts are created. If your domain is in native mode or higher, you should place the RID master in a site that has domain controllers where administrators are creating a majority of the accounts. This will allow the RID master to efficiently hand out allocations of RIDs to the domain controllers. If your domain is in mixed mode, consider placing the RID master on the same server as the PDC emulator. The PDC emulator is the only domain controller that can create accounts within the domain when the domain is in mixed mode.

Infrastructure Master

The infrastructure master holds a very important role within a multiple domain forest. If users from one domain are added to the membership of groups from a second domain, the infrastructure master is then responsible for maintaining any updates when changes occur within the remote domain.

For instance, if a user from domain A is added to a group in domain B, and the user's name changes because she gets married, the user account name in domain A does not match the entry within the group membership of domain B. The infrastructure master is responsible for reviewing the information from domain A and checking for discrepancies. If it finds that a change has been made, the infrastructure master updates the information in domain B so that the new name information within the group can be replicated to all of the domain controllers.

If the infrastructure master is located on a Global Catalog server, it will check for differences between domain A and domain B, but it will not notice any discrepancies because the Global Catalog server hosts information from domain A. Other servers that are not Global Catalog servers in domain B will not have the correct information for the group, and the infrastructure master will not update the other domain controllers. So, in a multiple domain forest, move the infrastructure master to a domain controller that is not a Global Catalog server. Of course, if you make every domain controller a Global Catalog server, you will not have to worry about the infrastructure master placement because every domain controller will host information from every domain and replicate changes whenever they are made.

When you are choosing the placement of the infrastructure master, place it within a site that also contains domain controllers from the other domains. This ensures that the queries and updates performed are local.

Primary Domain Controller (PDC) Emulator

The other master operations role that you need take into consideration is the Primary Domain Controller (PDC) emulator. Whenever Windows NT 4 Backup Domain Controllers (BDCs) exist within the domain, the PDC Emulator is responsible for keeping the Windows NT 4 BDCs and all other Windows 2000 Server or Windows Server 2003 domain controllers updated. The PDC emulator is also responsible for accepting password change requests from pre–Active Directory clients. If the domain is placed in Windows 2000 Native mode or the Windows Server 2003 functional level, the PDC emulator becomes the clearinghouse for password changes within the domain. Any time another domain controller receives a password change from a client, the PDC emulator is passed the change so that the other domain controllers can be notified of the change. If a user has entered a bad password, the PDC emulator is passed the authentication request to validate that the user's password was not changed on another domain controller prior to the authentication request.

Another important function of the PDC Emulator is time synchronization. All members of the domain, whether they are running Windows 2000, Windows XP or Windows Server 2003 as their operating system will synchronize their clocks according to time on the PDC emulator and use the timestamp to authenticate clients. This timestamp is then used with the Kerberos service to authenticate clients.

When deciding the most appropriate site for the PDC emulator role, choose a site that is close to the majority of users within the domain. Also, make sure that domain controllers placed in other sites have reliable links and available bandwidth to support the traffic that will be used by the PDC emulator.

The section that follows describes the options available when you are building domain controllers to support users and applications within the site topology that we have been designing.

Determining Domain Controller Creation Options

You have two options when creating domain controllers. The first option is to promote the member server to a domain controller and allow replication of the Active Directory objects to occur across the network. This is the default method and is the easiest to perform. The administrator who has the ability to promote the system to a domain controller only needs to provide the information required by the wizard. The promotion can even be automated so that the administrator will only have to provide the path to the answer file that contains the settings necessary to create the domain controller.

Promoting the domain controller and allowing the objects to be replicated works well because the data is up-to-date as soon as the replication is complete. However, this replication could cause a lot of network traffic. If this is the choice that you make, be sure that you have a high-speed connection between the two domain controllers where replication is occurring. If you are trying to build a domain controller within a remote site and the nearest domain controller is across a WAN link, replicating the objects may not be an option. You may need to perform the second option.

 Real World Scenario

Choosing How to Build a Domain Controller

Becca is the manager of the information technology division of an art supply retailer. The company has their headquarters in St. Louis, MO, and has five regional distribution centers. Each of the distribution centers services anywhere from 20 to 45 retail outlets. Each of the regional distribution centers hosts an Exchange Server 2003 server and an SQL 2000 Server database server. Some of the larger retail outlets, those with more than 200 employees, also host their own Exchange and SQL servers. Retail outlets that have fewer than 200 employees rely on the servers at the regional distribution center for e-mail and database services but will have a local domain controller to authenticate them.

After identifying the sites and the domain controllers that are going to be placed within each site, Becca devises a plan for the domain controller creation at each site. After installing the domain controllers at the company headquarters, she performs a system state backup of a Global Catalog server and stores the backup on a share on the network. Servers that will be used for domain controllers at the regional distribution centers and retail outlets are all delivered to the regional distribution center that services them.

During the night, the backup data is transferred to servers at the regional distribution centers. The following morning, the administrative staff at each of the regional distribution centers is told how to perform their domain controller promotion. Each server will be promoted using the advanced mode of dcpromo and the backed-up system state data will be chosen. Because each of the regional distribution centers will host Exchange Server 2003, the domain controllers at each will also be Global Catalog servers.

The administrators from the regional distribution center will then be responsible for building the domain controllers for the retail outlets. Because each of the retail outlet domain controllers will be identical, an answer file is created that will automate the domain controller creation. Once the domain controllers are ready, they will be shipped to the retail outlets where they can be connected to the network.

The second option is to perform what is referred to as an advanced install of Active Directory. An advanced install is initiated by using the dcpromo /adv switch when you are promoting a Windows Server 2003 system to a domain controller. When you are using the advanced mode, you use the system state information from an existing domain controller within the domain as the initial data to populate Active Directory. Once the initial population is finished, standard Active Directory replication updates the domain controller bringing it up-to-date. Using the advanced mode will drastically reduce the amount of data that will have to pass across a WAN link to the new domain controller.

If the system state information was taken from a Global Catalog server, you will be prompted to answer whether you would like the new domain controller to become a Global Catalog server. If you select Yes, a new Global Catalog server will be created. If you select No, only the objects for the local domain will be loaded onto the new domain controller. Do note that the system state backup that you are using to create the new domain controller cannot be older than the tombstone lifetime to ensure that old objects are not regenerated into the domain. The tombstone lifetime is the amount of time that a deleted object will remain within Active Directory. By keeping a deleted item within Active Directory, the object can be marked for deletion on all domain controllers before it is purged.

The older the backup media that contains the system state, the more replication that will occur when the data is restored. Make sure you back up the data regularly.

Summary

An efficient site design will allow users to authenticate using a domain controller close to their computer and applications to take advantage of Global Catalogs within the same site as the one in which they are located. When determining where you should create sites, you should map out the current network infrastructure to determine where the well-connected networks are and the WAN links that connect them. Once the network has been mapped, the initial site structure can be designed based on the network connections.

After determining where you need to control replication and application access to Global Catalog servers, you can create the site links that connect the sites. Site links allow domain controllers in two sites to replicate based on a scheduled time. Large amounts of replication traffic will be compressed to make the transmission of data as efficient as possible. Site link bridging, which is enabled by default, makes the site links transitive in nature and allows the replication traffic to pass through sites that do not have direct connections to each other.

You should consider domain controller specifications, and you should make sure that the domain controllers you are planning on using will support the number of users that you need to authenticate. Once you have chosen your domain controllers, you should place them close to the users who need to authenticate so that they will not have to pass the authentication request across a WAN link. If the WAN link were to fail, the users would not be able to access their network resources.

Global Catalog server placement should also be taken into consideration. Applications such as Exchange Server 2003 require a Global Catalog server, so you should have one in the same site as the server. Users request universal group membership from Global Catalog server when they log on. Sites where users perform many queries against the Global Catalog server should also have one located within the site.

In the next chapter, we are going to discuss network access and determine the required types of network access for all of the different users that will be using our network when accessing Active Directory resources. This will include local users and remote access users. We will also discuss placement of specialized servers such as routers, remote access servers, and servers that will be placed in perimeter networks.

Exam Essentials

Know the current network design.   If you do not understand the current network design, you will not have a foundation on which to base the new design. The current design will be the starting point for understanding where the LAN and WAN links are and where sites may need to be created.

Understand how authentication traffic is controlled within a site.   When a user authenticates, the authentication traffic is sent to a domain controller within the same site as the computer to which the user is attempting to log on, or a domain controller in a site that has been identified as the preferred site.

Understand site links.   Site links are created between sites to control the replication traffic between domain controllers in the sites. Site links have schedules as to when replication can occur, intervals during the schedule that specify how often replication can occur, sites that are connected through the site link, and costs that control which site links the replication traffic will use.

Understand site link bridging.   Site link bridging allows replication traffic to pass across two or more site links in order to reach domain controllers in sites that are either not physically connected or that have no domain controllers for the domain in the sites within the site link path.

Identify the domain controller specifications.   The number of users that are members of the domain will dictate how much drive space is required for the directory database on a domain controller. On average, every 1,000 users consume .4GB of drive space. Memory and processor speed are also factors in determining how many logon requests can be supported by the domain controller.

Understand domain controller placement options.   Domain controllers should be placed close to the users who need to authenticate. Other factors may dictate where the domain controllers are placed. If there is enough bandwidth on the WAN link to support all of the users, a domain controller in another site could be used. If the WAN link is not reliable or is over consumed, or if there are too many users in the site, you will probably want to place a domain controller in the same site as the user accounts.

Understand Global Catalog placement options.   Global Catalog servers are used when users authenticate and when users or applications query for Active Directory. If applications that use Global Catalog severs reside in the site, place a Global Catalog server there. If not many users are in the site and not many roaming users authenticate in the site, you could place the Global Catalog server on the other side of the WAN link. If there are several users, many roaming users, or the WAN link is not reliable or is over consumed, plan on placing a Global Catalog in the local site.

Understand master operations role placement options.   The infrastructure master should not be placed on a Global Catalog server if more than one domain is within the forest. The PDC emulator should be placed in a site that has the most users and has high-speed reliable connections to the other sites. The schema master and domain naming master roles should be placed close to the users that will be responsible for administering them. The RID master should be placed on the same domain controller as the PDC emulator if your domain is in mixed mode. Otherwise the RID master should be located within the site where the most account creation goes on.

Know the options available when creating domain controllers.   Domain controllers can be built using answer files to automate the promotion, or you can use the advanced mode, dcpromo /adv, to copy the directory database from backup media. The latter is preferred if the domain controller is being built in a remote site and you do not want to cause full replication across the WAN link.

Key Terms

Before you take the exam, be certain you are familiar with the following terms:

Intersite Topology Generator (ISTG)	site links
Knowledge Consistency Checker (KCC)	sites
site link bridges	universal group membership cacheing

Review Questions

1. Which of the following describes a group of well-connected subnets where the domain controllers replicate immediately and do not compress the data sent to other domain controllers?

    A. Site

    B. Site link

    C. Site link bridge

    D. Domain

2. Which of the following describes the object that controls replications between domain controllers in two sites?

    A. Site

    B. Site link

    C. Site connector

    D. Site connector bridge

3. Which protocols can be used between sites? (Choose all that apply.)

    A. IP

    B. SMTP

    C. ICMP

    D. POP3

4. What is the name of the first site link?

    A. DEFAULTSITELINK

    B. DEFAULTIPSITELINK

    C. DEFAULTFIRSTSITELINK

    D. DEFAULTLINK

5. What is the default cost value for a site link?

    A. 0

    B. 1

    C. 10

    D. 100

6.   What option is turned on by default that allows all sites to replicate to one another?

   A. Site link

   B. Site link bridge

   C. Site connector

   D. Site connector bridge

7.   Which of the following processor specifications will support 850 users? (Choose all that apply.)

   A. Single 566MHz

   B. Single 866Mhz

   C. Dual 899MHz

   D. Quad 899MHz

8.   How much drive space is required for a domain with 72,000 users?

   A. 28.8GB

   B. 28.8MB

   C. 288GB

   D. 288MB

9.   In which of the following sites should you place a Global Catalog? (Choose all that apply.)

   A. In a site with 10 users where the WAN link is considered reliable.

   B. In a site where Exchange Server 2003 exists.

   C. In a site with 620 users and the WAN link is utilized heavily during the day.

   D. In a site with 20 users but several roaming users visit the site on a daily basis.

10.   Within site A, there are 4 domain controllers: DC1.corp.com, DC2.corp.com, RDDC1.RD.corp.com, and RDDC2.RD.corp.com. DC2.corp.com and RDDC1.RD.corp.com are Global Catalog servers. You are trying to determine which server should hold the infrastructure master role for the corp.com domain. Which server would you place the role on?

   A. DC1.corp.com

   B. DC2.corp.com

   C. RDDC1.RD.corp.com

   D. RDDC2.RD.corp.com

Answers to Review Questions

1. A. A site is a replication boundary for domain controllers in which each domain controller will notify other domain controllers in the same site that there are objects to replicate. This replication occurs between all of the domain controllers without compressing the data. All of the subnets that make up the site should be well connected and have enough available bandwidth to support the uncompressed traffic.

2. B. Site links are used to create a replication path between domain controllers that exist in two sites. Site links can be created so that they control when the replication can occur and which sites are connected using the site link. They also have a cost value to control how the replication is directed.

3. A, B. When you create a site link, you can use IP or SMTP to deliver the replicated data.

4. B. The first site link that is created when Active Directory is installed is the DEFAULTIPSITELINK. You can rename this site link and use it as the site link to link all of the sites if the replication topology is similar among all sites.

5. D. If no changes are made to a site link, the default cost is set at 100. If all of the sites have the same available bandwidth and replication needs, this cost can be kept. If there are any differences, you will have to determine the replication path you want the replication to take.

6. B. Site link bridges are automatically enabled in Windows Server 2003 Active Directory. This makes all site links transitive in nature, which allows replication to occur even to sites that are not directly connected to other sites where a domain controller from their domain exists.

7. C, D. It is recommended that if there are 500 or more users within a site, the domain controller that is authenticating them should have at least dual 899MHz processors.

8. A. The formula that is used to determine the approximate amount of drive space that the directory database will consume is (number of users / 1000) * .4GB.

9. B, C, D. Global Catalog servers are used when users authenticate and when users or applications query for Active Directory. If applications that use Global Catalog servers reside in the site, place a Global Catalog server there. If not many users are in the site and not many roaming users authenticate in the site, you could place the Global Catalog server on the other side of the WAN link. If there are several users, many roaming users, or the WAN link is not reliable or is over consumed, plan on placing a Global Catalog in the local site.

10. A. The infrastructure master should not reside on a Global Catalog server if there are two domains within the forest. The infrastructure master for corp.com can only reside on the DC1.corp.com and DC2.corp.com domain controllers. Because DC2.corp.com is a Global Catalog server, the best domain controller to host the infrastructure master role is DC1.corp.com.

Case Study

You should give yourself 20 minutes to review this testlet, and complete the questions.

Background

Insane Systems builds custom computers for their customers. They specialize in building cases that are unique and support the latest in hardware technology. They started off as a small company that provided this service to gamers who would take their cases to LAN parties to show off. Because their systems were considered some of the most stable gaming platforms and they provided an impressive design that gamers could show off, they started to become popular. Insane Systems started mass manufacturing some of their more popular designs and began selling stand-alone cases along with their fully configured systems. As space at the company became a premium, the office was moved from the manufacturing facility. This allowed the company to add to the amount of space that was used for the mass production line.

Existing Environment

Over the past few months, Insane Systems has been developing plans to expand their company. They have identified San Jose, California, Atlanta, Georgia, and New York City as the locations with their highest customer base. The current Chicago location will remain the corporate headquarters, but they are opening branches in New York City and San Jose. They are also in the process of acquiring a competitor's business in Atlanta. These locations will provide retail outlets as well as support. Customers will have the option of sending their systems back to the corporate office for upgrades or repairs, or delivering them to one of the branch locations.

Because the company is planning on expanding, they want to make sure that the network infrastructure is in place to support their larger, distributed company. They are also concerned with the support lifetime of their current Windows NT 4 infrastructure. They realize they have the option of moving to a Windows 2000 or Windows 2003 infrastructure and are considering moving to Windows Server 2003 and Active Directory for two reasons: the expected support lifetime is greater than Windows 2000, and they are a technology firm that is not afraid of staying ahead of the technology curve.

Part of the expansion of the company is a complete overhaul of their current Internet presence. They are planning on bringing all of the web development and hosting in-house. Currently, a web hosting service is providing their Internet presence, and Insane Systems feels as though they could provide better marketing and support information for their customers if they had control over their own website. Insane Systems would also like to change the name of their website to better represent their name in the marketplace. They own the name `insane-systems.com`.

Interviews

Your company has been hired to design an Active Directory infrastructure and the network infrastructure to support it. During the interview process with some of the key stakeholders, you gathered the following information:

CEO   Currently we have a single location with all of our processes local. As we grow, we would like to keep all of the administration here in Chicago. Because the new branches are primarily retail and support offices, we will not need to have a large staff in those locations. The Atlanta office has an existing network that we would like to merge into our network. System design, research and development, and patent information come from the Atlanta office, so a secure connection from Atlanta to Chicago must be implemented.

CIO   Most of the infrastructure that we support is located here at the corporate office. We do support some key servers at the manufacturing location. We support these servers from our main office. Because the servers are nearby, if there is a problem, we can usually be onsite within half an hour.

The new branches are going to be another issue altogether. We would like to retain the same level of administrative control over the servers in the new locations that we employ currently. Due to the geographic limitations, we may need to have some support staff at those locations. Currently, the plan is to hire staff at those locations who can provide the support for the customers, but also have an understanding of the business systems we need to put into place. We would like to automate software installations to the remote office due to the lack of IT staff.

Manager of Information Technology   We have grown very quickly over the past three years and our current technologies have kept up with that growth. However we don't think the current infrastructure is ready for the amount of growth that we are expecting within the following year. We are not afraid of moving to the latest technology, but we want to make sure that the design is stable and makes sense for us, especially if we will continue growing in the upcoming months. And because we are losing support for NT 4, we want to make sure that we have an operating system that will be supported for a few years down the road.

Most of our processes are located here at this office and we would like to keep it that way. We know that some servers will need to be located at the remote offices, but we would like to be able to provide most of the support from this location. Remote administration tools will need to be included within the design so that we can keep our administrative costs to a minimum.

Currently, we have most of our servers located at the main office, and all are located on their own high-speed backbone. We do have a server at the manufacturing site that allows the staff there to have e-mail as well as plans and orders in case we lose connectivity between the offices. This server is running Exchange 5.5. Several times during the day we replicate the public folder information to this system so that they are always up-to-date and do not have to dial up to the main office using our 56Kbps modem.

The systems at the main office are all supported by our staff of four administrators. All of the administrators are cross-trained on Windows NT 4, Exchange 5.5, SQL Server 7, our accounting software, and each of our file and print servers. We currently have several Windows NT 4

servers in place, including one Exchange 5.5 server at both locations, one SQL Server 7 server at the main office, one server running our accounting package that interfaces with the SQL server, and one file and print server that is used by both locations. The Exchange server at the manufacturing location doubles as a print server also.

The Atlanta office currently has a Windows NT 4 domain, and we will migrate that domain into our forest. Although administration of the forest will be moved to the Chicago branch, administration of the Atlanta domain will reside in the Atlanta domain. We will have a very small IT staff in the Atlanta office who will need control all aspects of the Atlanta domain. Administrators of the Atlanta domain will have control over the Atlanta domain only and will not have administrator access to any other domain or any other part of the forest. All communication between the Atlanta office and the Chicago office will take place via an IPSec connection. The users in the Atlanta office will also require different password and lockout restrictions than the other offices.

Naming conventions for groups are very confusing right now, and adding the Atlanta domain only added to this confusion. Groups in the current domain are named Sales, IT, Accounting, and so on. Groups in the Atlanta domain are also named Sales, Accounting, and so on. We would like to rename groups to define the use of the group. All groups should be prefixed with the group type—Global, Domain Local, or Universal—so that it is easy to locate the group in Active Directory. Domain local groups should be named according to the location of the resource, the resource name, and the permissions granted. Global groups should be named according to the location of the users who are members of the group. When the domain is moved to Windows Server 2003 functional level, the universal security groups should be named for the groups that will be included as members.

LAN Administrators in the root domain of the forest are responsible for creating GPOs but do not have access to link them at any level. Domain Admins in each domain are responsible for testing and linking the GPO to their own domains only. Forest owners will also have access to link GPOs at any level of any domain in the forest.

Because all of the client machines are running Windows NT 4 Workstation, we do not have to worry about supporting different operating systems. We would like to maintain that same easy administration with the upcoming system. We would like to provide the same types of services at the remote locations that we provide at the home office, although accounting will remain at the home office and will not be spread out to all of the locations.

Current Infrastructure

After investigating the current infrastructure, you have determined that the following servers are in place:

Home Office

Primary Domain Controller (PDC)

Backup Domain Controller (BDC)

DHCP/DNS/WINS server

Exchange 5.5 server

SQL Server 7

Systems Management Server 2

File/Print/Antivirus server

Research and Development file server

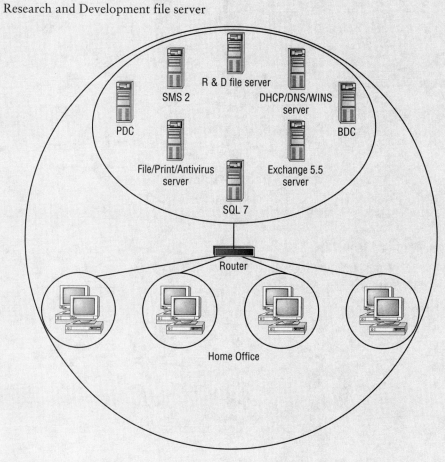

Atlanta Office

Primary Domain Controller (PDC)

Backup Domain Controller (BDC)

WINS server

File server

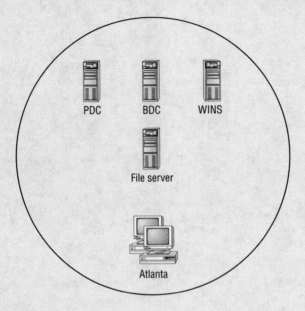

Manufacturing Facility

Backup Domain Controller (BDC)

DNS/WINS/DHCP Relay Agent server

Exchange 5.5/File server

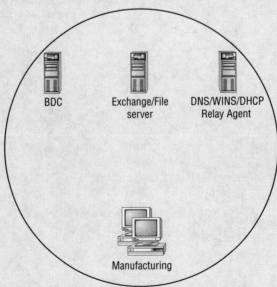

The Home Office hosts nearly 250 Windows NT 4 workstations at this point. They are interconnected by several 48-port 10/100Mbps switches. A router is used to divide the network into 4 VLANs. One of these broadcast domains is the 1Gbps backbone on which the servers reside. Each of the servers is connected to a 1Gbps switch port. This location takes advantage of private IP address ranges. The servers are located on the 192.168.1.0/24 subnet. The client systems are divided between network addresses 192.168.10.0/24, 192.168.11.0/24, 192.168.12.0/24, and 192.168.13.0/24.

The manufacturing facility contains 12 Windows NT 4 workstations connected to the same switch as the servers. Because Insane Systems does not want to slow down production due to a communication failure, they have taken advantage of Exchange 5.5's public folder replication. Public folders are continually updated with the latest orders. The crew foreman can access the orders locally from these public folders at any time, whether the communication link between the locations is up or not. This location uses another address range—192.168.20.0/24.

Case Study Questions

1. Using the supplied options, create a network map that identifies how Insane Systems is currently configured.

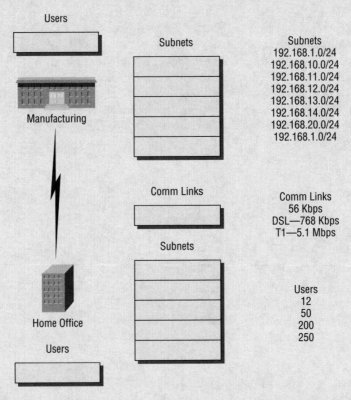

Users

Subnets

Subnets
192.168.1.0/24
192.168.10.0/24
192.168.11.0/24
192.168.12.0/24
192.168.13.0/24
192.168.14.0/24
192.168.20.0/24
192.168.1.0/24

Manufacturing

Comm Links

Comm Links
56 Kbps
DSL—768 Kbps
T1—5.1 Mbps

Subnets

Users
12
50
200
250

Home Office

Users

2. Within the existing infrastructure, where would you create sites?

   A. Home Office—1 site for users, 1 site for servers; Manufacturing—1 site

   B. Home Office—1 site; Manufacturing—1 site

   C. Home Office and Manufacturing—1 site

   D. Home Office servers and Manufacturing—1 site; Home Office users—1 site

3. After adding the additional locations, where should sites be located?

   A. Home Office—1 site; Manufacturing—1 site; New York—1 site; Atlanta—1 site; San Jose—1 site

   B. Home Office and Manufacturing—1 site; New York—1 site; Atlanta—1 site; San Jose—1 site

   C. Home Office and Manufacturing—1 site; New York and Atlanta—1 site; San Jose—1 site

   D. Home Office and Manufacturing—1 site; New York, Atlanta and San Jose—1 site

4. After the `insane-systems.local` domain is created, you want to add additional domain controllers for efficient user authentication. Where should you place domain controllers within the organization for authentication purposes? (Choose all that apply.)

   A. Home Office

   B. Manufacturing

   C. San Jose

   D. New York

5. When you are adding the domain controller at the remote locations, which of the following options would be the best for promoting the systems to domain controllers?

   A. Have the staff at each location run `dcpromo` on each domain controller at each location.

   B. Have an administrator from the Home Office run `dcpromo /adv` on each domain controller at each location.

   C. Install the servers at the Home Office and have an administrator run `dcpromo` on the servers and then ship them to each location.

   D. Install the servers at the Home Office and have an administrator run `dcpromo /adv` on the servers and then ship them to each location.

Answers to Case Study Questions

1.

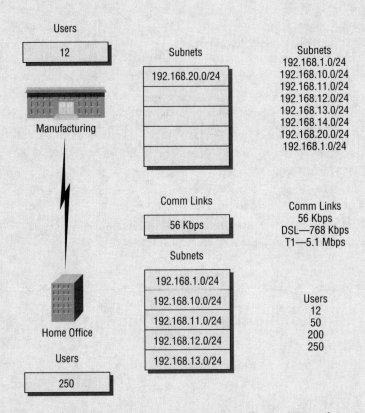

Users
| 12 |

Manufacturing

Subnets
| 192.168.20.0/24 |
| |
| |
| |
| |

Subnets
192.168.1.0/24
192.168.10.0/24
192.168.11.0/24
192.168.12.0/24
192.168.13.0/24
192.168.14.0/24
192.168.20.0/24
192.168.1.0/24

Comm Links
| 56 Kbps |

Comm Links
56 Kbps
DSL—768 Kbps
T1—5.1 Mbps

Subnets
| 192.168.1.0/24 |
| 192.168.10.0/24 |
| 192.168.11.0/24 |
| 192.168.12.0/24 |
| 192.168.13.0/24 |

Users
12
50
200
250

Home Office

Users
| 250 |

Insane Systems currently has two locations: the Home Office and Manufacturing. The Home Office has approximately 250 users and utilizes IP addresses 192.168.1.0/24, 192.168.10.0/24, 192.168.11.0/24, 192.168.12.0/24, and 192.168.13.0/24. Manufacturing has approximately 12 users and uses the IP address range 192.168.20.0/24.

2. B. Because the Home Office and the Manufacturing office are only connected by a 56Kbps dial-up connection, you should create two sites. You have no reason to create a site for the users because the domain controllers are located on the server subnet; the users will have to access that subnet for authentication anyway.

3. B. The new infrastructure is going to employ a 1.5Mbps SDSL connection between the Home Office and Manufacturing that will only have a 20 percent consumption. There will be enough bandwidth to consider having a single site. The other locations are connected to the Home Office via T1 connections that are going to have approximately 40 percent total network consumption on each. However, there are Exchange servers at each of the locations that will need to have local Global Catalog servers. Creating a site for each one will also guarantee that users will authenticate to a local domain controller.

4. A, B, C, D. Because you want to allow users to be able to authenticate and access resources at any time, you should locate a domain controller at each of the sites. Because not many users will be at each site, you could have them authenticate across the WAN links and centralize the servers, but if you want the sites to be autonomous and able to function without the Home Office connection, you should decentralize the resources and allow local authentication.

5. B. Because the staff at the remote locations have limited experience, you may not want to give them the ability to create domain controllers. An administrator can run the advanced mode for `dcpromo` in order to copy the directory database to the server, which will reduce the amount of replication required to bring the domain controller up-to-date.

Chapter 9

Designing Remote Access

MICROSOFT EXAM OBJECTIVES COVERED IN THIS CHAPTER:

- ✓ **Design the network services infrastructure to meet business and technical requirements.**
  - ▪ Create the conceptual design of the DHCP infrastructure.
  - ▪ Create the conceptual design of the remote access infrastructure.
- ✓ **Design security for remote access users.**
  - ▪ Identify security host requirements.
  - ▪ Identify the authentication and accounting provider.
  - ▪ Design remote access policies.
  - ▪ Specify logging and auditing settings.
- ✓ **Design a remote access strategy.**
  - ▪ Specify the remote access method.
  - ▪ Specify the authentication method for remote access.
- ✓ **Design an IP address assignment strategy.**
  - ▪ Specify DHCP integration with DNS infrastructure.
  - ▪ Specify DHCP interoperability with client types.
- ✓ **Design Internet connectivity for a company.**
- ✓ **Design a network and routing topology for a company.**
  - ▪ Design a TCP/IP addressing scheme through the use of IP subnets.
  - ▪ Specify the placement of routers.
  - ▪ Design IP address assignment by using DHCP.
  - ▪ Design a perimeter network.
- ✓ **Design the remote access infrastructure.**
  - ▪ Plan capacity.
  - ▪ Ascertain network settings required to access resources.
  - ▪ Design for availability, redundancy, and survivability.

In the previous chapter, we introduced the first piece of the physical aspects of the infrastructure design: the site topology, which controls the replication and application needs of a company and helps keep the Active Directory infrastructure running efficiently. Without a good site design, user authentication, application usage, and replication will not be as effective as a company needs.

In this chapter, you are going to learn how to allow users to connect to resources within the organization. Gone are the days of companies as autonomous units not needing access to other organizations' resources. Most companies today need to allow both internal and remote users to access data. They need that data to remain secure, while at the same time, allowing the users to perform their tasks in an efficient manner. The first section discusses available options for allowing internal users to connect to the resources they need to perform their job functions. The second and third sections deal with allowing remote users to connect to internal resources.

Before creating the design, you need to identify who will be accessing the organization's resources and how. Internal users accessing local resources will not take as much planning as users who connect remotely. Because local area networks (LANs) are generally allotted a generous amount of data throughput, concerns about data access requirements are not as much an issue as they are with wide area networks (WANs) or dial-up connections.

Users connecting remotely place additional demands on the designer. The available bandwidth on remote connections is usually not as high as that of the LAN. Depending on their connection method, users may not be able to access applications or data that they normally take advantage of while connected to the LAN. Plus, due to security requirements, they may need to use Virtual Private Network (VPN) technologies, which could slow down their connection due to the inherent nature of the overhead required to maintain a VPN connection.

Designing Network Access

In the typical company, internal users make up the majority of the user base. Internal users are those who show up at the office on a daily basis, log on to computers that have access to the networks, and access resources within the organization. For the most part, the network only needs the basic services that allow users to authenticate and access the resources. Specialized authentication servers that work in conjunction with a domain controller and security measures such as firewalls are not typically necessary to control users on the LAN.

As you will see when we start discussing allowing remote users access to internal resources, you need to take special security considerations into account. For an internal user accessing internal resources, however, the security measures are not as stringent.

That is not to say that you don't need security in these types of situations. Security breaches are common. As a matter of fact, it is usually far easier for an internal user to cause a security breach because they already have access to resources. When creating a secure infrastructure, the first rule you should follow is to make sure that the internal resources are secure before you allow access to outside influences. It is not uncommon to find firewalls within a company's internal network protecting the resources in case there is a breach of the external firewalls. Think of a castle with its moat, gates, and locked doors that you have to pass through to get to the King's chambers.

As with every chapter up to this point, you need to identify the information that will impact this portion of your design. You will need to review the initial discovery that you did when you were trying to determine how the current infrastructure is designed so that you can glean information that will help you determine what you have to work with. You will use the current network information along with the requirements that you have identified for the new Active Directory infrastructure when you develop the user access requirements.

Microsoft has identified a network access hierarchy that works for most companies. This hierarchy is composed of network access layers that not only control the data that is transmitted on the network segments, but identify how clients and servers are positioned within an organization so that the resources needed by users are readily accessible.

Identifying the Network Access Hierarchy

Microsoft's network access hierarchy is based upon a three-tier design that controls how the network infrastructure should be designed and where systems should be located in order to keep the network running efficiently. Figure 9.1 represents the basic layout of the network using this hierarchy. Note the three tiers that are used here:

- Core
- Distribution
- Access

The Core Tier

The core tier utilizes high-speed switching in order to keep segments connected. Typically, you won't find servers or client workstations at this tier; it is reserved for network devices that need high-speed access to unite the network segments together. This is usually seen as the "backbone" of the company.

When designing the core tier, you will take into account the network paths that define the backbone of the organization. An organization that hosts everything within a single building or campus may only utilize LAN technologies for their backbone. An organization that has many locations may use a metropolitan area network (MAN) or high-speed WAN to interconnect the locations. Figure 9.2 illustrates the core tier for an organization with five locations: three buildings within a campus, another connected through an ATM MAN connection, and another through a T1 WAN link.

FIGURE 9.1 Network access hierarchy

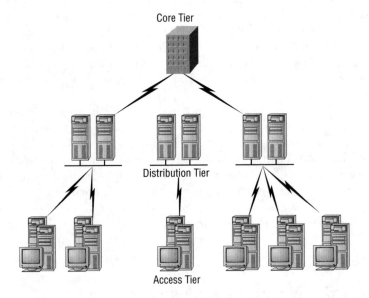

FIGURE 9.2 Example of the core tier

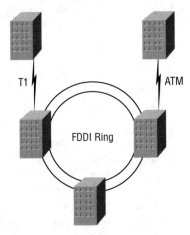

The Distribution Tier

You'll find network devices that define the network segments and servers that provide network resources to many segments in the distribution tier. Network devices found at this level are responsible for routing the data from segment to segment and controlling access to the servers that reside on the distribution tier. Network security and access control policies are implemented at this level also. Here you will find the firewalls and address translation servers that control access to other segments of the organization, along with access from remote users. Servers at this tier include domain controllers, and DHCP, DNS, and WINS servers to name a few. Figure 9.3 illustrates an organization's distribution tier and how it relates to the other two tiers.

The Access Tier

This is the layer at which the workstations and servers are connected. This tier is made up of network segments that are low- to medium-speed connections that allow several workstations to access the rest of the network.

When designing this tier, take into account the capacity of the distribution and core tiers so that you do not have more workstations connected to the access tier than the other tiers can support. You may also find that the access tier hosts servers that provide resources to a specific segment or workgroup, or you have an access tier segment that is made up of servers only.

When designing a segment for servers, you need to make sure that the network bandwidth will sustain the traffic from client workstations in other access tier segments. When placing servers in an access tier with client workstations, make sure that the resources provided by that server are not required by workstations that reside on segments in access tiers within other distribution tiers. Placing servers in the distribution tier would be preferable in such a case because the distribution tier has the capacity to handle the data.

Figure 9.4 illustrates the devices that are connected at the access tier and their relationship to the distribution tier of the hierarchy.

FIGURE 9.3   Example of the distribution tier

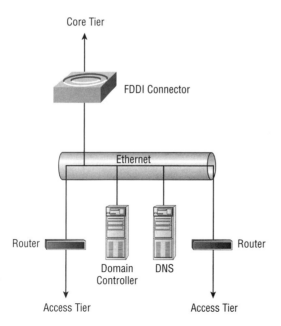

FIGURE 9.4   Example of the access tier

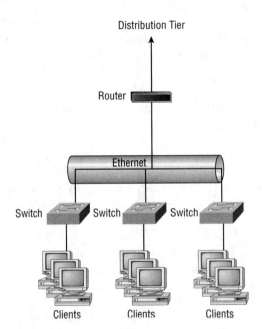

You should already have a diagram of the existing network infrastructure from when you performed the network discovery in Chapter 2, "Determining Business and Technical Requirements." This diagram holds the information that you need to determine how the existing infrastructure is tied together. Review the information on the diagram and determine where each of the tiers will be implemented.

When determining how the different tiers will be implemented for the organization, start by defining how users will access the network and the segments that host their workstations. User access will define the access tier. You will find that most organizations already have the access tier in place, although some organizations may have both the access and distribution tiers built as a single tier. If this is the case, inventory the resources and the servers that the resources reside on and try to determine if the users would be better served if the resources were located in the distribution tier. If the resources are used within a single workgroup or by a very small group of users within subnets that are all part of the same access tier segment, you could leave the resources at the access tier. However, if several users need access to the resources and the users reside in different access tier segments, consider relocating the resources to the distribution tier.

The routers or switches that define the segments that the workstation resides on will be connected to both the access tier to support the workstations and the distribution tier to support access to network services on the distribution tier. You should note the servers that are located within the distribution tier. Most of these servers will host resources that users from different access tier segments need to use. If a server is only used by users from one segment, you many want to consider relocating that server to the access tier so that a network failure at the distribution tier would not necessarily affect the resource access.

In the next section, we will discuss some of the security considerations when internal users are connecting to resources on the network.

Security Considerations

As mentioned earlier, it is far easier for an internal user to cause a security breach because they do not have to discover a method of accessing the network; they have already been granted this. The challenge for the network administrator is restricting the users to only those resources they need to use.

Once authenticated, an internal user is able to access any of the resources for which they have permission. Therein lies the one of the most important keys to security: permissions. NTFS permissions on file shares, folders, and printers, and permissions set on Active Directory objects are the primary security options available to network administrators. If the administrative team does not have control over the permissions that are assigned to network resources, they are not able to control what the users access, intentionally or unintentionally.

Sometimes setting permissions on objects and resources is not enough. In previous chapters, we discussed scenarios that organizations face when they have highly sensitive data. The organization may only want the data available to a specific group of users, or mandates due to governmental contracts may require you to control who can access certain resources. In this case, you will want to implement methods to secure the data, such as isolating a network from the rest of the organization or using security policies to restrict access to the resources.

For example, in the case of an organization that has a contract to manufacture equipment for the Department of Defense, the data that they use as the specifications when manufacturing equipment may be top secret and should be kept from prying eyes. The organization needs to guarantee that the data will be held in confidence. In this case, the server that holds the information could be configured so that an IPSec policy is used to encrypt the transmission of data, or the server could be isolated on its own network segment so that only workstations on that segment can communicate with it.

The best security comes from examining the data that the users need to access and determining how the data is utilized. Policies and procedures should be put into place that dictate how groups are created and how the permissions to resources are assigned to those groups.

Improving Availability

If users cannot access data, the network is useless. At the same time, guaranteeing that the data they are trying to access will be available can be a costly option. Reliable solutions and fault-tolerant solutions do not come cheaply. You need to consider several criteria when developing a highly available network solution.

When determining which solution you wish to implement, you should consider the cost of having the additional reliability against the cost of users not having access to their data. The following sections cover some of the topics to consider when determining how you are going to build your highly available infrastructure or services.

Mean Time Between Failures (MTBF)

Most devices are rated with a mean time between failures (MTBF) rating. This rating indicates how long, usually in hours, a device will run before you should expect it to fail. Of course this does not guarantee that the device will run for that many hours, but neither does it mean that the device will fail whenever it hits that time frame. Manufacturers run tests on systems and determine how long a device is likely to remain available. Usually, the higher the quality of the parts that makes up the device, the higher the MTBF. Although you should also take note of those manufacturers that skew the tests so that they represent the MTBF that they want to obtain.

Warranties on devices with a longer MTBF are usually longer as well. As a corollary, the longer the MTBF, the more money you can expect to shell out when purchasing it.

Mean Time To Recovery (MTTR)

The mean time to recovery (MTTR), or sometimes referred to as Mean Time To Repair, states how long you should expect an outage to continue when a device or system fails. The MTTR is harder to quantify than the MTBF.

Depending upon several factors—such as whether you have staff qualified to repair the device, or how long it takes to restart a system that was powered down—you need to determine how long it will take to return to normal operations. If you are working with outside vendors, make sure you have outage limits incorporated into the Service Level Agreement (SLA). Keep in mind that MTTR is the average time a repair will take to restore the entire system to its pre-failure state. If your design incorporates fault tolerance, your outage time will be less than MTTR.

Redundancy

One thing is for certain—equipment will fail. And more than likely, it will fail when you need it the most, or when you are on vacation. Having backup equipment for redundancy helps alleviate the problems associated with equipment failure. If the redundant equipment takes over automatically when the original equipment fails, you need to keep your users accessing their resources while you repair the failed device, thus reducing the downtime. If you do need to replace the failed equipment with the redundant equipment, you will reduce your downtime considerably. If you did not have the equipment available and you had to either order the equipment or repair the failed equipment, you would incur longer downtimes.

Secondary Paths

Even if you have redundant equipment, if you do not have additional network paths, a failure of the network connection keeps the users from accessing their resources and affects the services that need to use the connections. Planning for fault tolerance by having an additional network path allows users and services to continue processing if the primary connection goes down.

Some organizations have an identical secondary connection to the primary, but others have a less expensive connection type as a backup. Although the less expensive connection will not support the same amount of capacity that the primary connection would, the inconvenience of slower communication is overshadowed by the ability to continue working.

Load Balancing

Whereas secondary paths allow you to continue working when a primary connection fails, load balancing alleviates the load from one device so that all of the devices take on a fair amount of the workload. When load balancing, the user will not notice as much degradation in performance because more than one device is taking on its fair share of the workload. However, when a device in the load-balanced cluster fails, the other devices will have to take on the additional load, so for the remainder of the time that a device is down, the user may experience a drop in performance.

Building the network infrastructure to accommodate internal users is by far easier and usually less complex than designing for remote users. In the next section, we are going to discuss the options that are available when designing the network infrastructure to support remote user access to the network.

Considerations for Internet Access

Allowing users to have access to the Internet is a mixed blessing. Although many use the Internet as a resource and take advantage of the wealth of knowledge they can find there, others may waste time surfing and becoming unproductive. If you are going to allow access to the Internet, you need to design your network so that the users can gain access to the information they need to perform their job, while at the same time restricting them from causing harm to the organization's network.

Very few organizations allow users to have direct access to the Internet. While planning your Internet access, determine how much access you want the users to have and then choose a method of access that will help you maintain your security and network efficiency. You can use a network address translation (NAT) device that controls the Internet requests from your internal network while keeping the internal addresses from being seen by external users.

 **Real World Scenario**

Guaranteeing Connectivity

Tom needs to make sure that users in the Kansas City office do not lose access to their databases as they perform their end-of-the-month processing. Historically, the connection that had been used had proven to be about 80 percent reliable. Although the connection was not always down during the critical processing time, there were instances when the reporting was delayed due to the connection.

For the new Active Directory design, Tom has decided that he not only needs to make sure that the connection is available for the users, he also wants to make sure it is available for the replication traffic that will occur. Within the new design, Tom has identified the need for redundant connections to the Kansas City office as well as additional hardware to make the network infrastructure more fault tolerant. The existing dedicated T1 connection will remain, but he budgets an additional T1 and distributes the cost between the offices. Finally, to make sure that the connections are monitored and maintained better, Tom negotiates a SLA for the T1 connections.

To help alleviate some of the Internet traffic that your users will generate, and to better control which users can access the Internet, you can implement a proxy server. Proxy servers can cache pages that users have visited. If another user visits the same page, the proxy server can pull the data from its hard drive instead of having to request the data from the Internet. Another benefit of proxy servers is the ability to control access by using the user's account or group membership. NAT servers can control the addresses of the clients that can connect, but cannot control by user account.

Designing Remote User Connectivity

Remote users could be employees who are connecting to the network from their homes or hotel rooms, or they could be business partners who need to access specific resources within your organization. In any case, you need to make sure that the users are able to gain access to the resources they require while at the same time guaranteeing the safety of the data.

As we look at the options for remote user access, we will discuss considerations you should take into account, the connection types that are available, Internet and extranet considerations, and how to control and account for remote user access.

Identifying Remote User Access Considerations

Whenever you open up your network so that users can gain access from remote locations, you are endangering the data, resources, and computers that are part of your internal network. Prior to implementing a remote access solution, you should consider the effect that access to your network could have and assess any vulnerabilities in your infrastructure.

By allowing access to your network to external users you are possibly opening up the following vulnerabilities:

Exposure of network information   Any data that is accessible from a client on the network could be accessed from a remote client if not properly safeguarded. Make sure all of the network resources are secured; otherwise an outside entity could discover information that should be held in confidentiality.

Lack of control over infrastructure   Once you open up the network to the outside world, if you have not secured the infrastructure, you could be allowing too much access to outside attackers. If this is the case, the network could be modified in ways that allow the attackers to have control over your resources.

Exposure of computers to attack   As pathways to your network are opened, if you have not taken the appropriate steps to safeguard your computers, they are open to attacks such as denial of service attacks. Make sure that all of the appropriate security patches and precautions are in place before allowing any type of remote access into your network.

Organizations do not go to the trouble, nor do they take on the expense, to implement remote access if they do not have a good reason to do so. Employees may need to access the network from an outside location so that they can do their job. Partner companies may need to share information in order to work together. No matter what the reason for building a remote access solution, you should identify the following criteria:

- What functions do remote employees perform when connecting?
- What functions do remote non-employees perform when connecting?
- How long do they remain connected?
- How many users can connect concurrently?
- What types of clients are used when connecting?
- What type of encryption is required?
- What portion of the network do the remote users need access to?

The answers to these questions will aid you when you are trying to decide how to secure your infrastructure. If all of the remote users are employees in your company, you could mandate the use of a specific client that will support the encryption and authentication mechanisms you want to use. However, if you are working with another organization, you may not have the clout required to mandate that they upgrade their client systems to support a higher security level.

Identifying Connection Options

You have a choice of several connection options when you are designing a remote access infrastructure. One of the first things you need to consider is the amount of data that will be sent across the connection and the speed at which the connection can send the data. You also need to decide on whether or not you will use VPN connections.

Connection Types

Administrators who wish to interconnect remote locations and allow users to connect to resources or allow systems to interoperate have several options to choose from. Depending on the requirements and the budget that the organization wishes to use, you can use efficient high-speed connections, or you can choose slower connections if the connections do not need to have fast transfer speeds or support many users. The following are some of the connection types that are available for connecting locations and partner organizations together:

- Circuit Switched: Modem and ISDN
- Leased Lines: Broadband (T1, T3, etc.), DSL (ADSL, IDSL, SDSL)
- Packet/Frame Switched: X.25, Frame Relay, ATM
- Virtual: VPN technologies

When selecting the connection type, you should take the following information into account:

- Leased lines should be used for dedicated high traffic WAN links.
- Packet switching should be used for intermittent traffic
- Dial-up circuit switched lines should be used for secondary paths or connections that have minimal traffic.

These options are available to domestic administrators, but when interconnecting organizations that have offices outside of the United States, you need to take other criteria into account, the first of which is the interoperability of the connections. Will you be able to communicate effectively between the overseas connection and the domestic connection? And if they are compatible, what is the cost of the connection? You may find it prohibitive to maintain a high-speed connection in some locations and will be forced to use another slower method of connecting.

Make sure you are making decisions based on the business requirements of the organization. Although it may be nice to have a T3 connection to the Internet and other locations within your organization, you really need to define the bandwidth requirements. Paying for bandwidth that will not be used is not an efficient use of your company's financial resources. At the same time, if you are using dial-up to gain access to remote locations, the users may not be able to work with the resources that they need. You need to make a trade-off between cost and user productivity.

Before deciding on a connections type, determine what VPN options are available to you. If the connections are not secure and you are not able to implement a VPN connection, you may want to determine if another transmission media is more suited to your endeavor. Finally, if the connection is vital and you need to maintain it, you may want to determine what fault-tolerance options are available to you within the budget you have to work with.

VPNs

Using the Internet as an extension of an organization's network is an efficient and inexpensive way to connect locations. However, the Internet has never been a secure environment. Data that travels across the Internet is subject to capture by any number of disreputable users who could take advantage of the data they discover. Organizations that want to safeguard their data while taking advantage of the Internet use VPN technologies to encrypt the data.

There are pros and cons to using VPN technologies. You need to weigh each to determine if a VPN is the right solution for your organization's needs. Table 9.1 lists both the pros and cons.

TABLE 9.1 Advantages and Disadvantages to Using VPNs

Advantages	Disadvantages
The existing infrastructure can still be utilized.	You encounter extra overhead when using a tunnel.
An expensive private connection is not necessary.	The same protocol must be supported on both devices.
Will scale better than a dial-up solution.	Additional support is required to maintain VPN technologies.
	Packets could still be intercepted on the Internet.

Your VPN of choice will be limited to the clients that you allow to connect. Some earlier workstation clients are not able to take advantage of some of the newer technologies without having additional software added to them. This is a time where you may need to put your foot down and dictate which client operating systems can be used through a VPN to connect to your internal network. If you want to restrict VPN access to Layer 2 Tunneling Protocol (L2TP)–capable clients using IPSec encryption, you need to make sure that all of the remote workstations have the appropriate software. Windows 2000, Windows XP, and Windows Server 2003 have native L2TP/IPSec support, but other clients may need to have the additional software applied to them.

If you have to support Point-to-Point Tunneling Protocol (PPTP), make sure that the clients are using the most secure level of data encryption. The major drawback to PPTP is that it does not support mutual authentication of the client and server. Because L2TP does support mutual authentication, all of the packets passing between the client and the server are verified for authenticity. PPTP does not support this level of security.

Guidelines for Remote User Authentication and Accounting

As users connect to the remote access server, whether they connect through a dial-up connection or a VPN connection, they need to be authenticated before they are allowed to connect to network resources. You should also make sure you have a method of accounting for the users who connect to the network and the resources for which they gain access. Microsoft Routing and Remote Access Server (RRAS) can be used to authenticate users as they connect. If you employ a *Remote Authentication Dial-In User Service (RADIUS)* solution, not only will the users authenticate, but the RADIUS infrastructure will provide accounting for the users accessing data on the network.

RRAS has both authentication and routing capabilities built into it. You can configure the service to provide one or the other, or both. We discuss the router options in the section Designing Remote Site Connectivity.

A RADIUS-based infrastructure allows you to place servers close to the users who are attempting to authenticate to your network as well as the domain controllers that are used to authenticate the users. In a Windows Server 2003 network, the RRAS service that provides RADIUS server functionality is Internet Authentication Service (IAS). This is the service that accepts the user's credentials as they are passed from the RADIUS client, and authenticates the user by passing the credentials to the nearest domain controller. The RADIUS client is the RRAS server that has been configured to use a RADUIS server for user authentication.

You do not have to use IAS to have a RADIUS server, but there are some advantages of doing so. If you use the IAS as the RADIUS server, IAS will contact a domain controller in order to authenticate the user. If you use a third-party RADIUS server, you have to configure that server to either work with Active Directory as the account provider, or you have to maintain two authentication databases and determine how to keep them synchronized. With that being said, Microsoft RRAS servers have the ability to become RADIUS clients to third-party RADIUS servers; IAS also has the ability to interoperate with third-party RADIUS clients.

Design Scenario

Controlling User Access

Jessica has been evaluating her current environment in order to determine how she is going to design her network infrastructure to support her remote clients. All of the users who need to access the internal network have accounts within her domain. Of the 14 users, 10 have the same Internet Service Provider (ISP). This ISP supports UNIX RADIUS clients for other organizations; Jessica is interested in taking advantage of that.

1. **Question:** If Jessica wants to take advantage of the ISP's RADIUS clients, what services would she need to implement? **Answer:** The IAS server could be installed on a Windows Server 2003 system that will act as the RADIUS server.

2. **Question:** If the remainder of the remote users will access the network using a dial-up account, what service should Jessica add to her design? **Answer:** As long as the IAS server is not overloaded, it will be able to handle the additional traffic from the four remote users that need to dial in to the server. Jessica should configure a separate policy for these users.

One major advantage to using RADIUS is that it can centralize the remote access policies on the IAS server. If you are not using a RADIUS solution, or if you are not using IAS as your RADIUS server, you need to configure the remote access policies for each RAS server individually. This could be a time-consuming process, and if you make a change to a policy, you need to guarantee that each of the RAS servers have been updated correctly. Once you have IAS in place, you can store a remote access policy on the IAS server and all of the RAS servers acting as the RADIUS clients will use the master policy.

The same is true for monitoring the RADIUS implementation. The RADIUS clients can report auditing information to the RADIUS server so that an administrator can view the accounting information that was generated due to user access. If you are not taking advantage of the accounting feature that is built into RADIUS, you need to monitor your RAS servers using another tool such as the RAS Monitor, `rassrvmon.exe`, from the Windows Server 2003 Resource Kit.

In the "Controlling User Access" Design Scenario, you will make decisions on how to configure a RADIUS infrastructure.

Designing Remote Site Connectivity

For years, companies used WAN technologies to connect remote sites. These WAN connections were typically based on dedicated broadband connections. The drawback to these connections was their cost. As companies have tried to reduce costs, they have increasingly considered using the Internet to interconnect their remote locations. Of course the Internet has never been considered a secure method of communication. Virtual Private Technologies have matured over the past few years to where they are considered appropriate for businesses to take advantage of.

However, many companies are still using dedicated broadband connections, and many others will consider using them because of the inherent security that they provide. When designing your remote site connectivity, you need to determine what types of connectivity are appropriate for your infrastructure.

Determining Connectivity Needs

Depending upon how large your organization is, you may need connections between locations. Even some small organizations that have a single location may find themselves needing some type of external connection to a business partner. When you are designing your network infrastructure, look at your existing network map to determine which connections you need to retain, and then review all of the interview information to determine if you should add any new connections.

Once you have determined the connections you require in order to keep your locations communicating, you need to make another decision for each one: what type of routing you are going to use. Microsoft has offered software routing as part of the Windows server family for many years, but it does have its limitations. Under Windows Server 2003, RRAS can be used to provide routing functions within an organization, but it is not meant to be used for extremely large environments where the routing topology is complex. However, if you need to have a demand-dial router between your main office and an outlying office, it could very well suit your needs.

Hardware routers are more robust than what you find in RRAS. Most network administrators opt for dedicated hardware routers because they can provide all of the functionality that the administrator needs, and they do not have to use the Windows operating system as the platform on which the routing functions run. Plus, you will find that it is much cheaper to buy a router than it is to pay for server hardware and a copy of the operating system.

No matter which type of router you use, you need to decide upon a routing protocol. Routing tables contain two types of entries: static routes and dynamic routes. Using static entries in a routing table, you can determine where the packets should be forwarded. The drawback to static routing, just like almost any static method, is that you have to manually reconfigure the entries whenever a change takes place. That being said, if you have a demand-dial interface and you only need to provide information about the routing information on the other side of the link, a static routing table can be easy and efficient to use.

Dynamic routing protocols, in a Windows routing environment, is available in two types:

Distance vector   The distance vector dynamic routing option for RRAS is Routing Information Protocol (RIP).

Link-state   The link-state option is Open Shortest Path First (OSPF).

Before determining which routing protocol you will use within your RRAS server, find out which protocols are used within your existing environment. If the existing routers are broadcasting their routing information through RIP, follow suit with the RRAS server. The same is true for the OSPF capable routers; configure your RRAS server to use OSPF, but make sure you are configuring everything correctly so that you do not cause routing problems within your network due to an inappropriate routing table entry.

Other routing protocols that are used within enterprise level routers such as IGRP, EIGRP and BGP, are not supported on Windows RRAS.

Identifying Internet and Extranet Considerations

When connecting your internal network infrastructure to the Internet, you need to determine the best options for your organization. One of the primary challenges you will face is designing a secure solution while staying within the budget of the organization. You will also need to make sure that the solution you design restricts unwanted traffic while still allowing business-critical data to pass.

In the following sections we are going to look at how you should protect your network by using firewalls. Since firewalls come in many flavors, you will need to determine which is the best fit for your needs.

Determining Firewall Options

Firewalls are devices that control the network traffic into and out from a network. Several firewall options are on the market; some are dedicated hardware devices whereas others are software running on one of the operating system platforms. No matter which firewall type you use, each is usually a member of one of the following configurations:

- Bastion host
- Three-homed firewall
- Back-to-back firewalls

We will look at each in the following sections.

Bastion Host

A *bastion host* is a single firewall that is used to block traffic coming into the network. Usually found in small organizations, it is the primary means of making sure that only the appropriate traffic is allowed to gain access to the internal network. Although this is one of the least expensive methods of protecting your network, it is also one of the least secure. Because it is the only protection, if the bastion host is compromised, the entire network could be jeopardized. Figure 9.5 is an example of the bastion host.

Three-Homed Firewall

The *three-homed firewall* is a firewall that is connected to three networks and controls which traffic is allowed to pass to each of them. With this firewall type, one network connection is made to the Internet. The second network, sometimes known as the perimeter network, connection is made to a network that contains resources that can be accessed by users on the Internet. You will usually find web servers on this network. The third network connection is to the internal network. The firewall should not allow users on the Internet to access resources within the internal network, but it should allow resources within the perimeter network to access resources within the internal network. Figure 9.6 is an example of the three-homed firewall.

FIGURE 9.5   Example of the bastion host firewall solution

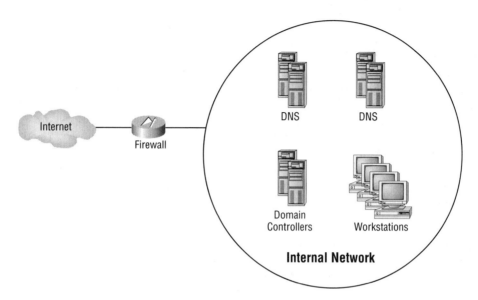

FIGURE 9.6   Example of the three-homed firewall solution

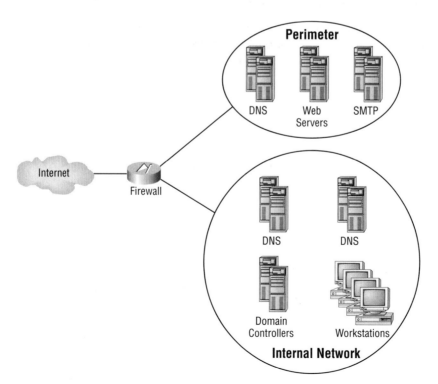

As with the bastion host, the cost of the three-homed firewall is usually one of the more inexpensive options, but you give up some of your security in using this option. If the firewall is breached, an attacker could gain access to the internal network.

Back-to-Back Firewalls

When you use the *back-to-back firewalls* option, sometimes referred to as a demilitarized zone (DMZ), two firewalls are employed to increase the level of security to the internal network. The first firewall allows users from the Internet to access the resources within the perimeter network. This front-end firewall has far fewer restrictions than the back-end firewall, whose job it is to block all traffic except the required traffic from the perimeter network. Figure 9.7 is an example of the back-to-back firewall approach.

Although this solution is more expensive than either the bastion host or three-homed firewall, it allows for extra levels of security. If the front-end firewall is compromised, the back-end firewall can stave off attacks.

 Ideally the internal firewall should be from a different manufacturer, or at the very least, the firewalls should be different model numbers, so that common flaws can't be used to attack both boxes.

In the "Building the Firewall" Design Scenario, you need to determine the best firewall solution.

Forest Firewall Considerations

Whenever a perimeter network is used, you need to determine how the accounts within the organization will be used. Four options are available for creating the accounts that will be used to authenticate to resources within the internal network and the perimeter network:

- A single forest design
- A multiple forest, no trust design
- A multiple forest, one-way trust design
- A multiple forest, two-way trust design

FIGURE 9.7 Example of the back-to-back firewalls solution

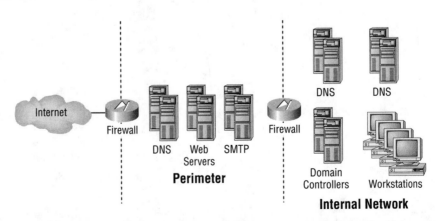

Design Scenario

Building the Firewall

Eros is concerned about the safety of his internal network. The previous administrator had configured a bastion host to protect the network from external users, but he had also opened ports to allow access to web servers and an SMTP server. Eros has called you to present options for a more secure network.

1. **Question:** What options would you present to Eros? **Answer:** A perimeter network needs to be created if the resources are to be secure. You can present the options of either using a three-homed firewall or a back-to-back solution.

2. **Question:** If you were designing the network infrastructure for Eros, which of the firewall options would you recommend and why? **Answer:** The back-to-back firewall option is always the preferred method, although it usually is more costly. If an attacker gains access to the forward firewall and breaks into the perimeter network, they still have another firewall to attack.

You should determine which of the scenarios works best for your organization so that you can have efficient administration of all resources while maintaining a high security level.

Single Forest Design

Most organizations take advantage of the simple *single forest design*. This is the easiest to administer because all of the accounts used within the internal network and the perimeter network belong to the same forest. However, if an attacker gains access to an account within the forest, they can also access internal resources. If a single forest is utilized, you may want to consider creating a separate domain for the perimeter network. In doing so, you can create accounts within the perimeter network that would not necessarily have access to any resources within the domain or domains used within the internal network.

Multiple Forest, No Trust Design

The *multiple forest, no trust design* is the most secure of all of the forest options. The perimeter network uses a different forest than the internal network. If an attacker is able to compromise the perimeter network, the accounts used within the perimeter network do not have permissions within the internal network. This is a very costly scenario to implement, however. Not only do you need additional domain controllers and DNS servers to support the infrastructure, the administrative costs increase greatly. Administrators need to maintain multiple accounts and manually maintain connectivity of resources.

Multiple Forest, One-Way Trust Design

The *multiple forest, one-way trust design* has most of the security benefits of the multiple forest, no trust design, while it alleviates some of the administrative concerns. Although not as easy to design as the single forest design, the multiple forest, one-way design allows administrators to create a one-way trust relationship between the forests so that accounts within the internal network can be added to groups within the perimeter network. Once added to the groups, administrative personnel from the internal network can maintain the resources within the perimeter network. If the perimeter network is compromised, the attackers would not have access to internal resources using the accounts from the perimeter network.

The multiple forest, one-way trust design is more expensive than the single forest design because it requires additional domain controllers and DNS servers to support both forests. The initial administrative overhead is also greater, because the required accounts need to be added to groups within the perimeter network to facilitate administration, but once this is designed and created, administrators don't need duplicate accounts to maintain the internal and perimeter networks.

Multiple Forest, Two-Way Trust Design

The *multiple forest, two-way trust design* allows trusts to be created between the internal and perimeter forests so that each forest trusts the other. This design allows for nearly the same level of interoperability between the resources of the two forests as the single forest design allows. Accounts from each forest can be added to groups within the other forest to facilitate efficient access to resources. This design allows extranet access to internal resources, but it also opens up security concerns because perimeter accounts can now access internal resources. If an attacker compromises the perimeter network, an account in the perimeter network that has privileges in the internal network could be used to compromise the internal network.

SID Filtering should be turned on between the internal and forests so that an attacker cannot take advantage of using the SIDHistory attribute to gain access to resources.

Designing Secure Replication Through Firewalls

For organizations that utilize the Internet to interconnect offices, firewalls are put into place to restrict access to resources. If the remote office has a domain controller, replication traffic needs to make its way through the firewall so that the domain controller can remain up-to-date. You need to design the network infrastructure to allow for this replication, and you must determine how domain controllers will be created. You must decide the method you are going to use to initially populate the directory service.

Identifying the Initial Promotion Options

Two methods allow Active Directory to be populated during the promotion of a Windows Server 2003 server to a domain controller. The default method involves allowing replication to populate Active Directory. If you choose the default method, the server locates a domain controller that is nearby and requests replication of the objects in Active Directory. The second method is to use the advanced method of promoting the domain controller. If you use the advanced method, the initial population of Active Directory is accomplished using data from

---

Real World Scenario

Easing Administrative Control

Penny is in the process of designing the updated network infrastructure to support her Active Directory design. Currently the design calls for a single forest with a single domain. She has eight locations, and tests have determined that the available bandwidth among all of the locations is sufficient to support the replication traffic that she is anticipating.

During the design of the infrastructure, she determines that she needs to implement a perimeter network to support her SMTP and web servers. After identifying the need for the perimeter network, she returns to the Active Directory design concerned about the security requirements for the perimeter network. Her main concern is the possibility of jeopardizing internal resources if an attacker gains control of a system within the perimeter.

After talking with the staff responsible for maintaining the perimeter servers, she determines that their highest priority is to maintain the security of the organization, but at the same time, they express a desire to make the administration of resources as easy as possible.

Penny's initial perimeter design document identifies the devices within the perimeter network as a separate forest. The domain controllers and DNS servers that support the devices within the perimeter are located within the internal network. The proper firewall rules are created to allow the perimeter devices to pass through the firewall to the domain controllers and DNS servers. Penny identifies that she needs a one-way trust relationship, allowing the administrative staff within the internal network to manage the resources within the perimeter. Penny discovers that she will need additional administration to keep the administrative accounts updated, and the users will need to use a different account when working with the perimeter resources, but she feels that is justified in order to keep the internal network resources protected.

---

the system state that has been backed up from another domain controller. Using the backed-up data, the domain controller does not have to replicate the data across network connections—the data can be imported locally.

Make sure the system state data that you are using for the initial population of Active Directory is as current as possible. The older the data, the more replication will be needed to bring the new domain controller up-to-date.

No matter which method you used, the server being promoted needs to be able to connect to a domain controller so that it can be authenticated to the domain that it is joining.

Identifying the Replication Options

No matter which of the promotion options you used, the replication of Active Directory objects between domain controllers is vital to the organization. Without this replicated information, the domain controllers in remote sites would not have accurate directory service information.

Active Directory replication between domain controllers within the same domain occurs using Remote Procedure Calls (RPCs). To allow replication to occur between domain controllers from the same domain in remote sites, you must configure the firewall to allow RPC data to pass. To do so, you must configure the firewall to either have RPC ports open or you must use IPSec to allow replication traffic to pass through the firewall.

USING IPSEC

When you use IPSec for secure replication, all of the replication traffic between the domain controllers is encapsulated in encrypted IPSec packets. Both domain controllers must be configured with the correct IPSec policies. Domain controllers can use a Group Policy object (GPO) that uses Kerberos for IPSec encryption, but any stand-alone server that is being promoted needs to use certificates because it will not be a member of the domain and cannot use Kerberos.

Using IPSec is the most secure way to transmit replication traffic over an insecure network like the Internet because the only ports that need to be opened on the firewall are those used by IPSec, DNS, and Kerberos.

The ports that you will need to open on the firewall in order to allow replication to occur are found in Table 9.2.

T A B L E   9 . 2   Ports to use for replication with IPSec

Service	Port/Protocol
DNS	53/tcp, 53/udp
Kerberos	88/tcp 88/udp
Internet Key Exchange (IKE)	500/udp
IPSec encapsulated security payload (ESP)	IP protocol 50
IPSec authenticated header (AH)	IP protocol 51

OPENING RPC PORTS

If IPSec is not used to protect the replication data, you have to configure ports to allow RPC traffic to pass through the firewall along with DNS and Kerberos. By default, you have to open all of the ports used by RPCs, including all of the dynamic RPC ports. This option opens too many holes within your firewall and could potentially allow undesirable traffic to enter into your internal network.

Microsoft has identified that allowing all of the RPC ports to be opened is not a desirable option, so they have issued a fix that allows you to define a single dynamic RPC port to use. To do so, you must edit the Registry to define the dynamic port. Although this reduces the number of ports that the firewall exposes, it is still not as desirable as using IPSec.

For more information on how to configure Domain Controllers to use fixed RPC ports, see www.microsoft.com/technet/prodtechnol/windows2000serv/ technologies/activedirectory/deploy/confeat/adrepfir.mspx.

Identifying Extranet Options

Using the Internet as an extension to your network in order to keep costs down is very popular. Extending it one step further by allowing a partner organization to access your internal resources is the next logical step. By allowing a partner organization to have access to resources within your organization, you can maintain the data and guarantee that it is valid, but at the same time, you need to exercise even greater control over the resources to keep them from becoming compromised.

As you design extranet access, you should determine who needs to access your resources. Only those external users who need access to your internal resources should be able to view the data. Consider creating accounts for each of the external users so they have to authenticate with when connecting. If you only use a single account for all external users, you will lose accountability.

If you have created separate accounts for each of the external users, you should then make sure that they can only access those resources they need in order to perform their job. When you are designing extranet access, it is a good idea to perform an audit of the resource access that is given to users. Having incorrectly applied permissions that allow an internal user to access resources could cause problems, but allowing external users to see confidential information could be disastrous to your company.

Finally, make sure you are only giving access to the correct users within the partner organization. There may be external users who you do not want to have access to your resources. You definitely don't want to allow users from other nontrusted organizations to have access. Part of the design criteria could identify an audit policy that is enacted to monitor access to resources that are made available to partner organizations. This helps you identify inappropriate access to your network.

Guideline for Server Placement

Determining where you are going to place your VPN and RAS servers takes a little planning. First you need to determine where your corporate policies allow you to place your server. Some companies do not allow a server to be placed outside of the perimeter network where it is exposed to the Internet. If this is the case, then you need to determine how you will implement firewall rules to protect the servers that do reside within the perimeter network and, at the same time, still allow efficient client access.

VPN Server Placement

You have two choices when you are implementing a VPN solution:

- You can use your firewall as your VPN server if it has VPN capabilities and can handle the processing of VPN client data.

- You can use a software solution. Windows Server 2003 RRAS will act as a VPN server and could potentially be more flexible and easier to deploy than a firewall-based solution.

You really only have two options when deciding where to place software-based VPN servers: either in front of the firewall, exposed to the Internet, or behind the firewall. The advantage of placing the VPN server in front of the firewall is that from there it can process the data as it comes from remote users or other locations and then pass it to the firewall to be directed within the intranet. The firewall should have rules in place that only allow traffic from the VPN server to pass into the perimeter network. The firewall can then scan the data for viruses and determine if the data is valid before it enters any part of your internal network.

More often than not, however, the VPN server is placed within the perimeter network where the firewall can protect it from attacks. The firewall has rules that direct the VPN traffic to the VPN server, which in turn processes the data and passes it to the correct servers within the intranet. Although placing the VPN server within the perimeter network is the preferred method, you have to expose the entire VPN IP address range through the firewall. You need to determine if exposing the entire VPN server to the Internet outweighs the risk of exposing the perimeter IP address range to attackers.

RAS Server Placement

Clients who connect to a RAS server in order to obtain access to their resources need to be assured that they have access to the same data as if they were working from the internal network. At the same time, you need to make sure that the clients, both internal and external, do not over consume the network when they are accessing their data. Try to place the RAS server as close to the resources as possible. When the client is accessing the network from a remote location, the traffic that it is causing will not be traveling across too many segments.

Just like any other service, though, make sure you are following corporate policies when you are determining where the RAS server can be placed. If your corporate policies do not allow you to have clients access your network segments directly, you may have to place the RAS server in the perimeter network. Of course, this is the safest location for those users who are using a VPN client to access the network from across the Internet. That said, if your corporate policies allow it, you could place a RAS server on the same segment as the resources that your dial-up clients need to access. You need to make sure that you can restrict access to only those parts of the network that the remote client needs to access.

Placing the RAS server within the perimeter network does have security advantages, of course. You can protect the RAS server from potential attackers through the use of firewall controls. You can also control access to resource that reside within the perimeter network and not allow users to access internal resources.

RADIUS Client Placement

As a rule of thumb, you should place the RADIUS client close to the user population that will use it. Doing so could potentially reduce the dial-up charges that are incurred because the users will dial a local point-of-presence (POP) instead of dialing a long distance number to gain access to a RAS server. This also allows the RADIUS client to be administered by staff who are located at, and are responsible for, the servers.

When users connect to the RADIUS client, they are connecting to a local system. They pass their credentials to the RADIUS client; the RADIUS client is then responsible for encrypting the data and passing it securely to a RADIUS server. Because the authentication is actually accomplished by a domain controller, the RADIUS client does not have to be configured with any user account information.

RADIUS Server Placement

Due to the fact that the RADIUS server needs to contact a domain controller in order to authenticate the remote users, it should be placed close to the domain controllers where the users' account information resides. If you place the RADIUS server within the local network, you can configure firewall rules that allow RADIUS clients to pass their information to the RADIUS servers. In this manner, you protect the account information within the internal network by using firewalls, and all of the communication between the RADIUS server and the domain controllers is protected there as well.

When it comes down to the lowest level of the network infrastructure, you need to understand the IP addressing options that are available to the network administrator. In the following sections, we are going to look at the options that are available when addressing host systems as well as efficient methods of assigning addresses.

Identifying IP Addressing Options

The first thing you should attempt to do when you design your IP addressing for your organization is decide which type of addressing you will use. Originally, IP addresses were grouped according to classes: Class A, Class B, Class C, Class D, and Class E. Although this worked out to be a somewhat efficient means of allocating IP addresses, as the Internet started to expand and more and more organizations needed to have addresses in order to communicate, the addresses started to become in short supply. Also, as more and more devices were introduced into the Internet, there needed to be a way to efficiently identify addresses within the routers that forwarded user requests through the Internet.

The standard classes were "modified" to allow for a more efficient use of network addresses. How many organizations really needed to have 65,000+, let alone 16 million, addresses within a network segment? Whereas many administrators understand how to create subnets so that they have an efficient use of their IP addresses, many others do not consider how to use *variable length subnet masks (VLSM)* to generate an efficient routing environment. VLSM allows you to use different subnet masks on a range of IP addresses so that you can create efficient subnets that use only the number of addresses that you need.

If you look at Figure 9.8, you can see a portion of a network where IP addresses have been configured to allow for efficient routing of information. Note that all of the addresses used within the distribution and access tiers of this design can be summarized into a range of 10.1.0.0/20. Because fewer entries are being used within the routing tables, the routing infrastructure is more efficient.

As you are developing your IP address scheme, make sure you do not have any network addresses that overlap. The best methodology to use is to consider the largest range that you need and create equal blocks of addresses. Once you have determined the largest block of addresses you need, set aside one range for the large number of hosts and then determine how many hosts you need in the next largest segment. Keep subdividing ranges until you obtain the desired number of addresses for your organization.

For example, if you look at Figure 9.8, one segment needs to have at least 500 host addresses available; 8 more need to have at least 200 addresses and 4 WAN links with 2 addresses each. If you were to determine the total number of segments required to support the number of hosts in this scenario, you would find that a 20-bit mask is most efficient. A 20-bit mask allows you to support upward of 4000 users in a single segment. This allows you to subnet the address space in order to partition the network for efficient communication and still have room for future growth.

FIGURE 9.8 IP address allocation

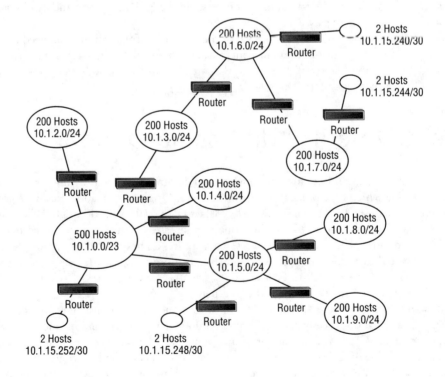

The largest address space that you need is 500 hosts. You can break your address range down from the 20-bit mask to a 23-bit mask for this range, which would give you the address ranges 10.1.0.1–10.1.1.254, or 510 effective host addresses. Doing so also gives you 7 other address ranges that will support 510 hosts. However, the remaining segments do not need to support as many hosts; remember, you only need 200 hosts on 8 other segments.

If you further break down the remaining segments into smaller units, you can create 8 segments from 4 of the segments by using a 24-bit mask. In doing so, you create the segments 10.1.2.0/24 through 10.1.9.0/24, which will host the required 200 hosts each.

For the final breakdown, you need four segments that will have only two hosts each. You can accomplish this by taking one of the remaining ranges and breaking it down using a 30-bit mask. Because these are such small segments, you use addresses at the end of the address range for this purpose, and leave larger blocks of addresses available for future use.

Once you have determined the address range that you are going to use, you will need to determine how you will apply those addresses to systems within your network. The following section details the options you have available when addressing your systems.

Allocating IP Addresses

Every system that uses TCP/IP needs to have an IP address configured so that is able to "talk" on the network. If the network on which the device is going to communicate is the Internet, the device must have an IP address that is considered "live," or one that is allowed to pass on the Internet routers. Addresses that are used on the Internet must be obtained from your ISP. You have to pay for the address in order to use it, but you should not have every device within your network directly connected to the Internet, so you will not have to purchase an address for every system. Instead, you should use private addresses that are reserved for use within an organization. These addresses are not allowed to travel through Internet routers, so you do not have to concern yourself with someone else using the same addresses.

 For more information concerning the private IP address ranges, see RFC 1918.

Configuring your systems so that they have the correct IP address for the subnet that they are on, and configuring all of the correct options that allow them to communicate with other systems throughout your infrastructure can be a daunting task. Some of your systems may be set to automatically obtain an address; others may be configured with static addressing. Your job is to make sure that all of the systems are properly configured so that all of the systems are able to reach the resources your users need to access. With Windows Server 2003, you have four IP addressing methods:

- Static
- Dynamic Host Configuration Protocol (DHCP)
- Automatic private IP addressing (APIPA)
- Alternate IP addressing

Using Static Addressing

Determine which devices need to have static addressing applied to them. You will find that certain servers, such as DNS and DCHP servers, are required to have a static address. Network infrastructure devices such as routers also require a static address. Once you have determined which devices need a static address, apply the appropriate static addresses to those devices only, leaving all other devices to use a dynamic configuration method such as DHCP.

Static addresses are more difficult to administer because you have to manually keep track of the addresses you assign, enter the addresses on each of the devices, and make sure you do not inadvertently enter a wrong number in an address. Then, if you need to move a device to another subnet, you have to manually reconfigure the address so that the device works properly on the new subnet.

Some companies have policies in place that do not allow DHCP assigned addresses for devices within a perimeter network. If this is the case, you are going to have to determine the addresses that are assigned to each of the devices, and then you'll need to maintain that list so that no other device conflicts with an existing system.

You should take a systematic approach to assigning the addresses. For example, many companies use the lower addresses within the range for static addresses only. This leaves the higher numbers available for use with DHCP.

Using DHCP

DHCP is favored by most administrators as the method of configuring addresses. Before you configure a DHCP server, you need to know the available addresses for the segment that it will be servicing. Take a look at all of the addresses that are assigned through static addressing and create your scopes to work around these addresses. If you follow the same systematic approach that we mentioned within the "Using Static Addresses" section earlier, you can assign the lower numbers within the address range to systems that need static address assignment and then use the upper range for DHCP. If you separate the addresses, you can minimize the need to configure exclusions within the DHCP address range.

If you do have systems that you would like to have configured with the same IP address all the time, but they are not required to have a static address, you can assign a reservation within the DHCP server so that the client's hardware address is associated with an IP address. Once configured within the DHCP server, the reservation only allows the system with the hardware address to obtain that IP address. This works out especially well for web servers or other servers that do not require a static address because you are able to change configuration options, and the system updates the setting during the next reboot or refresh interval.

You can also control how long the addresses are leased. If you have plenty of addresses to go around, you could configure the lease length to a long time frame, which would reduce the amount of DHCP related traffic on the network. If there are more than enough IP addresses for the hosts, increasing the lease length should not have any consequences for your systems with the exception of renewing the options for a client that has not rebooted recently.

On the other hand, if you are limited in the number of addresses you have available to lease, you can set a relatively short lease time, thus allowing the lease to expire more quickly and another system to use the freed-up address.

Finally, if you are using DHCP within an Active Directory environment, Windows 2000 and Windows Server 2003–based DHCP servers will need to be authorized. If the DHCP server is not authorized within Active Directory, the DHCP service will not start. Domain admins, enterprise admins, DHCP admins and any user who has been delegated permission will be able to authorize DHCP servers within Active Directory.

Using APIPA

The *automatic private IP address (APIPA)* range of 169.254.0.0/16 is a range of addresses that has been identified by the Internet Assigned Numbers Authority (IANA) that is not allowed to pass across routers on the Internet. This range is used for local access within a subnet only. In a Microsoft network where client operating systems support APIPA, which includes Windows 98 and newer operating systems, if a client is configured to automatically obtain an IP address and a DHCP server is not available, or the server does not have an IP address to lease from its scope, the operating system chooses a random address from the APIPA range. This automatically generated address does not configure any of the options for default gateway, DNS server, or any other option that you can configure from a DHCP server.

If you want to allow a system to automatically configure itself with an APIPA address, remember that the system is not able to communicate with any other system except for those that are also using an APIPA-generated address and are in the same collision domain. This usually doesn't do you much good because the computer is stranded on its own island, but it does add in a troubleshooting feature.

When a client is using an APIPA-assigned address, you can determine that there is either a network issue between the client and the DHCP server or the DHCP server does not have any available leases. On the other hand, if a client is using the 0.0.0.0 address, you can assume that there was a duplication of IP addresses on the network. By leaving APIPA enabled on the client system, you benefit.

Using Alternate IP Addressing

Whereas APIPA automatically configures a system with an address that is not viable for normal network communication, *alternate IP addressing* allows you to assign an address to a system so that it can still communicate normally on the network even if the DHCP server is unavailable. This gives you the added benefit of having a redundant IP address mechanism to keep your systems communicating properly; however, it adds in an additional level of administration.

For each system that you want to configure to use an alternate IP address, you have to set aside an address that will work on your network and you have to manually configure that address within the TCP/IP properties for your network connection. Using alternate IP addressing does give you the best of both the static and dynamic worlds, though. You can control the addressing based on a DHCP server, but still have the system function normally in case the DHCP server fails. Most companies do not configure servers this way, however; usually this is reserved for computers that roam from one location to another, like laptops, so that the computer can use DHCP at one location, such as the office, and then use the alternate IP address on a home network.

Defining Scope Options

TCP/IP configuration options that are available from a DHCP server allow an administrator to configure the systems to communicate with the correct DNS servers, WINS servers, and routers, as well as configure settings so that the system is identified correctly and communicates in the most efficient manner. You can configure these options in several places, and you need to determine which of the levels is the correct one for the clients that the option affects. Do take note that if you set any options static on the client, then DHCP-assigned options no longer apply.

Server Options

Server options become the default settings for all of the clients that receive a lease from the DHCP server. If you have settings that apply to many clients in every subnet, you should set them at this level, thus alleviating the need to configure the same setting within multiple scopes. Options that are typically set at this level include DNS and WINS server settings.

Scope Options

Scope options are settings that need to be applied to clients that reside within a specific subnet. These options override any option that is configured at the server level. If clients within a subnet have a specific setting they need applied that overrides the server level, apply it here. Also, if a specific setting needs to be applied to clients within a subnet, it needs to be applied here. Settings that you normally configure at this level include the default gateway address for the clients and DNS or WINS server settings, if they are different for the clients on this subnet than for those that are set as the defaults at the server level.

Reserved Client Options

The *reserved client options* are typically inherited from the subnet where the client's IP address is reserved. If you need to change the reserved client's options, you can configure the options within the reservation setting. Any changes at this level override any options that are set at the scope or server levels. One setting that you may want to configure at this level would be specifying a DNS server that the client uses that may be different than the ones other clients within the subnet use.

Class Options

Class options apply to specific client classifications to which a system is assigned. If a system is assigned a class ID, and the class ID is configured with options within the DHCP server, the client receives the options when it requests an IP address from the DHCP server. This comes in especially handy if you have a group of computers within a subnet that need to have specific options configured. Before the class options can be used, the client system needs to be configured with a class. For user classes that the administrator wants to use for specific systems, the `ipconfig` command is used to set the class ID; `ipconfig /setclassid 'classname'`. Options at the class level override options set at the scope and server level.

Determining DHCP Server Locations

Although it would be handy to place a DHCP server within every subnet where you are assigning IP addresses, you may not have that luxury. A single DHCP server can supply IP configuration options to systems within multiple subnets. You need to determine which subnets the server will work with, the scope of addresses for each subnet, the configuration options that will be used on each subnet and the method of relaying the settings to the DHCP clients.

Two distribution methods exist that allow a DHCP server to work with client systems:

- Connecting directly to the subnet
- Using a DHCP relay method

Because a DHCP server can be configured to have direct access to multiple subnets, it can respond to DHCP requests from clients on each of the subnets to which it is connected. Each of the scopes needs to have their own specific options applied so that the clients are able to communicate correctly.

If the DHCP server is not directly connected to the subnet in which a DHCP client exists, you have to use a DHCP relay method, either by configuring a router that supports forwarding of DHCP/BOOTP packets, or by configuring a system to perform as a DHCP relay agent. In either case, you set the DHCP relay device to forward DHCP requests, which are broadcast based, to a DHCP server as a unicast packet. The DHCP server would then assign the client an address based upon the subnet scope for the client system. The lease information is then sent directly back to the DHCP relay device which in turn broadcasts the information back out onto the subnet for the client to discover.

If you have a large client population on a subnet, you should consider configuring your DHCP servers to communicate directly on that subnet. However, if the subnet does not contain many DHCP clients, you may consider using a relay option so that you are not investing in the hardware. Do take note that if the network links between the client and the server fail, you need to have an alternate method of configuring the client in case the client's lease expires.

Summary

Active Directory relies on a stable and effective network infrastructure. Within the network infrastructure, you should make sure you have considered how the users will connect to the resources that they need. Every organization needs to have users that connect within the internal network, and most have some type of external user who needs to gain access to internal resources. Configuring the network to allow access and still maintain a high level of security can be a challenge.

After determining what kind of users you need to support, you need to design the network infrastructure to support the internal and remote access. Your infrastructure may use RRAS as routers, RAS, RADIUS clients, and RADIUS servers. It depends upon how you wish to implement each of the services to support your user needs.

IP address allocation is another item that you need to design so that you have the appropriate address structure to support all of your users within each location. Once you have determined the IP address ranges you will use, you need to determine how you will configure clients, either with a static address or using DHCP.

In the next chapter, we look at the part of the network infrastructure that drives most administrators insane—name resolution. In Chapter 10, we discuss DNS and WINS and make design decisions based upon the name resolution methods used within the network as well as the Active Directory requirements.

Exam Essentials

Understand the options available for a perimeter network.   When creating a perimeter network you have three options: a single firewall, known as a bastion host, to block all incoming traffic from accessing your network; a three-homed firewall that separates the internal network from a perimeter network that external users can access; or back-to-back firewalls that give you an added layer of protection and allow you to host servers within a perimeter network.

Identify the IP addressing needs.   Every device that uses TCP/IP needs to have an address for which it can communicate on the network. You can use either a private address or a public address when configuring the client systems. You need to determine if you want the systems to have direct access to the Internet or if you are going to use a NAT server or a proxy server.

Know the IP addressing allocation options.   Addresses can be assigned either manually or dynamically. Some systems, such as DNS servers, have to have a static address, but most systems can be dynamically assigned an address. A DHCP server can be used to assign addresses and configuration options to clients. If a DHCP server is not available, clients from Windows 98 on generate an automatic private IP address (APIPA). If the client system is a Windows XP workstation or Windows Server 2003 server, you can configure an alternate IP address within the TCP/IP properties that is used instead of APIPA.

Understand the remote access requirements for the organization.   You need to determine the users who will need remote access to your network and how they will connect. RAS servers can be used as dial-up solutions or as VPN servers. IAS can be used as the RADIUS server to RAS RADIUS clients. Using a RADIUS solution gives you better control over remote access policies and accounting information.

Know the Internet access options.   You can connect a user to the Internet with one of three methods: by configuring a router and giving them direct access; by configuring a NAT server, which will allow them to access the Internet but doesn't give you very much control; and by using a proxy server, which will give you additional caching mechanisms and user account control.

Know the forest design options that can be used with perimeter networks.   The servers in the perimeter network can be part of the same forest as the internal network, but if a system in the perimeter is compromised, finding information about the internal network, or access to the internal network is easier for an attacker. If you create a separate forest for the perimeter, you have the option of not creating a trust relationship between the two forests, which is the most secure method, or of creating either a one-way trust or a two-way trust, which make administration easier, but reduces security.

Understand the options that are available when promoting a domain controller.   When promoting the domain controller, you have the option of opening RPC ports on the firewall so that the domain controllers can communicate, or you can promote the domain controller from backup media, which will reduce replication traffic across the WAN link. The other option is to promote the domain controller at one site to allow the initial replication to commence on a fast network and then transport the domain controller to the other site.

Key Terms

Before you take the exam, be certain you are familiar with the following terms:

alternate IP addressing	Remote Authentication Dial-In User Service (RADIUS)
automatic private IP address (APIPA)	reserved client options
back-to-back firewalls	scope options
bastion host	server options
class options	single forest design
multiple forest, no trust design	three-homed firewall
multiple forest, one-way trust design	variable length subnet masks (VLSM)
multiple forest, two-way trust design	

Review Questions

1. When you are attempting to increase availability of network resources, which term defines how long a device is expected to function without breaking?

    A. Mean time to recovery

    B. Mean time before failure

    C. Redundancy

    D. Secondary paths

2. Which device type should Anna Beth choose if she wants to allow users to connect to the Internet, but she wants to control which user accounts will be able to connect?

    A. Router

    B. Proxy server

    C. Domain controller

    D. NAT server

3. Which of the following is considered a drawback to using a VPN?

    A. Existing infrastructure is used

    B. Scales better than dial-up

    C. Additional overhead

    D. Public connection can be used

4. What is Microsoft's service that acts as a RADIUS server called?

    A. NAT

    B. VPN

    C. RRAS

    D. IAS

5. If you want to centralize your remote access policies, what service will you use?

    A. IAS

    B. NAT

    C. RRAS

    D. VPN

6. Tina has a network that uses a link-state routing protocol that is compatible with the link-state protocol used in Windows Server 2003. If she decides to use Windows Server 2003 as a router, which protocol would she configure?

   A. IAS

   B. RIP

   C. OSPF

   D. NAT

7. Dan is designing his network infrastructure and is in the process of determining how he will allow access to web server, yet protect his internal network. Which of the following options will provide the best security?

   A. No firewall

   B. Bastion host

   C. Three-homed firewall

   D. Back-to-back firewalls

8. Toni is trying to determine which design to use for her perimeter network. She wants to have as much security as possible and is willing to forego ease of administration in order to get the security she wants. Which of the following models should she use?

   A. Single forest

   B. Multiple forest, no trust

   C. Multiple forest, one-way trust

   D. Multiple forest, two-way trust

9. Cheryl is designing the IP address allocation method for the web servers within the perimeter network. Which of the addressing methods should she choose?

   A. Static

   B. DHCP

   C. Reservation

   D. APIPA

10. When determining which IP address range to use between two Windows Server 2003 systems that are acting as routers between two of the company's locations, which address range would be the most efficient?

   A. 192.168.1.0/24

   B. 192.168.1.0/26

   C. 192.168.1.0/28

   D. 192.168.1.0/30

Answers to Review Questions

1. B. The mean time before failure is a measurement used to designate how long a device will typically function before it fails.

2. B. A proxy server can be configured to allow users to connect to the Internet and will cache the pages that the users visit so that Internet traffic can be reduced. With a proxy server, you can configure exactly which users will have the ability to connect to the Internet.

3. C. Whenever you use a VPN solution, you generate additional overhead on your server due to the encryption and decryption of the packets.

4. D. Internet Authentication Service (IAS) is Microsoft's implementation of a RADIUS server. Although IAS follows the RADIUS standards, it also has additional features such as the ability to centrally locate the RRAS policies.

5. A. If you do not use IAS, the remote access policies are held individually on a RAS server. By using the IAS, you can create a remote access policy and all of the RRAS RADIUS clients will use the policies from the IAS server.

6. C. If other routers within the network are using a link-state routing protocol, the only one that is supported by Windows Server 2003 RRAS is OSPF. Make sure you have configured the RRAS router correctly or you could cause routing issues within the network.

7. D. The back-to-back firewall option allows the devices within the internal network to be safe-guarded from attacks because two firewalls need to be hacked before the internal network is jeopardized.

8. B. With the multiple forest, no trust model, the perimeter network is a forest unto itself and no trust relationships exist with the forest for the internal network. When this model is used, there are added administrative costs because the users who need to access resources within both forests need to have a separate identity from the one used within the internal network. Also, if there is a reason that resources from one forest need to be used from the other forest, the accounts have to be set up to allow access, which could prove more difficult than the other models.

9. A. When placing web servers within the perimeter network, the best way to assign an IP address to them is to use a static address. If you use a static address, the IP address used by the web server will not have to be changed within the DNS servers that are accessible by Internet clients, and you will not have to open ports on the internal firewall to allow DHCP traffic to get to the servers.

10. D. When defining the addresses to use between routers, if you want to conserve the addresses available and use only the number required for the connection, you should use a 30-bit mask, which will give you the two addresses needed between the routers.

Case Study

You should give yourself 20 minutes to review this testlet, and complete the questions.

Background

Insane Systems builds custom computers for their customers. They specialize in building cases that are unique and support the latest in hardware technology. They started off as a small company that provided this service to gamers who would take their cases to LAN parties to show off. Because their systems were considered some of the most stable gaming platforms and they provided an impressive design that gamers could show off, they started to become popular. Insane Systems started mass manufacturing some of their more popular designs and began selling stand-alone cases along with their fully configured systems. As space at the company became a premium, the office was moved from the manufacturing facility. This allowed the company to add to the amount of space that was used for the mass production line.

Existing Environment

Over the past few months, Insane Systems has been developing plans to expand their company. They have identified San Jose, California; Atlanta, Georgia; and New York City, New York as the locations with their highest customer base. The current Chicago location will remain the corporate headquarters, but they are opening branches in New York City and San Jose. They are also in the process of acquiring a competitor's business in Atlanta. These locations will provide retail outlets as well as support. Customers will have the option of sending their systems back to the corporate office for repair, or delivering them to one of the branch locations.

Because the company is planning on expanding, they want to make sure that the network infrastructure is in place to support their larger, distributed company. They are also concerned with the support lifetime of their current Windows NT 4 infrastructure. They realize they have the option of moving to a Windows 2000 or Windows 2003 infrastructure and are considering moving to Windows Server 2003 and Active Directory for two reasons: the expected support lifetime is greater than Windows 2000 and they are a technology firm that is not afraid of staying ahead of the technology curve.

Part of the expansion of the company is a complete overhaul of their current Internet presence. They are planning on bringing all of the web development and hosting in-house. Currently a web hosting service is providing their Internet presence, and Insane Systems feels as though they could provide better marketing and support information for their customers if they had control over their own website. Insane Systems would also like to change the name of their website to better represent their name in the marketplace. They own the name `insane-systems.com`.

Interviews

Your company has been hired to design an Active Directory infrastructure and the network infrastructure to support it. During the interview process with some of the key stakeholders, you gathered the following information:

CEO   Currently we have a single location with all of our processes local. As we grow, we would like to keep all of the administration here in Chicago. Because the new branches are primarily retail and support offices, we will not need to have a large staff in those locations. The Atlanta office has an existing network that we would like to merge into our network. System design, research and development, and patent information come from the Atlanta office, so a secure connection from Atlanta to Chicago must be implemented.

CIO   Most of the infrastructure that we support is located here at the corporate office. We do support some key servers at the manufacturing location. We support these servers from our main office. Because the servers are nearby, if there is a problem, we can usually be onsite within half an hour.

The new branches are going to be another issue altogether. We would like to retain the same level of administrative control over the servers in the new locations that we employ currently. Due to the geographic limitations, we may need to have some support staff at those locations. Currently, the plan is to hire staff at those locations who can provide the support for the customers, but also understand the business systems we need to put into place. We would like to automate software installations to the remote office due to the lack of IT staff.

Manager of Information Technology   We have grown very quickly over the past three years and our current technologies have kept up with that growth. However, we don't think the current infrastructure is ready for the amount of growth that we are expecting within the following year. We are not afraid of moving to the latest technology, but we want to make sure that the design is stable and makes sense for us, especially if we will continue growing in the upcoming months. And because we are losing support for NT 4, we want to make sure that we have an operating system that will be supported for a few years down the road.

Most of our processes are located here at this office, and we would like to keep it that way. We know that sometimes servers will need to be located at the remote offices, but we would like to be able to provide most of the support from this location. Remote administration tools will need to be included within the design so that we can keep our administrative costs to a minimum.

Currently, we have most of our servers located at the main office, and all are located on their own high-speed backbone. We do have a server at the manufacturing site that allows the staff there to have e-mail as well as plans and orders in case we lose connectivity between the offices. This server is running Exchange 5.5. Several times during the day we replicate the public folder information to this system so that they are always up-to-date and do not have to dial up to the main office using our 56Kbps modem.

The systems at the main office are all supported by our staff of four administrators. All of the administrators are cross-trained on Windows NT 4, Exchange 5.5, SQL Server 7, our accounting software, and each of our file and print servers. We currently have several Windows NT 4

servers in place, including one Exchange 5.5 server at both locations, one SQL Server 7 server at the main office, one server running our accounting package that interfaces with the SQL server, and one file and print server that is used by both locations. The Exchange server at the manufacturing location doubles as a print server also.

The Atlanta office currently has a Windows NT 4 domain, and we will migrate that domain into our forest. Although administration of the forest will be moved to the Chicago branch, administration of the Atlanta domain will reside in the Atlanta domain. We will have a very small IT staff in the Atlanta office who will need control over all aspects of the Atlanta domain. Administrators of the Atlanta domain will have control over the Atlanta domain only and will not have administrator access to any other domain or any other part of the forest. All communication between the Atlanta office and the Chicago office will take place via an IPSec connection. The users in the Atlanta office will also require different password and lockout restrictions than the other offices.

Naming conventions for groups are very confusing right now, and adding the Atlanta domain only added to this confusion. Groups in the current domain are named Sales, IT, Accounting, and so on. Groups in the Atlanta domain are also named Sales, Accounting, and so on. We would like to rename groups to represent the name of the group, the home office of the user, the type of group (Global, Domain Local, or Universal), and then the job function of the user.

LAN Administrators in the root domain of the forest are responsible for creating GPOs but do not have access to link them at any level. Domain Admins in each domain are responsible for testing and linking the GPO to their own domains only. Forest owners will also have access to link GPOs at any level of any domain in the forest.

Because all of the client machines are running Windows NT 4 Workstation, we do not have to worry about supporting different operating systems. We would like to maintain that same easy administration with the upcoming system. We would like to provide the same types of services at the remote locations that we provide at the home office, although accounting will remain at the home office and will not be spread out to all of the locations.

Current Infrastructure

After investigating the current infrastructure, you have determined that the following servers are in place:

Home Office

Primary Domain Controller (PDC)

Backup Domain Controller (BDC)

DHCP/DNS/WINS server

Exchange 5.5 server

SQL Server 7

Systems Management Server 2

File server/Print/Antivirus server

Research and Development File server

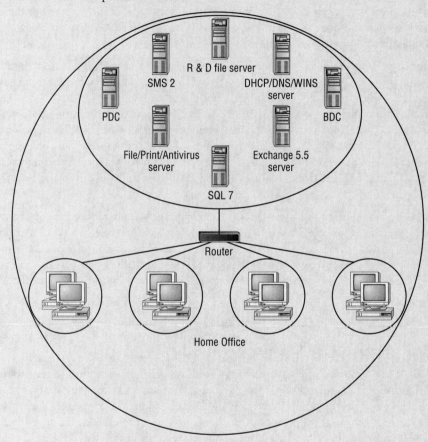

PDC

SMS 2

R & D file server

DHCP/DNS/WINS
server

BDC

File/Print/Antivirus
server

Exchange 5.5
server

SQL 7

Router

Home Office

Atlanta Office

Primary Domain Controller (PDC)

Backup Domain Controller (BDC)

WINS server

File server

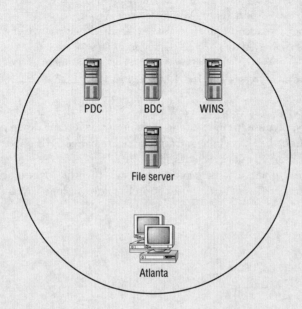

Manufacturing Facility

Backup Domain Controller (BDC)

DNS/WINS/DHCP Relay Agent server

Exchange 5.5/file server

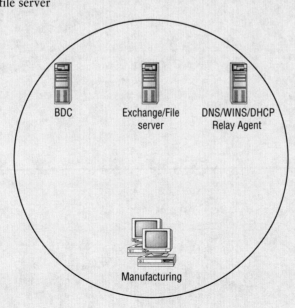

The Corporate Office hosts nearly 250 Windows NT 4 workstations at this point. They are interconnected by several 48-port 10/100Mbps switches. A router is used to divide the network into 4 VLANs. One of these broadcast domains is the 1Gbps backbone on which the servers reside. Each of the servers is connected to a 1Gbps switch port. This location takes advantage of private IP address ranges. The servers are located on the 192.168.1.0/24 subnet. The client systems are divided among network addresses 192.168.10.0/24, 192.168.11.0/24, 192.168.12.0/24, and 192.168.13.0/24.

The manufacturing facility contains 12 Windows NT 4 Workstations connected to the same switch as the servers. Because Insane Systems does not want to slow down production due to a communication failure, they have taken advantage of Exchange 5.5's public folder replication. Public folders are continually updated with the latest orders. The crew foreman can access the orders locally from these public folders at any time, whether the communication link between the locations is up or not. This location uses another address range—192.168.20.0/24.

Case Study Questions

1. When the web servers are moved so that Insane Systems host their own systems, what is the best option for supplying IP addresses to the servers?

   A. Use a DHCP server from the internal network to supply the addresses to the web servers.

   B. Use a DHCP server within the perimeter network to supply the addresses to the web servers.

   C. Use a static address for the web servers.

   D. Use APIPA for the web servers.

2. When designing how the web servers will be protected, how will you set up the firewall(s) so that you have the highest level of security for your internal network?

   A. No firewalls

   B. Bastion host

   C. Three-homed firewall

   D. Back-to-back firewall

3. Currently this scenario does not have any remote users, but administrators need to have remote administrative control of the servers at each location. What security measures should you take?

   A. Configure a dial-up connection on each of the servers

   B. Put each of the servers within the perimeter network

   C. Create a request IPSec policy and assign it to the servers

   D. Create a client IPSec policy and assign it to the administrator's workstations

4. When promoting the domain controllers for the San Jose and New York locations, which of the promotion methods would work the best?

   A. Have the new staff at each location promote the domain controllers.

   B. Have an administrator from the home office promote the domain controller at each site using remote control utilities.

   C. Have the new staff at each location promote the domain controller at each site and have them provide backup media for the initial replication.

   D. Have an administrator for the home office both promote the domain controller at each site using remote control utilities and specify the backup media for the initial replication.

5. Select the address assignment type and match it to the appropriate system(s).

System	Address Type
Intranet Web Servers	DHCP
DHCP Server	DHCP Reservation
DNS Server	Static
Workstations	APIPA

Answers to Case Study Questions

1. C. If you use static addressing, you will not have to open ports on the firewall to allow the requests to pass to the internal DHCP server, nor will you have to place a DHCP server within the perimeter, which could pose a security concern. The web server addresses should also be set static so that the entries within the DNS servers for the Internet will resolve correctly and not have to be updated. APIPA will not work because the APIPA address is not usable on the Internet.

2. D. By using a back-to-back firewall option, you will have two firewalls protecting the internal network.

3. C, D. To make sure that the administrators are using a secure connection when they are managing the servers, you could create IPSec policies for the servers and workstations that would use IPSec whenever the administrators connect to them.

4. D. Because the new staff at each location will have limited knowledge of Windows Server 2003 and Active Directory, the preferred method of promoting the domain controllers is to have a backup of Active Directory sent to each location and have the administrator promote the domain controller remotely. The staff at the location can insert the appropriate media when the system calls for it during promotion.

5.

Intranet Web Servers
DCHP Reservation
DHCP Server
Static
DNS Server
Static
Workstations
DHCP

When addressing client systems you need to identify which clients need static or dynamic addressing. Intranet web servers should be configured with either a static address or a reservation should be set within the DHCP server. Using a reservation, the web server will always obtain the same IP address, but you can control the configuration options from the DHCP server. Most of the workstations can receive DHCP supplied addresses. DNS and DHCP servers should have static addresses.

Chapter 10

Analyzing Name Resolution

MICROSOFT EXAM OBJECTIVES COVERED IN THIS CHAPTER:

✓ **Analyze DNS for Active Directory directory service implementation.**

  ▪ Analyze the current DNS infrastructure.

  ▪ Analyze the current namespace.

✓ **Design the network services infrastructure to meet business and technical requirements.**

  ▪ Create the conceptual design of the DNS infrastructure.

  ▪ Create the conceptual design of the WINS infrastructure.

✓ **Design an Active Directory naming strategy.**

  ▪ Identify Internet domain name registration requirements.

  ▪ Identify NetBIOS naming requirements.

✓ **Design a DNS name resolution strategy.**

  ▪ Create the namespace design.

  ▪ Identify DNS interoperability with Active Directory, WINS, and DHCP.

  ▪ Specify zone requirements.

  ▪ Specify DNS security.

  ▪ Design a DNS strategy for interoperability with UNIX Berkeley Internet Name Domain (BIND) to support Active Directory.

✓ **Design a NetBIOS name resolution strategy.**

  ▪ Design a WINS replication strategy.

✓ **Design a DNS service implementation.**

  ▪ Design a strategy for DNS zone storage.

  ▪ Specify the use of DNS server options.

- Identify the registration requirements of specific DNS records.

✓ **Design DNS service placement.**

In the previous chapter, we discussed how network access is designed for a network infrastructure. We discussed internal and remote access and IP addressing options along with the security options an organization can use when trying to protect its resources.

Every computer that needs to communicate with other systems on the network, whether it is internal to the network or a remote system, needs to be able to determine the network addresses of other computers. Systems are uniquely named so that they are differentiated from every other system within the organization. These names are easy for us to understand, but operating systems use other means of identifying themselves in order to communicate.

In this chapter, we are going to discuss the available name resolution design options. Although DNS is the preferred name resolution method in a Windows Server 2003 network infrastructure, numerous organizations are still supporting applications or operating systems that utilize NetBIOS naming and need to have a NetBIOS name resolution method. In a Windows environment, WINS is used as the NetBIOS name resolution service.

Examining the Current Name Resolution Infrastructure

Every network needs to have some method of resolving computer names to network addresses. Two name resolution methods exist within a Windows Server 2003 network infrastructure: the Domain Name System (DNS) and Windows Internet Name Service (WINS). We will look at each of these in the following sections.

The *Domain Name System (DNS)* is a name resolution method that is used extensively within Windows 2000 Server and Windows Server 2003 networks as well as the Internet and other network operating systems. Clients and servers can send queries to a DNS server in order to resolve a hostname to an IP address so that two systems can communicate with each other.

If you are going to implement Active Directory, you must have DNS within a Windows Server 2003 network. The Active Directory domain structure is based on the DNS domain structure. Domain controllers require DNS servers so that they can register service locator (SRV) records. Clients and applications will send queries for the SRV records when they are trying to locate a domain controller. Of course, many other applications need to have a DNS server so that they will function correctly, such as web services and e-mail systems.

Companies that have Internet access will have DNS servers that they use in order to access resources on the Internet. These DNS servers could be owned and maintained by the organization, but the servers could be maintained just as easily by an outside company like their Internet

Service Provider (ISP). You will need to determine how the company is currently using DNS as a name resolution solution.

If you currently host services that users from the Internet will access, or you are planning on allowing access to your resources at a later time, you need to make sure that the users will be able to locate your Internet name. You must register your Internet presence with an Internet registration authority so that you are ensured of owning your domain name. If you do not register your domain name, another company could register it and use it.

You essentially have two choices when determining how you will employ your DNS infrastructure: you could host your own DNS servers and maintain the DNS zones yourself, or you could have your ISP maintain your zones on their servers. For some companies, having an ISP host their DNS infrastructure may seem like the perfect fit. The ISP typically has administrators who are experienced with DNS and how to maintain it, and the organization does not have to support its own servers or train its administrative staff on another technology.

If you do decide to outsource your DNS implementation, you must make sure that the ISP has the appropriate DNS infrastructure to support your needs. You must also determine whether the ISP's infrastructure is secure enough to host critical information about your internal network. Chances are, you will not want an ISP to host your internal domain information. It is not advisable to have another organization hosting information on their servers that is critical to your network's availability. You should host your own DNS servers and make sure they are located close to the domain controllers and users that need them. Some of your domain controllers may also run the DNS service on them. As we discuss server placement options later in this chapter, we will look at how you should design your systems.

You could have a mixed environment that has internal DNS servers to support the organization's internal name resolution requirements and an ISP that hosts a DNS that the organization uses for external name resolution to Internet resources. Utilizing this method, the organization can outsource some of the DNS maintenance. Administrators from the organization can concentrate on maintaining their own infrastructure and allow the outside entity to maintain the services they are experienced in running.

Windows Internet Name Service (WINS) has been used extensively by Microsoft operating systems as a way to resolve computer names to IP addresses. Until the Windows 2000 product line, all of the Microsoft operating systems relied on NetBIOS name resolution from WINS servers. Therein lies the difficulty in trying to remove NetBIOS from a network so that it can rely solely on DNS for name resolution; too many applications and operating systems still *need* to use NetBIOS.

Because NetBIOS is so prevalent within today's networks, you will usually find a WINS infrastructure in place to assist with NetBIOS name resolution for clients and servers that reside in different subnets. Before you make any changes to the network infrastructure, you should determine where you have located WINS servers and which systems use these servers for name resolution.

The current DNS and WINS infrastructure will help you determine how the name resolution services are currently used by the organization. You should create a diagram of your name resolution environment that includes the DNS and WINS servers. This diagram should also specify which clients use each of the servers in your infrastructure. Chances are, the clients will continue to use the same servers.

Also take note of the types of DNS servers that are currently in use. Many companies have already implemented a DNS infrastructure using a third-party DNS solution. If this is the case, you may find yourself having to fight another battle—trying to get Microsoft DNS integrated into the environment. For years UNIX DNS solutions have controlled the DNS infrastructure in many organizations. If this is the case in your organization, you may find yourself having to use the existing infrastructure. In the next section, we will look at the options you have if a third-party DNS solution is already in place.

When diagramming the WINS solution, take note of the current replication topology. When you understand how the servers replicate to one another, you can better understand the importance of each site. For instance, you may have several remote locations that use WINS to register and query computer names. Two of the sites regularly share information. The replication schedule for these two sites is set so that replication occurs between them in short intervals. The other sites do not share as much data, so the replication interval is set so that the link is not used as often. Replication options are discussed in this chapter under the "Designing a Name Resolution Server Infrastructure" section.

In the next section, we will identify the options that make up a DNS namespace. Organizations that need to provide Internet users access to part of their organization's resources will need to determine how they are going to design their internal and external domain names. Once the domain name requirements have been determined, you will need to decide how the DNS infrastructure will support your requirements.

Designing the DNS Namespace

The DNS namespace that you choose for your organization will be used for more than identifying computers on your network. Internet users accessing web resources will identify you with your external domain name. Active Directory will be based on the name that you decide to use internally. The choices you make at the design level stage will impact the rest of the name infrastructure.

In Chapter 2, "Determining Business and Technical Requirements," and Chapter 3, "Designing the Active Directory Forest Structure," we discussed options for naming your forest root domain and the domains within that make up the trees within your forest. If you are working through this book from beginning to end, you should have already created a domain name design for Active Directory. Your DNS domain names will have to be identical to the domain names you have chosen for Active Directory.

Even if you have decided upon a domain name scheme for Active Directory, you should go back and review your decisions. As you are designing the DNS infrastructure to support your Active Directory design, you may find that the existing infrastructure is not conducive to the design that you wanted to put in place. Several things may get in your way, the first of which could be the political infighting you will encounter if you tell the current DNS administrators that you are taking over their DNS with yours. You may need to find a tactful method of working with the existing DNS administrative staff when you try to interoperate with their infrastructure. Depending on your current environment, you have the following options available to you:

The existing infrastructure uses a legacy Microsoft DNS implementation.   Windows NT 4 Server's DNS service conforms to DNS domain naming guidelines. The current namespace could be used if you are moving to a Windows Server 2003 DNS solution. If you are going to implement Active Directory, you will have to either upgrade the existing DNS servers to Windows Server 2003, or replace them with Windows Server 2003 DNS servers to support Active Directory within the network infrastructure.

The existing infrastructure uses a third-party DNS solution that adheres to standard DNS guidelines.   If the third-party DNS solutions follow the DNS domain naming guidelines, you will not have to change the namespace design. However, if you are going to use Active Directory, you will need to make sure that the third-party DNS server has the correct features to support Active Directory. If the server does not you are left with the option of upgrading the current server to a version that does support Active Directory or you will have to integrate Windows Server 2003 DNS servers into the infrastructure.

The existing infrastructure uses a third-party DNS solution that does not adhere to standard DNS guidelines.   If the third-party DNS solution does not conform to DNS domain naming guidelines, you will have to upgrade or redesign your DNS infrastructure to conform before implementing Windows Server 2003 DNS servers or Active Directory.

No DNS solution exists and you are implementing a new Microsoft Windows Server 2003 DNS. If you are simply implementing a DNS infrastructure, you need to design your domain names according to the organization's needs. If you are deploying Windows Server 2003 DNS to support Active Directory, follow your Active Directory naming requirements when you design the domain namespace.

The existing infrastructure uses a namespace that you do not want to use for Active Directory, but you do not want to redesign the current namespace.   Either create an Active Directory namespace that will be a child of the existing namespace so that you can separate the two namespaces, or create a new namespace that will be used in conjunction with the existing namespace.

Prior to implementing DNS zones, you need to know the names that you will need to support for your organization. In the following section we will take a look at the namespace requirements for internal and external domain names.

Determining Internal and External Namespace Requirements

You essentially have two options when you are creating a DNS namespace for your internal infrastructure and your Internet presence: you can use the same namespace internally as you do externally, or you can create a different namespace for each. Either way, you will need to support two DNS server infrastructures. If your internal and external namespaces are the same, you will have more administrative overhead as you synchronize data so that internal users are able to access your company's external resources.

In the following sections we will examine the options that can be used when designing the namespace and the root domain requirements.

Identifying Namespace Options

Most organizations will separate the domain names so that the internal DNS namespace is either a subdomain of the external namespace, or the two namespaces are completely different.

Although this will increase the administrative overhead because all of your internal and external resources will not be located in the same domain, you will add an additional level of security to your infrastructure.

Figure 10.1 illustrates a company that has used the same namespace internally as they have externally.

The primary problem with using the same namespace is that internal users will not be able to access the organization's external resources without additional administrative work. DNS records for the external resources will have to be added to the internal DNS server so that the users can access them, or the resources will have to be hosted on both internal and external servers and synchronized to keep them both up to date.

Figure 10.2 illustrates an organization that has implemented separate namespaces so that the internal and external domain names are not the same. This still adds security to your design due to the fact that external users will not have access to your internal namespace, yet you can configure DNS to allow internal users to access the external resources.

FIGURE 10.1   Using the same domain name internally and externally

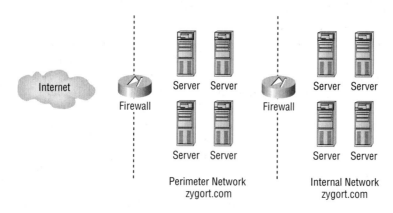

FIGURE 10.2   Using a separate domain name internally than is used externally

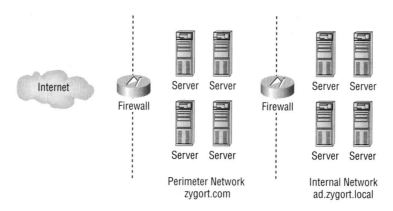

External users will be able to access your external resources, but they will not have access to the internal resources because the external DNS servers will not have records for the internal namespace. Internal users will have access to internal resources because the internal DNS servers will control the internal namespace. When internal users want to access external resources, the internal DNS servers can forward the request to the external DNS servers.

When separating the namespaces, a common practice is to use the subdomain "ad" for the internal namespace. For example, a company that uses zygort.com as their Internet presence could use ad.zygort.com as their internal namespace.

Another option when you are using a different namespace is to have completely separate namespaces. Whereas the aforementioned company could use zygort.com as their Internet presence, they may adopt zygort.local internally. The top-level domain "local" that is used here, or any name that is not defined as a top-level domain for the internet, will work to create a separation from the internal namespace and the external. You should try to determine a top-level domain name that you do not anticipate being used on the Internet so that you do not cause name resolution issues at a later date.

Identifying Root Domain Requirements

Using an *internal DNS root* allows you to implement a namespace that is identified as the only DNS infrastructure available. Instead of using top-level domains on the Internet, your DNS infrastructure would be seen as the highest level in the DNS hierarchy. When a client queries for a hostname, if the DNS server they are configured to use does not have entries for the domain of the host they are trying to contact, your DNS root will be contacted. If your DNS infrastructure does not have entries for the host, or forwarding of queries outside of your organization is not configured, the client will not be able to locate the host they are querying.

Because your DNS infrastructure is seen as the top level in the hierarchy, you will have to make sure that you have delegations for all of the domains for which you are authoritative. For example, if you have a company that hosts an internal DNS root, you would have to create delegations to each of the namespaces within your organization. Zygort, Inc. uses the domain name zygort.lcl. They also have a secondary company that uses the domain name bloomco.lcl. If a user with a computer in the zygort.lcl namespace wants to obtain the IP address for the computer with the hostname host1.bloomco.lcl, the DNS servers for zygort.lcl need to have a delegation record that identifies the name servers for the bloomco.lcl domain.

When you use an internal DNS root, the clients on your network will not use DNS servers on the Internet to resolve hostnames. This gives you an additional level of security because you will not pass any of your internal DNS information to servers on the Internet. At the same time, if your clients cannot access DNS servers on the Internet, they will not be able to resolve hostnames outside of your DNS infrastructure. You are not able to configure a DNS server that contains the root of the DNS hierarchy as a forwarder. If this is the case, you will have to determine another method of allowing clients to connect to Internet resources, such as using a proxy server like Microsoft's Internet Security and Acceleration (ISA) server.

If your organization hosts DNS hierarchies that are top-level DNS namespaces, you will need to design a method of interoperability between the namespaces. The easiest method of interoperating is to add a delegation to the root DNS zone. This will allow queries to be passed to the root zone, which will in turn send a response that identifies name servers authoritative for the zone in question.

Another method for allowing multiple top-level domains to interoperate is to add a secondary zone for each domain to each DNS server in the other domains. These secondary zones will then contain the DNS data for each of the domains in the organization. Zone transfers will keep them up to date and clients will have local name resolution from their preferred DNS server. Having secondary zones for the other namespaces also alleviates the wide area network (WAN) traffic that is generated when a client sends a hostname query, but you will have to take into account the amount of WAN traffic that is generated from the zone transfer.

The final options for top-level domain interoperability is to configure each of the DNS servers to forward requests to another DNS server. You could configure conditional forwarding for each of the domains within your organization. Conditional forwarding will send the query to a DNS server based on the namespace that the query is destined for. For example, if you create a conditional forwarder for the DNS servers in `zygort.lcl` to forward queries destined for `bloomco.lcl` to a DNS server authoritative for the `bloomco.lcl` domain, whenever your server receives a query for `bloomco.lcl`, the query will be forwarded to a `bloomco.lcl` DNS server. All other queries would be sent to the DNS servers defined for all other domain queries.

Identifying Naming Standards

There are two namespace considerations you need to take into account. Every company needs to determine what name they will use for internal resources. If you need to have an Internet presence, you will need to determine what name will identify you to the world. Each of these namespaces will then be integrated into your organizations identity. It is not easy to change either of these namespaces, so choose wisely.

In the following sections, external and internal namespace options are identified. Take these into account as you design the namespaces for your organization.

Identifying External Namespace Options

If you have determined that your organization will need an Internet presence, you need to determine what name you will be identified with. Your name should identify your company. Users who are accessing your external resources should find your name easy to understand. One guideline is to make your name short yet understandable. The easier it is to remember and type, the easier it will be for users to return to your site. The name zygort.com is much easier to remember and type than zygort-manufacturing-inc.com. Plus, if you are using a subdomain as your internal name, the longer the external DNS name is, the longer the internal namespace will be as you append the subdomain. Users will not appreciate having to enter accountspayable.accounting.corp.zygort.lcl.

Verify that the name that you would like to use for your Internet presence is available. You can search the whois databases on sites such as `www.networksolutions.com` to find out if another company has registered the name. If your name has not been registered, configure a DNS server to be authoritative for a zone, which will host your namespace or have an ISP host the DNS records for you. Then make sure you register your name for use and provide the registrar with the DNS server address that will be hosting the zone.

Even if you are not initially planning on an Internet presence, you should register a domain name for your company. It never fails—every time a company decides that they do not need to have an Internet presence, they turn around a couple of years later and change their minds. If someone else has previously registered the domain name that the company wants to use, they will have a hard time trying to obtain that name, or they will have to use another, less desirable name.

Identifying Internal Namespace Options

To keep your internal resources hidden from external users, you should keep the internal namespace different than the Internet namespace. If you wish to keep the two namespaces separate, you have the option of making the internal domain name a child domain from the Internet namespace or having two completely different namespaces.

Even if you never add any delegation records to the Internet domain so that the internal domain name is available from the Internet domain, you will still be using a domain name structure that will make sense to your users. If you decide to make the internal domain accessible, you can add a delegation record to the DNS servers that are used for your Internet presence or create a subdomain to allow specific servers to be accessed.

Make sure that you are not using a name that is already in use on the Internet. If you do, you could cause users to have name resolution issues. In addition to name resolution issues, if you were to decide to open up a portion of your internal network, you would not be able to because another entity owns the name.

You should also take some configuration options into account. First, you should not use one of the top-level domain names as the domain name of your internal network. Any of the top-level domain names like .com, .org, .edu, .us, and so on, should be reserved for top-level use only so that internal clients that have internet access do not become confused. You should also try to not use abbreviations or acronyms for any of your domain names that identify business units or divisions. Doing so could confuse your users when they are trying to locate resources, especially if separate business units use the same acronyms for different departments, or the department name changes during a reorganization. At the same time, you will have to make a trade-off when it comes to names that are difficult to spell or remember.

Businesses are in a constant state of flux. Attempt to use static identifiers so that reorganization will not adversely affect your domain design. A good example of a static identifier is a geographic location such as the city name where the office is located. This should safeguard you from having domain names that no longer describe their functions or use.

Identifying Computer Naming Options

Every computer within your infrastructure needs to have a unique name. Without a unique name, clients would become confused when they were trying to locate the host on which the resource they are trying to reach resides. Computers running Windows operating systems have two types of names within your network: hostnames or NetBIOS names.

Hostnames

Hostnames for systems that will be used with your DNS infrastructure should follow rules that you establish. If your organization already has a third-party DNS solution in place and you are going to continue using that solution or are planning on Windows Server 2003 DNS interoperating with that solution, you will need to follow the hostname naming conventions. Failure to do so could cause interoperability issues, such as records not being able to transfer from the Windows-based DNS servers to the third-party DNS servers.

To make migration from NetBIOS-based systems to DNS based, Windows Server 2003's DNS service allows you to use the Universal Multiple-Octet Coded Character Set (UCS) Transformation Format 8 (UTF-8) naming conventions. Most third-party DNS servers do not support UTF-8. Instead, most of them support the American National Standards Institute (ANSI) character set. If your organization is going to use Windows-based DNS services exclusively, you can use any valid character as long as it follows the Windows computer name conventions.

For more information about character sets that are supported by traditional DNS zones, see RFC 952, Requirements for Internet Hosts - Application and Support at `http://www.ietf.org/rfc/rfc952.txt`.

NetBIOS Names

NetBIOS names are the computer names that are configured for a system. When setting a computer name, you are allowed to use up to 15 characters, and every computer name must be unique. When designing the computer naming conventions that you will employ within your organization, you should first determine whether you will keep the computer name and the hostname the same. Doing so will make it easier for you to identify a system no matter which name resolution method is being employed.

For instance, if you want to keep the same names for both resolution methods, a server hosting e-mail for the Seattle office that is in the `seattle.corp.com` domain may be named SEAEXCH1 and its fully qualified hostname would be `seaexch1.seattle.corp.com`. Try to make the design as simple as possible so that your users will not have to be retrained on how to perform the tasks they are already familiar with.

Identifying Integration Options

The Windows Server 2003 DNS service was designed to interoperate with the latest DNS standards. It was also designed to support additional features that are only available to a Microsoft DNS implementation. These additional features are beneficial to administrators who want to have easier administration and additional security options.

Due to Windows Server 2003's compliance with DNS standards, it will interoperate with Berkley Internet Name Domain (BIND) DNS servers running versions 9.1.0, 8.2, 8.1.2 and 4.9.7. Windows Server 2003 DNS is also fully compliant with Microsoft Windows NT 4's DNS service.

As you will note in Table 10.1, Windows Server 2003's DNS service and BIND 9.1.0 support some important DNS features. Other versions of DNS do not support all of the options.

TABLE 10.1 DNS Features Supported on Multiple Platforms

	SRV Records	Dynamic Updates	Incremental Zone Transfer	Stub Zones	Conditional Forwarding
Windows Server 2003	X	X	X	X	X
Windows 2000	X	X	X		
Windows NT 4			X		
BIND 9.1.0	X	X	X	X	X
BIND 8.2	X	X	X		
BIND 8.1.2	X	X			
BIND 4.9.7	X				

Additional features are present in a Windows Server 2003 DNS environment that are not supported by other DNS servers. A list of additional features is presented in Table 10.2.

TABLE 10.2 DNS Features Not Supported on Non-Windows Platforms

	Secure Dynamic Updates	WINS Integration	UTF-8 Character Encoding	Active Directory Integrated Zones	Application Directory Support	Obsolete Record Scavenging
Windows Server 2003	X	X	X	X	X	X
Windows 2000	X	X	X	X		X
Windows NT 4		X				
BIND 9.1.0						
BIND 8.2						
BIND 8.1.2						
BIND 4.9.7						

When attempting to integrate Windows Server 2003 DNS into an existing environment, take the previously mentioned interoperability into account. If the existing infrastructure does not support some of the features, you may be forced to upgrade the current infrastructure to Windows Server 2003 DNS so that all of the features that you need for your design are met.

In many companies, a DNS infrastructure is already controlled by a DNS group. If this group is unwilling to relinquish control of DNS or will not allow you to implement your own Windows Server 2003 DNS server, you may be forced to use the existing DNS services. There are those organizations that have separate divisions that are responsible for specific portions of the network infrastructure. If your organization is one of these and you are not allowed to implement DNS due to departmental standards and regulations, you will be forced to use what the DNS administrative staff dictates. Be aware of the requirements for Active Directory, however. You may need to force them to upgrade their existing servers to handle the service locator (SRV) records and dynamic updates that Active Directory uses.

Designing Zones

After you have determined the namespaces that will support your DNS infrastructure, you will need to determine how your DNS servers will support the namespaces. Within a DNS solution, the records that are used by clients are stored in DNS zones. These zones are responsible for storing the records that identify the hosts and services within a DNS namespace. Because you have several zone type options, you need to understand how each of them functions and the advantages and limitations of each.

In the next few sections, we are going to look at the different zone types and how they can be used within your Active Directory infrastructure.

Identifying Zone Types

Three zone types are available within Windows Server 2003 DNS: primary, secondary, and stub zones. Any of these zones can be used as a standard zone type or can be integrated with Active Directory. Standard zones are stored as a file on the DNS server and are replicated to other DNS servers through a process known as a zone transfer. Active Directory–integrated zones store the zone information within Active Directory and replicate the zone information through Active Directory replication. If a non-Windows Server 2003 DNS server requests a zone transfer, an Active Directory–integrated zone will send the update via a zone transfer.

Primary zones are traditionally the zones in which changes to the zone data can be made. When a primary zone is a standard zone, that is, not Active Directory–integrated, it hosts the only modifiable copy of the zone. Any other DNS server that holds the same zone information would have to be a secondary zone. The secondary zone would then be updated through a zone transfer from the primary zone or another secondary zone acting as the master for the zone transfer. Once a primary zone is made Active Directory–integrated, the zone data is stored in Active Directory and all of the DNS servers hosting an Active Directory–integrated copy of the zone become peers. The zone data can be modified on any of the servers and Active Directory replication will keep all replicas of the zone up to date.

Traditional primary zones do have a very serious limitation when is comes to an enterprise-level environment; there is only one server within the zone to which changes can be implemented. In an organization that uses dynamic DNS in order to register the clients, each client will have to connect to the DNS server that hosts the primary zone to register. There are three main issues with this scenario. First, since each of the clients will have to contact the same server, you will have a bottleneck during busy registration periods. Secondly, if you are registering across WAN links, you will be using bandwidth for registration that may be needed for other services. Finally, the DNS server hosting the primary zone becomes a single point of failure. Active Directory–integrated zones alleviate each of these issues by making the primary zone redundant on each of the domain controllers that host the zone.

Secondary zones are read-only copies of the primary zone data. They are used to host a copy of the zone data close to the clients that need to use a local copy of the zone data so that WAN traffic is reduced or the client can access zone data from multiple zones on the same DNS server. You should use secondary zones at sites where you want to reduce the amount of Active Directory replication that is crossing WAN links or DNS servers that are not running Windows Server 2003 or Windows 2000.

Stub zones are new to Windows Server 2003. A stub zone is a zone that acts as a delegation to another namespace, but instead of an administrator having to update the delegation records every time an authoritative name server in the remote zone changes, the stub zone updates its entries by sending queries to a server that is authoritative for the remote zone. The stub zone only holds the start of authority (SOA) record, the name server (NS) records, and the address (A) records for the name servers. When the stub zone is created, a query is sent to the authoritative DNS server for the zone. This query asks for and populates the stub zone with the SOA, NS, and A records for the name servers. The refresh interval that is listed on the SOA record defines when the stub zone will request an update of the records. As with the primary zone, a stub zone can be either standard or Active Directory–integrated. Active Directory–integrated stub zones can be replicated to all DNS servers that are domain controllers.

Identifying Propagation Methods

As mentioned in the previous section, zone data can be passed from DNS server to DNS server in two methods: zone transfer and Active Directory replications. Depending upon your DNS infrastructure, you may not be able to use Active Directory–integrated zones. Even if all of your servers are running Windows Server 2003, if a DNS server is not a domain controller, you will have to use zone transfers to get data to it.

Zone Transfers

Zone transfers come in two flavors: *authoritative zone transfers (AXFRs)* and *incremental zone transfers (IXFRs)*. An AXFR, sometimes referred to as a complete zone transfer, transfers the entire zone database when the zone transfer is initiated. An IXFR only transfers the changes in the zone since the last zone transfer. As you can probably guess, the amount of data that is transferred during an IXFR transfer could be substantially less than that of an AXFR.

The choice to use zone transfers is usually made because the DNS servers in your environment are not Windows 2000– or Windows Server 2003–based. Third-party DNS servers do not participate in Active Directory replication, nor can they read the Active Directory database to determine the resource records that are used. To keep the network usage as low as possible, you should make sure the DNS servers all support IXFR. Otherwise, every time a zone transfer is initiated, the entire zone records will be passed to all of the appropriate DNS servers.

Active Directory Replication

Active Directory–integrated zones can take advantage of Active Directory replication to propagate the changes made to resource records. When you use Active Directory replication, not only do you have the additional benefit of only having one replication topology, but a smaller amount of data is usually passed across the network. For instance, take a record that changes a couple of times before the replication or zone transfer occurs. In the case of a zone transfer, if the record changes twice before the transfer is initiated, both changes have to be sent, even if some of the data is no longer valid. In the case of Active Directory replication, only the effective changes are replicated. All of the erroneous information is discarded.

You also gain the advantage of the built-in functionality of replication. In an environment where you have multiple sites, many of which could be connected through WAN links, if there is considerable amounts of zone information to be transferred, the replication traffic that is sent between domain controllers in different sites is compressed to reduce network overhead.

Windows Server 2003 DNS servers that host Active Directory–integrated zones also offer another feature that helps reduce the amount of traffic caused by keeping the DNS server in sync. Once you create an Active Directory–integrated zone, you have the option of determining the scope of replication for the zone. Four options are available:

- Replicating to all DNS servers in the forest
- Replicating to all DNS servers within a domain
- Replicating to all domain controllers within the domain
- Replicating to all domain controllers defined in the replication scope of a DNS application directory partition

If you choose the first option—replicating to all DNS servers within the forest—every DNS server within the forest will receive the DNS zone information. This will cause the most replication because every Active Directory–enabled DNS server within the forest will hold the records for the zone, but the only domain controllers that will receive the data will be those that host the DNS service. You cannot have any Windows 2000–based domain controllers in this scenario.

The second option—replicating to all DNS servers within the domain—will reduce the amount of replication traffic because only the domain controllers that are DNS servers for the domain in question will hold a copy of the domain records. Again, as with the previous option, you cannot have any Windows 2000–based domain controllers within the domain.

The third option—replicating to all domain controllers within the domain—essentially makes all of your domain controllers within the domain behave as if they are Windows 2000 domain controllers. Every domain controller, whether or not it is a DNS server, will hold the data for the zone. If you still have some Windows 2000–based domain controllers that are DNS servers, this is the option you will choose.

Real World Scenario

Separating Namespaces

Andrew was designing the DNS zones for his organization. He had decided upon using a completely separate namespace internally than was used externally. To compound problems, he had two companies within his organization and he needed to be able to resolve both domain names from all clients.

The first company, Robotic Concepts, had an Internet presence that was seen by external clients as robocon.com. The second company was a consulting company, Robotic Specialists, whose Internet presence was roboticspecialists.com.

To control access to internal resources, Andrew had designed the network infrastructure to include a perimeter network with a DNS server that hosted records for the servers within the perimeter and acted as a DNS server for external resolution. The DNS server within the perimeter was configured with root hints that pointed to the root DNS servers on the Internet.

Internally, Andrew configured a DNS server to be authoritative for the domain lcl. The DNS server did not host any root hints but did have a forwarder to the DNS server within the perimeter network. Within the .lcl zone, Andrew configured a delegation record for robocon.lcl and robospecs.lcl. He then created the zones for each of the domains and configured them for secure and nonsecure updates.

The final option—replicating to all domain controllers defined in the replication scope of a DNS application directory partition—is also an option that is only available to Windows Server 2003 domain controllers. Using an application directory partition, you can choose which of the domain controllers will host a copy of the partition. In this manner, you can control exactly which domain controllers that are also DNS servers will host the zone data. If you do not want to replicate the zone to a server that is across a WAN, you will not have to.

Identifying Migration Options

As with everything else, Microsoft wants you to leave third-party products and start using Windows-based solutions exclusively. You will find that Microsoft has included methods of easy migration from third-party services. With DNS, you can use two methods to migrate existing zones to the Windows Server 2003 DNS service: using a zone transfer and copying the zone file.

If you use a zone transfer, you can configure the Windows Server 2003 server with a secondary zone and choose the third-party DNS server's zone as the master. Once configured, you can initiate a zone transfer from the master zone to the secondary. This should populate the Windows Server 2003 DNS server with all of the records. Once the transfer has completed, you can decommission the original DNS server and change the secondary zone to a primary zone. Make sure that the SOA record reflects the correct server as the authoritative server.

The second method requires you to copy the zone files that are used by the third-party DNS server onto your Windows Server 2003 DNS server. Using this method, you could decommission the third-party system and put the Windows Server 2003 system in its place, using the same hostname and IP address. Before copying the file, you should always make sure that the data within the zone is correct and does not have any erroneous data.

Make sure that your migration to Windows Server 2003 does not alienate any of your users. Create a schedule for migrating and upgrading your servers so that the users will still have access to the existing DNS server while the server you are upgrading is offline. Once the upgrade has been completed, make sure you test the server prior to upgrading any other servers that the users are currently utilizing.

Identifying Delegation Options

In large organizations or organizations that have several locations hosting many users and servers, you may want to delegate the administrative responsibilities to administrators at each location. You can delegate the administration of the DNS zones by creating delegation records or stub zones within your DNS infrastructure that point to name servers that are authoritative for the subdomain.

The two methods of creating references to the subdomain are to create a *delegation record*, which is a resource record that identifies a server that is authoritative for the subdomain, or to create a stub zone that will hold the zone SOA, NS, and A records for the name servers. If you have a DNS infrastructure that supports the use of stub zones, you should seriously consider using them because the stub zone will automatically update and you will not be required to manually update as you would with a delegation record.

 Real World Scenario

Delegating with Stubs

Celia is the Windows administrator for an organization that has a large existing UNIX infrastructure. The organization has decided to move to Active Directory, and now it is Celia's responsibility to make sure that all of the systems she is putting in place will interoperate with the existing systems. The current DNS administrators have decided that they will not relinquish any control over the DNS infrastructure. Currently they run BIND 9.1.0. Celia wants to take advantage of Active Directory–integrated zones, so she knows that she will have to use a Windows DNS server. The meetings that follow are not very fruitful because the existing DNS administrators are being adamant that they will not have a Windows-based DNS server in the organization.

Finally Celia reached a compromise with the DNS administrators. Because her DNS servers will all be Active Directory–integrated, she will concede to using a subdomain within the existing namespace that the organization is using internally. Her group will be responsible for maintaining the Active Directory domain. To maintain name resolution within the entire organization for all services, the existing BIND servers will host a stub zone pointing to the new subdomain.

If your organization is already using a BIND DNS solution, and the administrators of the existing DNS infrastructure are leery of a Windows-based DNS solution, you can still use a Windows-based DNS to host your Active Directory integrated zones, and the current BIND administrators, if the BIND servers are running BIND 9 or later, can create stub zones that point to your zone. If the BIND servers are releases prior to 9 or a NetWare or Windows NT 4 solution is in place, you will have to create delegation records pointing to the new Active Directory zones.

The section that follows describes the options you have for implementing a name resolution infrastructure. Make sure you fully understand the options we have discussed up to this point before going on. Otherwise, you may find yourself designing an inefficient solution for your organization.

Designing the Name Resolution Server Infrastructure

The name resolution requirements for your organization may only include DNS and not WINS. Whereas DNS will be required for Active Directory and hostname resolution, you may be one of the lucky organizations that do not have to keep WINS running. If you are like almost every other organization that has been utilizing Microsoft operating systems and applications, however, you will need to keep WINS up and running for a while. Having these services running on your network will require you to make an investment in the hardware that will run the service. You will also need to determine where you will locate each of the servers so that they are used to their fullest capacity and are most efficient for your network.

Designing the DNS Infrastructure

After you have determined how you are going to name your domains and your clients within each domain, you will need to design the physical server structure to support the name resolution methods you will be employing. DNS servers will need to be deployed in a manner that will enable your users to have efficient name resolution, while at the same time, not cause adverse issues within the network infrastructure.

Determining the Number of DNS Servers

As with most servers, allocating the fastest processors, more memory, and faster, larger hard drives will improve the performance of a DNS server. By increasing the amount of memory that the server has, you will be able to more efficiently handle large zones since all of the resource records are pulled into memory as the system starts up and records are added to the zone. Each resource record will consume approximately 100 bytes of RAM, so you should be able to determine the amount of RAM that you will need based upon the number of records the zone will host. You will need to determine the number of clients that will be registering within the zone so that you will have an estimation of the total amount of RAM dynamic updates will consume.

Along with the client registrations, remember that each domain controller will register many SRV records in order to identify the domain controller and Global Catalog server services within the forest, domain, and site.

Tests have shown that a DNS server running on a server with a Pentium III 800MHz processor with 512MB RAM can support nearly 10,000 queries per second. Always test the systems you are putting into place to make sure that they will support the client base that you are assigning to them. If you find that the servers are having a hard time keeping up with the queries, add an additional server to take on some of the client query load. You can change the primary DNS server settings on some of the clients to direct their queries to the new server, thus relieving the load from the original DNS server.

If you are planning on creating Active Directory–integrated zones within your design, remember that the DNS service will have to be located on a domain controller. Make sure that the domain controllers you are planning to use as DNS servers are able to take on the additional DNS traffic load and still efficiently respond to clients needs.

Determining DNS Server Placement

Placing DNS servers could be as easy as putting one in each subnet so that every client has a local DNS server, but this is probably not a realistic option for most companies. However, it does address the first rule of DNS server placement: make sure the DNS service is highly available. DNS is used by servers and clients alike; they both rely on the service to be available so that they can perform the functions they are called upon to do. Try to place DNS servers close to the clients that will use them the most. You should always have redundancy built into your namespace design, giving each of the clients at least two DNS servers to call upon.

Most organizations cannot afford one server per subnet, let alone two, so you will have to design the placement of servers where they can be the most effective for the most clients. In Figure 10.3, DNS servers are placed at each of the locations that need to have local name resolution. In this example, each of the segments contains servers that the workstations need to locate, even if the network links to the other locations fail.

There could be instances where a remote site needs to have name resolution, but it may not have any resources local to the site. To reduce the amount of name resolution traffic that is sent across the WAN link, you could implement a caching-only server. A caching-only server does not have any zones created on it; it simply forwards queries to another DNS server to resolve on its behalf. The results that are returned are cached for future requests for the same information. As the cache is built, fewer and fewer queries are sent across the WAN link, reducing the overhead on the link. There is a downside to using a caching only DNS server: if the actual IP address for an external resource changes after the external resource's IP address has been cached, the external resource will be unavailable to your internal users until the data in your cache expires and a new query is sent to the outside DNS server.

Now that we have taken a look at the DNS infrastructure, let's turn our attention to the WINS infrastructure. If you are an administrator for an organization that still supports NetBIOS within their infrastructure, you will need to take what we discuss next into account.

FIGURE 10.3 DNS server placement to support username resolution queries

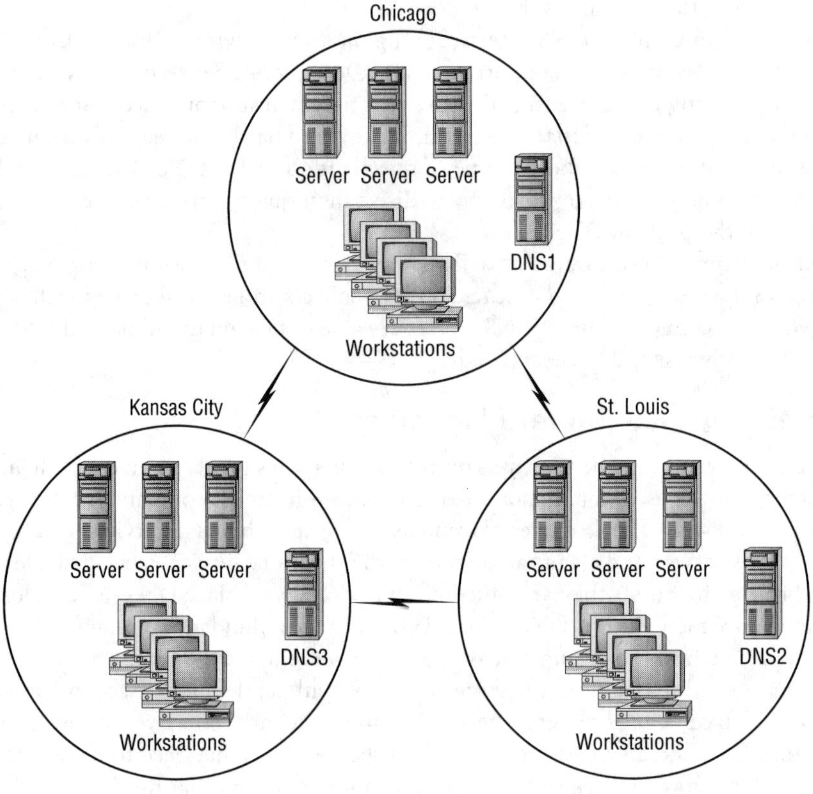

Designing the WINS Infrastructure

The WINS infrastructure will be based upon the computer and application needs. If any of the operating systems or applications within your organization has a NetBIOS dependency, you will have to make sure they are able to resolve names and locate services. Once you determine the extent of the NetBIOS infestation, you can then determine how many WINS servers you will require and where you will place them. If you deem that multiple servers are necessary, you will also need to configure the replication between the servers to allow all of the clients to interoperate within the network.

Determining the Number of WINS Servers

As with any service, you should always test to see how your servers will handle any type of service. Microsoft has identified that a typical WINS server can support approximately 1,500 name registrations per minute or respond to 4,500 queries per minute. If this is the case with your hardware, you should be able to host approximately 10,000 clients per WINS server.

However, other issues come into play when you are trying to determine the number of WINS servers you should deploy.

The first thing you should consider is the WAN links that you have. Depending upon the current level of traffic on the link, you may not want to have WINS traffic passing across it. Plus, you may want to have the WINS server local for the users in case of a WAN link failure. This way, if a WAN link were to go down, the clients would have local name resolution and could continue with any work they need to perform locally. At the same time, you may not want to put a WINS server in an office that only hosts five systems. You will need to determine what the trade-off limit is going to be.

 Design Scenario

Determining WINS Population

Michelle is trying to determine how many WINS servers she will need for her organization. Currently, she has four sites, each of which will have domain controllers from her domain. The corporate office consists of 15,000 users and each of the regional offices employs between 5,000 and 10,000 users. Four regional offices exist: Washington, DC, with 5,000 users; Los Angeles with 6,500 users; Atlanta with 8,000 users; and Houston with 10,000 users. All of the offices are connected to the corporate office through T1 connections. In order to control the replication of Active Directory objects, sites have been created for each location. She has already decided upon the hardware that she is going to use for the WINS servers: a Pentium 4 2.4GHz processor, 512 MB RAM, and 100 Mbps network cards. A performance test on the hardware has proven that the servers can handle more than 20,000 queries per second in the lab, while the anticipated peak query rate is 13,000 queries per second.

Michelle wants to make sure that each of her locations has a level of redundancy that will guarantee name resolution in case of a link failure between locations or a server failure within the site. She also wants to keep the WINS traffic that has to pass across the WAN links to a minimum.

1. **Question:** Where should Michelle locate WINS servers to meet her needs? **Answer:** She should place a WINS server at each location to make sure that she has name resolution capabilities even if the WAN link fails.

2. **Question:** How many WINS servers are required at each location to support queries? **Answer:** The hardware specifications will allow one server to support all of the users at the same location as the WINS server; however, you may need to add additional hardware to support redundancy.

3. **Question:** To support all of the requirements that she has identified, redundancy, and efficient use of the WAN link, how many WINS servers should Michelle implement? **Answer:** She should implement at least ten WINS servers, two at each location. When she locates the WINS servers at each site, she is reducing the query traffic on the WAN links. By implementing two WINS servers at each site, she will also meet her specification that name resolution will survive if a WINS server fails.

Identifying WINS Replication Options

WINS replication is enabled by choosing which servers will be made replication partners of one another. With the exception of automatic partner replication, the administrator is responsible for determining which servers will replicate with each of the other servers in the organization. Automatic partner replication, if turned on, will find other WINS servers within the same subnet and automatically create replication connections to them. WINS servers in other subnets are not detected and will not participate in the automatic partner replication. The administrator must explicitly configure the replication between two servers. Replication can be configured as push replication, pull replication, or push/pull replication.

 If your infrastructure allows multicast forwarding between subnets, the WINS servers will configure automatic partner replication.

In *push replication*, the replication partner that is the owner of records is configured to wait until a specific number of record changes has occurred before notifying its partners that there are changes they need to accept.

In *pull replication*, the replication partner is configured to wait a specific amount of time before requesting a list of the changes from its partners with which it is configured to replicate.

Push/pull replication configures a partner to utilize both options when working with its partners.

Whenever possible, you should try to configure your WINS replication partners to use push/pull replication. Using push/pull replication will allow you to maximize the replication topology. If several record changes exist, the push partner will notify the pull partner that it needs to request the changes. During slow times when there are not very many changes to the WINS database, the pull partner will still request the changes, but only after a certain time interval has passed. Having each of the WINS servers configured in this manner will allow you to preserve the WAN traffic while minimizing false responses from the WINS server when a client queries.

You will need to determine the maximum amount of time you will allow before changes should be replicated to each partner. The longer you wait before implementing pull replication or the more changes you allow before you initiate push replication, the more out of sync the WINS servers will be. In order to maintain a consistent WINS topology, you need to take into consideration the convergence time that will occur as the WINS servers replicate all of the changes. The more hops a record needs to take going from WINS server to WINS server, the longer the updates will take to reach every server within the organization. Try to use a *hub-and-spoke* method of propagating the changes. Figure 10.4 shows an example of the hub-and-spoke method of replicating changes.

When you use the hub-and-spoke method, servers in the hub are responsible for replicating changes to all of the WINS servers at the spokes. In addition, each WINS server passes their replication data to the central WINS server, which is responsible for replicating the data to the other servers in the organization. This reduces the maximum number of replication hops to 2. If each of the replication partners is configured to pull every 15 minutes, the convergence time would be 30 minutes.

Figure 10.5 illustrates another method of replicating data between WINS servers—the *linear model.*

FIGURE 10.4   WINS hub-and-spoke-replication-topology

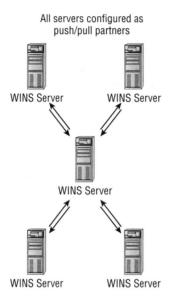

FIGURE 10.5   WINS linear replication topology

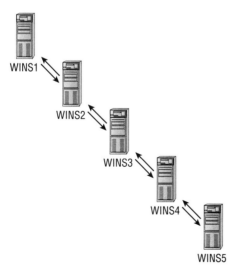

If we still have a 15-minute pull replication cycle, data from WINS1 will not reach WINS 5 until an hour has passed. As you can see, the hub-and-spoke method is more efficient. However, there is a problem with either of these methods. If communication to along any of the network links is lost, replication traffic will not make it to the other servers. If you decide to build a WINS hub-and-spoke or linear topology into your design, you should also build in redundancy and fault tolerance within your network infrastructure.

The larger your organization is, the more challenging it will be to design a functional WINS topology. Review the resource usage patterns of the clients to determine where the changes within the WINS database will need to be replicated. Make sure that those servers can replicate efficiently with one another and then configure replication to the other WINS servers on a schedule that will keep the users happy.

In Figure 10.6, a company that has several locations uses a two-level hub-and-spoke topology.

Each of the sites where users need to be updated on changes is tied to the others by a hub system. WINS servers at each of the spoke sites are configured as primary WINS servers for the clients and the hub system is defined as the secondary in case the primary WINS server fails. Each of the hub WINS servers is interconnected to the other hub servers to guarantee that all of the changes within the organization are replicated throughout. If you configure each of the servers within the spokes to replicate with two WINS servers in the hub, you will increase the total amount of replication traffic, but you will ensure that each spoke WINS server will have a partner to replicate changes from if one hub server were to fail.

FIGURE 10.6   Multi-level WINS hub-and-spoke topology

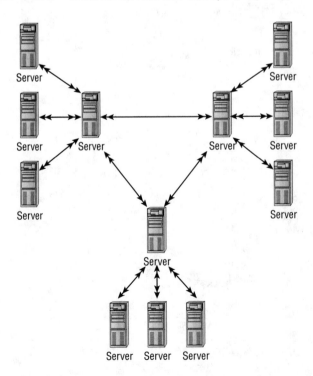

One thing that you can do to make sure that the hub WINS server is available is to implement a clustering solution. Because the WINS service is cluster aware, you can put a clustered system in place that hosts the WINS service. If one of the nodes fails, you will still have the remaining node online. You should determine if the cost of building a clustered solution is worth the uptime that you will achieve from the fault tolerance that is gained. You should also determine how you will keep the systems communicating, because the clustering solution will only protect the servers, it will not guarantee that the communication lines will remain available.

 Design Scenario

Determining WINS Replication Paths

Acme Creations has four offices within its organization: the corporate office in New York, and three regional offices located in Hawaii, Taiwan, and Japan. Each of the WAN links has approximately 1Mps available, but due to additional anticipated client traffic, Acme wants to reduce the total query traffic across the WAN links. The regional offices in Japan and Taiwan are connected to the Hawaii office through dedicated WAN links that have traditionally held an 88-percent uptime. The corporate office in New York is connected to the Hawaii office through a WAN link that has maintained an uptime rating of 96 percent, whereas the WAN connections from New York to Japan and Taiwan have proven to be less reliable, with an uptime rating of only 73 percent.

Joel is trying to determine the best method of keeping the WINS servers synchronized. He has placed two WINS servers at each location and made them replication partners of each other. Now he needs to determine how the rest of the WINS topology will be designed.

1. **Question:** How should Joel implement the replication topology if he wants to use the most reliable communication paths? **Answer:** Hub-and-spoke topologies allow for the most efficient replication of database entries because each of the sites has a maximum of one server to pass the replicated data through before it reaches the intended WINS server.

2. **Question:** Which of the locations would make the best hub? **Answer:** Hawaii has the most reliable links to all of the other locations, so it would make the most sense to implement the hub there and make the other three spoke locations.

3. **Question:** What options should Joel consider for guaranteeing the WINS service at the hub location? **Answer:** Because Joel is already planning on having two WINS servers at each location, each of the WINS servers within the Hawaii site could be configured as push/pull partners with the WINS servers from the other locations. This would allow all the records to be replicated to each of Hawaii's WINS servers and would guarantee that replication could continue if one of the servers failed. He could also use a clustered solution if he wanted to go to the added expense of installing clustered equipment.

As with many Microsoft products, the name resolution services can be used in conjunction with one another so that you have a comprehensive name resolution strategy. Both services will also take advantage of the DHCP service to help an administrator configure the infrastructure.

Integrating Name Resolution Services

DNS, WINS, and DHCP are all important services within an network. Each of them provides functionality that makes networks more efficient and easier to administer. When using them, you should take advantage of their interoperability. DHCP provides functionality that makes using WINS in your network easier, and DNS and WINS work together to create a solid name resolution topology.

Through the following sections we are going to discuss how each of the services interact with one another.

Integrating DNS and WINS with DHCP

DHCP is the service that provides IP configuration settings to DHCP-enabled clients. DHCP can also be integrated with the DNS service to assist in the dynamic registration of clients. If the two services are integrated, the DHCP server can be responsible for updating and removing the PTR record for the DHCP client, which is the default setting for Windows 2000 or later clients, or, with a small configuration change, both the A and PTR records.

The DHCP server can assign WINS and DNS server addresses and WINS node types to DHCP clients. As a result, you will not have to configure each of the clients manually; you can centralize the control. Since the client will receive the WINS server address from DHCP, you can make changes to your infrastructure and not have to reconfigure the client. The node type controls how the clients will query for name resolution. On each of the DHCP servers, make sure the entries for each of the subnets is valid and that the clients are directed to the correct WINS and DNS servers on their subnet.

Integrating DNS with WINS

If you still have systems within your network that register computer names with your WINS server and do not support dynamic DNS registration, you can allow the DNS server to perform WINS lookups to locate computer names that match the hostname for which another system has sent a query. This configuration is especially convenient if your environment supports clients who cannot perform a WINS lookup and clients who cannot dynamically register within DNS.

You may also need to support clients that do not interact with WINS servers. If you have clients that only broadcast for name resolution, you can configure a WINS proxy agent on the segment where the non-WINS client resides. The WINS proxy will intercept the queries and will send the query to the WINS server for processing. Once the WINS server responds, the WINS proxy will broadcast the response for the client to receive. For other clients to locate the non-WINS clients, you can add static entries within the WINS server.

However, this scenario has a caveat. If the third-party DNS servers that you are using do not support WINS referrals, you may elicit errors in the zone when zone transfers occur. To alleviate this issue, you can create a zone on the Windows-based DNS server that is used for WINS referrals.

Then, configure the clients to search both the original DNS zone and, if they are unable to locate the appropriate record there, they will issue a request to the zone enabled for WINS referrals. The third-party DNS server will host the original zone and a delegation to the server hosting the WINS-enabled zone. Records that are transferred to the third-party DNS server will not cause errors because of the unknown record types.

You will find that there are very few, if any, services that will not have to be secured. The name resolution services are no exception. You need to determine the level of security you need to provide each of the services with based upon where they will be used.

Securing the Name Resolution Infrastructure

Both the DNS and the WINS service, by their nature, contain information about the organization's infrastructure. Failure to secure either of these two services could compromise your infrastructure by allowing an attacker to discover information about your company or by allowing them to create an attack that will cripple the name resolution services, thus stopping your clients from being able to perform their functions.

Identifying Security Considerations

As with any network service, you need to identify potential security threats. The buzz around Microsoft recently has been their implementation of security at all levels of their products. This security initiative is a good thing for administrators because now the software giant is trying to plug the holes that attackers like to take advantage of, which makes the administrator's job that much easier.

Although many key features of Windows Server 2003 have taken on a secure-by-default posture, DNS is not one. Some of the settings are turned on by default, such as the Secure Cache Against Pollution setting, but due to the open nature of DNS, you will have to perform some tasks to lock down your DNS infrastructure.

DNS attacks come in the following forms:

Data Modification   *Data modification* is also known as IP spoofing. An attacker modifies the IP address in IP packets that are sent to a DNS server. Because the IP address appears valid, the data is accepted on the network and passed to the DNS server where its attack can be implemented. If this type of attack is successful, data can be modified or damaged, a denial-of-service (DoS) attack can be implemented, or the attacker can implement the first step of a redirection.

Denial-of-Service Attacks   When an attacker attempts a *denial-of-service (DoS) attack*, the DNS server is inundated with queries. The attacker is hoping that the DNS server will not be able to handle all of them. When the server cannot handle all of the requests, valid requests may not be able to be processed and the services that rely on DNS for name resolution will not be able to function correctly.

Footprinting   *Footprinting* is the process of capturing enough DNS data to build a network map that includes IP addresses, computer names, and domain names. Once this data is collected, the attacker can try to determine which computers are running services within the infrastructure and target attacks at vital services. One of the easiest methods of footprinting a network is for an attacker to request a zone transfer from a DNS server. If the DNS server is not secured and allows the attacker to successfully obtain the zone file, the data could point the attacker directly to important systems. The SRV records that are contained in the zone data will give the attacker the names of the domain controllers and global catalog servers, and the address records will supply the attacker with the IP addresses.

Redirection   Clients rely on the data from a DNS server to be accurate. When a client receives a response to a query, they use the information in the response to locate the correct server for which they are trying to connect. If an attacker is able to change the data in a DNS server, the record could direct the attacker to a server that is under the attacker's control. If the attacker successfully changes the data and the client is unaware of the change, the client has been the victim of a *redirection* attack.

If you want to protect yourself from any of these attacks, you need to identify which systems are susceptible to each type of attack and determine what level of protection you will apply. The level of protection you decide upon will become your DNS security policy. Although this is not a policy that you apply to a system as you would the local security policy or a Group Policy object, it is a written policy that you need to follow for each of the DNS servers. A DNS security policy identifies the level of protection you need to apply to your DNS server infrastructure to keep it protected from attacks. You could have multiple DNS security policies that identify the security that will be applied to DNS servers that are used internally and those that are accessible from the Internet. Microsoft has identified three levels of DNS security, appropriately named low-level, mid-level, and high-level.

Low-Level DNS Security Policy

The *low-level DNS security policy* is not concerned about attackers gathering data about your internal network or attacks that could damage the DNS infrastructure. Organizations that do not have any type of connectivity to outside networks, the Internet especially, can take advantage of this policy. However, if you are at all concerned about the integrity of your DNS data and DNS infrastructure, and external users have access to your network, you should not use this policy level.

When using the low-level DNS security policy, you allow all of the servers to perform standard DNS name resolution. This means that the DNS servers listen for queries on all of the IP addresses bound to each network card, will respond to queries from all clients, and are configured to point to the root servers on the Internet for all external name resolution. At the same time, zone transfers are allowed to any server that requests the transfer. This policy level does not take advantage of the Secure Cache Against Pollution setting and allows dynamic updates for all zones. Your infrastructure will also allow port 53 to remain open on the firewall so that all UDP and TCP traffic bound for the DNS server is allowed through.

Mid-Level DNS Security Policy

The *mid-level DNS security policy* increases the level of security from what is allowed with the low-level DNS security policy. The mid-level DNS security policy allows an administrator who is running third-party DNS servers or DNS servers that are not domain controllers to have more control over their DNS infrastructure. Although this policy level does give you more control over your DNS environment, it still leaves a few security holes. You may want to implement this policy level if you still want to maintain some level of communication with the Internet.

Standard DNS resolution is not allowed at this policy level. Instead, the DNS servers are configured to use forwarders to assist in resolving hostnames. Conditional forwarding can be designed to allow the queries to be sent to the DNS servers that are name servers for specific domains. Zone transfers are not allowed to all servers, only those that are name servers for the domain. Only internal clients are allowed to send queries to the internal DNS servers because the DNS servers are configured to listen for queries only on specific IP addresses. To control the data that is within the DNS server cache and to protect the clients from redirection attacks, the Secure Cache Against Pollution setting is enabled on all zones.

The network infrastructure is designed to control access to the DNS infrastructure by placing servers that can perform Internet resolution within a perimeter network. The internal DNS servers are configured with forwarders that will forward queries to the DNS servers in the perimeter network that have root hints configured. The firewall is configured with rules to control the DNS traffic so that only the DNS servers are allowed to communicate with one another through the firewall. Client access to the Internet is controlled by using proxy servers.

High-Level DNS Security Policy

The *high-level DNS security policy* is the extreme lock-down policy. When using this policy, access to the Internet is extremely limited. You may have users who need to access websites and e-mail that needs to be routed, but other means of performing those tasks are configured instead of allowing the DNS infrastructure to be visible.

A typical high-level DNS security policy does not allow any type of Internet access through the internal DNS server. The DNS servers are configured to have their own DNS root namespace so that they can provide resolution for internal clients to internal resources. All DNS servers are configured to listen for queries on specific IP addresses. To protect from any type of redirection attacks, the Secure Cache Against Pollution setting will remain on.

This policy level controls who is allowed to configure and modify the DNS server and the zones. All zones at this policy level are Active Directory–enabled so that the data is not stored as a file, it is secured within the Active Directory database. Because the DNS zone is stored in Active Directory, permissions can be set that will control which users have the ability to create, delete, or modify DNS zones and records. Rights can be assigned to control who has the ability to administer the DNS server also.

If clients do need to have access to websites, a proxy server is configured to control Internet access. Placing the proxy server in the perimeter network will allow it to use an external DNS server for resolution. For e-mail, the internal e-mail servers will use internal DNS to route messages within the organization, any external e-mail can be forwarded to a smart host within the perimeter that is configured to resolve Internet addresses from an external DNS server. The firewalls can be configured to limit traffic only from specified servers over specific ports.

Securing DNS Servers

Once you have chosen the policy level that you want to use for you DNS infrastructure, your need to determine how you will design the security for both internal and external DNS servers.

Because the external DNS servers are exposed to the Internet, you will want to pay special attention to them, especially because you will want to secure them as much as possible. But to allow them to perform the functions that they are intended to perform, they will need to have lighter security settings in some cases. Internal servers could be placed under a lighter policy, but make sure that they are properly protected from outside influence.

Designing Secure External DNS Servers

If you have to host DNS servers that are exposed to the Internet, make sure they reside within the perimeter network. If they are on the internal network, you will have to open up ports on the firewall that will allow unwanted traffic into your infrastructure. If you have servers within the perimeter network that need to resolve hostnames for internal resources, plan on deploying multiple DNS servers, one for public information and another that hosts private information. You can allow Internet resolution to the public DNS server so that your web servers and SMTP mail servers can be found by external users, and have another DNS server that will host internal DNS records so that the servers residing in the perimeter can resolve internal names of servers that they need to interact with. Figure 10.7 illustrates a perimeter network that hosts two DNS servers and the servers that provide functionality for external users.

Always make sure that you have redundancy built into your design. If you do not, you run the risk of alienating users when they cannot resolve hostnames for your organization. You can host multiple DNS servers that share the same zone information, or you could have an ISP act as your backup should your DNS server fail. In either case, if you are the recipient of a DoS attack, you will have additional servers to take over should one become unavailable. And remember, if you want to your data to be available at all times, you should have redundant hardware.

FIGURE 10.7 DNS servers in perimeter network

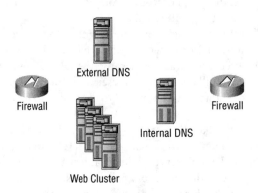

Secure communication between DNS servers that reside within the perimeter network and those that reside in the internal network should be maintained. Most of the DNS servers within the perimeter network will not be Active Directory–enabled; the zone transfers between DNS servers should use IPSec or a VPN technology to encrypt the data. Using an encryption method keeps attackers from intercepting packets and footprinting the internal network. This also allows you to open IPSec or VPN ports on the firewall instead of UPD and TCP port 53. Once you have protected the zone transfer traffic, don't forget to restrict the servers to which zone transfers are allowed. You can allow transfers to all name servers, but the more secure method is to control by specific IP addresses instead.

If you are allowing zone transfers to DNS servers that reside within a perimeter network, make sure that none of the SRV records that are used for Active Directory are included within the zone data.

Designing Secure Internal DNS Servers

Internal DNS servers are critical to the operation of your network. Without them, Active Directory will become useless. As with any critical resource, you should have redundancy built in so that the failure of a single component will not cause the entire infrastructure, or even a portion of the infrastructure, to become unavailable. All servers and clients should be configured to use multiple DNS servers for name resolution. Also review the network infrastructure to make sure that the devices that interconnect the clients and servers can withstand the loss of a service.

You should plan for all of your zones within the internal network to be made Active Directory–integrated as soon as possible. This will alleviate the need for zone transfers; all of the updates will be sent by Active Directory replication. Using Active Directory–integrated zones will also allow you to enforce secure dynamic updates, which give you the ability to control the clients that can update resource records within your zone.

With either of the external or internal DNS servers, you should make it a point to continually monitor the DNS logs and the Event Viewer for DNS-related exceptions. Proactive management can aid you when you are determining if your DNS infrastructure is failing or compromised.

Securing WINS

As with the DNS service, you should make sure that the WINS servers are secure. For the most part, WINS is not utilized for Internet access and by nature, the WINS servers are usually protected because they reside within the internal network. However, you may have WINS servers placed within the perimeter network to assist with NetBIOS name resolution for computers and applications that rely on NetBIOS. You may also have parts of your organization located in different geographic locations that communicate through the Internet. If replication between the WINS servers at these locations is required, you will need to find a method for securing the communication. Failure to do so could compromise the data being sent and the WINS server could fall victim to the same types of attacks that are listed previously for DNS servers.

As mentioned previously in this chapter, WINS replication is controlled by the administrator. Once the replication partners have been identified, the administrator creates the replication connections. Unless an attacker has already gained access to the internal network, the servers should not be replicating with any other servers than those identified in the design. If you must use a NetBIOS name resolution method and the LMHOSTS file will not accommodate it, you should place the WINS server that the perimeter clients will use within the perimeter network so that none of the internal data will be available from the perimeter network.

The replication data passing between servers in different sites could become compromised if an attacker captures it. For this reason, any replication data that travels on an unsafe network should be encrypted. Consider using a VPN to encrypt the contents of the replication traffic. Make sure that you take advantage of the highest level of encryption available for the VPN solution that you are using.

Summary

DNS is an essential service when you are using any TCP/IP-based environment. DNS provides hostname to IP address resolution as well as a method of locating services within your infrastructure. In an Active Directory network, DNS is required, otherwise Active Directory will not function. Along with its counterpart WINS, DNS acts as the centerpiece to the name resolution infrastructure.

When designing the name resolution infrastructure, your primary design goal is to make sure you have servers to support the name resolution needs of your users and the systems within your organization. You will need to determine where you will place the DNS and WINS servers, how many you will need to support the clients, and how you will integrate then into the network.

When designing for DNS, make sure that you place DNS servers where they can function on behalf of clients trying to locate servers and services on the network. At the same time, make sure that you have DNS servers that support your domain controllers because Active Directory requires DNS in order to function.

Design your namespace to support both your internal name and the Internet presence that you use. Your internal namespace should be different than the namespace you employ on the Internet; however, some organizations wish to have both the same. Using the same namespace is more difficult to manage.

You will need a WINS infrastructure if you wish to support NetBIOS-based operating systems or applications. If this is the case, you will need to determine where you will place the WINS servers to support your clients and how you will manage replication between all of the WINS servers. A hub-and-spoke topology will usually work the best for any organization, but you can enhance the design based upon the replication needs of the organization.

Both name resolution methods require you to understand the security requirements needed to secure your systems. Attackers can discover information about your network if they intercept packets transmitted from your DNS or WINS servers. If an attacker gains access to your DNS or WINS server, they could enter false records and cause clients to receive incorrect information.

In the next chapter, we are going to take a look at how you will implement an efficient IP addressing infrastructure. This will include designing your subnets for IP addressing and working with addressing assignment types—both automatic and static.

Exam Essentials

Understand the current DNS infrastructure.   If you do not understand the current DNS infrastructure, you will not know what types of DNS servers are in place and how they interact with the internal and external domain names.

Identify the current namespace.   You will need to determine if the company is using a namespace that will work for your design. If is will, you will need to determine if you will use the existing namespace internally, externally, or both.

Identify the Internet domain name registrations requirements.   If the organization is using an Internet presence, you could continue to use that name. If you do not, you will need to determine what you will use for your Internet presence, register it, and then determine how you will use it in conjunction with your internal namespace.

Identify NetBIOS naming requirements.   Determine if you have clients or applications that require NetBIOS. If you do, you will need to determine how you will provide name resolution for those clients and where the WINS servers that provide that functionality will be located.

Identify interoperability with Active Directory, DNS, WINS, and DHCP.   DNS is required for Active Directory to function and DNS zones can be made Active Directory–integrated. DNS and WINS can be used together to provide a fully functional name resolution method between clients that support hostname and computer name resolution. DHCP can provide clients with configuration options that make assigning DNS and WINS servers more efficient for administrators. DHCP can also register clients within a dynamic DNS zone so that the administrator does not have to manually enter the host information in DNS.

Understand zone requirements.   Active Directory requires that the DNS server supports SRV records. Although not a requirement, to ease the administrative load, the DNS server should also support dynamic DNS registrations.

Understand name resolution service security.   DNS and WINS servers need to be secured from attacks so that attackers are not able to footprint the infrastructure, cause DoS attacks, redirect users to the wrong servers, or modify the information within the zone to cause resolution issues with the clients.

Understand DNS strategies for interoperability with UNIX BIND.   BIND servers can be used to host Active Directory records, but the zones cannot be Active Directory–integrated. BIND servers and Windows Server 2003 DNS servers can be used together within the same infrastructure. Either server type can be delegated control of a zone from the other type, and zone transfers from either one can go to the other.

Identify WINS replication strategies.   WINS replication should be configured to be as efficient as possible so that clients can locate the correct resources. Push/pull replication can be used to keep the servers synchronized. Designing an efficient replication topology should involve a hub-and-spoke topology to keep the replication convergence time to a minimum.

Identify DNS zone storage.   DNS zones can be stored as files if they are primary or secondary standard zones. They can also be Active Directory–integrated if they are primary or stub zones.

Identify server placement options. Servers should be placed close to the users that will use them but should not consume more traffic on a WAN link when replicating data than would be used when querying the zone. In the case of a remote site where name resolution for resources in the site does not occur, you should consider creating a caching-only server.

Key Terms

Before you take the exam, be certain you are familiar with the following terms:

Active Directory–integrated zone	linear model
authoritative zone transfer (AXFR)	low-level DNS security policy
data modification	mid-level DNS security policy
delegation record	primary zone
denial-of-service (DoS) attack	pull replication
Domain Name System (DNS)	push replication
footprinting	push/pull replication
high-level DNS security policy	redirection
hub-and-spoke method	secondary zone
incremental zone transfer (IXFR)	stub zone
internal DNS root	Windows Internet Name Service (WINS)

Review Questions

1. Which DNS security policy specifies that zone transfers are only allowed to specific IP addresses?

   A. Low-level

   B. Mid-level

   C. High-level

   D. Secure-level

2. You want to control the replication of WINS records so that they replicate every hour. What type of replication should you use?

   A. Push

   B. Pull

   C. Time-initiated

   D. Dynamic

3. What DNS options allow you to direct client queries to servers that are authoritative for a zone? (Choose all that apply.)

   A. Primary zones

   B. Stub zones

   C. Delegations

   D. Zone transfers

4. Which zone type is used to identify a server that is authoritative for a zone, and will automatically retrieve the SOA record for the zone, the NS records for the name servers within the zone, and the A records for those name servers?

   A. Delegation

   B. Primary zone

   C. Secondary zone

   D. Stub zone

5. How does WINS interoperate with DHCP?

   A. The DHCP server assigns the WINS server address and node type options to clients.

   B. The DHCP server registers the computer name of clients within the WINS database.

   C. The WINS server provides remote clients with access to the DHCP server.

   D. The WINS server receives IP address information from the DHCP server and then passes the address information to the client.

6. To which of the following types of attacks are DNS servers susceptible? (Choose all that apply.)

   A. Footprinting

   B. Data modification

   C. Denial of Service

   D. Redirection

7. Becca is designing her name resolution infrastructure and is trying to determine how she is going to design the DNS solution for Active Directory. She plans on installing several Windows Server 2003 domain controllers and she wants to take advantage of Active Directory–integrated zones. Which of the following DNS server types will accommodate her needs?

   A. UNIX BIND 8.1.2

   B. UNIX BIND 9.1.0

   C. Windows NT 4

   D. Windows Server 2003

8. Leon is designing the DNS infrastructure and need to determine the namespace that will be used for his organization. The design calls for a back-to-back firewall to define a perimeter network and protect the internal network. Currently the organization is using `bloomco.com` as the external name for their internet presence. In order to protect the internal network and keep administration costs to a minimum, which of the following options should Leon consider using? (Select all that apply)

   A. `bloomco.com`

   B. `ad.bloomco.com`

   C. `bloomco.net`

   D. `bloomco.lcl`

9. Sally is designing the WINS replication topology for her company. Seven offices have been identified as locations for WINS servers and all of the servers need to have records replicated to them so that the clients can find the resources they need. She has identified the Austin location as the hub for the replication topology and wants to make sure that the WINS service is available at all times. What can she do to increase the reliability of the WINS server?

   A. Increase the memory on the server.

   B. Put the WINS service on clustered hardware.

   C. Put the WINS service on domain controllers.

   D. Increase the number of processors.

10. Tom is concerned that an attacker may be able to discover the addresses of servers on his network by using zone transfers. To alleviate his fears, what should be included within the DNS design? (Select all that apply.)

   A. Allow zone transfers only to systems identified by their IP address within the SOA record.

   B. Do not allow zone transfers to DNS servers within the perimeter network.

   C. Allow zone transfers to all servers.

   D. Use Active Directory-integrated zones within the perimeter network.

Answers to Review Questions

1. C. The high-level DNS security policy, as defined by Microsoft, states that zone transfers should only be sent to other DNS servers that are configured through their IP address. The low-level DNS security policy allows zone transfers to any other DNS server whereas the mid-level DNS security policy allows zone transfers to any DNS server defined on the Name Servers tab of the SOA record. The secure-level policy does not really exist.

2. B. Pull replication is configured to wait for a specified amount of time before requesting changes within the partner's database.

3. B, C. Stub zones and delegations are methods for identifying DNS servers that are authoritative for a specific zone if the zone in question is not located on the current DNS server.

4. D. A stub zone is responsible for redirecting clients to a name server that is authoritative for the zone they are querying. When a stub zone is created, it will copy the SOA record as well as the NS and A records of the name servers for the zone for which it is configured. The records will be refreshed based upon the time-to-live of the SOA record.

5. A. DHCP clients can be configured to receive the IP address of the WINS server along with the node type, or resolution method, from the DHCP server.

6. A, B, C, D. You will need to make sure you take the four attack types into account when designing the DNS infrastructure. Base your security requirements for each DNS server upon the attacks that are most likely to occur against that server.

7. D. From the available options, only Windows Server 2003 will support Active Directory–integrated zones. Of the other options, both of the UNIX BIND systems will support Active Directory, but only on primary and secondary zone types. Windows NT 4 DNS servers will not support Active Directory.

8. B, C, D. By using names that are not the same as the Internet presence, the internal network is then separated from the internet presence, yet the administration is simplified since you can create delegation records, stub zones, or forwarding to allow internal users to gain access to external resources.

9. B. The WINS service is cluster-aware and the only fault-tolerant option listed is the clustering solution.

10. A, B. If you select to allow zone transfers to DNS servers that are identified by their IP address within the properties of the SOA record, you will only transfer zone data to those servers and not to all name servers within your network. You should not include servers within the perimeter if at all possible so that internal records are not hosted on a DNS server within the perimeter. You should not allow zone transfers to all DNS servers because that is an open door for an attacker to request and receive zone transfers. Active Directory–integrated zones are more secure because you host the zones within Active Directory instead of within a text file on the server. However if you place a server that has an Active Directory–integrated zone within the perimeter, you are placing a domain controller within the perimeter that will then be accessible to attackers who access your perimeter. Also, Active Directory–integrated zones need to have zone transfers configured just like primary zones since they allow the zone data to be replicated to secondary zones.

Case Study

You should give yourself 20 minutes to review this testlet and complete the questions.

Background

Insane Systems builds custom computers for their customers. They specialize in building cases that are unique and support the latest in hardware technology. They started off as a small company that provided this service to gamers who would take their cases to LAN parties to show off. Because their systems were considered some of the most stable gaming platforms and they provided an impressive design that gamers could show off, they started to become popular. Insane Systems started mass manufacturing some of their more popular designs and began selling stand-alone cases along with their fully configured systems. As space at the company became a premium, the office was moved from the manufacturing facility. This allowed the company to add to the amount of space that was used for the mass production line.

Existing Environment

Over the past few months, Insane Systems has been developing plans to expand their company. They have identified San Jose, California, Atlanta, Georgia, and New York City as the locations with their highest customer base. The current Chicago location will remain the corporate headquarters, but they are opening branches in New York City and San Jose. They are also in the process of acquiring a competitor's business in Atlanta. These locations will provide retail outlets as well as support. Customers will have the option of sending their systems back to the corporate office, or delivering them to one of the branch locations for repairs or upgrades.

Because the company is planning on expanding, they want to make sure that the network infrastructure is in place to support their larger, distributed company. They are also concerned with the support lifetime of their current Windows NT 4 infrastructure. They realize they have the option of moving to a Windows 2000 or Windows 2003 infrastructure and are considering moving to Windows Server 2003 and Active Directory for two reasons: the expected support lifetime is greater than Windows 2000, and they are a technology firm that is not afraid of staying ahead of the technology curve.

Part of the expansion of the company is a complete overhaul of their current Internet presence. They are planning on bringing all of the web development and hosting in-house. Currently, a web hosting service is providing their Internet presence, and Insane Systems feels as though they could provide better marketing and support information for their customers if they had control over their own website. Insane Systems would also like to change the name of their website to better represent their name in the marketplace. They own the name `insane-systems.com`.

Interviews

Your company has been hired to design an Active Directory infrastructure and the network infrastructure to support it. During the interview process with some of the key stakeholders, you gathered the following information:

CEO   Currently we have a single location with all of our processes local. As we grow, we would like to keep all of the administration here in Chicago. Because the new branches are primarily retail and support offices, we will not need to have a large staff in those locations. The Atlanta office has an existing network that we would like to merge into our network. System design, research and development, and patent information come from the Atlanta office, so a secure connection from Atlanta to Chicago must be implemented.

CIO   Most of the infrastructure that we support is located here at the corporate office. We do support some key servers at the manufacturing location. We support these servers from our main office. Because the servers are nearby, if there is a problem, we can usually be on site within half an hour.

The new branches are going to be another issue altogether. We would like to retain the same level of administrative control over the servers in the new locations that we employ currently. Due to the geographic limitations, we may need to have some support staff at those locations. Currently, the plan is to hire staff at those locations who can provide the support for the customers, but also understand the business systems we need to put into place. We would like to automate software installations to the remote office due to the lack of IT staff.

Manager of Information Technology   We have grown very quickly over the past three years and our current technologies have kept up with that growth. However, we don't think the current infrastructure is ready for the amount of growth that we are expecting within the following year. We are not afraid of moving to the latest technology, but we want to make sure that the design is stable and makes sense for us, especially if we will continue growing in the upcoming months. And because we are losing support for NT 4, we want to make sure that we have an operating system that will be supported for a few years down the road.

Most of our processes are located here at this office and we would like to keep it that way. We know that sometimes servers will need to be located at the remote offices, but we would like to be able to provide most of the support from this location. Remote administration tools will need to be included within the design so that we can keep our administrative costs to a minimum.

Currently, we have most of our servers located at the main office, and all are located on their own high-speed backbone. We do have a server at the manufacturing site that allows the staff there to have e-mail as well as plans and orders in case we lose connectivity between the offices. This server is running Exchange 5.5. Several times during the day we replicate the public folder information to this system so that they are always up to date and do not have to dial up to the main office using our 56Kbps modem.

The systems at the main office are all supported by our staff of four administrators. All of the administrators are cross-trained on Windows NT 4, Exchange 5.5, SQL Server 7, our accounting software, and each of our file and print servers. We currently have several Windows NT 4

servers in place, including one Exchange 5.5 server at both locations, one SQL Server 7 server at the main office, one server running our accounting package that interfaces with the SQL server, and one file and print server that is used by both locations. The Exchange server at the manufacturing location doubles as a print server also.

The Atlanta office currently has a Windows NT 4.0 domain, and we will migrate that domain into our forest. Although administration of the forest will be moved to the Chicago branch, administration of the Atlanta domain will reside in the Atlanta domain. We will have a very small IT staff in the Atlanta office who will need to control all aspects of the Atlanta domain. Administrators of the Atlanta domain will have control over the Atlanta domain only and will not have administrator access to any other domain or any other part of the forest. All communication between the Atlanta office and the Chicago office will take place via an IPSec connection. The users in the Atlanta office will also require different password and lockout restrictions than the other offices.

Naming conventions for groups are very confusing right now, and adding the Atlanta domain only added to this confusion. Groups in the current domain are named Sales, IT, Accounting, and so on. Groups in the Atlanta domain are also named Sales, Accounting, and so on. We would like to rename groups to represent the name of the group, the home office of the user, the type of group—Global, Domain Local, or Universal—and then the job function of the users whose user objects are in that group.

LAN administrators in the root domain of the forest are responsible for creating GPOs but do not have access to link them at any level. Domain Admins in each domain are responsible for testing and linking the GPO to their own domains only. Forest owners will also have access to link GPOs at any level of any domain in the forest.

Because all of the client machines are running Windows NT 4 Workstation, we do not have to worry about supporting different operating systems. We would like to maintain that same easy administration with the upcoming system. We would like to provide the same types of services at the remote locations that we provide at the home office, although accounting will remain at the home office and will not be spread out to all of the locations.

Current Infrastructure

After investigating the current infrastructure, you have determined that the following servers are in place:

> **Home Office**
>
> Primary Domain Controller (PDC)
>
> Backup Domain Controller (BDC)
>
> DHCP server
>
> DNS/WINS server
>
> Exchange 5.5 server
>
> SQL Server 7

Systems Management Server 2

File server

Print/Antivirus server

Research and Development file server

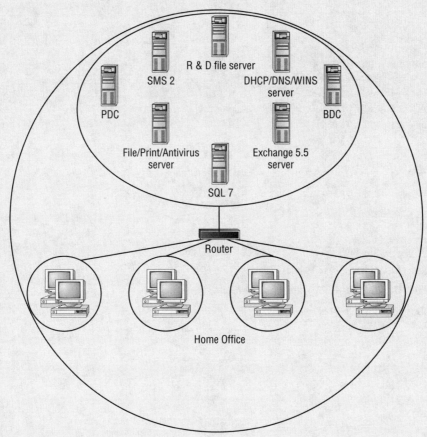

Atlanta Office

Primary Domain Controller (PDC)

Backup Domain Controller (BDC)

WINS server

File server

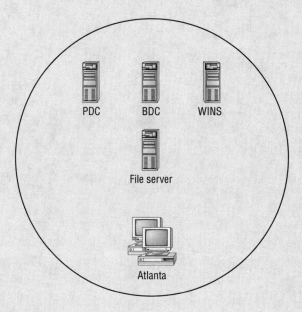

Manufacturing Facility

Backup Domain Controller (BDC)

DNS/WINS/DHCP Relay Agent server

Exchange 5.5/file server

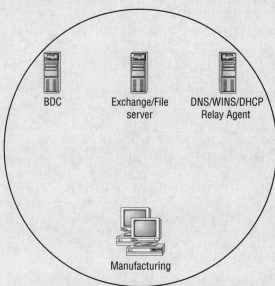

The Corporate Office hosts nearly 250 Windows NT 4 workstations at this point. They are interconnected by several 48-port 10/100Mbps switches. A router is used to divide the network into 4 VLANs. One of these broadcast domains is the 1Gbps backbone on which the servers reside. Each of the servers is connected to a 1Gbps switch port. This location takes advantage of private IP address ranges. The servers are located on the 192.168.1.0/24 subnet. The client systems are divided between network addresses 192.168.10.0/24, 192.168.11.0/24, 192.168.12.0/24, and 192.168.13.0/24.

The manufacturing facility contains 12 Windows NT 4 workstations connected to the same switch as the servers. Because Insane Systems does not want to slow down production due to a communication failure, they have taken advantage of Exchange 5.5's public folder replication. Public folders are continually updated with the latest orders. The crew foreman can access the orders locally from these public folders at any time, whether the communication link between the locations is up or not. This location uses another address range—192.168.20.0/24.

Case Study Questions

1. What types of DNS servers are identified in the current infrastructure?

   A. UNIX BIND

   B. Novell NetWare

   C. Windows NT 4

   D. Windows 2000

2. What DNS namespace should be used internally if Insane Systems wants to have the most secure namespace?

   A. `insane-systems.com`

   B. `insanesystems.com`

   C. `insanesystems.lcl`

   D. `insanesystems.org`

3. Prior to installing a Windows Server 2003 domain controller, which service or services need to be upgraded?

   A. At least one Windows Server 2003 DNS server needs to be installed.

   B. At least two Windows Server 2003 DNS servers need to be installed.

   C. At least one Windows Server 2003 WINS server needs to be installed.

   D. At least one Windows Server 2003 DHCP server needs to be installed.

4. At which locations should you deploy DNS and WINS servers?

   A. DNS and WINS servers at the Home Office to support all sites

   B. DNS servers at the Home Office, WINS servers at all offices

   C. DNS servers at all offices, WINS servers at the Home Office

   D. DNS and WINS servers at all offices

5. Diagram the WINS server locations and the replication topology.

| Chicago Home Office | | Chicago Manufacturing |

| Connection Types:
Push
Pull
Push/Pull | New York | San Jose | Atlanta |

Answers to Case Study Questions

1. C. Each of the DNS servers that are currently in place are running Windows NT 4 as the operating system.

2. C. When planning the internal namespace, you should consider using a namespace that is different than your Internet presence. Although you could use any of the options, having an internal namespace that is not available from the Internet is the most secure option.

3. A. For Active Directory to be supported, a DNS server that supports SRV records needs to be installed. A single Windows Server 2003 DNS server will be sufficient when installing Active Directory, but you will want to make sure your design calls for multiple DNS servers in your infrastructure, especially as you install domain controllers at the remote sites.

4. D. Because each of the offices needs to have the services provided by both name resolution services, you should locate them close to the systems that will access them. If you do locate them at each location, and if the WAN link fails, local resolution can still continue.

5.

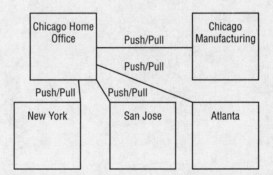

To keep the WINS query local, WINS servers should be located at each of the locations. To allow all of the users within the organization to be able to locate resources from all locations, the WINS servers should be configured in a hub-and-spoke topology to reduce the convergence time.

Glossary

A

account/discretionary access control list (A/ACL)   Resource access method that enters the account directly into the discretionary access control list of an object to either allow or deny access.

Account group   Term used to describe an Active Directory group object that is used to organize user accounts that have the same resource access requirements.

Account group/discretionary access control list (AG/DACL)   Resource access method that uses global groups and includes them in the discretionary access control list of the object to which the users need access.

Account group/Resource group (AG/ RG)   Resource access method that nests global groups within domain local or local groups in order to allow user accounts to have access to resources.

Account Lockout Duration setting   The setting used to determine the amount of time that an account will remain locked after a prespecified number of bad passwords has been attempted to log on to a user account. If set to 0, the account will remain locked out until an administrator unlocks the account.

account lockout restrictions   The settings that specify when an account should be locked when the password is entered incorrectly. These security measures protect from brute force or dictionary attacks.

Account Lockout Threshold setting   The setting used to set the number of failed logon attempts that are allowed before the account is locked out.

account OUs   Organizational units that are created to hold User, Group, and Computer accounts.

account policies   The password, lockout, and Kerberos policies. These policies can be applied at the domain level or on a stand-alone system.

Active Directory–integrated zones   DNS zones that have the resource record information stored in Active Directory. These require a DNS server that is also a DC. The DNS zone data is then replicated to other Active Directory–integrated DNS servers via Active Directory replication.

Active Directory Migration Tool (ADMT)   A utility that administrators can use to move accounts from one domain to another. This tool can be used to move accounts between Windows NT, Windows 2000, and Windows Server 2003 domains.

A/DACL   See *account/discretionary access control list (A/DACL)*.

ADMT   See *Active Directory Migration Tool (ADMT)*.

AG/DACL   See *Account group/discretionary access control list (AGDACL)*.

AG/RG   See *Account group/Resource group (AG/RG)*.

alternate IP addressing   IP addressing option that allows an administrator to enter an IP address into a DHCP client that will be used whenever the DHCP client cannot obtain an IP address from a DHCP server. This IP address will be used instead of APIPA.

APIPA   See *automatic private IP address (APIPA)*.

attributes   Properties of an Active Directory object.

authoritative zone transfer (AXFR)   DNS zone transfer that sends the entire zone datafile to another DNS server in order to keep it updated.

automatic private IP address (APIPA)   An address that is automatically generated by a DHCP client when it is unable to obtain an IP address and it is not configured to use an alternate IP address.

automation tools   Tools that allow an administrator to remotely administer computers

autonomous model   This model lets you have control over resources so that administrators from outside of your domain, with the exceptions of the forest-level administrators, will not have any control over resources within your domain.

AXFR   See *authoritative zone transfer (AXFR)*.

B

back-to-back firewalls   Firewall solution that places two firewalls in front of the internal network. This allows for resources to be placed between them in a perimeter network so that external users can access them safely. These types of setups are also known as DMZs.

baseline   Initial sampling of data that is used as a comparison point for troubleshooting system performance.

bastion host   Firewall solution that uses a single firewall in front of the internal network but does not allow for a perimeter network.

Block Inheritance   The method of stopping GPOs from upper levels within the Group Policy hierarchy from being processed unless the upper-level GPOs are enforced.

brute force attack   Attack type that attempts to break the security of a system by continuous attempts at discovering the password or encryption key.

C

centralized administration   Controlling and maintaining resources from one central location.

change management   Rules that control how changes to an infrastructure are allowed to occur.

change policy   The rules that are enforced for change management.

class options   DHCP client configuration options that are applied to systems based upon vendor- or user-supplied configurations.

coerced administrators   Administrators who are forced by an outside entity to perform an attack upon network resources.

collaborative model   Sharing administrative responsibilities within a domain, tree, or forest.

complex passwords   Passwords that use a combination of character types and are not words. When enforced, the password has to contain at least three of the following four character types; uppercase character, lowercase character, numeral, and special character.

connection types   The wide area link types that are available for an organization to use in order to connect their locations.

corporate standards   The policies that control user environments so that the company's rules and regulations are enforced.

cost center model   Business model that allows departments to "charge" one another for use of their resources.

cryptographic export laws   Laws that govern what level of encryption can be transferred to other countries.

D

data administrators   Members of an organization who are responsible for the resources within a domain or forest.

data autonomy   The ability to have control over the resources you maintain but not have the ability to isolate those resources from forest owners.

data modification   An attack method that manipulates data so that the attacker can either harm the data or change the way the data works.

decentralized model   Controlling and maintaining resources from more than one location, or having different administrative groups perform management of resources at different locations.

Default Domain Policy   The policy that is enacted on a domain and enforced on all users by default. This is where the account policies that control password, lockout, and Kerberos settings are located by default.

delegation record   DNS record that defines the name servers that are responsible for lower-level domains.

Denial-of-Service (DoS) attack   Attack type that interferes with the normal operation of a system so that it cannot perform the functions for which it is configured.

departmental model   Based on the structure of the business units, this model reflects the internal organization of the company and the clearly delineated lines between job responsibilities.

demilitarized zone (DMZ)   See *back-to-back firewalls*.

DHCP   See *Dynamic Host Configuration Protocol (DHCP)*.

dictionary attack   Password cracking method that uses words from a dictionary to determine what password is used.

DMZ   See *demilitarized zone (DMZ)*.

DNS   See *Domain Name System (DNS)*.

Domain Name System (DNS)   Hierarchical name resolution method that allows clients to resolve a system's IP address from its hostname or its hostname from an IP address.

domain owners   The administrative staff who have been assigned the full control of the domain. Domain admins are the default domain owners.

domain restructuring   Changing the original domain structure, usually by collapsing multiple domains into a single domain.

DoS attack   See *Denial-of-Service (DoS) attack*.

Dynamic Host Configuration Protocol (DHCP)   Service used to configure IP address and TCP/IP options to network clients.

E

Enforce Password History setting   Password policy option that dictates the number of passwords a user has to use before they can reuse the same password again.

Enterprise Admins group   Forest-level group that has the ability to control all resources within the forest.

extendable database   A database that can be modified so that additional attributes and object classes can be created.

external trusts   One-way trust relationship that is built between two Active Directory domains residing in separate forests, or an Active Directory domain and a Windows NT 4 domain that enables users to access resources within the remote domain.

F

filtering   When used with Group Policy, filtering is used to specify which accounts will not have the GPO applied to them.

footprinting   Attack type in which an attacker gleans information about the systems that exist on a companies network, either the perimeter, or more than likely, the internal network.

forest owners   The administrative staff who have been assigned the full control of the forest. Members of the Enterprise Admins group or Domain Admins from the forest root are forest owners.

forest root domain   Initial domain that is created when the first domain controller is promoted. Holds the Enterprise Admins and Schema Admins groups and is also the default location for the Schema Master and Domain Naming Master master operations roles.

forest trust   Transitive trust relationship that is created between two forests that are running at the Windows Server 2003 functional level.

G

GPO   See *Group Policy object (GPO)*.

Group Policy   Change and configuration management tool that is tied into Active Directory to manage and control users and computers within the Active Directory infrastructure.

Group Policy Management Console (GPMC)   Administrative tools that allows administrators to view the Group Policy infrastructure and perform modeling and testing of Group Policy options.

Group Policy object (GPO)   Collection of Group Policy settings that are applied to computers and users.

H

hardware requirements   The minimum system performance level that software needs to run on.

high availability   Criteria that specify that a service is available to users or other systems nearly all of the time, usually at a higher cost than systems with less reliability.

high-level DNS security policy   Rules that dictate how the DNS server is used within the organization. These rules dictate that absolutely no Internet interoperability is available through the DNS infrastructure.

hub-and-spoke method   WINS replication topology that uses centralized WINS servers as hub servers that are responsible for maintaining the replication to all other push/pull partners, or spoke WINS servers.

hybrid   Administration method that uses a combination of centralized and decentralized administration to allow the network to be managed efficiently.

I

incremental zone transfers (IXFR)   DNS zone replication method that sends only the updated records to the secondary DNS zones.

inheritance   Group policy settings that are applied to users and computers in lower-level containers.

internal DNS root   A DNS zone for an organization that becomes the highest entity within the DNS namespace.

Intersite Topology Generator (ISTG)   A function of the Knowledge Consistency Checker that generates the replication paths for Active Directory replication between sites.

isolated administration model   Administration term that is used to identify that the administrative staff has control over resources and no other administrative staff has access to those resources.

ISTG   See *Intersite Topology Generator (ISTG)*.

IXFR   See *incremental zone transfers (IXFR)*.

K

Knowledge Consistency Checker (KCC)   Service that determines the replication topology between domain controllers.

L

L2TP   See *Layer 2 Tunneling Protocol (L2TP)*.

local area network (LAN)   Communication system that typically has 10Mbps or higher bandwidth for the devices to communicate with one another.

Layer 2 Tunneling Protocol (L2TP)   VPN protocol that is used to authenticate the end points of a VPN.

linear model   Replication path in which the replicated data has to pass through multiple servers to reach the final server in the chain. Chaining the systems together in this fashion will cause propagation delays.

line-of-business applications   Applications that have been approved for use within the organization.

lockout policy   Settings that determine how many password attempts a user can make before the user's account becomes unavailable, and the length of time the account will remain unavailable.

loopback processing   Group Policy processing mode that specifies how the GPOs will be applied if the user and computer accounts do not reside within the same OU. The default setting is to use the GPO settings that apply to the computer's OU. You can configure the loopback processing to merge the settings from the user's OU with the computer's OU or completely replace the settings with those applied at the computer's OU.

low-level DNS security policy   Rules that dictate how the DNS server is used within the organization. These rules allow the DNS server to interact with the Internet.

M

Master User Domain (MUD)   Windows NT 4 domain that was used exclusively for user and group accounts in a multimaster domain environment.

Maximum Password Age setting   The setting that determines the longest amount of time that a password is allowed to be used within a network before the user is forced to change it.

Microsoft Management Console (MMC)   Software that allows an administrator to add snap-ins to it so that they can manage and maintain the systems and services for which they are responsible.

Microsoft Point-to-Point Encryption (MPPE)   40-bit or 128-bit encryption algorithm that uses RC4 and provides confidentiality between clients and servers when IPSec is not available.

mid-level DNS security policy   Rules that dictate how the DNS server is used within the organization. These rules dictate that limited Internet interoperability is available through the DNS infrastructure.

Minimum Password Age setting   This setting sets the amount of time that a user must use a new password before they are allowed to change it.

Minimum Password Length setting   This setting specifies how many characters must be included in the password.

MMC   See *Microsoft Management Console (MMC)*.

most-restrictive/most-inclusive strategy   Group nesting method that dictates that you should first add users to groups that are most restrictive for their needs and then add those groups to other groups that allow large groups of users to access resources.

MPPE   See Microsoft Point-to-Point Encryption (MPPE).

MUD   See *Master User Domains (MUDs)*.

multifactor authentication   Using additional methods, in addition to passwords, to authenticate, such as biometrics and smart cards.

multiple forest, no trust design   Perimeter network design option that creates a forest for resources within the perimeter network, but no trust relationship exists between the perimeter forest and the internal forest.

multiple forest, one-way trust design   Perimeter network design option that creates a forest for resources within the perimeter network and allows a trust relationship to be created so that administrators from the internal network can access perimeter resources.

multiple forest, two-way trust design   Perimeter network design option that creates a forest for resources within the perimeter network and allows a two-trust relationship to be created so that administrators from the internal network can access perimeter resources and systems within the perimeter network can access internal resources.

N

naming strategy   Designing a method of naming groups so that they are descriptive enough to identify their purpose.

O

object autonomy   The ability to have sole control over objects without allowing other administrators, with the exception of domain or forest owners, to have access.

object visibility   Using OUs and permissions to allow only authorized users to view objects.

object-based delegation   Administrative delegation method that assigns permissions to perform functions within a domain or OU.

Operations Masters   Functions that are only performed on a single domain controller at a time. The operations masters are the Schema Master, Domain Naming Master, Infrastructure Master, Primary Domain Controller Emulator, and Relative ID (RID) Master.

organization-based forest   Forest design option that creates a forest based upon the organizational needs of the company.

organizational unit (OU)   Logical container within Active Directory used to organize Active Directory objects for administrative purposes and GPO assignment.

OU   See *organizational unit (OU)*.

OU administrators   Users who have been delegated permissions to perform specific functions within an OU.

OU owners   Users who have been granted full control over an OU.

outsourced method   Administration method that uses administrators from another company to complement the organization's administrative staff.

P

Password Must Meet Complexity Requirements setting   Password policy setting that, if enabled, requires a user to use at least three of the four following options: uppercase character, lowercase character, numerical character, and special character.

Point-To-Point Tunneling Protocol (PPTP)   VPN technology used in Microsoft networks that uses Microsoft Point to Point Encryption (MPPE), but does not perform mutual authentication.

political boundaries   Governmental jusridictions that are used to enforce laws and regulations.

PPTP   See *Point-to-Point Tunneling Protocol (PPTP)*.

primary zones   DNS zone type that allows for management of the resource records.

processing priority   When you are linking multiple GPOs to the same site, domain, or OU, the processing priority determines in which order the GPOs are processed.

product/service-based model   Administrative design model that breaks out administration of resources based upon the product or service for which the staff is responsible.

project-based model   Administrative design model that breaks out administration of resources based upon a project.

pull replication   WINS replication method where the WINS replication partners will wait a specified period of time before requesting the changes to the WINS database.

push replication   WINS replication method where the WINS server will notify the partners after a specified number of changes to the WINS database have occurred.

push/pull replication   WINS replication method that uses both the push and pull replication methods between the partners.

R

realm trusts   One-way non-transitive trust relationship that can be created between an Active Directory domain and a UNIX realm.

redirection   An attack type that sends a user's request to a server that is under the attacker's control instead of to the system that the user intended.

regional domain model   Domain structure that is based upon the geographic regions the domains represent.

reliability   Describes how dependable a system is. Redundant hardware will increase the reliability of a system.

Remote Authentication Dial-In User Service (RADIUS)   Remote user authentication technology that allows a remote user to connect to a local server (a RADIUS client), which then sends the authentication request to a RADIUS server, that is responsible for authenticating the user.

reserved client options   DHCP client configuration settings that are applied to the individual system that receives the reserved IP address from the DHCP server.

Reset Account Lockout Counter After setting   Account lockout policy option that resets the number of failed logon attempts to zero after the administrator-configured time has passed.

resource forest   Forest that is created to host specific resources. This is usually created so that a failure of a directory service–related system within another forest will not affect the resources.

Resource group   Group type that has permissions assigned to resources. Other groups are added to the Resource group in order to give the users within those groups the appropriate permission to access the resource.

resource OUs   Organization units that are designed to host resources that specific users will administer.

restricted-access forest   A forest that is created in order to keep unauthorized individuals from having access to specific resources.

rogue administrator   A user who has administrative capabilities and uses them to gain access to resources they are not supposed to access.

S

schema modification policy   Administrative policy that defines who will authorize a schema change, who will make the change, and when and where the change will be made.

scope options   DHCP configuration options that are applied to all systems within an IP subnet that receive IP configurations from the DHCP server.

secondary zones   DNS zone type that receives its zone data through a zone transfer from a master DNS server. This zone type is read-only—the records can only be changed through a zone transfer.

security identifier (SID)   Unique descriptor used to identify users, groups, and computers.

server options   DHCP configuration options that are applied globally to all users who receive IP configurations from the DHCP server.

service account   User account that is used to allow a service or software to operate on a system.

service administrators   Administrative staff who are responsible for maintaining the directory service and the services that the directory service relies upon.

Service Level Agreement (SLA)   Contract that specifies the requirements for a system's responsiveness and the responsibilities of the administrative entity of the system.

shortcut trusts   One-way or two-way transitive trust relationships that are created between two domains within the same Active Directory forest.

SID   See *security identifier (SID)*.

SID filtering   An option on trust relationships that blocks the SIDHistory attribute from being used in a remote domain.

SIDHistory   Attribute of a user account when a domain is in Windows 2000 native mode or higher that allows previous SIDs to be associated with the user account.

single forest design   Active Directory design option that uses one forest for the organization to ease administrative costs.

site link bridge   A logical path between two sites when you are using multiple site links.

site link   The connector that allows Active Directory replication to pass between two sites. The site link is based on an interval within a schedule that an administrator controls.

sites   A collection of well-connected IP subnets.

snap-ins   Software that can be added to the MMC in order to give administrators the ability to control services and software.

software reliance   Software that must be in place for applications or services to function.

software requirements   The system options that will need to be met for software to function on a system.

stakeholders   Anyone who is responsible for, or needs access to, a resource.

Store Passwords Using Reversible Encryption setting   Option that is required when you are using digest authentication so that the user's password can be correctly identified.

strong passwords   Passwords that contain at least three character types, (i.e., uppercase, lowercase, numerical, and special characters), and are not common words or reiterations of the same password (i.e., P@ssw0rd1, P@ssw0rd2, and so on). See *complex passwords*.

stub zones   DNS zone type that contains the name server (NS) and host (A) records for the name servers that are authoritative for the zone. These records are dynamically updated so that the administrator does not have to update them manually.

T

task-based delegation   Assigning permissions to perform specific tasks based on specific object types.

temporary employees   Users who are not employed long term but need to have accounts for the time that they are members of the organization.

Terminal Services   Software that allows multiple user sessions to run on a single system. Administrators use Terminal Services for remote administration.

three-homed firewall   Firewall option that uses a single firewall to protect both the perimeter network and internal network.

total cost of ownership (TCO)   The complete cost of maintaining a system—not just the dollar amount spent on purchasing the system, but the additional costs that are incurred through the administration and maintenance of the system.

U

universal group membership caching   The option that allows domain controllers within a site to cache the universal group membership of users in that site so that a Global Catalog server is not necessary.

user restrictions   Group Policy settings that limit what actions a user can perform on their workstation or control the applications that are allowed to run.

V

variable length subnet masks (VLSM) IP addressing method that allows administrators to make more efficient use of IP addresses.

Virtual Private Network (VPN) Method of encrypting data between two parties on an insecure connection so that attackers will not be able to intercept and view the data as it is transmitted.

W

WAN See *wide area network (WAN)*.

wide area network (WAN) Connection between two locations that typically does not have the same bandwidth as the local area network (LAN).

Windows Internet Name Service (WINS) Name resolution method that is used to locate a NetBIOS-based system.

WINS See *Windows Internet Name Service (WINS)*.

Index

Note to the reader: Throughout this index **boldfaced** page numbers indicate primary discussions of a topic. *Italicized* page numbers indicate illustrations.

E

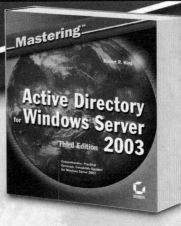

TELL US WHAT YOU THINK!

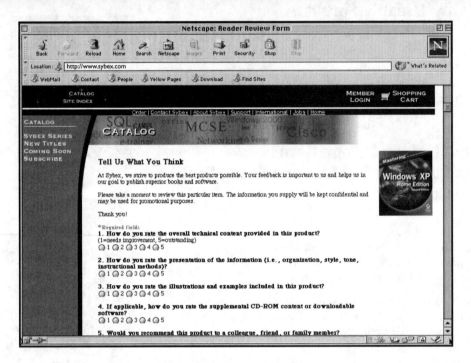

Your feedback is critical to our efforts to provide you with the best books and software on the market. Tell us what you think about the products you've purchased. It's simple:

1. Go to the Sybex website.
2. Find your book by typing the ISBN or title into the Search field.
3. Click on the book title when it appears.
4. Click **Submit a Review**.
5. Fill out the questionnaire and comments.
6. Click **Submit.**

With your feedback, we can continue to publish the highest quality computer books and software products that today's busy IT professionals deserve.

www.sybex.com

SYBEX Inc. • 1151 Marina Village Parkway, Alameda, CA 94501 • 510-523-8233